The Life and Times of Soviet Socialism

Alex F. Dowlah and John E. Elliott

PRAEGER

Westport, Connecticut
London

Library of Congress Cataloging-in-Publication Data

Dowlah, Alex F.
    The life and times of Soviet socialism / Alex F. Dowlah and John
E. Elliott.
        p.   cm.
    Includes bibliographical references and index.
    ISBN 0–275–95629–6 (alk. paper)
        1. Soviet Union—Economic conditions.   2. Soviet Union—Economic
policy.   3. Socialism—Soviet Union—History.   I. Elliott, John E.
II. Title.
HC335.D744   1997
335.43—dc20   96–24358

British Library Cataloguing in Publication Data is available.

Library of Congress Catalog Card Number: 96–24358
ISBN: 0–275–95629–6

First published in 1997

Praeger Publishers, 88 Post Road West, Westport, CT 06881
An imprint of Greenwood Publishing Group, Inc.

Printed in the United States of America

The paper used in this book complies with the
Permanent Paper Standard issued by the National
Information Standards Organization (Z39.48–1984).

10 9 8 7 6 5 4 3 2 1

To my parents (in memoriam), Jheshan, my son and Panna, my wife
  —AFD

To Rosie —my soulmate and life's companion
  —JEE

Contents

Tables

Preface

The life and times of Soviet socialism are by no means over. Its legacy—as context, as historical example, as inspiration for partial restoration—will continue to have a profound impact in the former Soviet Union in particular and around the world in general. Moreover, the dissolution of the USSR as a geopolitical entity in 1991 has not been accompanied by or, thus far, followed by the successful establishment of a market-driven and western-style democratic society. The former Soviet Union remains in "transition" and "transformation," although to what is not clear. The accomplishments and inadequacies of a 74-year long experiment by the Soviet people will continue to stimulate both academic and non-academic inquisitiveness throughout the world. No matter what happens to the post-Soviet, post-Cold War world, it is unlikely that the effects of that experiment will dissipate quickly or entirely.

This book attempts to provide a comprehensive but reasonably succinct analysis of the Soviet politico-economic system. The Soviet system was initiated under the exigencies of war, revolution, and civil war. Over the course of time, it evolved through several models or stages until its ultimate dissolution in 1991. It is the authors' intent to examine herein the several variants of the Soviet experience with a post-Cold War objectivity and professional integrity. Of course, no claim is made here to the effect that the book provides the final truth on its subject—readers will judge to what extent that goal has been accomplished.

The authors have benefited enormously from the vast literature on the Soviet politico-economic system. Our special thanks, however, go to prominent authorities in this subject: Alec Nove, Ed Hewett, Stephen Cohen, Moshe Lewin, Archie Brown, Jerry F. Hough, Stephen White, Paul R. Gregory, Robert C. Stuart, Nikolai Shmelev, Vladimir Popov and Abel Aganbegyan.

We wish to thank Jim Ice, Economics Editor, and David Palmer, Production Editor of Greenwood Publishing Group for the interest they have taken in this project and for their editorial assistance. Finally, we thank our family members for their invaluable support throughout the long and arduous period of this project.

Chapter 1

Introduction

This chapter identifies the major stages (and substages) in Soviet politico-economic development since 1917. In doing so, it summarizes the leading features in both the historical evolution of the Soviet system and the different models or forms of the Soviet version of socialism.

MODELS OF SOVIET SOCIALISM AND STAGES OF SOVIET DEVELOPMENT

The several variants of Soviet socialism examined in succeeding chapters—war communism, the new economic policy or NEP, the classical Soviet system of totalitarian state-directed economy, the authoritarian reform economy, bureaucratic collectivism, and democratizing socialism—may be simplified around three broader headings: the preclassical system of revolutionary transition to classical Soviet socialism engineered by Vladimir I. Lenin and his Bolshevik followers, from the revolution in 1917 until the consolidation of power by Joseph Stalin in the late 1920s; the classical Soviet system, or totalitarian state-directed economy, associated notably with Stalin, from the advent of Stalin to power until his death in 1953 (with continuing influence beyond, especially into the Brezhnev regime); and reform socialism, beginning with Stalin's death and culminating in the democratizing and marketizing reforms of the Gorbachev era in the late 1980s and early 1990s. A final variant may be identified as transformation and transition out of the Soviet system into its successor(s), which is beyond the scope of this book, although some aspects of this topic emerge naturally out of an examination of the disintegration of the Soviet politico-economic system in the final chapter.

The characterizations of experience suggested by these variants serve as alternative conceptualizing models of the Soviet system. As such, they provide three main functions. First, they describe or explain the relationships among the phenomena under investigation. Second, they envision the possibility or likelihood of future changes in these relationships. Third, they justify or advocate the kind of politico-economic system and human being considered good or socially desirable. In the 1920s, for example, the early Bolsheviks spoke of constructing or "building" socialism. Socialism was considered as a desirable, and prospective future, rather than an actually existing, system. By the mid-1930s, with the widespread adoption of government ownership, centralized planning, and programs for health, education, and social welfare, Stalin officially characterized the actual Soviet system as "socialist."

These comparative and contrasting models of the Soviet politico-economic system are also historically successive stages of Soviet development. As political philosopher C. B. Macpherson (1977, 7) aptly puts it, "using successive models reduces the risk of myopia in looking ahead. It is all too easy, in using a single model, to block off future paths; all too easy to fall into thinking that [the current system], now that we have attained it, by whatever stages, is fixed in its present mould." An additional reason for perceiving the Soviet system in terms of historically successive stages is that "their use is more likely to reveal the full content of the contemporary model, the full nature of the present system. For the presently prevalent model is itself an amalgam, produced by partial rejection and partial absorption of previous models" (80).

Thus, in succeeding chapters (1) the underlying causes of each stage of Soviet development and (2) its institutions and policies are found in (3) consequences and (4) tensions and contradictions of the preceding stage. The institutions and policies of the stage under study, in turn, are seen as generating their consequences and tensions, which serve as the underlying causes of the transformation to the institutions and policies of the next stage.

THE PRECLASSICAL SOVIET SYSTEM

War Communism

Sustained by the expectation that their revolution would inspire Communist revolutions in industrially advanced countries, which then would come to their aid, the Bolsheviks turned enthusiastically to the tasks of organizing the economy and, within limits, incorporating certain of the dimensions of the prerevolutionary Marxian visions of socialist economic society, including worker control of industry, expropriation of property and reduction of inequality in wealth and income, supersession of money economy, and decentralization in government and economic administration. In the countryside, the peasantry interpreted Lenin's revolutionary slogans ("peace, land, and bread") literally and took over the landed estates of aristocrats. Lacking government machinery to coordinate agricultural production, the Bolsheviks relied on stringent emergency measures, including forced requisitioning of grain. Nationalization of industry, which was widespread and often indiscriminate, was not accompanied by any genuine planned coordination of production decisions.

When the Bolshevik Revolution did not trigger other (successful) revolutions in Western Europe, Soviet leaders found themselves isolated, surrounded by unfriendly powers abroad and confronted with discord and civil war at home. Faced with the unlikelihood of foreign assistance and the exigencies of civil war and foreign intervention, the Bolsheviks increasingly shifted away from the more decentralized, democratic, and egalitarian qualities of the early months following the revolution. Worker control over industry was increasingly replaced by centralized and hierarchical government direction. Labor unions increasingly lost any semblance of independence and autonomy and became part of the apparatus of government-party control. The government bureaucracy expanded and became more centralized. The Bolshevik party extended its control over the economy and society. Former tsarist managers, technicians, specialists, and government officials were drawn back into management of industry and government with steadily increasing salaries relative to the general body of industrial workers.

Civil war brought confusion and dislocation as well. By 1921 the economy was in virtual collapse. Output was lower than pre-World War I levels, trade was almost completely disrupted, and inflation was rampant. The peasantry, scattered throughout the countryside and beyond effective party-government control, became increasingly restive and uncooperative in response to food requisitions. With food supplies uncertain and tightening, the regime could no longer count on even the tenuous, continued support of the small urban proletariat. With increasing disenchantment and growing worker-peasant opposition, symbolized by the Kronstadt sailors revolt of 1921, the very survival of the regime came into question.

Beyond the immediate issues was a more fundamental problem. Without assistance from friendly, developed countries, industrialization in Russia, regarded as an imperative precondition to the full establishment of socialism, had to be mobilized by internal efforts by imposing heavy sacrifices on the worker and peasant populations. But the burdens of the civil war, increasing hostility of the peasantry to forced requisition of grain, lack of a developed, sophisticated system of governmental and industrial administration, and general disruption and dislocation of the economy made immediate frontal assault on the industrialization process impracticable.

New Economic Policy

The New Economic Policy, commenced in 1921, constituted an attempt to create a Bolshevik version of a "mixed economy." It represented both a reaction against the dislocations and extreme institutional forms of war communism and a commitment to a more or less extended period of transition during which the economic foundations for building socialism could be laid. Retaining control over the "commanding heights," the Bolsheviks released agriculture, wholesale and retail trade, and services to private enterprise, relying on market motivations and processes to coordinate supplies and demands. The rationale was to save the revolution by giving the economy an opportunity to rebuild, and the party leadership a breathing space to determine its strategy for constructing the socialist society of the future.

The NEP was highly successful on both counts. By the mid-1920s, the dislocations of war and Civil war had been overcome, the economy had expanded vigorously within the framework of its inherited industrial capacity, and government-party control became organized, centralized, disciplined, and sophisticated. Although politics became increasingly authoritarian, the Soviet Union during the 1920s approximated a Bolshevik "Golden Age" in terms of combining a liberalized economy, social and cultural pluralism, and considerable opportunities for intraparty discussion, debate, and dissent.

During this same period, the perceived logic of their position became increasingly clear to the Bolshevik leadership. Protection of the revolution from hostile powers abroad, maintenance and extension of political support at home, and creation of the preconditions for an effective and efficiently functioning socialist economy and society all combined to make industrialization a high strategic priority, even if that meant incorporating substantial capitalist elements (for example, one-man management, industrial hierarchy, capitalist modes of the division of labor, inegalitarian incentive schemes) into the system.

Strategies for fostering higher economic growth ranged from the Right to the Left. The Rightists, led by Nikolai Bukharin (1982), propounded either a "balanced growth" strategy, focusing on gradual and simultaneous development of both agriculture and industry, or an "unbalanced growth," agriculture-first strategy, featuring the greater capacity and income-creating qualities attributed to agriculture and its larger benefits in the context of international comparative advantage. The Leftists, led by E. A. Preobrazhensky (1965), proposed an "unbalanced growth" strategy, emphasizing a faster pace and higher rates of investment, especially in heavy industry, initially propelled by a "primitive socialist accumulation" financed by the agricultural sector. The Rightists generally espoused more incrementalist strategies and stressed the need for voluntarism and sustenance of the *smychka* or alliance between the peasantry and proletariat. The Leftists typically supported more vigorous proposals and an industrialization which imposed its greatest sacrifices and costs on agriculture and the peasantry. Because each side of what came to be called the Great Industrialization Debate identified serious negative consequences of the opposing strategies, as well as positive benefits from the adoptions of its own proposals, the Party, by the end of the 1920s was caught on the horns of a dilemma that demanded immediate resolution.

STALIN'S TOTALITARIAN STATE-DIRECTED ECONOMY

The Stalinist solution to the dilemma posed by the great industrialization debate of the 1920s was eventually adopted in the late 1920s after several years of skillful political maneuvering in which Stalin disposed, first, of Leon Trotsky and his other left-wing opponents and, finally, of his right-wing opposition. This solution constituted an abrupt break with the NEP and a commitment to radical reconstruction of Russian institutions, politico-economic life, and social values. It has been candidly described, in an official Soviet publication edited by Stalin himself, as a "profound revolution, a leap from an old qualitative state of society to a new qualitative state, equivalent in its consequences to the revolution of October 1917." Its most "distinguishing feature is that it was accomplished *from above*, on the initiative of the state." (cited in Bettleheim and Chavance 1981, 52). Stalin's revolution applied centralized methods of political control to the industrialization process. It supposed that rapid, large-scale industrialization was essential for the progress and survival of Soviet socialism.

The Stalinist industrialization strategy was one of *extensive* development; it focused on mobilizing resources and manipulating savings and investment. This strategy had two major facets: first, the transfer of peasant labor to cities and factories and their transformation there into a disciplined force of industrial labor and, second, the transformation of the industrial labor force thus created into capital goods.

For the system as a whole, the strategy maximized the output of capital goods and thus, within strategic limits, minimized the output of consumption goods.

Transfer of the saving-investment process from the private sector to government permitted savings and investment to be set at levels substantially above those that presumably would have been forthcoming if businesses, workers, or households had had an effective voice in the matter. For the two major sectors of the economy, the strategy involved maximization of the transfer of labor, food, and raw materials from agriculture to industry, combined with minimization of investment of human and capital resources in agriculture and minimization of provision of food and other consumer goods to the peasantry.

Apparently, Stalin and his associates believed that implementation of this ambitious strategy, especially in a short period of time, required important institutional innovations. These innovations, which emerged in the late 1920s and early 1930s, were essentially completed by 1937. Taken together, they transformed the Soviet Union from the mixed NEP economy to one characterized by comprehensive governmental direction and control of the economic system. These dramatic institutional changes had several leading elements. First, the collectivization of agriculture provided the basic institutional mechanism for eliminating the economic power and resistance of the peasantry, for ejecting peasant labor from agriculture, and for organizing production and distribution within the agricultural sector to keep peasant consumption at minimum levels. Rapid and massive collectivization created extreme dislocation and disruption and threatened the very survival of the Soviet system. Entire villages were deported to eliminate or absorb middle-class and kulak peasants. Collectivization was extended to farm animals as well as the physical means of production, which caused peasant resistance and large-scale slaughtering of livestock. Agricultural output and income plummeted. Several million people died, largely from the famine that accompanied collectivization. The Russian peasant was subdued and agriculture was brought within the rubric of planned economy only at a steep price, with repercussions down to the present.

Second, government ownership of the means of production, centralized physical allocations of resources to managers in accord with plans for industrial development, and controls over labor and management provided the institutional mechanism for disciplining workers and managers and inducing concentration of emphasis on production of investment goods and utilization of investment goods primarily within the industrial sector. As noted earlier, the government sector had retained ownership of the commanding heights in industry during the NEP period. As the economy stabilized during the 1920s, the government sector expanded, in trade as well as industry. This process continued in the 1930s. By 1937 government-owned enterprises accounted for virtually 100 percent of the Soviet national income, gross industrial product, and retail trade.

Another major element in Stalin's institutional transformation was a shift to overall economic planning as the dominant social process for economic coordination and implementation of developmental strategies. In part, this involved elimination or emasculation of market exchange relations. This antimarket bias, though reflecting traditional Marxist and socialist critiques (notably the perceived "anarchy" of the market and its tendencies toward crisis under capitalism), was undoubtedly reinforced by the view, nurtured by the experiences of the NEP period, that market forces were an obstacle to the Soviet leadership's aspiration to rapid, large-scale industrialization guided from above.

Money, markets, and prices were not eliminated, but they were restricted and became limited compared to capitalist (or socialist) market economies. The domain for market exchange was restricted to relations between government and collective farms and between government enterprises and households (as consumers and workers), supplemented by sales by peasants from their private garden plots and by a very small amount of exchange activities undertaken by private craftsmen or professionals. Moreover, prices, in most instances, were set by government agencies, based on nonmarket criteria, and used to pursue collective purposes designed by Soviet leaders and planners. (For example, prices of certain necessities were set below cost, while prices of automobiles and other luxuries were set at levels substantially above cost to discourage their consumption.) In the industrial sector, prices served essentially modest accounting purposes, assisting in plan formulation and in testing consistency of plans, rather than as information signals guiding resource allocation decisions.

The most important control hierarchy was provided by the Communist party. First, the party determined overall planning objectives and targets. Through the *nomenklatura* system, the party appointed ministers and labor union officials and filled other posts of significance. Local party officials kept an eye on plan fulfillment and mobilized, through labor unions and educational programs, worker enthusiasm and productivity. A final component in the transformation to the centrally directed economy of the Stalin years and beyond was the establishment of tight government controls over the monetary, fiscal, and pricing systems. These controls enabled Soviet planners and administrators during (and since) the Stalinist era to establish a financial mechanism to supplement and complement their physical and labor plans and allocations.

REFORM SOCIALISM

Much of the Stalinist approach to economic theory and policy died along with Stalin. After his death, there were substantial changes in economic thought and, to some extent, in practice in the Soviet Union and Eastern Europe. In part, the increasing emancipation of Soviet thought from Stalinist orthodoxy was attributable to Stalin's death and the lessening fear of party-government reprisals, especially in the light of denunciations by Nikita Khrushchev and his successors of the "excess" of the Stalinist era. Economic development also led to shifts in goals and to new theories and approaches to running the economy. In particular, Soviet leaders committed themselves more concretely to the idea that the goal of growth was to raise the standard of living. Also, they concluded that both growth and allocative performance could be improved by at least some decentralization of decision making and by releasing initiative at the lower levels of the system, rather than by sweeping, strategic-style decisions.

The very success of the Stalinist development strategy altered key conditions, which contributed to growing obsolescence of the strategy. These altered conditions have been interpreted by revisionists as being inconsistent with the highly centralized processes and institutions for economic planning and decision making of the Stalinist era: (1) Whatever the suitability of Stalinist methods for transformation from an underdeveloped, dominantly agricultural society to a significantly higher level of economic development, that task was largely accomplished by 1953; (2) the greater size and complexity of the postwar economic organization required more sophisticated and finely tuned instruments and methods; (3) Draconian sacrifices of consumption in favor of investment, and accompanying institutional processes to enforce them, had a logic and rationale in the 1930s that no longer existed. Increased emphasis upon consumption and an increased quality and variety of consumer goods accelerated the obsolescence of Stalinist planning from the center and increased the need for institutional mechanisms to relate production decisions more closely to consumer preference; (4) the lack of a skilled and loyal managerial corps and the need to create a disciplined labor force could no longer be credibly used as rationales for concentrating and centralizing power and authority for planning and administrative decisions, for these needs had been largely attained; (5) similarly, revolution, war, civil war, radical institutional transformation, and the danger of counterrevolution no longer credibly justified the maintenance of highly centralized planning structures. With the passage of time, new generations emerged for whom the revolution was but history, who more or less accepted the basic institutional structure of the society, but were willing to support reforms or changes.

Acknowledgment of altered conditions and willingness to consider revisions of the Stalinist model were prompted most directly by deceleration of growth. The rate of growth in the Soviet economy dropped markedly after the late 1950s. In the Soviet Union, it has been estimated that, during most of the postwar period, the gross national product (GNP) grew at a rate of about 7 to 8 percent per year; since 1958, it fell to more nearly 5 percent per year. An explanation for this deceleration of growth is that the Stalinist strategy ran into diminishing returns. First, productivity gains from transferring peasant labor to urban factories was much reduced. Labor became a scarce factor and needed to be economized. Second, agriculture was shorn of economic surpluses. Indeed, large-scale investments in agriculture were needed to maintain and expand food production. Third, capital was characterized by diminishing marginal productivity. Opportunities for substantial economic growth merely by expanding the capital stock (capital widening) were distinctly limited. Economic growth increasingly required technological improvements and careful choice among alternative investments (capital deepening). The investment policy of the past (neglect of investment in agriculture, transportation, and housing, as well as neglect of obsolescence) needed overhaul. Fourth, the policy of autarky denied Soviet development the advantages of international division of labor. This policy was never as applicable to the smaller and less self-sufficient Eastern European countries as it was to Soviet Union and was increasingly being abandoned, as demonstrated by burgeoning East-West trade.

With increasing size and complexity, the informational problem of accounting for production plans and performance mounted steadily. The number of firms, commodities, resources and commodity combinations, and technological possibilities increased markedly with industrialization. Moreover, interactions among economic units tended to grow more rapidly than their number. Thus, much more information was needed to make rational choices. There was also an increased awareness of the need for better economic calculations. This implied a need for new kinds of and better information. The emphasis upon *quantities* in the economic plans of the Stalinist era and the inadequacies and inaccuracies of the price system compounded the problems of economic calculation and coordination by excluding, for all practical purposes, comparisons of the *values* of alternatives foregone in production and consumption.

During the Stalinist era, when economic decisions were made at the center, the magnitude of decisions was large, the scope of any decision was relatively wide, and revisions of strategic decisions were apt to be infrequent. With increasing size and complexity and increasing problems of coordination and efficiency, each of these dimensions of the Stalinist planning methodology became increasingly questioned. The centralization of decisions tended to overlook the concretized knowledge of "time and place" of local administrators or managers. Big, overall decisions applied indiscriminately to wide areas of the economy tended to neglect special features of particular cases and microeconomic interdependencies. Infrequent revision of strategic decisions created an institutional mechanism insufficiently flexible and adaptable to changing circumstances.

The Stalinist economy, with its hierarchically structured vertical information channels and chains of command, tended to maximize responsiveness of lower level administrators and managers to directives of political leaders and planners and to minimize responsiveness to laterally related enterprises, sectors, regions, or consumers. Rational as this structure might have been at an earlier stage of economic development, it was characterized by bottlenecks and inefficiencies with the increasing size and complexity of production and the increasing importance of consumption.

The "success indicators" of the Stalinist regime had a distorted impact on any incentive system. For example, if the planning target for nails was fixed in terms of weight, big and heavy nails were produced. If the target was put in terms of number, large numbers of small nails were produced. Quantity and quality moved in opposite directions. In general, classical Stalinist socialism had no integrating, synthesizing success indicator (such as profitability) to enable planners and administrators to evaluate economic performance in a comprehensive way that would not distort local decision making.

At a later stage, Soviet leaders reordered their priorities somewhat and attached greater importance to improving living standards. This stemmed partly from the fact that the level of per capita output became high enough both to satisfy the goals for investment and military expenditure which the leaders saw as necessary and to provide higher consumption levels. Without any change in the relative shares of consumption in total output, growth creates a rising level of per capita consumption, so that the task of satisfying consumer demand took on new dimensions. When per capita consumption was extremely low, it was enough to turn out standard necessities; later, it became necessary to think more about quality and variety and about providing more service and convenience. These new desiderata required a much more flexible system of allocating resources and making production decisions. There was thus a need to reform the motivation and control system that governs production decisions so that the consumers' share of total resources could be turned into consumer goods in a way more subtly responsive to the wishes of consumers.

Changes in circumstances and goals within the Communist world also called for corollary changes in the strategy of growth. The rationale for many characteristics of the command economy was to insulate production decisions against the ways by which consumers might hamper the allocation of resources to investment. With that motive attenuated, there remained little reason to suffer misallocation and inefficiency. These changes also suggested that new strategy must ensure better use of existing capacity, better allocation of resources, and more rapid and flexible adaptation to changing opportunities. Economic growth could no longer mean just an increased volume of output of the standard mix of commodities characteristic of the past; it required improvement in productive efficiency and intensification of the production processes.

The Khrushchev Era

Reforms in the Soviet version of socialism occurred during the regimes of Khrushchev, Leonid Brezhnev, and Mikhail Gorbachev. Khrushchev orchestrated the sharpest break from the classical Stalinist model prior to Gorbachev. The Khrushchev period retained essentially intact, albeit with attempts at reform, the main elements of the institutions—collectivized farms, state-owned enterprises, bureaucratic coordination, national economic planning, and a dominant position of the Party and state in economy and society—that constituted the core of the "politically-directed" economy (Solo 1967). At the same time, Khrushchev significantly modified those features of the system inherited from the Stalinist era, notably the personal tyranny of the dictator and the systematic use of terror as a means of political power, that were perceived by the post-Stalinist collective leadership, which Khrushchev represented, to constitute the most objectionable elements of Stalin's totalitarian rule.

Thus, largely because of changes initiated in the Khrushchev era, several of which were more or less retained by subsequent administrations, "the Soviet Union ceased to be a totalitarian political system after Stalin's death." The "most important and decisive change" was the "retreat from terror" and its sharp reduction as "an instrument of state power." Perhaps the second most significant change was that, although the system continued to generate single, dominant leaders, none of them from Khrushchev onward held power or authority approaching that of Stalin, and all "had to operate through collegial decision-making organs." In addition, partly because of Khrushchev's critique of Stalin's "personality cult," the Stalinist ideology lost much of its "normative popular appeal." The declining credibility of the Soviet ideology, which, if anything, steadily continued in the Brezhnev period, meant that "this pillar of the totalitarian system ceased to play its former role," as evidenced by the perceived need to rely more heavily on material incentives (Rutland 1992, 7-9).

Even those elements of the totalitarian state economy that survived more or less intact from the Stalinist years (dominance of the single party, monopoly control over the media of mass communication, centralized economic institutions) were modified. The role of the central party leadership decreased in the Khrushchev period because "economic administration was radically decentralized, and local party organs played a vital role in holding the economy together." The role of market processes, in both labor and consumer goods, expanded relative to party and state command and control. The organization of work and production was characterized by a significant "de-Stalinization " and strengthening of workers' control. Critiques of Stalin's errors stimulated greater openness, especially in scientific and scholarly work, including economics. The Khrushchevian variant of authoritarian state socialism was a "post-totalitarian society;" it retained significant vestiges of its Stalinist past and differed in various ways from common garden variety conservative authoritarian systems, which tend to "leave large parts of civil society more or less intact, from religious groups to private business interests." But overall, the institutional and policy innovations of the Khrushchev period marked a "clear qualitative break from the Stalinist past" and made the post-Stalinist Soviet Union, notably its pattern of leadership, look "much more like an authoritarian regime than a totalitarian one" (Rutland 1992, 6, 8, 23).

The Brezhnev Period

The Brezhnev period was characterized by some of the same pressures for economic and political reform found during the Khrushchev era. Theoretical arguments proposing economic reforms were prominently associated with the ideas of Evsey Liberman, a noted economist and engineer. Economic reforms in practice occurred especially under the auspices of Premier Aleksei Kosygin, who provided the main challenge to Brezhnev's leadership as well as the major critique among top political leaders of centrally planned economy. Kosygin sought to enhance the authority and responsibilities of enterprise managers by reducing the number of success indicators and giving managers greater latitude in the use of resources. Economic reforms remained relatively conservative, however. Enterprise autonomy was restricted in two major ways. First, output mix and input mix (what and how to produce) remained under centralized oversight. Second, prices were set administratively, based on the traditional cost of production approach rather than on market criteria. Moreover, during the 1970s, many of the modest Soviet economic reforms of the 1960s were modified or reversed. At most, the reforms in the system of economic management strove to improve the quality of economic performance within the framework of an essentially unchanged system of centralized planning, administration, and allocation.

The Brezhnev regime strongly emphasized institutional continuity and political stability. The result was an oligarchic, bureaucratic, collectivist rule in which all powerful interest groups were represented and major decisions were reached on the basis of consensus among the leading participants. This oligarchic leadership pattern originated in an attempt to dismantle Khrushchev's "harebrained schemes," for example, his bifurcation of the party into rural and urban components. It persisted because, among other reasons, political leaders were fairly evenly balanced in power and shared common values. Bureaucratic collectivism was characterized by a diminution in personal tyranny and dictatorship and an enhancement in intraparty democracy, by comparison with the classical Stalinist model. But it also constituted a bureaucratic predilection toward the status quo and an aging of the Soviet leadership, which contributed to the severe economic stagnation of the Brezhnev regime, especially in its later years.

The Gorbachev Era

The Gorbachev era in Soviet development was the most advanced version of reform socialism, which led to the disintegration of the politico-economic system of the Soviet Union. It was an exemplar of a self-declared movement toward a more democratic and humane socialism. Economically, it embodied perestroika, or the restructuring of economic institutions, priorities, and policies. Politically, it incorporated glasnost (openness), or liberalization of social and cultural life, and demokratizatsiya or democratization. According to Gorbachev and his supporters, the variant of Soviet socialism that emerged in the late 1980s and early 1990s constituted "a qualitatively new state of society" which renounced the classical or "deformed" model of the 1930s and the political bureaucratism and economic stagnation of the 1970s. It inherited the "best elements" of both its founding fathers (Lenin and Bukharin) and of other societies and systems. It would be based on diverse modes of ownership, including cooperative, local, and individual as well as state forms, would enhance democratic workers' self-management, would make a "stage-by-stage transition to a market system," and would retain a significant role for central planning but abandon the "command-administrative" methods of the past (Gorbachev, cited in White 1992, 223-29).

Among the underlying causes of perestroika was the economic slowdown of the later years of the Brezhnev period, attributed to excessive centralization, domination by party and state authority, extensive modes of development, over-emphasis on state forms of ownership and management, excessive priority on military spending, and some external factors, such as falling oil prices and escalation of military spending by Western powers.

Perestroika, itself an evolutionary phenomenon, proceeded through several stages. In an initial stage (1985-1987), Gorbachev tinkered with the system by shifting priorities (from the military sector to consumption, from extensive to intensive development) and improving labor discipline. In a second stage (1987-1989), moderate reforms prevailed. These included greater delegation of decision-making powers, expansion in private and hybrid forms of ownership, and extension of glasnost and demokratizatsiya. In a third stage (from late 1989 on), the party relinquished its monopoly power position, the state monopoly in ownership was abandoned, and the centralized system for resource allocation and administrative direction of the economy ended (Dowlah 1992a, 150-52).

Gorbachev's "humanistic" and "democratizing socialism" succeeded in reducing some of the problems associated with earlier, more centralized, and more authoritarian modes of political economy. Yet at the same time, the attempt to construct a "third way," in between a statist society and market capitalism elicited tensions and problems of its own. Despite its problems and defects, the "classical system," like a market capitalist society, "forms a coherent whole." An affinity applies between the elements of it, so that they mutually complement and attract each other. The reform destroys the coherence of the classical system (Kornai 1992, 370-71). Depending on circumstances, it may be extremely difficult to establish an intermediate, or mixed economy, new order.

Economically, two examples will suffice here. First, the attempt to foster simultaneously higher economic growth and substantial economic restructuring proved to be unrealistic. Even if economic reforms are economically progressive in the long run, they are often dislocative in the short run, causing even lower growth, to say nothing about inflation, unemployment, inequality, and poverty. Second, market economy is not automatically self-emergent; nor does it develop rapidly. It requires institutions and attitudes which, in Western societies, took positive action and emerged slowly. Therefore, under reform socialism, old institutions tend to be dismantled before new ones have emerged to supersede them, with growing chaos as a result.

Gorbachev's attempt to guide the Soviet Union to a qualitatively new version of socialism also encountered major political impediments. First, perestroika was imposed from above. Although some of its aspects, notably glasnost and demokratizatsiya, were highly popular, others were not. The result was vacillation in the content and pace of economic reforms, reflecting a fundamental ambivalence among the Soviet population as well as the party-state elite concerning the reforms and their trade-offs. Second, the party, in the late 1980s, and early 1990s, buffeted by the pressures of economic slowdown and the challenges of reform, including threats to the power and status of the politocracy, lost the consensus forged during the Brezhnev years. It increasingly divided into factions, with conflicting opinions on reforms and with linkages to and support from different groups and elements in Soviet society. Gorbachev was caught in these contradictions, and he walked a tightrope between his more radical advisers and conservative defenders of the (modified) classical system, trying, largely unsuccessfully, to create a new consensus. Third, glasnost and democratizatsiya served to some extent as vehicles for criticizing the surviving elements of the classical system and thereby contributed to the reforms. But they stimulated additional forms of liberalization and democratization, hence challenging the power monopoly of the political leadership, indeed, eventually contributing to the disintegration and demise of the system itself. Hence, the end result of reform socialism in the Soviet instance was disintegration of the system.

Chapter 2

War Communism:
Transitional Command Economy

INTRODUCTION

The first model of political economy that the revolutionary Bolshevik leaders attempted to establish in the Soviet Union has generally been called "war communism." During the period of war communism, the Bolsheviks consolidated power over a country and a population that had been ravaged without interruption for years by World War I, the October Revolution, an excruciating civil war, and external hostility and intervention. Transforming themselves into the ruling power by November 7, 1917,[1] the Bolsheviks, under the leadership of Vladimir Ilyich Ulyanov (Lenin), had to fight against internal and external forces and enemies until the end of 1920 to save the revolution, build a new state, and commence a transition to a new form of economy and social order. The Bolshevik leaders accomplished these goals by orchestrating a powerful combination of strategies—dictatorship of the Communist party in the name of the proletariat, a warlike administrative mechanism, centralized economic planning, suppression of opposition, emergency mobilization of resources, and a form of egalitarianism characterized by the virtual disappearance of class distinctions.

The politico-economic model that emerged out of these strategies and circumstances may be described as a revolutionary transitional command economy. The period of war communism has been interpreted variously both in terms of content and duration.[2] For our purposes, war communism covered roughly the period from November 1917 to the Tenth National Congress of the Bolshevik party held in March 1921.[3] Basic features of the model are discussed below using the four criteria developed in Chapter 1.

UNDERLYING CAUSES

War communism was rooted in several interrelated factors: (1) revolutionary and ideological aspirations, (2) wartime exigencies, (3) needs and concerns for state building and economic development, and (4) the Russian tradition and legacies. Each factor, in various degrees, was significant in determining the character of political and economic organization during this period.[4]

Revolutionary and Ideological Aspirations

Certainly, the aspirations and revolutionary zeal of the Bolshevik leaders played a powerful role in shaping the policies of war communism in the immediate aftermath of the revolution. The Bolshevik Revolution, inspired by Marxian socialism, was aimed at overthrowing existing capitalist and landowning classes and replacing them with the rule of workers and peasants—officially described as a "revolutionary democratic dictatorship of the proletariat and the peasantry" (Corrigan, Ramsay, and Sayer 1978, 36). Because the revolution occurred in a semifeudal, largely agricultural, peasant-based, and economically backward country, it was believed necessary to catch up with the material advancements attained in the Western countries. For the revolution to succeed, the Bolsheviks, in addition to abolishing the bureaucratic and military machine of the tsarist empire, had to promise peace, redistribution of land, and an adequate supply of bread. Moreover, like many ordinary people, a significant component of the Bolshevik leadership, largely buoyed by revolutionary euphoria, also expected an early establishment of requisite conditions for socialism even in Russian preindustrial economy.

Swept by such revolutionary zeal, the Bolshevik leaders also brushed aside traditional Marxian schema of stages of development that made a highly industrialized economy a necessary prerequisite for socialist revolution. Most Bolshevik leaders, including Lenin and Leon Trotsky, discounted the necessity in Russia of a bourgeois-democratic revolution substantially prior to a socialist revolution. To Lenin, the Russian Revolution symbolized both the completion of Russia's bourgeois revolution and the inauguration of the socialist revolution.[5] Challenging other Bolshevik leaders, including Leonid Kamenev, who insisted that a socialist revolution could succeed only at a relatively high stage of economic development, Lenin declared, "Theory, my friend, is grey, but green is the eternal tree of life" (cited in Hough and Fainsod 1979, 46). Lenin insisted that, in postrevolutionary Russia, the rule of the bourgeoisie could be rapidly succeeded by a dictatorship of the proletariat and peasantry.

Within months of the revolution, in *The ABCs of Communism* (1969), Nikolai Bukharin and Evgeniee Preobrazhensky declared that the "practical" and "immediate" responsibility of the new Soviet power was to establish the dictatorship of the proletariat and, to organize all economic activities under a centrally controlled national plan. Such centralized national planning would replace capitalistic market processes by an elaborate governmental machinery. The plans and visions of the victorious Bolshevik leaders, as discussed below, revolutionized both the expectations and the actions of many common people throughout the postrevolutionary period.

War and Civil War Exigencies

A second set of factors responsible for the emergence of the war communism model was the wartime exigencies that Bolshevik leaders and the Russian population faced in the immediate aftermath of the Revolution. The Soviet Union emerged as the first country in the world that claimed to be a workers' and peasants' state. Although the Bolsheviks succeeded in quickly overthrowing the Provisional Government,[6] virtually without bloodshed, consolidation of Bolshevik power took three years of eventful, uncertain, and violent struggles against internal propertied classes, counterrevolutionary ("White") armies, and external aggressors. The Brest-Litovsk treaty (signed in March 1918 to concede defeat in World War I) cost dearly in terms of population, agriculture, industry, and mineral resources.[7] Moreover, throughout the war communism period, the newly born state was under constant attacks by allied forces from both inside and outside the country, and a substantial part of its territory was under foreign occupation. In addition to the occupying powers, the Bolshevik Revolution was threatened by pro-tsarist White generals and anti-Bolshevik and pro- nationalist forces within the country. Thus, "survival was the categorical imperative of socialist construction after the Bolsheviks seized power in a collapsing Russian state," and military and political factors were "dominant in the initial stages of the socialist experiment." War communism "was the creation of military necessity, though some Bolshevik leaders saw a virtue in it independent of necessity" (Cox 1991, 171-72).

External and internal threats to the survival of the fledgling Bolshevik regime had the effect "of privileging those internal forces that appear[ed] effectively to respond to them." Bolshevism in practice, consequently, was not "the gradual putting into effect of a socialist idea." Instead, military and political pressures intermingled with Russian versions of socialist ideology to provoke responses from the postrevolutionary leadership "in the realms of foreign policy, production, and the form of state that [had] nothing intrinsically to do with the socialist idea *per se*" (Cox 1991, 172). Specifically, needs and concerns arising from internal and external exigencies contributed heavily to the formation of the revolutionary transitional command model.[8] Internally, civil war called for tight organization of a relatively underdeveloped and unorganized proletarian class against the tsarist and anti-Bolshevik forces. External threats and aggression called for centralization of scarce economic resources and for command and control strategies. Moreover, creating, organizing, and feeding a revolutionary military force, the Red Army, to fight against both internal and external enemies in a war-devastated shortage economy required centrally controlled diversion and management of food, fuel and other materials. These contributed to centralized, even militarized, administration and control throughout this period.

Russian Tradition and Legacy

No doubt the policies of this period also originated in the centralized and authoritarian tradition and legacy of imperial Russia. The centralized variant of socialism that the Bolsheviks sought to establish during this period was deeply rooted in Russian experience. Politically, prerevolutionary Russia was ruled by a monarchy. It was never a democratic society and had no tradition of political pluralism. The first political party that emerged in Russia was only about two decades old when the October Revolution took place, and it was not until 1906 that an organized political party (the Kadets) assumed a formal role in the operation of the Russian government.[9] And it was not until the Revolution of 1905 (which followed the defeat of Russia in the Russo-Japanese War of 1904) that the tsar granted the Russian population a representative assembly, called the duma, universal suffrage, and freedom of speech and association.[10] Economically, prerevolutionary Russia had several characteristics conducive to centralized decision making. Its population, as Maurice Dobb (1928, 123) remarks, had "none of the essential conditions" for the success of a decentralized economic system. In the immediate aftermath of the revolution, for example, the Russian population did not have "a fairly high standard of education, intelligence, and integrity" (122). Also, as mentioned above, in prerevolutionary Russia, industry and finance capital achieved a considerable level of concentration and monopolization. Moreover, much of the prerevolutionary Russian industry was owned and operated by foreigners.[11] Consequently, the Russians had little administrative or economic knowledge and experience of modern industrial management. On the other hand, although on a limited scale, in prerevolutionary Russia the traditions and forms of communal economic organizations, such as the mir and various types of cooperatives, were very much alive. As well as a preference for communal and cooperative ownership and management, considering their country's backwardness compared to the Western countries, many Soviet people aspired for a stronger and more effective role for government in the economy (Hutchings 1982, 23-24).

Finally, Lenin and other Bolshevik leaders did not trust the independent ability of the working masses. The peasants, especially, were regarded as potential adversaries, although they were included in an extended concept of a worker-dominated proletariat to encourage them not to take sides with anti-Bolshevik forces.[12] Bolshevik leaders were also disturbed by the dwindling morale and support of economic experts and other professionals. Surveys revealed that almost 90 percent of state officials had little or no sympathy for, or were hostile to, the Bolshevik government.[13] Having little faith in the integrity and support of administrative personnel and little confidence in the independent ability of relatively uneducated and unorganized workers and peasants, Bolshevik leaders, being a small minority, believed that they were left with only one option: centralization of all important decisions. As the prerevolutionary Russian tradition was much the same, especially in respect to centralization of power, such efforts met little resistance. Of course, other factors such as wartime exigencies, shortages of resources, chaos in economic management, and armed opposition to the Soviet government, also contributed to continuation of a centralized and authoritarian tradition.

State Building and Economic Development

A fourth set of factors underlying war communism included the needs and concerns for state building and economic development. The Bolshevik leaders well understood that they had orchestrated a revolution in an economically backward country with a small, underdeveloped, and relatively unorganized proletariat.[14] Also, they comprehended that defending the revolution in an internally and externally hostile environment would be far more difficult than overthrowing an already substantially weakened imperial power. The burden of rebuilding a war-devastated economy with a war-torn population was overwhelming. The destruction of bourgeois bureaucratic, commercial, and agricultural classes and interests, and the establishment of a new class rule and power out of relatively inexperienced and unorganized peasants and workers posed an almost unsurmountable problem to the Bolshevik leaders, especially in a chaotic, postrevolutionary environment. In addition, Bolshevik leaders were committed to rapid economic development. Ideological aspirations to build socialism, the need to recover from the devastation of war, economic backwardness, and the dependence of the popular sense of legitimacy, perhaps survival, of the new regime, on raising mass living standards, all contributed to making economic development a leading Bolshevik priority.

The commitment to economic development and its relationship to state building were also affected by Bolshevik ideology. As noted earlier, prominent Bolsheviks such as Lenin and Trotsky rejected the mechanistic view that capitalism, by providing objective and subjective prerequisites, must necessarily precede socialism in a particular country. According to Lenin's theory of imperialism, the "chain" of world capitalism will be broken at its "weakest link," in a country like Russia. Nonetheless, for most Bolsheviks, capitalist modernization was paradigmatic for development of the productive forces, and socialism was subordinate to the developmental imperative. Although socialism may not require a precedent capitalism, Bolsheviks believed that it "cannot be built except on the foundation of levels and paths of development comparable to those enforced by capitalism." In short, modernization, incorporating such elements as capitalist-style divisions of labor, industrial hierarchy, and focus on investment and industry over consumption and agriculture, "must come before socialism." If capitalist forms of property relations are rejected as a means to foster modernization, the strategic question then becomes what is to substitute for those capitalist property (and associated political) relations? The Bolshevik answer, in the practical reality of the postrevolutionary situation, was to capture and "wield the machinery of State" (Corrigan, Ramsay, and Sayer 1978, 41-43). Thus, the high priority given to economic development, in the crucible of Soviet practice, became indissolubly linked with the extension of the scope and intensity of party/state direction of economic life.

The need for a powerful state, led by a vanguard party, was reinforced, in Bolshevik ideology, by the transitional problems of the war communism period. Bukharin, whom Lenin later called the "favorite of the party," provided the most sophisticated analysis of war communism made by the early Bolsheviks. According to Bukharin (1964), authoritarian and centralized methodologies are essential during the transition to socialism. First, war and proletarian revolution engender economic dislocation and declines in production, which require careful husbanding of resources by the revolutionary regime. Second, tight discipline and state control are also needed to achieve rapid and large-scale mobilization of resources to defeat counterrevolutionary and hostile external forces. Third, "because negative reproduction was necessarily concentrated in the more interconnected urban economy, and because the *petit-bourgeois* structure of agrarian production precluded effective nationalization, …coercive appropriation of surpluses was initially required" (Howard and King 1989, 293). After civil war was successfully concluded, the agricultural sector eventually socialized, class divisions and inequalities reduced, and planned economy (and thereby supersession of capitalist economic crises and depressions) successfully inaugurated, the state and its coercive agencies could wither away and participatory democracy could prevail. But the transition period was necessarily one of proletarian dictatorship over landowners, capitalists, and small business and farm proprietors, and centralized, authoritarian control over the working class by the state and vanguard party (Bukharin 1982).

INSTITUTIONS, PROGRAMS, AND POLICIES

Establishment of One-Party Monopoly

As mentioned above, by November 1917, the Bolsheviks had succeeded in overthrowing the Provisional Government which had assumed power following the successive events of the defeat of the tsar in World War I, the abdication of Nicholas II, and the refusal of the throne by his brother Michael. Immediately after seizing power, the Bolsheviks created the *Sovnarkom* (Council of People's Commissars) to run the revolutionary government in the name of the dictatorship of the proletariat.[15]

In the name of the dictatorship of the proletariat, the Bolsheviks established a dictatorship of the Communist party over the state and economy. For them, the Communist party stood for the interests of the workers and peasants; therefore, power exercised by the Communist party implied power of the workers and peasants. Moreover, they politicized the meaning of the proletariat by including everybody who was pro-Bolshevik as proletarian, and declaring that everybody opposed to the revolution was antiproletarian. The meaning of the term proletariat became further complicated by the fact that the Bolsheviks completely ignored social mobility during the period of war communism. Although many prerevolutionary workers and soldiers moved to white-collar jobs during and after the Revolution, they were perceived as proletarian, while many prerevolutionary bourgeoisie were identified as remaining nonproletarian, although it was often true that their class position was deliberately or forcibly changed during the course of the period.[16]

Prominent leaders of the *Sovnarkom* included Lenin as the chairman, Trotsky as the commissar for foreign affairs, and Joseph Stalin as the commissar of nationalities. No non-Bolshevik leaders were included in the *Sovnarkom*. Claiming to be the true representatives of the workers and peasants, the Bolshevik party declared it to be counterrevolutionary to share power with other political parties that represented other interests and classes. They established their own version of the dictatorship of the proletariat by cementing power under the Bolshevik party alone. Immediately after the seizure of power, however, the matter of coalition with other socialist parties arose prominently. This issue divided the Bolshevik party. Lenin and Trotsky, representing the majority, favored a party dictatorship, and Lev Kamenev, Gregory Zinoviev, and other Bolshevik leaders representing a moderate minority view, advocated a coalition with Mensheviks and Socialist Revolutionaries. But the majority view prevailed.[17]

Subsequently, in January 1918 the Bolshevik government dissolved the Constituent Assembly,[18] a remnant of the Provisional Government, on the alleged ground that it stood for bourgeois interests and betrayed the cause of the proletariat. Instead, the Third All-Russian Congress of Soviets assumed the supreme governing authority of the country and changed the name of the Provisional Workers' and Peasants' Government to the Workers' and Peasants' Government of the Russian Soviet Republic. The Russian Soviet Republic vested its supreme power in the Congress of Soviets and proposed a parliamentary form of federation consisting of all Soviet republics. Therefore, theoretically, the *Sovnarkom* was supposed to be appointed and removed by the Congress of Soviets. In practice, however, the Bolsheviks "even violated their own claimed attachment to Soviet authority and legality. Within months of the Revolution, the Party organs usurped the Soviets, curtailed or repressed pluralism within the revolutionary camp, manipulated elections, permitted or encouraged lawless repression, [and] prevented the development of an independent press or system of justice" (Blackburn 1991, 190). The Central Executive Committee of the Soviets, supposedly the permanent expression of the sovereign institution of the country, only rarely met in 1918 and not at all in 1919 (Farber 1990, 29). In March 1919, the Eighth Party Congress claimed the power of undivided political supremacy in the Soviet Union. Thus, the dictatorship of the Russian Communist Party was established over all political affairs in the country.[19]

Comprehensive Nationalization of Industries

War communism was characterized by a widespread nationalization of production and trade in the country.[20] Such government ownership of enterprises, however, did not occur immediately after the revolution. Lenin's initial position espoused a gradual and peaceful transition to socialism. In the early days of the revolution, recognizing the backward economic conditions and the relatively unorganized and undeveloped proletarian culture in the country, Lenin was inclined to introduce "state capitalism" for the transition period. The concept of "state capitalism" stood for a combination of government ownership in leading industries, state-regulated private enterprises, and state-leased and privately run factories and industries. The state-regulated and state-leased enterprises, however, would have a substantial degree of workers' control in management and operation. In the meantime, workers were expected to learn production, management, and accounting techniques from domestic and international capitalists.

But several circumstances forced a dramatic reversal from this stand by Lenin and the Bolshevik regime: a breakdown of industrial management, the strength of counterrevolutionary forces, problems associated with employer-worker relationships in the nonnationalized enterprises, strengthening of Leftist dominance in rural areas, and, above all, threats that former capitalists might be reinstalled with external help as owners of enterprises (Dobb 1928, 58-60).

The Soviet government's first nationalization decree came on June 28, 1918. It brought enterprises of over 1 million rubles of capital under state ownership and control. Widespread unauthorized nationalization of factories and industries went on throughout the country even before the national decree came into effect. Indeed, the first enterprises nationalized did not belong to the commanding heights that Lenin often emphasized and were of no particular national significance (Malle 1985, 49). An earlier decree of December 18, 1917, provided that enterprises could be nationalized if they were considered important from the viewpoint of state interest; if enterprise owners refused to accept workers' control over enterprise management; or if produc-

Table 2.1
Number of Industrial Units Nationalized by Initiatives of Various Institutions, 1917-1918

Institutions	Nov.-Dec. 1917 N	S	M	Jan.-Mar. 1918 N	S	M	Apr.-Jul. 1918 N	S	M	After Jul. 1918 N	S	M	Total
Sovnarkom	10	-	-	17	1	-	247	3	-	177	1	-	456
Vesenkha	4	11	-	12	1	-	104	4	164	3	-	-	292
Local Soviets	136	11	61	208	16	76	251	24	147	197	10	88	1,225
Local *Sovnrakhozy*	18	2	4	56	6	4	264	13	31	417	18	28	861
Trade Unions	3	2	4	14	2	17	24	10	26	20	1	18	141
others	23	3	17	94	1	13	56	6	12	96	12	30	363
TOTAL	194	18	86	401	27	110	946	60	216	1,071	45	164	3,338

Source: Malle (1985, 54).

tion units were abandoned or closed down by former owners. By July 1918, out of a total of 1,071 expropriated enterprises, only 341 were nationalized by the central authorities; the rest were socialized by local organizations and labor unions. As Table 2.1 shows, out of 3,338 enterprises nationalized, confiscated, or municipalized by 1920, less then 14 percent, only 456, were handled by the *Sovnarkom*. On the other hand, the local Soviets' share was 36.6 percent. In fact, one of the main reasons for promulgation of a national decree was to stop unauthorized expropriation by local organizations.

After promulgation of the nationalization decree, however, the nationalization process went so far that, by the beginning of 1919, more than 1,000 enterprises were nationalized; by the end of 1920, out of a total of 37,000 enterprises nationalized with 1,615,000 workers, almost half were nonmechanical, 3,492 employed only one worker, and 3,676 employed only two workers. The number of state enterprises that employed fewer than five workers totaled 12,077. Enterprises that did not employ hired labor at all, which totaled about 185,727 in 1920, however, were not nationalized or considered in the category of state enterprises. Table 2.2 shows the number and percentages of enterprises nationalized by 1920. It also shows the number of workers affected by such nationalization.[21]

Administration of the nationalized enterprises was organized both horizontally and vertically under the overall guidance and direction of *Vesenkha* (the Supreme Council of National Economy), formed in December 1917.[22] *Vesenkha* was responsible, among other things, for guiding national economic policies, overseeing nationalization efforts, and coordinating the functions of factory committees. Vertically, all enterprises under an industry were brought under the control of *glavki* (intermediate economic organizations) created for that industry; and horizontally, industries in a province were placed under the control and guidance of local economic councils called *sovnarkhozy*. Such a vertical, or centralized, and a horizontal, or decentralized, coordination and control of enterprises and economic activities resulted in tensions and contradictions. We shall focus on this issue below.

Table 2.2
Nationalization of Enterprises in the Soviet Union, 1917-1920

Branches	Number of Enterprises	Number of Workers	Number of Nationalized Enterprises	Percent of Nationalized Enterprises
Quarrying clay, earth moving	998	187,487	445	44.5
Metal Working	1,155	243,547	582	50.4
Wood Working	242	9,984	157	64.9
Chemicals	261	45,735	244	93.5
Food-Processing	2,639	161,551	1,946	73.7
Organic materials	421	43,322	228	54.1
Textiles	847	454,639	629	74.2
Paper & Printing	146	32,684	146	100.
Mineral-metal	133	91,963	127	95.5
Various	66	6,600	43	65.1
Total	6,908	1,277,515	4,547	65.7

Source: Malle (1985, 62).

After initial experiments with control by workers' councils over industrial management, by 1920 individual factories and production units were placed under one-man management (OMM). Introduction of OMM radically shifted emphasis to the productivity and technical skills of workers. Initiated under the dominant influence of Trotsky, OMM sought to institute military-like order and discipline on the relatively unorganized and chaotic economic management of the country. Emphasis was placed on organizing labor so as to bring every able-bodied person under a system of universal labor mobilization aimed at increasing productive efficiency and output. The Bolshevik leaders justified such mobilization of labor on the grounds that, because Russia lacked what Marx called "primitive" (precapitalist) capital accumulation and was economically backward, it was necessary to resort to labor conscription to create the foundations of a socialist economy.

Indeed, most of the Bolshevik leaders were preoccupied with the idea of economic development. Bukharin (1964, 11-12), for example, described mobilization of labor as the "basic moment of socialist primitive accumulation." Lenin's preoccupation with development was paramount, as illustrated by his repeated emphasis on electrification. He sided with Trotsky's emphasis on military-style organization and discipline of labor. Dissatisfied with rapidly deteriorating economic conditions, Trotsky criticized workers' councils and insisted on their replacement by competent technical authorities. To him, competent and skilled people constituted national capital, which should be exploited for building socialism like any other means of production. Neither OMM nor other measures, however, succeeded in halting the decline of the industrial sector or the economy as a whole. On the contrary, these policies had many unintended consequences, tensions, and contradictions, which will be discussed below.

Sweeping nationalizations of almost all sectors of the economy—from handicraft enterprises to machine building, from engineering to chemical industries—were not accompanied by an efficient administrative machinery or adequate planning. Establishment of collective ownership over almost all means of production in a war economy called for central control and direction of production and distribution. Indeed, central planning or centralized administrative machinery of this period, which some refer to as the genesis of the Stalinist model,[23] emerged during this period as offshoots of central control of most of the productive units.[24] As the workers and peasants, the driving force of the revolution, had little experience in running such a gigantic administration, the Bolshevik leaders sought support of bourgeois specialists in running the economy. Indeed, confronting harsh realities, the Bolsheviks largely continued the existing infrastructures and patterns of administration. According to some estimates, carryover personnel from the old regimes at the upper and middle reaches of the Bolshevik government ranged between 50 and 80 percent.[25]

Food Requisitioning

Another feature of this period was forced requisition of food from the peasants. The exigencies of the civil war made it imperative for the Bolshevik regime to collect grain from the peasants to feed the Red Army, the workers, and the urban population. Thus, the desired distribution of food was critical, even at the expense of production. Records show that as a result of land reforms agricultural production did rise in the early days of the revolution. Indeed, the Bolsheviks championed—one might say acquiesced—in a sweeping land reform in the country that evicted large landowners and redistributed land among the former landless peasants. Nationalization of land was proclaimed on the second day of the Bolshevik Revolution, November 8, 1917. Although serfdom had been abolished in 1861, large estates survived until the October Revolution. In addition, between 1861 and 1917, a class of wealthy peasants, later called kulaks, emerged and prospered up until Stalin's agricultural collectivization in the late 1920s.[26]

The November Land Decree nationalized the remaining large estates, and abolished private ownership of land altogether. Bolsheviks acceded to the redistribution of land among the peasants, which allowed landless agricultural laborers to get a share of the redistributed land. In return, the Bolsheviks expected peasant cooperation. Although the former landless peasants largely remained allied to the Revolution, problems continued with the rich peasants, or kulaks, throughout this period. As hyperinflation transformed money into worthless paper, the peasants became increasingly reluctant to exchange their products for rubles. When initial efforts, based on monetary transactions, to collect agricultural goods from the peasants failed, in May 1918, the disenchanted Bolshevik regime resorted to *prodrazverstka* (the system of food requisitioning).[27] The *prodrazverstka* made it mandatory for the peasants to deliver a specified "surplus" agricultural production to the government for a nominal price. The government employed police (the *Cheka*) and party activists for requisitioning and did not hesitate to use force if necessary to extract the agricultural surplus from unwilling peasants. But since the surplus was arbitrarily decided by the government, the peasants often responded by concealing production or by refusing to produce more than their

Table 2.3
Percentage of Soviet Population in Ration Categories, 1918-1920

Category	Oct. 1918	Jan. 1919	Jan. 1920	April 1920
1	52.3	*81.1	63.0	63.0
2	38.6	16.5	7.0	6.5
3	8.9	2.2	.2	.1
4	.2	---	30.0	30.0

* Of the 81.0 percent, 20.0 percent were children.

Source: McAuley (1989, 164).

own requirements. The government, faced by the overpowering need to feed the Red Army and workers, eventually succeeded by coercive measures, in confiscating minimally necessary supplies of food.

An almost unsurmountable food shortage also compelled the government to resort to a rigid food-rationing system in the urban areas.[28] For the purpose of rationing, the entire adult population was divided into four categories according to their occupations. People engaged in heavy labor belonged to category 1; less heavy manual labor and white-collar employees belonged to category 2; the intelligentsia belonged to category 3; and the bourgeoisie (renters, house owners, stall owners, and so on) belonged to category 4. Following socialist egalitarianism, such categorizations were intended to make sure that category 1 members received the most food and category 4, the least. Although this rationing system worked initially, it soon became largely ineffective in the face of increasing pressures for reclassification.

By October 1918, as Table 2.3 shows, a little more than half of the population was categorized as heavy laborers and therefore was entitled to higher ration benefits. Only 0.2 percent were in the category of "bourgeoisie" and therefore subjected to the minimum of rationed goods. All this happened at a time when almost no one in urban Russia could live on the meager rations. Subsequently, the percentage of people in category 4 increased dramatically, reaching 30 percent, meaning almost one in three received the lowest amount of rations. On the other hand, categories 2 and 3, although they constituted 47.5 percent of the population in October 1918, by April 1920 constituted only 6.6 percent. A large section of these groups, apparently, ended up either in category 1 or category 4, depending on the degree of their support for or opposition to the revolutionary forces.

Elimination of Money and Market Relations

Nationalization of industry was also accompanied by efforts to eliminate money and market relations altogether. To many of the revolutionary Bolshevik leaders, nationalization and elimination of market mechanisms constituted core tasks for establishing socialism. Moreover, in a climate of postrevolutionary chaos and mismanagement of the economy, they appeared to be natural twins, one necessitating the other. War exigencies required centralized control and direction of nationalized enterprises, and the task of centralization of control could be easier, it was widely assumed, in a nonmonetized and administratively activated economy. Accordingly, *Vesenkha* was made responsible for centralized control of enterprises, along with supply of inputs and distribution of finished products of enterprises. Such monopoly power, Dobb (1928, 101-3) observes, transformed *Vesenkha* into a giant "merchant manufacturer" which gave out work and organized a nationwide division of labor among numerous dependent producers.

Vesenkha, in turn, exercised strong control and supervision over enterprises through a nationwide administrative network that brought all nationalized enterprises under a giant barter system, in which state orders, not money, served as instruments of transactions. Even smaller enterprises were brought under state control so that monetary transactions could be eliminated and a barter system could be extended to smaller transactions.[29] Between 1919 and 1921, workers were paid mainly in kind. In many places they received rationed goods, including food and consumer goods, free of charge. As money lost its importance as a medium of exchange and monetary calculations were gradually replaced by simple bookkeeping, enterprises, in turn, had to make no payments for raw materials or wages for labor services. Non-monetization was not confined to the state sector but was extended among the rural and nonpublic sectors as well (Nove 1969, 64-65).

Coupled with dependence on the printing press, the Bolshevik government's drive to replace monetary transactions with calculations and allocations in kind resulted in both economic decline and a high rate of inflation. Between March and November of 1917 alone, the currency in circulation nearly doubled, and prices rose 224 percent. Prices multiplied three times in the course of 1919 and over four times in 1920 (Dobb 1928, 81). Overall, as Table 2.4 shows, compared to 1913, the price level in Russia rose by more than 1,000 percent by 1921. The table also shows how the rapid rise in prices was accompanied by increasing circulation of money during this period. As the following section shows, attempts to abolish monetary processes had far-reaching repercussions on the overall performance of the economy, in particular, on the evolving relationship between the rural peasants and urban workers.

CONSEQUENCES

Political Consequences

Besides a decisive victory in the civil war, the policies of this period brought for the Bolsheviks a number of often overlooked but far-reaching accomplishments. The most significant among them was state building. In the ruins of the inherited imperial state machinery, the Bolsheviks had to build a new state structure and apparatus completely from scratch. Extinction of the tsarist monarchy, a proletarian revolution, and the dislocations and turmoil of civil war paralyzed the Russian state apparatus. The Bolsheviks, as professional revolutionaries, organized and presided over the state with strict military discipline. In addition to fighting internal and external enemies, they had to organize, feed, equip and run an army of about 5 million people; mobilize labor nationwide; establish and sustain the legitimacy of proletarian rule (in the absence of which the crucial support of the peasants could well go to White generals); and, above all, keep the revolution alive and attain victory in a savage civil war (Dowlah 1993).[30]

Table 2.4
Volume of Currency Growth and Price Level in Soviet Economy, 1916-1921

Year	Volume of Currency	Price Level	National Income
1916	3.40	1.43	-----
1917	5.57	2.94	0.75
1918	16.60	20.76	-----
1919	36.80	164.00	-----
1920	135.20	2,420.00	-----
1921	702.00	16,800.00	0.38

Source: Shmelev and Popov (1989, 6)

All these developments had far-reaching implications for subsequent periods of Soviet society. Some of the by-products of the state-building process, such as politically commanded central planning, centralized and bureaucratic administrative machinery, militarization of labor, and coercion of peasants, profoundly affected Soviet economic and political history. Continuity theorists claim that the Stalinist programs of mass collectivization, rapid industrialization, and even the establishment of a totalitarian state system had their origins in the state-building processes of the war communism period. While the continuity theorists find strong similarities between Stalinism and war communism, and believe the former was the continuation of the latter, their opponents oppose this strand of thought with equal force. Opponents to the continuity thesis argue that, although there were significant similarities between Stalinist programs and war communism, the former significantly differed from the latter, especially in respect to the comprehensive scope of Stalinist party and state structures and the Stalinist personal tyranny and personality cult.[31]

Economic Consequences

Economically, this period brought excruciating suffering to much of the population. The industrial sector, including communication, transportation, and distribution systems, almost completely collapsed. Policies of war communism alienated the peasants by forcing them to submit to an arbitrarily defined food requisition policy, caused massive migration of urban people to the villages in search of food and security, and created nationwide economic chaos compounded by serious dislocations and an illegal underground economy.

The dimensions and magnitude of the catastrophic decline of the industrial sector can be seen in Table 2.5. As it shows, gross industrial production by 1921 fell to 31 percent of 1913 levels. In such large-scale industries as coal and steel, the decline was more dramatic. Compared to 1913, production fell to 21 percent, exports and imports fell to less than 1 percent, and output of bricks, cement, iron ore, pig iron, and railway carriages fell to below 5 percent. In 1920 production of fully manufactured goods and semimanufactured goods reached only 12.9 percent and 13.6 percent, respectively, of the 1913 value (Carr 1952, 195). By 1920 the total shipments of goods carried by

Table 2.5
Performance of Soviet Economy in 1921 Compared to 1913

Indicators	1913	1921
Gross Output of all industry (index)	100	31
Large-scale industry (index)	100	21
Coal (million tons)	29	9
Oil (Million tons)	9.2	3.8
Electricity (milliard Kwhs)	2039	520
Pig Iron (million tons)	4.2	0.1
Steel (million tons)	4.3	0.2
Bricks (millions)	2.1	0.01
Sugar (million tons)	1.3	0.05
Railway tonnage carried (millions)	132.4	39.4
Agricultural production (index)	100	60
Imports (1913 rubles)	1374	208
Exports (1913 rubles)	1520	20

Source: Nove (1969, 68).

railway and waterway amounted to only one-fifth of 1913 levels. Overall industrial production ranged between 0 percent and 43 percent of 1913 levels, and overall labor productivity declined sharply (Dowlah 1992a, 69).[32]

The collapse in industrial production and labor productivity was compounded by sharp reductions in the agricultural sector. The harvest of major grain crops in Russia fell by 36 percent between 1917 and 1920, and total agricultural output in 1920 was only half the prewar quantity (Hutchings 1982, 31).

Demographic Consequences

War communism policies also created serious problems concerning migrations of urban people.[33] Although Russia was far from a fully industrialized capitalist economy at the moment of the October Revolution, its overall degree of urbanization in 1917 was about 20 percent.[34] There were more than fifteen cities with populations greater than 100,000, with the main concentrations of urbanization in St. Petersburg (formerly Petrograd) and Moscow. Confronted by food shortages, in St. Petersburg, 2 million people left the city by 1918. Moscow lost about 40 percent of its total population during the war communism period.[35]

Decline of the urban population was not, however, uniform in all cities. As Table 2.6 shows, emigration was very significant in the northern food-importing cities and less significant in the southern food-producing cities. The average decline of the urban population was only 14 percent in the latter cities, but was 24 percent in the former cities. Overall, smaller urban areas (less than 10,000 population) lost on the average

Table 2.6
Change in Population of Major Russian Cities, 1910-1920

City	1910	1920
St. Petersburg	1,962,000	722,000
Moscow	1,533,000	1,028,000
Odessa	506,000	435,000
Kiev	505,000	366,000
Khar'kov	236,000	284,000
Saratov	206,000	190,000
Ekaterinoslav	196,000	164,000
Tiflis	188,000	327,000
Kazan	188,000	146,000
Baku	167,000	256,000
Astrakhan	150,000	123,000
Rostov-On-Don	121,000	177,000
Nizhnyi-Novgorod	109,000	70,000
Ufa	103,000	93,000
Minsk	101,000	104,000
Samara	96,000	177,000
Taritsyn	78,000	81,000
Perm	50,000	74,000

Source: Koerner (1989, 82).

10 percent of their inhabitants, intermediate size cities (10,000 to 50,000 population) lost 17 percent of their population, and major cities (with over 50,000 population) lost 25 percent of their population. Table 2.6 also shows the magnitude of deurbanization of major Russian cities between 1910 and 1920.

The migrations of the 1917-1920 period caused serious problems for the Bolsheviks because they threatened the proletarian base of Bolshevik power and the working-class content of the Soviet state. The October Revolution was primarily based on the support of urban workers, and most of the urban industrial workers supporting the revolution lived in the two biggest cities of the country: Petrograd and Moscow. In 1915 about 75 percent of Petrograd province's population and 53 percent of Moscow province's population lived in these cities. Now that almost half of these people had left the cities, many, especially the Mensheviks, began to interpret this event as a withering away of the social base for the legitimacy of Bolshevik rule. Lenin himself proclaimed at the Tenth Party Congress in 1922, "People have run away from hunger; workers have simply abandoned their factories, they set up housekeeping in the countryside and have stopped being workers" (quoted in Dowlah 1993, 71).

Lenin was partly right in pinpointing hunger and shortage of food as major reasons for such a huge migration to the countryside. But other conditions of this period, including the worsening terms of trade in agricultural products, the disorder of civil war, the disappearance of consumer goods, the closing out of enterprises, the disappearance of employment opportunities in urban areas, the disappearance of oil supplies and the dwindling of coal supplies, the epidemics of communicable diseases in the absence of health care and presence of unsanitary conditions, and the relatively better food and employment opportunities in the rural areas, also contributed heavily.[36]

Workers, disgruntled by industrial and commercial depression in the urban areas, also found it attractive to move to villages where they could claim communal land. Indeed, throughout the period of war communism, the workers suffered the most. The peasants were relatively better off—they got land, they had food, and most of the battles were fought in urban areas. Therefore, the attraction of land, food, and security all played important roles in the deurbanization during this period. This can be gauged from the fact that much of the disappearing urban workforce showed up in the countryside, in the army, in the workers' communes and Soviet farms, or in rural industry and producers' cooperatives, and in state services such as food detachments and inspection (Carr 1952, 195).

Conditions of Workers and Labor Unions

War communism succeeded in accomplishing one working-class aspiration: a remarkable degree of egalitarianism in society. Private properties in land and capital were largely abolished, and property incomes (rents, interest, profits, dividends) were essentially eliminated. The state controlled almost all the means of production, and monetary transactions were either eliminated or reduced to insignificance. Workers confiscated factories and sharply curtailed wage differentials. Rationing ensured egalitarian modes of food distribution. By these various means, class distinctions and inequalities in wealth and income were largely abolished. The upper and middle classes simply disappeared, and workers' emancipation from class exploitation and liberation from the tsarist state and social machineries were accomplished.[37]

But as we have seen, war communism imposed excruciating economic hardships on the working class. Moreover, the costs of war communism were not only economic ones. Soviet workers were also subjected to undemocratic political processes. Labor unions, workers' committees, and Soviets—the proletarian organizations that played key roles in the Bolshevik Revolution—were all substantially weakened in terms of prestige and status by the end of the war communism period. Indeed, the Bolshevik government, shortly after the revolution, turned the labor unions' role upside down. Instead of their traditional role in a capitalist society, that is, protection of the rights of labor against employers, the Bolsheviks turned labor unions into instruments to carry out state policies more effectively. Unions were effectively utilized for nationwide conscription and mobilization of labor and for enforcement of stricter labor discipline in industries and factories. Such statization of labor unions caused serious erosion in their ability to influence working conditions or to limit wage differentials. Subsequently, by the end of 1920, the appropriate role of labor unions in a socialist state became a subject of acrimonious debate among top Bolshevik leaders. Although both Lenin and Trotsky considered labor unions as instruments of government to be commanded by the Communist party or the party-run state, they differed in terms of (relatively more) dictatorial versus more democratic means of accomplishing it.[38]

Although it is tantalizing to speculate, we do not know what would have happened in the relationship between the party and the working class (or the party and society generally) had there been no civil war and accompanying decimation of the working class. Conceivably, some variant of "guided democracy," more akin to Lenin's characterizations of the working class and state in *The State and Revolution,* qualified by his belief that workers need education and direction by professional revolutionaries, might have emerged. In fact, the practical exigencies of war, revolution, and economic underdevelopment paled by comparison with the chaos of the war communism period. What actually occurred constituted a metamorphosis between the new party-state and workers as well as society at large.

Throughout the period of war communism, the Bolshevik party significantly strengthened its bureaucratic and coercive machineries. When the Bolsheviks seized power in October 1917, there were only 240,000 members of the Communist party. By the year 1920, the number of party members had increased to 600,000, only about 33 percent of whom had participated in the revolution, and only about 40 percent of whom were officially classified as "workers" (Schapiro 1984, 193). Moreover, the elimination of the control exercised by workers' councils over industrial management, the introduction of OMM, and differential wages for specialists were some of the policies the Bolshevik regime carried out that departed from more egalitarian and democratic aspirations of the prerevolutionary period.

TENSIONS AND CONTRADICTIONS

War communism succeeded in winning the civil war, and thereby was able to save the October Revolution from internal and external enemies. But it, or more precisely a combination of its programs and the civil war, also plunged the country into catastrophic economic decline. Production and productivity fell critically in all indices. Politically, almost all spheres of the country—peasants, workers, labor unions—reached potentially explosive points. Besides, throughout the period pro-tsarist elements or anti-Bolshevik forces remained alienated and hostile to the Bolshevik regime. These economic, political, and social conditions created many problems in postrevolutionary Russia. In this section we shall explore some of the tensions and contradictions that eventually led to the abandonment of this model.

The Peasant Question

The policies of war communism alienated the peasants. At first, the peasantry sided with the Bolsheviks because they promised them land. Few doubted that they had little commitment to a socialist society or to the Bolshevik Revolution.[39] As the White Army generals threatened to return lands to the old landlords, the peasants, primarily to protect their newly acquired land, found it a marriage of convenience to support the Bolsheviks. During the period of war communism, Bolsheviks figuratively waged a war against the recalcitrant peasants to ensure requisite supplies of food for the Red

Army and the urban population. As the peasantry received few industrial goods in exchange for food and as money progressively decreased in value, the peasants grew increasingly hostile to the Bolshevik regime. This hostility was further sharpened by the fact that the threat from the White Army generals was diminishing at the same time.

On the other hand, the Bolsheviks also grew impatient with the peasants. In prerevolutionary Russia, most of the peasants were landless. It is the Bolsheviks who supported the peasants' takeover of the lands, but the peasants' cooperation with the Bolshevik regime was, at its best, less than satisfactory. The rebellious peasants responded to the Bolshevik policy of forced requisition of food in three ways: they started to sow less, so that less could be confiscated; they substantially concealed their actual sowing, so that determination of confiscable amounts could be manipulated;[40] and they resorted to illegal private trade to sell food while the Bolshevik regime was trying to abolish money and market relations.

Although in an extended conception of the dictatorship of the proletariat, the Bolsheviks included the peasants as a partner of the new ruling class, the majority of the peasantry never considered themselves to be proletarian.[41] They rather considered themselves to be small land-owning proprietors, and they were vehemently opposed to exchanging agricultural produce without what they considered to be adequate compensation.[42] Although the Bolshevik onslaught on the peasants, organized by armed detachments of workers and poor peasant committees, went far beyond the kulaks and affected the intermediate peasants too, such sufferings, instead of weakening the peasants, hardened their opposition. As a result, peasant resistance to the Bolshevik regime became stronger and sometimes violent.[43]

Rights of Workers and Labor Unions

The Bolsheviks came to power in the name of the proletariat—proclaiming the working class as the core component of the new ruling power. But, as noted, workers suffered the most during the War communism period. They fought the war at all fronts: to drive out external enemies, to subdue the internal forces opposed to the revolution, to ensure a supply of food and fuel for the army and the urban population, and to increase production in the industries. Half-fed workers endured warlike mobilization of labor, stricter labor discipline, and large numbers of war casualties throughout the period. According to Schapiro (1984, 188), food consumption fell to 41 percent of prewar levels in the urban areas during the war communism period.[44] Workers, in effect, were militarized, and labor unions, as mentioned above, were transformed into an extension of the Bolshevik party or, in Lenin's expression, "transmission" belts from the Communist party to the masses (1922, 382).

But as hostilities with internal and external forces came to an end, the exhausted and weary workers became more defensive concerning their rights. The ensuing tensions can be illustrated by the fact that, while the first All-Russian Congress of Trade Unions in 1918 acceded to the declaration that the unions were organs of state power, the Eighth Congress held in 1919 declared that the unions should "concentrate de facto in their hands the whole administration of the whole national economy as a single economic entity." Tension between the government and labor unions intensified with a catastrophic transportation crisis in 1920 that threatened the breakdown of the whole economy. Instead of greater concessions to workers' demands and needs, it was resolved, mainly at the behest of Trotsky, to establish firm discipline under the dictatorship of the Bolshevik party.

At the Third All-Russian Congress of Trade Unions in 1920, the Mensheviks demanded freedom of the working class from the policies of the "militarization of labor." This issue, as mentioned before, paralyzed the Bolshevik leadership at the top. Lenin emphasized that with the change of internal conditions, new strategies were called for to ensure labor discipline. Trotsky, following his views of militarization of labor, saw the solution to these problems along military lines. As mentioned above, neither Lenin nor Trotsky was opposed to strict Party control over labor unions. Therefore, the Mensheviks' proposal for the freedom of workers from compulsory work or Trotskian type "labor armies" failed. But attempts were made to mitigate labor union problems more tactfully, as suggested by Lenin. Because the working class, however, was less and less willing to accept such militarization of labor with the end of the civil war, this issue emerged as a formidable source of tension between workers and the Bolshevik regime.

Ideological Contradictions

War communism generated considerable ideological controversy. As noted, it was a revolutionary transitional command model aimed at rapidly establishing a highly centralized and statist variant of socialism. Economically, it emphasized that all means of production ought to be nationalized, a central plan ought to control the economy from the top, money and market relations should be abolished, workers ought to be mobilized as in a war, and an egalitarian wage system ought to be established. Politically, a dictatorship of the Bolshevik party was to exercise power in the name of a loosely defined proletariat. All organizations, including political opposition and labor unions, were to be strictly subordinated under the supreme command of the Bolshevik party. The Bolshevik leaders promoted all these changes in the name of Marxian socialism. As we indicated above, these policies diverged in various ways from classical Marxian expectations concerning a postcapitalist, socialist society. Contradictions and tensions emanating from these policies, as will be explored in subsequent chapters, had far-reaching implications during the entire history of the Soviet Union.

Gaps Between Prescriptions and Practices

The Bolsheviks, as the above discussion shows, attempted to establish their first, early version of socialism through various shortcuts. These shortcuts created a number of unintended and dysfunctional consequences. Although some of these consequences were mere by-products or side effects of the ill-conceived or accidental policies of war communism, they engendered disturbing tensions.

First, for some Bolsheviks, the nationalization of industries, a centralized administrative system, central planning of production, consumption and allocation of resources, and replacement of money and market mechanisms constituted requisite conditions for building socialism, if not defining properties of socialism itself. Bolshevik leaders pursued all these innovations forcefully, although they created extreme forms of bureaucratization and statization. Indeed, during war communism, statism became de facto a virtual synonym for socialism. On the other hand, traditional socialist thought had never stated, as Lewin (1974, 82) remarks, "that the process of expanding socialism would become tantamount to the growth of state machinery." Indeed, in his critical notes on *The Gotha Program*, Marx (1973, xxiv: 94) contended that "freedom consists in converting the state from an organization superimposed on society to one completely subordinate to it." Just before the Bolshevik Revolution, in *The State and Revolution*, Lenin (1974), echoing Marx and Engels's line of thought, professed a limited and demising role for centralized state institutions under socialist society. Moreover, the early Bolshevik image of socialism, certainly by rank-and-file revolutionaries, included egalitarianism, democracy, and workers' control, as well as social ownership and overall planning. Although Lenin (and, especially, Trotsky) favored essentially centralized modes of decision making during this period, the party's left wing criticized the emergence of the party-state bureaucracy and employment of former tsarist officials and managers, and proposed control over production decisions by a cooperative association of workers, democratic election of officials and managers, and income equality.

Massive growth of a centralized administrative apparatus in a chaotic state and economy created two sets of unintended consequences. On the one hand, overcentralization prevented Bolshevik leaders "from centralized control over the chaotic sprawl of official agencies"; therefore, it became "progressively less capable of responding to progressively greater crises." On the other hand, as the Bolshevik regime stripped away workers' rights, the workers themselves resorted to counter mobilizations against the proletarian government which had been established in their name (Remington 1984, 20-21).

As markets and money relations were replaced by bureaucratic administration, and as forced requisition of food and conscription of labor followed, both the peasants and the workers were turned into instruments of production under the control of state machineries. On the other hand, many of the people who acquired positions in the new administrative machineries were tsarist or antirevolutionary elements. Therefore, class relations were not eliminated but were sustained or reinforced by the Bolshevik regime. In the management boards of nationalized enterprises in 1919, the share of labor unions dropped to 3.1 percent, and workers and full-time factory committee members constituted 20.2 percent, while administrative technicians accounted for more than 50 percent (Malle 1985, 126). Such policies created a particular kind of "dual society" in which one society dominated the other by creating a "walled fortress of state power, with its official doctrine and its bureaucratic solidarity" (Remington 1984, 21).[45]

War communism apparently brought about "the most accomplished form of the proletarian natural-anarchistic economy" (Kritsman, quoted in Lewin 1974, 80), embodying significant egalitarian elements as emphasized above. But as a matter of fact, much of the egalitarian character of this period was elicited by the collapse of the monetary system, not by intended consequences of the Bolshevik regime. Bolshevik leaders clearly favored policies that could sustain inequality for a long time. As mentioned above, the Bolsheviks restricted workers' councils, introduced one-man management, and emphasized productivity and differential wages.

Second, by the end of this period, the Bolshevik government had nationalized almost all industrial enterprises and means of production. But the Bolsheviks neither had cadres at the top levels nor an adequate administrative machinery or central planning for the management of nationalized industries. Therefore, nationalization, in many cases, was accomplished only on paper. Although a vast administrative apparatus was erected, it failed increasingly to manage the enormous network of large and small enterprises. Surpluses accumulated in one area, for example, while production was halted for lack of raw materials in another. Such administrative inability was compounded by the fact that the Bolshevik regime did not resolve the conflict between horizontal and vertical management of enterprises as represented by *sovnarkhozy* and *glavki*. The losses that the Russian economy suffered because of the peace treaty with Germany, and through the ravages of civil war, also added to the chaos (Schapiro 1984, 188).

The countryside, meanwhile, remained in the hands of an untrustworthy partner of the revolution—the peasants. The peasantry, as discussed above, was joined by many urban dwellers during the period of war communism. As state management of industries showed an increasing inability to meet growing consumer demands, small-scale, individualized, illegal private business activities sprang up, primarily in the rural areas. Such illegal private trade sustained what Lenin called the "souls of petty bourgeoisie" throughout the countryside. Indeed, one might say that it was the "souls of petty bourgeoisie" that triumphed during the next stage of Soviet development.

NOTES

1. Old style October 25, 1917, hence the name the October Revolution. In 1917 there had been two revolutions in Russia: the February Revolution, the first, deposed the tsar; and the October Revolution, the second, brought the Bolsheviks to power.

2. The term "war communism" was first introduced by Lenin in "The Tax in Kind," published in 1920. He wrote this pamphlet to acknowledge the "mistakes" of the war communism period and to reverse those policies. Therefore, for Lenin and other Bolshevik leaders, the period of war communism effectively had ended by the end of 1920. But to some scholars, this period continued up to 1922 (Lewin 1989, 399).

3. Strictly speaking, the period from the revolution to the onset of the civil war in mid-1918 should be distinguished from that which followed. In the early months succeeding the revolution, formal land nationalization essentially legitimated de facto peasant seizures of the land and its redistribution along "traditional communal principles." Nationalizations in the urban industrial sector were few, and most resulted from "spontaneous local action." Workers seized factories and established "workers' control" over them and their private owners, managers, and technicians by factory committees and local Bolsheviks. Lenin characterized the ensuing rather chaotic and quasi-anarchic situation as (a variant of) "state capitalism" and the "principal mode" for transition to socialism, at least during "its earliest stage." Lenin's basic presupposition was that "proletarian political power" would be sufficient to "re-establish production and distribution until international revolution provided an environment in which more systematic progress toward socialist construction could be undertaken." These beliefs were "quickly falsified by events," however, notably, the catastrophe of the war, the regime's "tenuous hold on power," the uncooperativeness of private capitalists, governmental and business bureaucrats, and peasants, and the failure of (successful) international revolutions. With the out-

break of civil war in mid 1918, the Bolshevik regime shifted to a program incorporating widespread nationalizations, the forced requisition of food, and tighter, more centralized control by the Party and state over labor and production, which characterized war communism sensu stricto. (See Howard and King 1989: 287, 290-91.)

4. Emphasizing the ideological determination of Bolshevik leaders to establish socialism rapidly, Wiles (1962, 29-30) describes the policies of this period as "naive communism." Dobb (1928, 61), emphasizing war exigencies, declares that war communism was "the product, not of theories, but war-time improvisation." A similar standpoint can be seen in Carr (1952, 2:260-68). Nove (1969, 40-45) maintains that Soviet leaders seized power without having a clear idea about socialist economic organization, and therefore, the policies of war communism ranged from sheer dogmatism to merely a response to emergency situations. Moore (1967, 39), on the other hand, rejects such interpretations and emphasizes historical and ideological factors in shaping the policies of this period. Roberts (1971) similarly emphasizes an ideological commitment by the Bolsheviks to a conception of socialism as highly centralized, centrally planned, and antimarket in his interpretation of war communism.

Soviet historians put forward two different approaches to war communism. The first approach tended to emphasize revolutionary and ideological aspirations by depicting the policies of this period as logical and conscious efforts to build socialism. Especially during the Stalinist era, this approach attempted to show that war communism's emphasis on economic autarky, electrification, and industrial development represented cautious efforts at establishing centralized institutions of socialist government. A second approach characterizes the period of war communism as a temporary break necessitated by such factors as civil war and foreign intervention. All these strands of thought have their strong supporters. See Remington (1984, 6-7) and Malle (1985, 3-16).

5. Claiming that Russia had already entered the stage of monopoly capitalism and imperialism in 1917, Lenin declared:

> For socialism is merely the next step forward from state-capitalist monopoly. Or in other words, socialism is merely state-capitalist monopoly *which is made to serve the interests of the whole people and has to that extent ceased* to be capitalist monopoly.... no revolt can bring about socialism unless the economic conditions of socialism are ripe—but because state-monopoly capitalism is a complete *material preparation of socialism, the threshold of socialism,* a rung on the ladder of history between which and the rung called socialism *there are no intermediate rungs.* (Quoted in Medvedev 1979, 80)

According to Lenin, in 1894 and 1895, one-tenth of Russian factories employed three-quarters of the total labor force and produced seven-tenths of the total industrial output in the country. According to Malle (1985, 42-43), on the eve of the October Revolution, out of fifty joint-stock banks, twelve controlled 80 percent of the country's banking capital. Powerful cartels controlled 45 percent of the nation's iron and steel output. In 1912 large-scale metal, textile, and food-processing firms produced, respectively, 83, 82, and 92 percent of the total output.

6. The Provisional Government, headed by Prince G. E. Lvov, had a cabinet consisting of ten liberals and six socialists—three Socialist Revolutionaries (including Alexander Kerensky as minister of war), two Mensheviks, and one Populist-Socialist. Subsequently, Kerensky succeeded Prince Lvov as the head of the Provisional Government. For details see Hough and Fainsod (1979, 47-55) and Schapiro (1984, 55-72).

7. According to Hough and Fainsod (1979, 81), by signing this treaty with Germany, Russia lost 34 percent of her population, 32 percent of her agricultural land, 54 percent of her industry, and 89 percent of her coal mines. At one point 75 percent of Soviet territory was occupied by the opponents of Bolshevik authorities (Gregory and Stuart 1990, 52).

8. For example, Lenin argued in "The Tax in Kind" that the centralized economic organization and warlike policies of the period up to the year 1920 were "more" consequences of the war exigencies than "the economic tasks" that confronted a postrevolutionary proletariat.

9. The term organized party here refers to Kadets (the Constitutional Democrats), who formed the first duma in 1906. One of the first formal political organizations of Russia was the Social Democratic party, which was formed in the late 1890s. The Mensheviks (Social Democrats) and Bolsheviks (Communists) were two factions of this party. Both the Mensheviks and the Bolsheviks stood for socialist revolution and building socialism in the Soviet Union, but while the former preferred a gradual approach, the later switched to a more radical approach. This distinction caused the split in their parent political organization in 1903. Socialist Revolutionaries (SRs), on the other hand, emerged out of the Narodnik movements of the 1880s and 1890s. The SRs lacked commitments to Marxism and preferred democratic and socialist reforms.

10. Initially, the rights and powers of the duma, as defined by the Imperial Manifesto of August 6, 1905, were seriously limited. But by the end of 1905, with the introduction of universal suffrage, and freedom of speech, assembly and organization, the duma was transformed from a loyal advisory body into a somewhat more powerful representative organization having the power to investigate the legality of governmental actions (see Hough and Fainsod 1979, 26-27).

11. During 1916 and 1917, foreign capital constituted 91 percent of mining, 42 percent of metal working, 28 percent of textiles, 50 percent of chemicals, and 37 percent of wood-working industries. Among the foreign capital, Germany's share was 20 percent, and French and English companies had shares of 33 and 23 percent, respectively. (See Malle 1985, 41-45.)

12. Lewin (1989, 413-414) observes that, in practice, the peasants' support for the Bolshevik regime was "no more than a marriage of convenience related to the possession of land" and that the peasants sided with the Bolsheviks because the Whites stood for returning their newly acquired land to the old landlords.

13. Dobb (1992, 124-25) refers to a survey conducted by a noted Soviet economist in 1922. According to the survey, 25 percent of those who had held responsible posts in capitalist industry before the war, and 67 percent of those who had been employed as technicians, had no faith in their work, and 67 percent of both groups expressed an unwillingness to discontinue accepting bribes. Dobb maintains that in 1918 and 1919 the proportion of such persons hostile to the Bolshevik regime had been greater than in 1922.

14. According to W. W. Rostow's (1990) theory of the stages of economic development, Russia's industrialization began in the 1870s and, by the early twentieth century, Russia was still at the infancy of the take-off stage.

15. The concept of the dictatorship of proletariat in this context is controversial because the Bolsheviks attempted to establish such a dictatorship in the name of Marx and Engels. For Marx and Engels, dictatorship of the proletariat meant proletarian democracy, not the establishment of a regime of professional revolutionaries or a party in the name of the proletariat as Lenin and other early Bolsheviks envisaged. For details see Dowlah (1992a, 20-21).

16. See for details Fitzpatrick (1989) and Koerner, Rosenberg and Suny (1989).

17. Medvedev (1979, 97), however, argues that the postrevolutionary Russian government was a "coalition" government that "significantly strengthened its overall position in the country." Perhaps Medvedev is referring to the brief membership of three left SRs in the *Sovnarkom* from the period of December 22, 1917, to March 15, 1918. It is true that, although no non-Bolsheviks were included in the *Sovnarkom* afterward, a temporary alliance with the left SRs allowed the Soviet government to gain substantial following in the countryside. At the same time, by carrying out sweeping land reform and accepting distribution of the land among the previously landless peasants, the Bolsheviks also succeeded in obtaining the support of the peasants.

18. The Bolshevik government's dissolution of the Constituent Assembly was a landmark. In the election of the assembly held just after the October Revolution, the Bolsheviks received only one-quarter of the votes. Therefore, it remained a minority. Even including an alliance

with the left SRs, their total number of votes was 136, while the right SRs had 237 votes. Failing to get approval of the Bolshevik programs by the Constituent Assembly in its first meeting held on January 18, 1918, the Bolsheviks forcibly dissolved the assembly. By doing so the Bolsheviks succeeded in saving the revolution, but questions remained about its commitment to democratic values.

19. It should be noted that the Socialist Revolutionaries and the Mensheviks had nominal representation in the Central Executive Committee, and for a brief period, from December 22, 1917, to March 15, 1918, three SRs held portfolios in the Council of People's Commissars. But by June 1918, the Bolsheviks excluded right SRs and Mensheviks from their ranks on the grounds that they were engaged in counterrevolutionary and anti-Soviet activities. By the end of 1918, the left SRs were also ousted from their ranks. But scholars generally agree that opposition political activities had not completely been eliminated at this stage.

20. Nationalization of leading industries was one of the central pieces of Lenin's famous "April Theses" presented at the Seventh All-Russian Conference of the Bolshevik party in April 1917, just months before the revolution. In it, Lenin proclaimed that an "immediate task" to introduce socialism in Russia was "to bring social production and the distribution of products at once under the control of the Soviets of Workers' Deputies." The Bolshevik party's program, in this context, based on the April Theses, emphasized amalgamation of all banks in the country into a single national bank and strict control of large capitalist syndicates, but not massive nationalization. See Dowlah (1992a, 13-33, 57-65) and Brus (1973, 13-18).

21. These figures are based on Carr (1952, 174-75); Cliff (1978, 82-83); Dobb (1928, 33-34); and Dowlah (1992a, 33-34). It should be noted that Soviet economic historians present different figures in this context. The confusion is further compounded by the absence of any reliable official census. *Vesenkha* sources show that a total of 6,908 industrial enterprises were subject to its control, out of which 4,547 were effectively state owned and controlled. This figure indicates that 65.7 percent of total enterprises were nationalized, and such state enterprises employed 1 million workers.

22. The genesis of *Vesenkha* can be traced to the days of the provisional government. However, whereas the earlier economic councils were merely consultative bodies, the *Vesenkha* under Bolshevik rule was primarily responsible for the overall economic management of the country. Indeed, *Vesenkha* constituted the central control and coordination organization of economic activities in Russia.

23. Those who trace the origin of the Stalinist model to the centralized control and planning structures of war communism are known as continuity theorists. We shall discuss their arguments at a later point.

24. Although Marx provided penetrating criticism of the anarchic character and vulnerability to crises of a capitalist system and emphasized conscious channeling of scarce resources to productive sectors, he did not embrace comprehensive micro planning by a centralized bureaucracy. But immediately after the revolution, in *The ABCs of Communism*, Bukharin and Preobrazhensky (1969) called for a centralized plan that would control the allocation of resources, channel investment funds, and determine the national output under a comprehensive organization of national economy.

25. See Orlovsky (1989) for details in connection with the primacy of what he calls "lower-middle strata" in the postrevolutionary administration of the Bolshevik government. Such claims also have some foundation in Lenin's writings during this period. Although in *State and Revolution* (written immediately before the revolution) Lenin was optimistic that anybody with average intelligence could run industrial administration, in *Will the Bolsheviks Retain the State Power?* (written immediately after the revolution) he emphasized the need for utilizing bourgeois specialists during the period of transition, if necessary at higher wages than those of ordinary workers.

26. The term kulak refers to rich peasants. During the revolutionary period, Russian peasants were divided into three categories: the well-to-do (wealthy) peasants or kulaks, who employed some labor and produced a surplus for sale; the poor peasants or *batraks*, who were either landless or possessed little land, and often hired themselves out as agricultural labor; and an intermediate category of peasants (middle peasants), who could maintain their families from their small farms but did not produce a surplus or hire labor. According to Lenin, Malle (1985, 335-36) maintains, in 1905 more than 80 percent of the Russian peasantry were poor, only about 8 percent were middle peasants, and about 12 percent could be considered wealthy peasants. But in postrevolutionary Russia, (Carr 1952, 160), the kulaks constituted approximately 10 percent of the peasants, *batraks* accounted for about 40 percent, and the rest, that is, 50 percent, belonged to the middle class. As the movement of socialization in the rural areas was mainly orchestrated by committees of poor peasants, it was directed against both the middle and upper class peasants.

27. A centralized food procurement drive under governmental initiative was provoked by a number of other factors, such as the independent use of industrial products by factory committees, the lack of financial means, the fear of counterrevolutionary movements, and social pressures (see Malle 1985, 345). It should also be noted that the Bolsheviks tried such alternative means as a fixed amount of grain as a tax in kind. All such policies of the government were vehemently opposed, especially by the kulaks.

28. In fact, the Bolsheviks inherited a rationing system from the Provisional Government and retained many of its features of distribution.

29. That, however, did not happen instantly. The process began, immediately after the revolution, with the efforts of Bolshevik leaders to meet state expenditures and to make wage payments and other expenses of enterprises through the printing press. This soon made rubles worthless. It worked in two directions: hyperinflation diminished the ruble's worth as a store of value, and official elimination of monetary exchange made it almost useless as a means of payment.

30. Such state building, as Lewin (1989, 400) argues, involved speedy transformation in "all facets of party life and in many of its principles, such as ties with the masses, organizational structure, modus operandi, social composition, ways of ruling, and style of life."

31. A rich literature exists on this controversial issue. For details see Dowlah and Elliott (1991); Lewin (1989); Fitzpatrick (1989); Dowlah (1992a, 116-124); Tucker (1977) and Cohen (1977).

32. Indeed, by the end of the civil war, many key industries absolutely vital for the functioning of the economy had reverted to their pre-1861 levels (Lewin 1989, 404).

33. The discussion of migration problems is based on Koerner (1989) and Brower (1989).

34. Lewin (1974, 53) estimates the urban population of Russia at only 18 percent in 1917. It rose to 24 percent in 1939, largely due to Stalin's agricultural collectivization and rapid industrialization programs.

35. Carr (1952, 195) estimates that St. Petersburg and Moscow had lost 57.5 percent and 44.5 percent, respectively of their total population by the end of 1920.

36. Schapiro (1984, 188) estimates that over 7 million died from malnutrition and epidemics alone between January 1918 and July 1918.

37. Rosenberg (1967, 140) observes that a worker "should have lived through the greatest revolution in history appeared in the eyes of the Russian workman like a glorious vision. As soon as the Civil war and the miseries to which it had given rise had passed away the road would be open for the free development of the paradise of a society freed from class distinctions."

38. For details see Carr (1952, 222-27) and Schapiro (1984, 192-93).

39. This can be gauged from the fact that in the election in the immediate aftermath of the October Revolution, few peasants voted for the Bolsheviks. The Bolsheviks got most of their votes in the urban areas.

40. According to the Central Statistical Bureau, concealment of actual sowing amounted to about 14 percent of the sown area in 1920. In terms of gross harvest, the amount concealed reached about 33 percent. See Nove (1969, 145).

41. As Lewin (1989, 405) remarks, "Notwithstanding all the forcible measures employed against them by a militarist communism, millions of small peasants remained in the country, who formed part of the declining middle class not of the proletarian state."

42. Dobb (1928, 145) refers to Soviet economist Larin's estimates that peasants actually gained out of the exchange, and secured twice as many manufactured goods as they received before the war. Nove (1969), however, maintains that during the years 1919 and 1920, towns received from state collections about one-third of their prewar agricultural supplies, while the villages received manufactured goods about 12 to 15 percent of the prewar level.

43. Schapiro's (1984, 188) remarks in this context are worth mentioning: "The peasants, having obtained the land under the distribution effected by the Bolsheviks in one of their first acts, the land decree, no longer had anything to hope from the new rulers."

44. As suggested earlier, relatively speaking, the peasants were far better off during this period. They obtained rights to land, had enough food for themselves at least, sent smaller numbers of offspring to the Red Army, and bore a smaller number of war casualties.

45. It should be noted, however, that although the Bolsheviks emphasized specialists over workers in industrial management, they expected that this would be a temporary measure and, furthermore, Bolshevik leaders expected that the specialists would themselves be transformed into proletarians under the rule of the proletarian state.

Chapter 3

New Economic Policy: Bolshevik Mixed Economy

INTRODUCTION

This chapter examines the New Economic Policy (NEP) period of Soviet development as an exemplar of socialist mixed economy. The NEP period began with the Tenth Congress of the Bolshevik Party, held in March 1921 and extended up to the party's Fifteenth Congress held in 1928.[1] The NEP comprised a series of governmental policies that constituted a spectacular about-face in the position of the Bolshevik regime. It dramatically reversed and replaced many of the policies that were ardently pursued during the war communism period. Major features of the war communism period that were recast under the NEP included forced requisitioning of agricultural produce, attempts to abolish monetary transactions and market relations, wholesale nationalization, and centralized control over national economic and business activities. The NEP, instead, emphasized mutual coexistence of a state-owned and state-controlled sector of "commanding heights" (as explained below) and a robust private agricultural, trade, and small business sector. In the political sphere, contrastingly, the NEP stood for retaining, even strengthening, the authoritarian character of the political system inherited from war communism.[2] It is this combination of a relatively liberal economic system and a relatively authoritarian political system, what Lewin (1974, 96) has called a "liberal dictatorship," that distinguishes the NEP as a socialist mixed-economy model.

Like war communism, the NEP remained controversial in former Soviet literature. Western scholars also differ sharply in their interpretations of its origins, character, performance, and consequences. The main features of the NEP model are discussed below using the four criteria developed earlier.

UNDERLYING CAUSES

Contending Perspectives

At least three distinguishable interpretations can be identified concerning the origins of the NEP among Western scholars. One school emphasizes the objective situation in the country that called for a dramatic shift from the policies of the previous period. This approach points to several factors that demanded the immediate attention of the Bolshevik government. First, the standoff between the Bolsheviks and the peasants had to be resolved. Growth in agricultural production could not be expected without substantial policy changes. The rebellious peasants, either by concealing output or by not producing, thwarted the Bolshevik regime's efforts to collect food through forceful requisitioning. Therefore, concessions and compromises were in order to persuade the peasants to resume normal agricultural production. Second, the Bolshevik government realized that the workers, who made tremendous sacrifices throughout the war communism period, had to be persuaded, through greater reliance on economic relative to heroic, political incentives, to put factories back in motion and get the industrial economy growing. Third, the role of central planning, partly because of the lack of necessary administrative and scientific skills, had to be recast. War communism's reliance on crude forms of central planning contributed to economic dislocations and administrative chaos. According to this school of thought, the NEP was needed as a "breathing space" to foster economic recovery from war, the civil war, and disruption; to achieve full employment and full capacity production; and to establish infrastructural preconditions for a robust economic development. The NEP's aim was thus seen as creating a solid economic foundation so that appropriate strategies could be worked out to move to socialism at a more expedient time. In this view, the NEP was perceived as a stage of transition from economic backwardness to a takeoff stage of industrialization needed for establishing socialism.[3]

Another prominent approach interprets the NEP as a "strategic retreat" from the policies of war communism to utilize capitalist instruments for socialist construction. In this perspective, the NEP was a temporary retreat from socialism to lift the country from the morass of economic backwardness and thus better lay the foundations for socialism. This interpretation attributes the origin of the NEP to the realization by the Bolshevik regime that it had orchestrated a socialist revolution in a primarily precapitalist economy, and the country needed capitalist means and Western technology for modernization so that subsequently it could be moved to socialism. The NEP retreat, a "peasant Brest-Litovsk," in the words of Ryazanov (Carr 1952, 2:278), was regarded as "a temporary truce, not a surrender or admission of defeat" (Treadgold 1972, 204). It was a tactical maneuver to achieve development and modernization by selectively using capitalist ways and means under a proletarian government. Once the usefulness of the capitalists and capitalist methods were exhausted with the achievement of modernization in the country, such institutions could be eliminated, and a relatively developed economy could be moved forward, rather speedily, to establish full-scale socialism.[4]

A third perspective argues that the NEP was introduced, in earnest, as a long-term strategy to build socialism, gradually, with the active cooperation of and alliance between workers and peasants through what was called *smychka*. This approach maintains that, given a predominantly peasant society, the Bolshevik leaders realized that the processes of urbanization and modernization of the country depended heavily on a mutually supportive relationship between workers and peasants. This approach believes that the NEP in part provided an opportunity to return to "state capitalism," "the path which was being trodden in the spring of 1918" (Dobb 1928, 165) and which was abandoned only temporarily during the war communism period due to civil war exigencies. A return to the NEP's "state capitalism" now had, Maurice Dobb asserts, a "surer tread and less encumbrances" as the civil war came to a victorious end, a reasonably strong state apparatus was in place, and, above all, resistance and sabotage by the bourgeoisie had largely subsided. Such a sea change in objective conditions enabled the Bolsheviks to embark on a more flexible and decentralized strategy for the reconstruction of the country by utilizing existing productive capacities in a harmonized fashion. Therefore, proponents of this viewpoint believe that the Bolshevik leaders conceived of the NEP as a long-term strategy. Theodore Draper (1988, 287), for example, maintains that V. I. Lenin introduced the NEP "in March 1921, defended it to his last breath, and died in January, 1924, while NEP was still untouchable."

Bolshevik interpretations of the origins and basic elements of the NEP were characterized by diversity and change over time. War communism, as noted in Chapter 2, was regarded as "the creation of military necessity, though some Bolshevik leaders saw a virtue in it independent of necessity." Similarly, the NEP "was also a creation of necessity; and some other Bolshevik leaders saw virtue in it independently of its necessity" (Cox 1991, 172). Lenin, the NEP's founder, provided the most sophisticated Bolshevik explication of its origins, basic character, and relationships to war communism, state capitalism, and socialism. His interpretation of the NEP incorporated elements from all three of the overlapping, but distinguishable, viewpoints just discussed.

Lenin vigorously pursued the NEP, repeatedly characterized it as a long-term strategy to remain in operation for an indefinite period, and emphasized the need for a "'reformist', gradual, cautious, and roundabout approach to the solution of the fundamental problems of economic development" (cited in Tucker 1975, 511). First, Lenin held, the experience of war communism demonstrated that, given Russia's low level of economic development and crude methods of public administration, the Bolsheviks "cannot run the economy" (521). Russia unsuccessfully "tried alone directly and at one stroke" during the War communism period to establish "new links between industry and agriculture." Having "failed to achieve this task by 'direct assault' it must now try to achieve it by a number of slow, gradual, and cautious 'siege' operations" (515).

Second, by 1921, Lenin was persuaded that a gradualist strategy for building socialism was also warranted by the international situation. One vital international development was the "delay in the world revolution" (509). Ultimately, Lenin contended, in his last article in 1923, the "complete victory of socialism is fully and absolutely assured." But the worldwide movement toward socialism will not be consummated through the "gradual 'maturing' of socialism" via internal evolution within industrially advanced capitalist countries. Indeed, the Allied powers, flushed from their victories over Germany in World War I, coupled with gains from world-wide imperialism, were able to make modest concessions to their "oppressed classes" which served to "retard the revolutionary movements in those countries and create some semblance of class truce." Instead, Lenin claimed, socialism will come on to the agenda of social change through the imperialist "exploitation of some countries by others" and by the drawing into the "maelstrom of the world revolutionary movement" of such Eastern countries as Russia, China, and India. Because these countries "account for the overwhelming majority of the population of the globe," there "cannot be the slightest doubt what the final outcome of the world struggle will be." In the meantime, for an indefinite period, the appropriate strategy for Bolshevism is to "hold on" and "keep going until the socialist revolution is victorious in more developed countries" (743-45).

Third, according to Lenin, through its revolution, the Bolsheviks had brought an "epoch-making change": the establishment of working class rule through the "Soviet system, as a form of the dictatorship of the proletariat" and thereby the "political requisites" for socialism (513-14). But, Lenin stated, postrevolutionary Russia lacked sufficient "civilization" to "pass straight on to socialism." Examples abounded: the general low level of economic development; the "deplorable" and "wretched" "state apparatus"; the extremely low productivity of labor in small and very small peasant farming; and the survival of cultural qualities from the prerevolutionary society, notably traditionalist attitudes among the large majority of the peasantry (735, 743, 745). It would take "decades" or "generations" (though not "centuries"), Lenin declared in introducing the NEP at the Tenth Party Congress in 1921, to "remold the small farmer and recast his mentality and habits" (505).

Fourth, given this "objective situation," Lenin believed, it was necessary to accede to "a certain freedom to exchange, freedom for the small private proprietor" and the freedom of the small peasant proprietor to obtain industrial commodities by free exchange with businesses. Otherwise, it would be "economically impossible— in view of the delay in the world revolution, to preserve the rule of the proletariat in Russia" (506, 509). Confiscation of agricultural surpluses through state monopoly, Lenin argued, needed to be superseded by a moderate tax in kind, leaving remaining surpluses for consumption or sale by peasant proprietors, thus giving the small farmer an "incentive and spur to till the soil." "State economy" needed to be adapted to the "economy of the middle peasant, which we have not managed to remake in three years, and will not be able to remake in another ten" (509). The survival of the revolution thus required use of "all transitional economic forms for the purpose of strengthening the link between the peasantry and the proletariat," promoting economic recovery from the "ruin" of the 1918-1921 period, developing industry, and fostering modernization, specifically electrification (517).

At the same time, Lenin held, by thus permitting private property and free exchange, the NEP constituted a partial "turning back towards capitalism" and a "retreat" from the "victorious advance" of the heroic days of revolutionary civil war (506, 324, 330). It meant significant concessions to a nonproletarian majority of small farm and business proprietors and to the vagaries of the market economy. Moreover, private property and free exchange "inevitably lead to a division of commodity producers into capitalists and wage-workers" and thereby to the revival of capitalism, not merely to trade and petty proprietorship (506, 512). In addition, in order to obtain the commodities needed by the peasantry, in the absence of large-scale machinery and electric power in Russia, imports from and thus foreign trade with and loans from capitalist countries are also necessary, at least for a "decade or two." To "organize competition properly," mixed enterprises, in which "private capitalists, Russian and foreign, and Communists participate," are also needed (515, 521).

In response to criticism from within the Bolshevik party, "probably strongest among cadres formed by the wartime experience of 1918-20, and the younger party generation" (Cohen 1977, 23), Lenin maintained that the concessions to the peasantry and the partial "retreat" to capitalism embodied in the NEP could be permitted "to an appreciable extent, without destroying but actually strengthening the political power of the proletariat." The "main economic power," that is, the "vital large enterprises, the railways, etc.," were under Bolshevik control, thereby preventing restoration of capitalist property relations in industry and ensuring the "irrevocable" quality of the revolution. Small-scale private property and market economy are "not at all dangerous for socialism," Lenin averred, "as long as transport and large-scale industry remain in the hands of the proletariat," thereby ensuring the economic dominance of the revolutionary government. Moreover, the "proletarian government can control trade, direct it into definite channels, keep it within certain limits." In 1918 the Bolsheviks "retreated to state capitalism, but we did not retreat too far. We are now [1921] retreating to the state regulation of trade, but we shall not retreat too far." In any event, the NEP's mixed economy, "controlled and regulated by the proletarian state (i.e., state capitalism in this sense of the term), is advantageous and necessary in an extremely devastated and backward small peasant country." A "legitimate breathing space" is "necessary," both to prevent "utter defeat" through fullbodied capitalist restoration and to utilize capitalist methods to foster industrialization and modernization, thereby "laying the foundations for socialist economy," permitting the retreat to mixed economy to be stopped "in the not too distant future," and enabling a "subsequent victorious advance" toward socialism (515, 517, 506, 527, 529, 641). In short,

> Inasmuch as we are as yet unable to pass directly from small production to socialism, some capitalism is inevitable as the elemental product of small production and exchange; so that we must utilize capitalism (particularly by directing it into the channels of state capitalism) as the intermediary link between small production and socialism, as a means, a path, and a method in increasing the productive forces. (Quoted in Dowlah 1992a, 53)

Finally, we should make explicit a point already implied above: In his later writings beginning with the autumn of 1921, Lenin began to reconceive the NEP as a "new road to socialism," based on a "new class strategy and a new economic strategy," not merely as a means of temporarily coping with an emergency situation so as to save the revolution and strengthen Soviet power (Bettelheim 1976, 477-78). The peasantry, Lenin proposed, if educated and led by the advanced members of the working class and their vanguard, the Bolshevik party, through a "cultural revolution," potentially could be political, as well as economic allies. From this perspective, one of the major defects of war communism was that it adversely affected political, not merely economic, linkages between workers and peasants.

Through such an alliance, the appropriate strategy for building socialism is to encourage the voluntary establishment of a system of producer cooperatives organized and conducted by their members. Although "it will take a whole historical epoch to get the entire population into the work of the cooperatives through NEP," in this way "NEP is an advance because it is adjustable to the level of the ordinary peasant" and thereby constitutes a mode of "transition to the new system by means that are the *simplest, easiest, and most acceptable to the peasant*" (Lenin in Tucker 1975, 708-9). Under a system of private property, worker and peasant cooperatives would retain many elements of exploitation and class conflict. But, given state ownership of land and other physical means of production and a dominant political role by an active working class, a "system of civilized cooperators *is* the system of socialism" (Lenin in Tucker 1975, 710). Thus, the NEP can potentially evolve into a transitional society that goes beyond concessions to a recalcitrant peasantry and regulation of petty bourgeois and residual capitalist trade and industry (state capitalism) and becomes a vehicle for constructing over time the institutions of a socialist economy themselves.

Most Bolshevik leaders, particularly Lenin, thus considered the NEP primarily as a long-term, gradual approach/model to build socialism in a relatively underdeveloped economy and polity. The objective conditions in Russia in the aftermath of war communism provided the Bolshevik regime the opportunity to return to a conciliatory strategy similar to the one they anticipated immediately after the revolution. In this sense, the NEP was actually not so much a "retreat," as what Alec Nove (1969, 120) calls a return to the "status quo ante" and, at best, an "advance" to a transitional mode of society instrumental in the process of building socialism. Lenin defended the NEP until his death. During his lifetime, the NEP was generally visualized as a gradual, rather than radical, approach to achieve socialism in Russia with the harmonious cooperation of all segments of the postrevolutionary society. The NEP, however, symbolized disenchantment with several policies of the 1918-1920 period. The main reasons for the NEP's emergence out of war communism can be summarized as follows.

Economic Causes

War communism ended with widespread devastation and dislocation throughout the economy and excruciating suffering for all segments of the Russian population. In all indices—industrial, agricultural, transport, and communications—the economy was in shambles. As discussed in Chapter 2, compared to the 1913 level, in 1921 overall industrial production amounted to 31 percent. In 1920, compared to 1913 levels, fuel output was 30 percent, power generation was 25 percent, iron ore production was 2.5 percent, and steel output was only 5 percent.

Agricultural production amounted to little over 50 percent of the 1913 level in 1920. Compared to the annual average of the 1909-1913 level, in 1920 and 1921, the grain harvest reached 54 percent and 43 percent, respectively, and cotton and sugar beet production fell to less than 4 percent and 8 percent, respectively.[5] Furthermore, the policies of forced requisitioning caused a conspicuous reduction in sowing areas, especially in provinces of the Russian Federation, the Ukraine, and Byelorussia. Sharp declines in agricultural production and marked reductions in sowing areas were also accompanied by a severe drought in the east and southeast of the country that resulted in widespread famine and millions of deaths.

This catastrophic decline in production and the resulting economic retardation and political chaos powerfully threatened the existence of the country and the revolution. Millions of people died of famine, starvation, and disease; and chronic food shortages crippled the country, especially the urban areas. As both external and internal hostilities dwindled, alarmingly deteriorating economic conditions forced the Bolshevik regime to espouse more receptive strategies so that the recalcitrant peasants could be motivated to plough the fields, and the disenchanted and strained workers could be reactivated to run the factories and thereby launch national reconstruction in earnest.

Political Causes

Years of civil war, external threats and aggression, and the policies of war communism, especially food requisitioning and labor mobilization, had decisive and far-reaching adverse effects on Soviet economy and society. Worse still, successful international socialist revolutions, upon which the Bolsheviks had counted on so heavily, especially in Germany, did not occur. Throughout war communism, the Bolsheviks clung to the hope of such revolutions to come to their aid. Internally, the disastrous economic consequences of war communism, compounded by administrative chaos and rudimentary central planning machineries, brought formidable internal pressure on the Bolshevik regime as its own rank-and-file members were less and less willing and less able to sacrifice further for the sake of the revolution alone. By the beginning of 1921, workers in many industrial centers of the country were on the verge of revolt. Bad working conditions, unemployment, and endemic scarcities of the basic necessities of life fueled industrial unrest. The climax of the anti-Bolshevik protests occurred in Kronstadt in March 1921.[6] Sailors at the Kronstadt naval base, who previously had been ardent revolutionaries and mostly were Bolsheviks themselves, seized the island fortress to demand "land and bread" and a Soviet government without Bolsheviks.[7]

Peasant resistance to the Bolshevik regime also grew stronger in the latter part of the war communism period. Peasants from the very beginning of the revolution had been untrustworthy partners of the Bolshevik regime. As previously pointed out, peasants found it convenient to support the Bolsheviks against White generals and foreign aggressors in order to sustain their new de facto ownership of land. But the relationship between the peasants and the Bolsheviks soured with the introduction of forceful requisitioning of agricultural produce in May 1918. The problem was further compounded by the Bolshevik government's antimarket policies. The climax of peasant resistance to the Bolshevik regime erupted in the south and east of Russia. One massive uprising occurred in Tambov province late in 1920 even before the successful completion of the civil war.

Peasant revolts, as demonstrated in Tambov and the Ukraine; large-scale industrial strikes, especially in Petrograd and Moscow; armed rebellion; and splits in the rank and file of the Bolshevik party, as manifested by the Kronstadt revolt, cumulatively had overpowering effects on the perceived legitimacy of the regime and the survival of the revolution. Initially, demands of the striking workers were economic in nature. They largely concentrated on the basic necessities of life; food, clothing, the freedom to trade with villagers, and the elimination of special rationing privileges for a few. But gradually the workers' demands included political issues, including removal of special squads of armed Bolsheviks from the factories, the disbanding of labor armies, and the restoration of political and civil rights (Farber 1990, 188-92). Moreover, the industrial unrest and strikes were often fueled by the Mensheviks and the Workers' Opposition. Both capitalized on the dissent of workers and, in turn, gained significant momentum in the main industrial centers of Russia.[8]

As a result, Bolshevik leaders came to realize that more relaxed and conciliatory policies were needed for the recovery of the country. Lenin provided an ideological justification that, in the desperate economic and political conditions of the post-civil war period, the issues of ideology must be subordinated to the more fundamental tasks of survival of the regime and economic reconstruction of the country. To Lenin, the NEP was basically a political decision, rather than an economic one.[9] To strike a compromise with opposed political forces, especially the peasants and petty bourgeois elements, Lenin relaxed the rigors of war communism by incorporating significant doses of capitalist institutions.

INSTITUTIONS, PROGRAMS, AND POLICIES

The NEP constituted a sharp turn from the practices of war communism. It introduced a series of agrarian, trade, industrial, and fiscal policies that included resumption of money and commodity relations; emphasis on private trade, small-scale manufacture, and cooperatives; concessions to foreign capital and joint ventures; denationalization of state trusts and enterprises; large-scale discontinuation of state-subsidization and introduction of self-accounting *(khozraschet)* systems for state enterprises; and a less egalitarian distribution system than that of war communism.

Introduction of Food Tax

The replacement of forcible requisitioning *(prodrazverstka)* by a tax on surplus food *(prodnalog)*, on February 24, 1921, marked the official beginning of the NEP era in Russia.[10] The new tax measure, a tax in kind, provided an incentive to the farmers to grow food because they were allowed to sell their surplus output in the open market after making a payment of a previously arranged amount of taxation on their products.[11] The food tax was progressively designed so that well-to-do peasants, that is, the kulaks, paid the highest tax while poor peasants paid the least.[12] The tax rate also had regional variations; it was high in some regions and low in others. The NEP decrees also brought an end to the practices of arbitrary confiscation; peasants now paid a fixed tax and retained at least half of their products. Moreover, the tax in kind was fixed substantially below the "requisitioning targets" of the previous year. The NEP decrees specified that the new tax should not exceed half of the former requisition. For example, the delivery quota for 1920-1921 was 423 million puds, whereas the grain tax in kind was fixed at 240 million puds in 1921.[13] By 1922 peasants were guaranteed rights to lease land and hire labor and to choose land tenure systems.[14] In

1924, as the national economy approached price and monetary stabilization, the tax in kind was replaced by a monetary tax. After the payment of the monetary tax, the peasants were allowed to sell the rest of their products in open markets.

Denationalization of Industry

The NEP allowed a dominant position for private enterprise in agriculture, trade, and small-scale manufacturing. Except for the commanding heights—primarily transportation, banking, communication, foreign trade, and large-scale industry—the NEP denationalized most of the previously nationalized industrial enterprises. In May 1921 the earlier decree that nationalized all small-scale industries was formally revoked. Two months later, a privatization decree permitted private undertaking of handicraft and small-scale industrial production.

Under the NEP, the *Vesenkha* leased out a large number of previously nationalized enterprises. By 1922 over 10,000 such enterprises were leased out, of which 3,800 employed fifteen to twenty persons. About 50 percent of these leases went to private individuals including some foreigners. By October 1923, the number of leased enterprises that employed sixteen workers on the average rose to 5,698. Out of these enterprises, 1,770 were in food processing, and 1,515 were in hides and skins. The NEP policy of *khozraschet* (discussed below), which called for self-accounting in state enterprises, also contributed to the momentum of denationalization. As enterprises were called upon to meet their own expenses and run on a profit basis, some enterprises sold off some of their fixed capital assets to private buyers in order to be more market competitive. Such fixed capital assets amounted to about 6 percent of the basic capital belonging to industry controlled by *Vesenkha*.[15]

It should be noted, however, that the NEP's denationalization was less sweeping than was often perceived. As Nove (1969, 22-23, 86-87) points out, only seventy six enterprises were returned to their original owners by the *Vesenkha*. In most cases, small enterprises employing twenty workers or less were denationalized. By 1924-1925, there were only eighteen private enterprises that employed between 200 and 1,000 workers. The NEP's denationalization was mainly carried out in terms of workshops rather than factories. The economic significance of such denationalization was moderate, and many of the denationalized entities went to industrial cooperatives rather than to individual owners. Quoting the spring 1923 industrial census of the Soviet Central Statistical Department, Dobb (1966, 142-43) claims that private enterprises covered only 12.5 percent of all workers employed in enterprises covered by the census. Moreover, private enterprises employed only two persons on the average, and the overall contribution to the gross national product of denationalized enterprises was only 5 percent. According to Blackwell (1970, 81), foreign firms accounted for less than 1 percent of the total number of industrial enterprises, workers, and value of production. Privately financed industrial stock corporations were similarly insignificant.

Currency Reforms

Along with denationalization of enterprises, the NEP also struggled to achieve monetary stabilization. Under the NEP the Bolshevik government pursued a policy of decontrolling prices. But it had to remove price controls in a condition of acute shortages of the basic necessities of life and widespread infrastructural disloca- tions. Therefore, the NEP's price decontrol resulted in a sharp increase in aggregate price levels. To check inflation, the Bolshevik government introduced what came to be known as "bipaperism." In July 1922 a new currency called *chervonets* was in- troduced. Unlike the old currency *sovznaki*, *chervonets* were backed by gold and for- eign exchange. Interestingly, *sovznaki* (old currency) was not replaced. Throughout the years of 1922 and 1923, both *sovznaki* and *chervonets* were in operation simultaneously. *Chervonets*, issued in large units and restricted quantity, served primarily as a means for hoarding and holding values in stable form; *sovznaki* still required for smaller transac- tions, primarily as means of payment, was subject to inflationary pressures and con- tinual depreciation (Dobb 1928, 225). The discriminatory monetary policy of 1922 and 1923 made the *sovznaki* worthless. By February 1924 *chervonets* became the sole cur- rency in the country, and monetary stabilization was achieved.

The NEP's initiatives to stabilize the money supply and monetary conditions were associated with simultaneous efforts to institute a network of banking and credit facili- ties throughout the country. Several specialized banking institutions that NEP had es- tablished by 1922 included *Agrobank*, which supplied credit to peasants; *Prombank*, which extended credits to state and private industries; *Electrobank*, which funded na- tional electrification efforts; and *Tsekombank*, which financed municipal enterprises.

Self-Accounting for State Enterprises

Simultaneously with the promotion of private trade and small-scale industry, the NEP attempted to reduce the state's support to nationalized enterprises. NEP poli- cies encouraged state enterprises to adopt self-accounting, which became known as the *khozraschet* model. The *khozraschet* model emphasized that state enterprises run efficiently, compete in open markets as commercial entities, and become self-reliant. During war communism, state enterprises ran under the direction of administrative authorities, that is the *Vesenkha* or *glavki*. As most industrial trans- actions were carried out through bookkeeping under the direction of these authori- ties, state enterprises were not required to pay serious attention to the cost of production or the relevance of their products and services to market demands.

The NEP divided state-owned enterprises into two major categories. Large-scale industries, known as the commanding heights of the economy, constituted a part of the state budget and remained dependent upon relatively rigid centralized control and direction. The remaining nationalized enterprises were organized into trusts, which enjoyed substantial financial and commercial autonomy[16] and had to operate on a *khozraschet* basis. In order to be cost effective and more efficient, enterprises had to get rid of surplus staff and often, as mentioned above, were forced to sell off some of their fixed capital assets.

The *khozrascht* model was also promoted by conditions evolving in the economy at this point in time. By 1922 the free rationing system was abolished, and workers, once again, were largely paid in cash.[17] Government subsidy and easy credit (later known as "soft budgets") were largely eliminated. Moreover, as retail trade was pri- marily dominated by private markets, state-owned trusts and enterprises had to compete with each other. By 1922-1923, the NEP brought an end to the state preference system in receiving supplies. Therefore, enterprises and trusts had to compete in buying necessary inputs as well.

Foreign Trade

One of the objectives of the NEP was to open the economy to international markets, especially to obtain desperately needed technology and equipment from Western companies and countries.[18] With that objective, the NEP directed its foreign trade primarily at accumulating locomotives, farm machineries, and electrical or other equipment critically needed for the reconstruction of the national economy.

The NEP also granted broad concessions to foreign governments and companies. According to Nove (1969, 89), during the NEP period forty two such concession agreements were made, of which thirty one were in the timber industry. During 1924 and 1925, thirteen significant concession enterprises employed 4,260 workers. The share of these concession enterprises in the national output was, however, insignificant. In 1928, for example, such enterprises contributed only 0.6 percent of industrial output in the country. However, the volume of foreign trade during the NEP grew rapidly from 8 percent of the prewar level in 1921 to 44 percent in 1928 (Gregory and Stuart 1981, 51).

Political Measures

The NEP's economic liberalization was, however, accompanied by political authoritarianism as the Bolshevik party further consolidated its power over the country. Ironically, the same Tenth Congress of the party that abandoned war communism's command economy approved more authoritarian measures in the political sphere.[19] The internal discussions and dissent that had earlier characterized the party decreased significantly with the banning of factional politics within the party. The purge that followed the Tenth Congress, according to Robert Service (1979, 160), ejected fully a quarter of the total membership of the Bolshevik party by the end of 1921.

In addition to stern measures against political opposition, the Tenth Congress restricted the participation of non-Bolsheviks in the elections of local soviets and other political institutions. Immediately after the congress, Bolsheviks resorted to "a complete and systematic repression of opposition parties and groups" (Hough and Fainsod 1979). Mensheviks and Socialist Revolutionaries, who continued to oppose the Bolshevik regime, were particularly targeted for such political repression.[20] By 1922 the last opposition newspapers and journals in the country had been shut down. Also, the Bolsheviks' commitment to clean out all undesirable elements, as well as their adamant application of antifactional and other organizational measures, "considerably accelerated the process of converting the trade unions into transmission belts for Communist Party policies" (Farber 1990, 196).[21]

Other important political developments of this period included the formation of the Union of Soviet Socialist Republics (USSR) in December 1922 and the appointment of Joseph Stalin as the general secretary of the Bolshevik party in the same year.[22] Previously the country was officially known as the Russian Socialist Federated Soviet

Table 3.1
Soviet Production and Trade Indexes: 1913, 1920, and 1928
(1913=100)

Years	Industry	Agriculture	Transportation	Exports	Imports
1913	100	100	100	100.0	100.0
1920	20	64	22	0.1	2.1
1928	102	118	106	38.0	49.0

Source: Gregory and Stuart (1981, 52).

Republic (RSFSR), as adopted in July 1918. The RSFSR was composed of six separate republics: Russia, Byelorussia, Ukraine, Azerbaijan, Georgia, and Armenia. In late 1922 the last three were amalgamated into a Trans-Caucasian Republic.[23] Also, a new constitution, authoritatively resolving the relations between the center and outlying regions, was ratified by the Eleventh Party Congress held on January 31, 1924, ten days after Lenin's death. The constitution came into force in 1924.

These tendencies toward authoritarian politics in the 1920s, however, must be seen in perspective. Many economically underdeveloped societies have exhibited authoritarian political institutions. Tsarist regimes prior to the Bolshevik Revolution, for example, were typically autocratic and repressive. Industrially advanced capitalist societies, which demonstrate a better record concerning democratization than less developed countries, do not invariably succeed in achieving or sustaining robustly democratic institutions; Nazi Germany is the classic example. Finally, although Bolshevism during the NEP period consolidated and strengthened the grip of the party oligarchy, it fell significantly short of the extremes of the Stalinist totalitarianism of the 1930s and after.

Lenin was clearly the dominant figure within the Bolshevik party. But he never established the definitive personal tyranny, or *fuhrerprinzip,* quality of Stalin, later characterized by Nikita Khrushchev and others as "the cult of personality." Moreover, the scope of party control over society was quite limited during the NEP period, in contrast to the "totalist" comprehensivity of a totalitarian regime, whether of the Left or the Right. This is illustrated by the "officially tolerated social pluralism in economic, cultural-intellectual, and even (in local Soviets and high state agencies) political life" (Cohen 1977, 21). In addition, despite the attempts to constrain party factionalism, party organization in the 1920s was oligarchic, not monolithic. In Nikolai Bukharin's characterization, in 1925, the Bolshevik party remained a "negotiated federation of groups, groupings, factions, and traditions" (cited in Cohen 1977, 17). This was especially true regarding intraparty debates over new directions in instances where the top leadership had not yet made up its collective mind, as illustrated vividly by the Great Industrialization Debate (see below).

CONSEQUENCES

Economically, the NEP was highly successful. By 1928 the NEP not only succeeded in attaining economic recovery, but it also brought the economy to the threshold of large-scale industrialization.[24] By 1928, as Table 3.1 shows, while industry and transportation only slightly exceeded their prewar levels, performance of the agricultural sector was 20 percent above its prewar level.[25] Although the foreign trade sector did not recover the prewar level, it made substantial headway given the record of war communism. Some of the far-reaching consequences of the era are discussed below.

Expansion in Private Trade

Private trade and small-scale industry became the hallmark of the NEP era. During war communism, the bourgeois class either lost its businesses or emigrated to other countries. Therefore, the number of people capable of operating large businesses was very small during the NEP period. A new class of people, however, sprang up to fill the vacuum and to gain from the NEP concessions. Indeed, many of the "new bourgeoisie" came from the lower echelons of Soviet society.[26] Several factors contributed to the dramatic growth of private trade during this period: (1) small-scale trade required little business experience or capital; (2) government policy favored small-scale private trade and business; therefore, they were controlled less; and (3) such trades promised rapid return on investments whereas long-term and large-scale business and trade were associated with many uncertainties (Ball 1991).

Private business activities during the NEP were categorized hierarchically into ranks depending on the size of the trade and the number of persons employed. They ranged from rank 1, businesses owned and managed by the same individual, to rank 5, large private businesses employing the largest number of workers. The NEP permitted both wholesale and retail trade and allowed hiring of more than ten workers for wholesale trade and more than twenty workers for retail trade.[27] As Table 3.2 shows, an overwhelming percentage of the new bourgeoisie had little or no previous business experience, while the upper ranks, that is, larger business enterprises, were dominated by experienced traders.

Private trade dominated the NEP economy. In 1922 the private share of retail sales exceeded 80 percent. Even government employees and workers made from 36 to 40 percent of their purchases from private traders during 1925 and 1926. Private traders maintained dominance over marketing of manufactured goods, for instance, in textiles, common hardware and other metal products, and leather goods. Muscovites bought about 70 percent of their bread from private traders in 1924, and in trades of dairy products, eggs, meat, fruits, and vegetables, often the share of private traders rose to 80 percent or more even toward the end of the decade. Private traders also dominated the peasant market as they supplied almost the same percentage of manufactured goods, such as agricultural and construction tools, clothing, footwear, dishes,

Table 3.2
Previous Occupation of Private Traders during the NEP

Ranks	Traders	Peasants	Workers	Handicraftsman	Office Workers	Housewives	Others
Rank 1	20%	31%	10%	4%	5%	18%	12%
Rank 2	38%	27%	9%	5%	6%	7%	8%
Rank 3	59%	15%	5%	6%	5%	2%	8%
Rank 4	67%	6%	3%	3%	6%	1%	14%
Rank 5	78%	4%	1%	2%	6%	1%	8%

Source: Ball (1991, 94).

Table 3.3
Share of Different Sectors in Small-Scale and Handicraft Industry, 1923-1927

Sectors	1923-24	1924-25	1925-26	1926-27
State	2.2	2.6	2.5	2.3
Cooperative	8.1	20.4	19.8	20.2
Private	89.7	77.0	77.7	77.5

Source: Nove (1969, 104).

soap, and processed food products, to the peasants. Private traders also were strik-ingly successful in the procurement of agricultural commodities. In 1924 and 1925 they handled from 40 to 50 percent of all procurement of agricultural commodities in the country (Ball 1991, 96-97). The percentage, however, fell to from 30 to 40 percent during 1925 and 1926, and to the neighborhood of 30 percent in the next two years.[28]

The private sector also dominated small-scale and handicraft industry during the NEP period. As Table 3.3 shows, it constituted 89.7 percent of the industry in 1923-1924, and more than 77 percent in the following years up to 1927. The share of the state sector in this industry declined to 2.2 percent in 1923-1924, and remained below 3 percent throughout the same period. Employment in the private sector in-creased 13 percent in 1924-1925, 20 percent in 1925-1926, and from 2 to 5 percent the following year. Overall, Nove (1969, 137) maintains, the share of the socialized sector in the national economy was 45.9 percent in 1925-1926, 48.7 percent in 1926-1927, and 52.7 percent in 1928. The share of the private sector in the national economy was 54.1 percent, 51.1 percent, and 47.3 percent respectively, for the same years. The gradual decline in the share of the private sector and the simultaneous rise in the share of the state sector were associated with a gradual strengthening of the state vis-a-vis private interests, that is, the NEP men, during the last years of the NEP.

Agricultural Boom

The NEP's policy to abandon forced requisitioning of food elicited an immedi-ate favorable reaction from the peasantry. As discussed above, the NEP initially re-placed food requisitioning by a tax in kind and later by a monetary tax. In both cases, the agricultural tax was far below the level of war communism. In addition to reduc-ing the tax, the NEP promoted agriculture by extending credits and supplying such agricultural implements as tractors and other instruments.

Such measures were taken favorably by the peasants. As a result, the agricultural sector registered a spectacular recovery by 1925. As Table 3.4 shows, the sown area in 1925 reached almost the level of 1913, and the grain harvest reached 90 percent of the 1913 level by the same year. Also by 1925, the number of sheep, goats, cows, and pigs exceeded the 1916 level, and the number of horses reached 75 percent of the 1916 figure.

Industrial Recovery

The NEP policies also contributed to a rapid recovery of the industrial sector. As mentioned earlier, by 1928, Soviet industrial output exceeded the prewar levels (see

Table 3.4
Soviet Agricultural Recovery under the NEP Compared to 1913

	1913	1922	1925
	(all numbers in millions)		
Sown area (hectares)	105.0	77.7	104.3
Grain harvest (tons)	80	50.3	72.5
Horses (heads)	*35.5	24.1	27.1
Cattle (heads)	58.9	45.8	62.1
Pigs	*20.3	12.0	21.8

* 1916 figures.

Source: Nove (1969, 110).

Table 3.5
Sectoral Industrial Growth in the Soviet Union, 1913-1928

	1913	1916	1921	1925	1928
Pig Iron*	4216	3804	117	1309	3282
Steel*	4231	4276	220	1868	4251
Oil*	9234	9970	3781	7061	11625
Coal*	29117	34482	9531	16520	35510
Electric Power**	1945	2575	520	2925	5007
Paper*	197.0	---	---	211.5	284.5
Cement*	1520	---	64	872	1850
Granulated Sugar*	1347	1186	51	1064	1283
Peat***	1.7	1.6	2.0	2.7	5.3

* thousand tons, ** million kilowatt hours, ***million tons.

Source: reproduced from Hutchings (1971, 42).

Table 3.1). Several factors contributed to the robust recovery of the industrial sector, including the competitive business environment, the *khozraschet* model, increased private trade and business, the government's explicit policy of promoting
industrial growth, extension of easy commercial and industrial credit and banking
facilities, and tightening of state support for noncompetitive enterprises. According
to official estimates, Russian industrial production, which in 1920-1921 stood at 18
percent of the prewar level, rose to 27 percent in 1921-1922, and 35 percent the
following year. By 1925, as Table 3.5 shows, industrial production nearly reached
the prewar level and, in some sectors, even exceeded it. By 1928, as the table shows,
Soviet industrial production exceeded the prewar levels in almost all indices.

It is notable that, although the 1913 level of large-scale industrial production was
exceeded in 1926, the growth of large-scale industry fell to less than 15 percent in
1927. As Table 3.6 shows, the high rates of growth in industry up to 1926 were made
possible by bringing many factories into operation, or by greatly expanding the operation of existing enterprises and by fuller utilization of unused plant capacity, thus
requiring relatively small inputs of new fixed capital (Jasny 1972, 24). A great drop
in the rate of growth in 1924 (to 16.4 percent) was the result of the scissors' crisis
(discussed below). Table 3.7 illustrates the outcome of the preferential treatment for
heavy industry over agriculture (as advocated by Evgeniee Preobrazhensky and Leon

Table 3.6
Output of Large-Scale Industry in 1913 and from 1921 to 1927 (in 1926-27 prices)

Year	Million rubles	Percent of 1913	Annual Increase
1913	10,251	100	---
1921	2,004	19.5	42.1
1922	2,619	25.5	30.7
1923	4,005	39.1	52.9
1924	4,660	45.4	16.4
1925	7,739	75.5	66.1
1926	11,083	108.1	43.2
1927	12,679	123.7	14.2

Source: Jasny (1972, 23).

Table 3.7
Comparative Growth Rates in Heavy and Light Industries, 1924-1927

Year	Heavy Industry	Light Industry
1924	9.7	22.8
1925	59.3	71.9
1926	37.9	38.4
1927	24.8	11.8

Source: Based on Jasny (1972, 25-26).

Trotsky during the scissors' crisis). The rate of growth of large-scale industry, which averaged 52.4 percent in 1923, was composed of a 63.8 percent growth in heavy industry and a 43.7 percent growth in light industry. The rate of growth was larger in light than in heavy industry for three years in succession. But the gap again increased somewhat in 1927 when heavy industry grew by 24.8 percent and light industry by 11.8 percent.

TENSIONS AND CONTRADICTIONS

The NEP succeeded in what it was intended to accomplish—economic recovery and political stability. But the policies pursued by the Bolshevik government for recovery had both intended and unintended consequences. The tensions and contradictions of the NEP may be summarized as follows.

Ideological Contradictions

Perhaps the sharpest criticism that the NEP faced, both internally and externally, was its ideological character.[29] The NEP's efforts to restore money and monetary relations, to foster substantial private trade, to make concessions to foreign companies and governments, to denationalize formerly nationalized enterprises, to tighten state subsidies, legalization of hiring wage labor, and above all, to relinquish war communism's egalitarian principles were some of the policies that were construed in many circles to be a restoration of capitalism and therefore drew fierce criticism.[30] Under ground political parties, disenchanted ex-Communist members, and disgruntled workers began to proclaim that the NEP stood for a "New Exploitation of the Proletariat." In 1917 about 60 percent of the members of the Bolshevik party belonged to manual occupations; by mid-1923 their number fell to only 15 percent. Bolshevik party composition underwent significant changes between 1917 and 1927. Whereas in 1917 more than 60 percent of its rank-and-file members belonged to the working class, their number had decreased to less than 40 percent by 1927. While peasants constituted only 7.5 percent of Bolshevik party membership in 1917, their number had increased to more than 27 percent by 1927. A similar transformation occurred in respect to white-collar membership: their share, 32 percent in 1917, had risen to 47 percent by 1927 (Rigby 1968).[31]

In addition to a class composition in the party that increasingly departed from its working class origins, the Bolshevik regime of the NEP era was criticized for critically degrading labor unions. By transforming labor unions into an integral organ of the Bolshevik party, the NEP succeeded in undermining their importance both in terms of utility and prestige. Labor unions were deprived of the right to intervene in the management of state-owned industries. Also, their rights to intervene in the affairs of privately owned industries were seriously curtailed. Labor unions, therefore, had the responsibility to represent workers but were stripped of adequate power because they had to function as subordinate units of the party. Worse still, they often had to support the party's cost-cutting and labor-intensification measures, which were strongly opposed by the working class. Such policies resulted not only in the loss of legitimacy by the labor unions, but in relegating workers to a status similar to that under nineteenth-century capitalism, as opposed to their elevation to the role of owners and rulers—as official and ideological statements often claimed. According to E.H. Carr, "There had been no time since the Revolution when discrimination was so overtly practiced against him (worker), or when he had so many legitimate causes of bitterness against a regime which claimed to govern in his name" (quoted in Cliff 1979, 151).

Another formidable ideological contradiction of this period emanated from the bureaucratization of the Bolshevik party. From the beginning, the Bolshevik party was led by professional revolutionaries, the so-called vanguard of the revolution. But during the revolution and war communism period, ordinary workers were the driving force of the party's rank and file. During the NEP period, the internal affairs of party cells became more and more bureaucratic, and rank-and-file members increasingly lost their voice to an administrative stratum which had little sympathy with the immediate aspirations of the working class. Also, by 1922, elections to party and committee positions were replaced by appointments, although formal adherence to democratic centralism, that is, the claim that Party officials were elected from below, was maintained.[32] The contradiction stems from the fact that workers were consciously relegated to back seats by a professional bureaucracy and political leadership in a state ruled by what had been called a dictatorship of the proletariat.[33]

The NEP also came under scrutiny for failing to instill a "socialist" consciousness among workers and for creating industrial strife between workers and management. First, the interests of the NEP and workers, in fact, collided head on. The NEP was primarily aimed at reconstruction of the war-devastated economy; therefore, emphasis was on increasing production and raising workers' productivity. Workers, on the other hand, exhausted by years of war and scarcities of basic needs, emphasized consumption and higher wages. Second, NEP management was criticized for promoting labor intensification and creating division among the labor force. This battle was fought on two fronts. Relatively new urban workers, who demonstrated better adaptation skills, were ardent supporters of raising productivity and intensifying production processes. Management used them against those older and privileged workers who opposed this move. On the other hand, NEP management systematically discriminated in favor of rural workers against the urban proletariat. Taking advantage of peasant migration to the cities, management was able to hold down wage costs and lessen skilled workers' prospects of defending their positions. Such industrial strife contributed to "a general worsening of worker-management relations and exacerbated social antagonisms between workers and technical personnel, and, at times, gave way to incipient politicization" (Nove 1969, 114).

Besides holding it responsible for undermining and dividing the working class, for the bureaucratization of party and state, and for the failure to integrate harmonious and "socialist" relationships between workers and management, the NEP was criticized for reinvigorating a wide range of traditional social outlooks and customs, tensions and attitudes in the party and society, which were considered by many old-time Bolsheviks to be antisocialist in content and spirit.

Social Stratification

The NEP's economic success was associated with sharp stratification in Soviet society. The egalitarian spirit, a hallmark of war communism, vanished with the NEP. As Tony Cliff (1979, 152) remarks, "Inequality became widespread. Wealth and luxury became legitimate. There was no longer any need for concealing opulence." Several factors contributed to this situation. First, the NEP's concessions to and compromises with the peasantry were made at an enormous cost to industrial workers. Workers had made tremendous sacrifices during the civil war. They were called upon to continue to sacrifice to pacify recalcitrant peasants. Second, not only were industries transferred to *khozraschet* models, so that they had to operate in open markets, but the powers of managers (professionals, predominantly drawn from the traditional managerial class) were also massively increased. Workers were increasingly subjected to layoffs, work speedups, and other work-intensifying efforts. In addition, managers were increasingly integrated into the Communist party hierarchy.

Third, the NEP's industrial recovery was achieved less by a numerical expansion of the workforce than by success in raising productivity. Therefore, unemployment was rampant during the whole period of the NEP. Unemployment began to rise rapidly in 1923, reached 1.24 million in January 1924; and, except for the year 1925 when it fell to 0.95 million, it remained a serious problem until the end of the NEP. In 1929 unemployment reached a figure of 1.46 million, about one-sixth of the employed labor force in the country (Nove 1969, 115). Fourth, the NEP has also been accused of opening doors for a plethora of administrative and political abuses, nepotism, and discrimination that adversely affected the working class. Therefore, although the standard of living of workers during the NEP period was much better than it had been during the previous period, antigovernment feelings were the strongest among the industrial workers, as demonstrated by workers' unrest over wages and other issues.[34]

The NEP has also been accused of promoting social stratification among the peasants because some peasants fared better than others under its concessions. While war communism promoted almost universal equalization in agricultural units, under the NEP many poor families had to sell their labor power to richer neighbors in order to survive the rigors of the postwar reconstruction.[35] As forcible requisitioning of food was replaced by (a more acceptable form and level of) taxation, the NEP succeeded in restoring confidence in the countryside and thereby taking the steam out of peasants' material discontent.[36] But NEP policies resulted in social stratification in rural areas and the ability of rich peasants to accumulate wealth again.

The Scissors' Crisis

The scissors' crisis,[37] a severe price imbalance between manufacturing and agricultural goods that surfaced in 1923-1924, was the first serious demonstration of the contradiction between the NEP's industrial and agricultural policies. Both these policies were surprisingly effective in rejuvenating industrial and agricultural production. But soon recovery of the agricultural sector proved to be inimical to industrial growth. The problem reached crisis scale when the industrial sector in general, with the exceptions of rural and consumer industry and handicrafts, failed to match the growth in the agricultural sector. Industrial production was up, but costs were high, wages were low, and industrial unemployment expanded substantially. On the other hand, an abundant supply of agricultural produce drove grain prices down while prices of manufactured goods rose, with accompanying reductions in the purchasing power of the peasantry relative to the industrial sector. The consequent moving of the rural-urban terms of trade against the countryside came to be known as the "scissors' crisis," which reached its widest gap in October 1923. Such disparity between industrial and agricultural sectors was also caused by the government's encouragement of privatization and *khozraschet* principles for state enterprises. These policies, in particular, were responsible for promoting higher profits and higher industrial prices compared to agricultural produce so that industrialization could be financed at the expense of the peasants.

The Bolsheviks solved the scissors' crisis in favor of the peasants.[38] Strong administrative measures were taken to bring manufacturing prices down. Besides direct orders to government sector enterprises to reduce the prices of industrial goods, the government initiated measures to control credit supply and regulate prices. The government also imported lower priced foreign goods to close the gap of the scissors. By October 1923 the crisis was largely surmounted, and by 1923-1924 the economy returned to a stable condition.

THE GREAT INDUSTRIALIZATION DEBATE

Competing assessments of the NEP's problems and prospects, known as the Great Industrialization Debate, played a crucial role in shaping Soviet society. Beginning shortly after the death of Lenin in January 1924, this debate occupied years of rigorous attention by the Bolshevik leadership in particular and the Soviet intelligentsia in general. The debate reached a critical stage in 1926 when the Soviet Union approached full-scale industrial and agricultural recovery. The crux of the problem was that after achieving a spectacular recovery, the NEP policies lacked the means to promote further substantial economic growth. It was, indeed, the NEP's success, not failure, that made it dispensable, or at least debatable, for subsequent stages of Soviet economic growth.

The NEP's fundamental inability to meet the changed needs and demands of the Soviet economy began to surface by the mid 1920s. First was the scissors' crisis. After this crisis had been resolved in favor of the peasantry, a series of other crises emerged to disrupt the economy. By 1926 the Soviet industrial sector had very nearly attained its prewar capacity and required further investment for expansion and modernization. But, at the same time, Soviet agricultural production began to decline, becoming less and less capable of providing the resources that could be shifted for industrialization. In fact, in 1926, Soviet agriculture experienced an ominous decline, and in 1926-1927 only 13 percent of peasant production reached the market. As a result, the country plunged into severe grain shortages.

A number of factors can be held responsible for the lackluster performance of the agricultural sector. First, since the revolution, Russian agriculture underwent drastic structural and institutional transformation. The large estates and farms that had produced almost all of Russia's cash and export crops had disappeared, and smaller units of individual farms dominated the agricultural sector. According to Nove (1969, 106), the number of households rose to 23 million in 1924, to 25 million in 1927, from roughly 17 to 18 million on comparable territory in 1917. Moreover, in 1927, shares of state and collective farms (all types) of the entire sown area were 1.1 percent and 0.6 percent, respectively, while individual peasants' share in the total sown area was 98.3 percent. Second, agricultural implements remained largely preindustrial. Although the NEP supplied credit as well as a large number of tractors, even as late as 1928, 5.5 million households still used the *sokha* (wooden plough) and half the grain harvest was reaped by sickle or scythe. Forty percent was threshed with flails.

Third, many blamed the kulaks for their noncooperation. The number of alleged kulaks seemed to be growing. Their share of leased land increased form 2.8 percent in 1922 to 6.1 percent in 1925. The share of employment of labor by kulaks ranged from 1.0 percent to 1.9 percent during the same period. But, as the above figures show, small households dominated the agricultural sector. Fourth, the government shared some of the blame for the crisis because it failed to develop policies that could foster technical improvement, land consolidation, and voluntary collectivization among the poor. NEP government, instead, followed an erratic price policy (Blackwell 1970, 87).

By 1926, the NEP had restored the prerevolutionary levels of industrial and agricultural output and had achieved full capacity production. The question now shifted to how to augment production capacity and industrialize the economy. But questions of large-scale industrialization and rapid economic growth brought forward a whole series of controversial issues, such as the type of economic system to be adopted, long-run industrial strategies, balanced versus unbalanced growth, mobilization of agricultural savings, investment capital for industrial growth, overall accumulation of capital, the scope of government and central planning, and the national and international character of socialist revolution and economic development. Before we move to these controversies, a brief discussion of some of the major factors that constrained the industrialization debate is in order.

Inflationary Pressures

The industrialization debate was sparked by the inflationary threat of 1924.[39] This threat occupied a central position in the debate because the NEP had succeeded in bringing the nation's aggregate demand back close to the capacity limits of the economy. But the NEP had accomplished industrial recovery by regaining the prewar level of output, not by making up for the loss of industrial capital stock. Therefore, further expansion of the industrial sector required substantial net investment. Such large industrial investment plausibly would create inflationary problems because its capacity-creating effect would be felt only after a time lag,[40] while the economy would experience its income generation effect immediately. Therefore, massive industrial investment would fuel inflationary pressures. That, in turn, would worsen the scissors' crisis further by contributing to a rise in the prices of industrial goods. And that would jeopardize the *smychka* between the peasants and workers since agricultural prices might not rise proportionately.

An alternative to this was to move to industrialization with a slow rate of capital accumulation. That would avoid excessive inflation and thereby could preserve the *smychka*. But this strategy would fail to generate substantial industrial capacity and at the same time would leave the economy vulnerable to inflationary pressures because of capacity constraints on expanding production.

Marxist-Leninist Prescriptions

The industrialization debate was also linked to Marxist and Leninist prescriptions. According to Marxian schema of economic development, societies move from primitive agricultural society to feudalism, then to capitalism, then to socialism, which in turn transforms into communism. But at the time of the revolution Russia was a semifeudal, semi-industrial society. Marx, in the nineteenth century, had largely (though not definitively) discounted Russia as a prime candidate for socialist revolution. Now that revolution under proletarian socialist auspices had occurred in Russia, debate centered on whether the Soviet Union needed a stage of capitalism (as proxied by the NEP through state capitalism) or whether it could skip this stage and move directly to socialism.

Also, several Marxian concepts had relevance to the industrialization debate of the 1920s. First, Marx's expanded reproduction scheme provided a conceptual model for determining sectoral priorities. Marx's sectors A and B could be superimposed on Russian agriculture and industry in order to determine which sector should be given priority over the other. Second, the Marxian concept of "primitive capitalist accumulation" was relevant to the industrialization debate as some of the Bolshevik leaders were looking for socialist parallels to "primitive capitalist accumulation." For Marx, early capitalism was characterized by "original" or "primitive," that is, precapitalist, accumulations, for example, the slave trade and such expropriations of the property of the weak as the enclosure movement. In the absence of external assistance for an emerging socialist society, the agricultural sector might serve as an analogous source of "primitive socialist accumulation." Third, Marx's concept of conscious planning of production and distribution during the transition period also had relevance to the industrialization debate. During the transition period, Marx emphasized, sectoral imbalances can be consciously planned for rapid growth. Such growth can be accelerated by giving priority to the investment goods sector over the consumer goods sector. Fourth, Marx's notion of transition into socialist economy contained significant capitalist elements, notably, distribution of goods to individuals according to their labor contributions, not according to their needs, which was projected as possible and desirable only at the "higher" stage of communism.[41]

Lenin's contributions to the industrialization debate were minimal. But his positions during the war communism and NEP periods provided ample references for participants in the debate to defend their respective positions in his name. Lenin, as elaborated in Chapter 2, identified a period of transition between capitalism and socialism, which, in the Soviet context, he designated as "state capitalism." State capitalism, as explained earlier, stood for a state-controlled mixed economy that would utilize many capitalist elements, such as the services of specialists, concessions to foreign capital, and private trade, for achieving socialist goals. As to whether socialism could be built in one country, Lenin's position oscillated between the polar positions taken by Trotsky and Bukharin. Trotsky emphasized "permanent revolution" and the international character of socialism, while Bukharin argued that the Soviet Union's resource base and economic potential were strong enough to build socialism alone. Although Lenin believed that the ultimate success of Soviet socialism would depend on the spread of socialism in advanced countries, he emphasized that a "breathing space" would be required to allow consolidation of revolutionary gains in the USSR before worldwide socialist revolution would occur.[42]

Strategies for Industrialization

The Great Industrialization Debate, given its crucial, sensitive, and far-reaching character, divided the Bolshevik leaders, mainly into two opposing groups: those who represented the right wing of the party; and those who represented the left wing of the party. Both agreed that transition to a socialist society must be based on a substantially higher level of economic development and industrialization, that economic recovery within the limited confines of the industrial capacities of the NEP period had been pretty well exhausted, and that further economic progress would depend on strategies to expand industrial capacity (and thereby reduce the pressures for inflation that had increasingly plagued the Soviet economy as the 1920s proceeded). They differed, however, in their assessments of the magnitude and rapidity of the needed economic transformations, the "balance" (or "imbalance") between industry and agriculture, the relationships between workers and peasants, and their specific strategies for growth.

The Leftist Strategy. The left wing of the Bolshevik party was represented by such party leaders as Gregory Zinoviev, Lev Kamenev, and, to some extent, Trotsky; its economic arguments were provided by an economist, E.A. Preobrazhensky (1965). Preobrazhensky argued that the Soviet Union had two major options: to continue to stagnate, or even retrogress to lower levels of industrial capacity under continuation of NEP-type policies; or to move forward with an "unbalanced" growth focused on industry, especially heavy industry, relative to agriculture and a program of capital accumulation that was both massive in scale and rapid in pace. Preobrazhensky justified a strategy of rapid, large-scale accumulation and industrialization by the need to replace obsolete and depreciated capital stock; adopt higher ratios of capital to output under conditions of full capacity and higher ratios of capital to labor in investment, as compared to consumption and goods industries; incorporate the latest technologies (utilizing capital-intensive modes of production) to achieve high efficiency and productivity; and to provide large investments in many different areas simultaneously. Preobrazhensky explicated his proposal for simultaneity of accumulation projects on the basis of perceived interdependencies of investments and the need to make what today would be called a "big push" to generate a critical minimum amount of investment to catapult the Soviet economy rapidly out of the lethargy of underdevelopment. In the context of the 1920s, the Leftists were typically characterized as "super-industrializers."

In the absence of external assistance, Preobrazhensky contended, a rapid and large-scale industrialization program would require a substantial shift of resources from the agricultural sector. As noted in Marx's analysis of the historical transition to capitalism, a "primitive" (or precapitalist) accumulation of capital—through piracy, conquest, colonization, the slave trade, and enclosure of former public lands—helped to establish the foundations of investment and industry from which capitalism's own accumulation process could then continue. By analogy, Preobrazhensky argued, the establishment of a socialist economy, with its accumulation processes, in the setting of economic underdevelopment required a sort of "primitive socialist accumulation," that is, harsh measures to impose a rate of capital accumulation (and its concentration in heavy industry) significantly beyond that which would be spontaneously forthcoming from peasant saving and which would extract from agriculture the resources needed to set socialism on its feet by a "discontinuous spurt" of investment. In brief, "the position of the Leftists was that industrialization would require tremendous savings, that these would have to come mostly from the peasantry, but that the peasants would never voluntarily make this sacrifice if the government continued to follow a policy of encouraging peasant agriculture" (Campbell 1960, 18-19).

Preobrazhensky's analysis also responded to the problem of inflation. Inflationary pressures in the Soviet economy in the mid 1920s, he argued, had two causes: the low capacity of the industrial sector, and a loss of saving ability caused by institutional changes in Soviet agriculture since the revolution. He contended that postrevolutionary redistribution of land among the peasantry had substantially increased the aggregate demand of the peasants while industrial capacity, although increased somewhat, could not keep pace with that of agriculture. Closing this inflationary gap, he argued, required a significant increase in industrial investment that could come from a restructured aggregate demand that would discourage consumption and encourage saving. The state, through a process of "nonequivalent exchange" (Preobrazhensky 1965, 271), should purchase raw materials from the peasants at low prices and sell manufactured goods to them at high prices. The saving generated through such a process of primitive socialist accumulation would then be channeled by the state to the industrial sector, especially heavy industry. Such a strategy, he stated, would cause a temporary reduction in the standard of living of the peasants, but the long-term benefits from this would far outweigh the short-run benefits of investing in agriculture or light industry.

The "super-industrializers," therefore, condemned the NEP's concessions to peasants and private trade and maintained that socialism could be established in the Soviet Union without going through the capitalist stage of economic development. The Leftists, notably Trotsky, also denounced the concept of building socialism in one country, while insisting on international socialist revolution. They argued that capitalism was an international system that could be overturned only by an international socialist revolution. Trotsky emphasized the international character of socialism and the international role of the Soviet Union in supporting the workers' revolution abroad.

The Rightist Growth Strategy. The Rightists, on the other hand, favored the avoidance of super-industrialization, preservation of *smychka*, and efforts toward rapprochement with the capitalist world. *Pravda* editor Bukharin, labor union leader Mikhail Tomsky, and generally party general secretary Stalin, and many party bureaucrats responsible for government policy during the NEP were generally associated with the right wing of the party. The Rightists began with recognition of the government's weakness relative to the peasants and, to a lesser degree, the workers, and thus, the need to make accommodations for continued political support. The institutional form of economy envisaged by this group consisted essentially of a continuation of the NEP: a socialized public sector, a governmentally controlled private sector, private enterprise coupled with free agricultural markets for the peasantry and NEP tradesmen, and liberal wage policies, shorter hours, improved working conditions, and support of labor unions and their demands for some degree of worker control over industry. As a corollary, suggested Bukharin (1982), the excessive centralization, officious government bureaucracy, and tendency toward autocracy inherent under Russian conditions in the urge to rapid, large-scale industrialization could be at least blunted.

The Rightists propounded a balanced growth strategy resting on the mutually supportive evolution of agriculture and industry. The expansion of industry was expected to provide industrial goods in exchange for food and raw materials from agriculture. Technological improvements in industry would lower costs, raise profits, and provide funds for investment in industry. As agricultural output and income expanded, peasant saving would rise voluntarily, augmenting saving and investment within the industrial sector. Unlike the leftists, they believed in deterministic interpretations of Marx and insisted that "economic laws" could not be circumvented or necessary stages of historical development avoided. They also emphasized measures to transform small-scale manufacturing and handicraft industries into producers' cooperatives and maintained that, during the early stages of industrialization, the Soviet Union must import large quantities of industrial equipment from abroad and pay for those commodities with agricultural exports.

Extreme Rightists proposed a growth strategy discriminately based on agriculture. They argued that the Soviet economy had traditionally enjoyed a comparative advantage in agriculture; therefore, industrialization should be based on an agriculture-first strategy. Led by Lev Shanin, this group argued for an unbalanced growth of agriculture within an essentially free market economy. According to Shanin, first, given a huge surplus population and very low capital intensity, the marginal output-capital ratio was higher in agriculture than in industry. Soviet agriculture thus possessed greater growth potential than the industrial sector. Second, Soviet peasants traditionally had a higher propensity to save than the industrial sector; therefore, increased investment in agriculture would lead to higher savings than a similar investment in industry. Among other benefits, inflationary pressures would be minimized. Third, Soviet agriculture had a comparative advantage; its outputs could be efficaciously exchanged for industrial goods in foreign trade. These benefits, he argued, would industrialize the Soviet Union in a shorter time, eliminate inflationary pressures, and do all this without much dislocation. The main difference between Shanin's extreme Rightist position and Preobrazhensky's Leftist position is that Shanin emphasized the income generation side of capital investment while Preobrazhensky emphasized its capacity-creating effect (Gregory and Stuart 1981, 76).[43]

NOTES

1. The Fifteenth Congress of the Bolshevik Party reversed many of the policies of the NEP and introduced the First Five Year Plan aimed at rapid industrialization of the Soviet Union. Although official documents still referred to a continuation of the NEP, it is commonly believed that this congress effectively terminated it.

2. It should, however, be noted that the NEP emphasized a relatively decentralized governing system in which local, regional, and central administrative bodies enjoyed greater functional autonomy than during the period of war communism.

3. For details on this school of thought, see Fitzpatrick (1991) and Rosenberg (1991).

4. Prominent members of this school of thought include Blackwell (1970); Tucker (1977); Kolakowski (1978); Treadgold (1972). For details see Dowlah (1990b) and Dowlah and Elliott (1991).

5. These figures are based on Dobb (1966); Nove (1969, 86); and Table 3.5.

6. Kronstadt was a naval base located in the Gulf of Finland about twenty miles west of Petrograd. In 1921 it had a population of about 50,000, of which approximately half were military personnel.

7. This happened during the session of the Tenth Party Congress held in March 1921, in which Lenin proposed substitution of a food tax (*prodnalog*) for confiscation of food surpluses (*prodrazverstka*). Some authors erroneously credit the Kronstadt revolt as the genesis of such a dramatic policy change. In fact, the proposal to abolish *prodrazverstka* was initiated before the Kronstadt rebellion occurred. See, for example, Nove (1990, 58-59) and Getzler (1983).

8. Nove (1990, 58) remarks that, by the end of 1920 and early 1921, massive peasant resistance and risings brought the country to a condition so catastrophic that the survival of the Bolshevik regime came "ever more clearly to depend on the relaxation of the rigors of War communism."

9. Blackwell (1970, 76-77) puts it succinctly: "The foremost questions before the Bolshevik leaders were: to preserve their power, to avert the impending food crisis in the short-run, and rebuilding the Russian economy in the long-run."

10. Poor Peasant's Committees, formed for the requisitioning of food at the early stages of revolution, had already been abolished by November 1918.

11. Treadgold (1972, 197) claims that Trotsky sought to replace the requisitioning of agricultural surplus with a tax in kind one year earlier, but his proposal was watered down by other Bolshevik leaders, including Lenin.

12. The immediate implications of food tax progressivity were not economically significant. According to Carr and Davies (1969, 291), because of war communism, policies there had occurred a "striking equalization of the size of the unit of production" among the peasants, and

small-holding had become a predominant feature of Russian agriculture by 1920. Therefore, food tax progressivity did not have much effect. But during the NEP era, as Nove (1969, 108) points out, the number of alleged kulaks increased. Their share of leasing land increased from 2.8 percent in 1922 to 6.1 percent in 1925. Therefore, such tax policy had significant effects. The following table demonstrates the government's tax revenues based on progressive tax policies.

	1925-1926	1926-1927
Poor peasants*	1.83	0.90
Middle peasants	13.25	17.77
Kulaks	63.60	100.77

*all amounts are in million rubles per annum.
Source: Nove (1969, 137).

13. In practice, however, as Blackwell (1970, 78) notes, the tax rates for most important agricultural goods like grain, potatoes, and eggs, were slightly higher than 50 percent during 1921 and 1922.

14. The Fundamental Law on the Exploitation of Land by Workers, enacted in May 1922, gave the peasants the right to choose among individual, communal, and other kinds of land tenure systems.

15. According to Hutchings (1971, 38), such sales of nationalized capital assets to private individuals touched on a sensitive chord in the country. As a result, a decree in April 1923 restricted the rights of trusts to sell their property and abolished rights to dispose of certain types of capital assets.

16. Enterprises, however, did not have commercial or financial accountability. Trusts were solely responsible for the functioning of enterprises. This system functioned until 1927 when the enterprises themselves were guaranteed defined rights and duties.

17. Nove (1969, 114), however, maintains that the conversion of workers' pay into purely money wages did not happen at once. Even in the first quarter of 1921, he maintains, only 6.8 percent of wages were paid in money; the rest was issued in the form of goods and services. By the middle of 1922, over half of the wages were paid in the form of money, and even in the first quarter of 1923, 20 percent of the wage was paid in kind.

18. Britain was the first country to sign a foreign trade agreement with Russia in 1922. Soon, other European countries, including Germany and France, followed suit.

19. It should, be noted, however, that an extraordinarily chaotic administration, the turbulent and volatile political situation in the country, and an increasingly activist role of anti-Bolshevik ultraradical forces, might have left the Bolsheviks without any other viable political option at this juncture.

20. One such example was the show-trial of central committee members of the Socialist Revolutionaries in 1922. The defendants were accused of collaborating with the White generals during the civil war, and they were sentenced to death by the Revolutionary Tribunal. See Service (1979, 160).

21. Such an about-face in the political sphere of the NEP has been explained differently. One strand of thought blames the Bolsheviks themselves. According to this view, it was largely the work of a small but tightly knit faction of Bolshevik leaders who had an extreme leaning toward authoritarian method, and who outmaneuvered rival groups. This view also cites the prerevolutionary tradition of the Bolsheviks, which, indeed, emphasized a radical approach and elitist leadership. Another school identifies objective circumstances as the great molder of the Bolshevik party's internal transformation. They believe that the changes that occurred after the revolution and the collapse of revolutionary stirrings in the rest of Europe were primarily responsible for increasingly rigid party politics during the NEP. (See Service 1979, 3-4).

22. Stalin was appointed general secretary because Lenin had been incapacitated by a stroke earlier the same year. Although Stalin's appointment as general secretary evoked sharp controversy in 1922, he held this position for three decades to come.

23. The amalgamation was carried out at Stalin's behest. Stalin, at this time, was in charge of nationality problems, and he orchestrated this amalgamation, brushing aside serious opposition, especially from the Georgians. Stalin himself was a Georgian by birth.

24. In Rostow's (1990) theory of the stages of economic development, this is described as the "take-off" stage of Soviet economy. As Cohn (1974, 326) remarks, in terms of factor availabilities and motivation on the part of the regime, the thesis that the Russian economy was ready for a takeoff is even more applicable to the Soviet economy of 1928 than that of 1913.

25. Gerschenkron (1965), however, maintains that by 1926 Russian industrial production was roughly back to the prewar level. By 1927 the gross value output of large-scale industry was 123.6 compared to 1913, and by 1928 the index had risen to 154.3.

26. Some of the new bourgeoisie were government officials. It is striking that much like present-day marketization in Russia, some of the very first sizable private stores opened during the NEP period were owned by former state employees. Such employees used their official positions to acquire goods and then sell them in private markets. Another category of officials remained in service, registering their shops under someone else's name and supplying the stores with products they controlled as government officials. (See Ball 1991, 91).

27. The ranks were organized as follows: Rank 1: trade by an individual, generally in market squares, bazaars or along streets; rank 2: trade by an individual, or no more than two people, from small permanent facilities, which the customer does not enter; rank 3: retail trade, by the owner of the business and no more than four hired workers or family members, conducted from a permanent facility, which the customer can enter; rank 4: partial wholesale trade from enterprises with no more than ten workers, or retail trade employing from five to twenty workers; rank 5: wholesale trade or partial wholesale trade employing more than ten workers, and retail trade employing more than twenty workers (Ball 1991, 93).

28. According to *Vesenkha*, in 1927, about half the output of state consumer goods eventually reached the population through private traders. Urban private traders received approximately 40 percent of their merchandise from state and cooperative factories, agencies and stores in 1925 and 1926. The percentage fell to 33 percent in 1926 and 1927, 25 percent in 1927 and 1928, and 17 percent in 1928 and 1929. The share declined as the state tightened its control over the private sector.

29. For ideological contradictions of the NEP see Dowlah (1990b, 222-26) and Dowlah (1992a, 32-33).

30. As Blackwell (1970, 82) remarks: "Fears and hopes were sounded throughout the world, mainly by apprehensive socialists and dispossessed capitalists, about the restoration of capitalism in Russia."

31. These numbers, however, should be read carefully. Between 1917 and 1923 Russia, experienced a dramatic social metamorphosis. Many working-class members moved upward on the social ladder but still remained members of the Bolshevik party. Indeed, the revolution was supposed to change the fate of the working class. For social mobility of classes during war communism and the NEP see Rigby 1968; Orlovsky 1989; Service 1979.

32. At least until 1921, and to a lesser but significant extent throughout the 1920s, the Bolshevik party was characterized by robust discussion and even dissent. Not only top level party officials, but even rank-and-file members, could express their views in party meetings.

33. In fact, Lenin believed this metamorphosis within the party and society had dysfunctional consequences. In the last years of his life, especially after 1922, he was preoccupied with the bureaucratization of the party and state. He demonstrated his disapproval of the bureaucratization of the *Sovnarkom* machine and made resolute efforts to dissociate party and state business. Rigby (1979) provides a useful examination of these issues.

34. Hatch (1991), in his study of Soviet workers between 1921 and 1925, however, maintains that during the latter part of the NEP (presumably by 1924 or 1925), in conjunction with economic improvements that affected many workers, strike actions rapidly declined.

35. Social differentiation of this kind was not to the liking of the Bolsheviks, but they had to tolerate it as long as the concessions given to private enterprise in the countryside still seemed unavoidable. Even radicals like Trotsky and Preobrazhensky recognized that an all-out drive toward equalization was impracticable for the time being.

36. As Service (1979, 162) remarks, "Most rural households were much more interested in getting a good price for their wheat, potatoes or milk than in contemplating armed insurrection."

37. It is believed that this term has its origin in a diagram that Trotsky used in a speech showing the intersection of a falling rural price curve and a rising urban price curve. The curves intersected, according to Trotsky, in September 1922.

38. Policies pursued for such a resolution, however, remained instructive for the Bolshevik regime for subsequent periods, as will be discussed in the following section.

39. Eventually, the debate extended far beyond inflation to cover a number of critical issues involving alternative strategies for the large-scale industrialization of the Soviet economy, which we shall discuss below.

40. Such a time lag occurs because industrial investment soon generates new income through multiplier effects, while the extension of industrial capacity and its application to industry requires a more or less longer period of time.

41. For literature on the economics of the transition period, see Bettleheim (1975); Bukharin (1964); Day (1973); Deutscher (1960); Dowlah (1992a); Elliott (1984).

42. Gregory and Stuart (1981, 66-69) provide a useful analysis of the relevance of Marx's and Lenin's prescriptions for the Soviet Great Industrialization Debate of the 1920s.

43. In addition to the major debate between left and right perspectives, as described in the body of the text, there was a third group in the party's extreme left wing. Known generally as the Workers' Opposition, it consisted of idealistic, old-time Bolsheviks influenced by democratic, egalitarian, and communitarian strains in the prerevolutionary Marxian vision of the future socialist society. For them, the NEP policy and positions of the Rightists combined capitalist economy and authoritarian politics by the government and party elite, each problematic and neither expressive of authentic socialist revolutionary aspirations. Leftist policies and strategies were also criticized, but for their overcentralization, harshness, and dictatorial implications. This group proposed a genuine proletarian revolution to overturn the increasingly concentrated and centralized power of the party and to establish a version of socialism from below, embodying democracy, equality, and decentralized institutions for workers' control of industry. (See Horvat 1982).

Chapter 4

Stalin and Totalitarian State-Directed Economy: Origins, Institutions, and Policies

INTRODUCTION

This chapter and the next examine the Stalinist model of Soviet socialism. The Stalinist era marks a watershed in Soviet history. Much of the economic, military, and industrial might of the former Soviet Union has its origin in the Stalinist model. Elected general secretary of the All Union Communist (Bolshevik) party in 1922, Joseph Stalin[1] had consolidated his power by 1929 and transformed a semiindustrial Soviet Union into the second mightiest industrial and military power of the world in record time.[2] The model that evolved during three decades of Stalinist rule brought thoroughgoing and far-reaching changes in Soviet society, polity, and economy. The rapidity and magnitude of these changes, cumulatively known as the "revolution from above,"[3] succeeded in repudiating the institutions and processes of capitalism and building the Stalinist version of socialism in the Soviet Union.[4]

The Stalinist politico-economic model had five tightly knit characteristics: (1) dictatorship by the Communist party over the state; (2) personal tyranny by Stalin over the Communist party; (3) a closely knit set of institutional innovations for party/state control and coordination of the economy, namely, collectivization of agriculture, state ownership of the means of production, centralized planning, and a strong bureaucratic machine; (4) rapid industrialization, with emphasis on investment in heavy industry and shifts in resources from agriculture to industry; and (5) domination by the dictator, party, and state over society through monopolization of control over the armed forces, the media of mass communication, ideology, and education and the systematic use of secret police terror (Elliott 1989). These draconian measures, which constituted a complete reversal of the NEP, a sweeping revision of the Bolshevik (Leninist) tradition, and comprehensive control over Soviet society in the name of socialism, can be described as a totalitarian party-state-directed economy.[5] The Stalinist model is discussed below using the four criteria developed in earlier chapters.

UNDERLYING CAUSES

As discussed in Chapter 3, the NEP achieved considerable economic and political success. Economically, both agriculture and industry in the Soviet Union had recovered almost completely to the prewar level by 1926-1927 (see Tables 3.4-3.6). However, the Soviet economy was shattered for seven years by World War I, civil wars, and other disruptions. Through the NEP's success in economic recovery, the Soviet Union attained the prewar level of economic condition; however, it was still as backward and semiindustrial as it was in 1913. Compared to the advanced capitalist countries Soviet production and technological progress remained outmoded. The Bolsheviks castigated the economic backwardness of prerevolutionary Russia and remained committed to socialism's superiority over capitalism. The NEP's recovery thus brought them to the threshold of their perceived historic mission to move the economy forward. Moreover, the NEP's success was based on a compromise with the peasantry. The NEP's mixed economy relied heavily on market instruments such as price, tax, and fiscal and monetary policies rather than on administrative means. Consequently, the agricultural sector thrived in the economy predominantly under private ownership. Indeed, the share of private ownership in agriculture in 1927 exceeded that of the prerevolutionary Russia of 1914. Therefore, many Bolshevik leaders believed that fruition of the October Revolution, or establishment of socialism, required resolute government control along with greater public ownership in the agricultural sector.

Politically, the NEP succeeded in restoring a normal, even optimistic, mood in the country. The NEP's conciliatory policies toward agriculture dissipated much of the steam of disgruntled peasants. Moreover, the economic success of the NEP made it possible to feed urban dwellers and industrial workers with relative ease. These factors contributed to a greater political stability in the country after years of wars and other disruptions. At the same time, the dominance of agriculture in the economy, the rise in private ownership of agriculture, and the peasantry's resistance and apparent inability to contribute significantly to the industrialization process created strong political pressure on the Soviet leadership to restrict or eliminate the role of the private sector in the economy. Moreover, as discussed below, the NEP was increasingly showing signs of exhaustion in the industrial sector.

All these contributed to a pervasive feeling, especially among the leadership, that the country needed a new and bolder approach to move forward to large-scale industrialization in order to catch up with the Western capitalist countries. Although this goal was hardly contested, Bolshevik leaders bitterly disputed over the right course to follow. The dispute essentially boiled down to two sharply opposed alternatives: either a complete replacement of the NEP, which would call for rapid industrialization at the expense of the peasantry, or continuation of a rejuvenated the NEP, which would emphasize gradual industrialization based on balanced development of agriculture and industry. Stalin's victory in the power struggle settled the matter in favor of the former. Among others, the following four factors played crucial roles in the eventual replacement of the NEP and the triumph of Stalinism.

The Exhaustion of the NEP

By 1926-1927, signs of the NEP's exhaustion were clearly discernable in both agricultural and industrial sectors. Agriculture's recurring inability to provide a substantial surplus, as demonstrated repeatedly throughout the 1920s, was perceived to be a crucial impediment to large-scale industrialization. Although agricultural production had reached prewar levels by 1927, in respect to marketed or state-requisitioned surplus of grains the progress was less than satisfactory. For example, Russia exported 12 million tons of grain in 1913, but during the NEP years annual exports never exceeded 3 million tons. In addition, the agricultural sector showed little promise of supplying raw materials and manpower for industry or contributing substantially to the national objectives of industrialization, capital accumulation, and international trade.

Several factors contributed to agricultural weakness in the late 1920s. First, the NEP agriculture was dominated by a stubbornly noncooperative private peasantry in terms of ownership, cultivation, consumption, and trade. In 1929 state and collective farms together contributed less than 2 percent of the total grain crop and covered little more than 1 percent of the cultivated area. Moreover, agricultural resources were heavily owned by richer peasants who remained opposed to the socialist project.[6] Second, increased fragmentation of agriculture after the revolution contributed to its relatively poor performance. As discussed previously, the Bolshevik government's land distribution policy created millions of new landholding peasants. Such small peasant households were less able to contribute to marketing foodstuffs for domestic or foreign markets.[7] Third, the government pricing policy, which strongly discriminated against agricultural goods (that peasants sold) relative to manufactured goods (that peasants bought), played a crucial role in the weakening of agricultural performance. Throughout the NEP period, as demonstrated by the scissors' crisis, the grain crisis, and other events, the Soviet government ignored forces of demand and supply and deliberately set policies to pay low prices to the peasants for agricultural goods and maintain high prices for manufactured goods. Fourth, Soviet agriculture of the late 1920s remained traditional in its mode of production. The peasantry still used largely primitive cultivation methods, overall agricultural productivity was less than satisfactory, and most peasants remained conservative in their attitudes (Dobb 1948, 208-25).

But in the absence of foreign aid or large-scale domestic savings, an expansion of agricultural production and consequent increased flow of agricultural products to domestic and foreign markets remained the most viable option open to the Soviet leadership for industrialization. In addition to providing a supply of foodstuffs for urban dwellers and workers to industries, the agricultural sector was expected to provide raw materials and necessary capital to acquire machineries for industrial expansion. Realization of such ambitious goals called for considerable capital investment in agricultural equipment and productivity, which, some Bolshevik leaders believed, could be accomplished only by the state through a thoroughgoing reorganization of the agricultural sector itself.[8]

The NEP industrial sector also showed signs of exhaustion; by 1926, it had reached an upper limit of existing capacities. New investments were needed to move beyond the existing capacity.[9] Both industrial and political leaders—committed to a policy of transforming the Soviet Union into a self-sufficient, modern, industrial nation—believed it was essential to expand industrial capacities significantly. In the absence of any other viable or acceptable alternative, agriculture remained the only sector to provide a major source of capital accumulation for industrial prosperity.[10]

Grain and Price Crises

The NEP's agricultural problems were intensified by the grain crises of 1923-1924 and the food shortages of 1926-1927. These crises brought to the surface more crucial facts pertaining to the character of the Soviet peasantry. In addition to the agriculture sector's perceived inability to cope with the increasing demand for industrialization and urbanization, these crises demonstrated an unmistakable tendency of the peasants not to cooperate with the Bolshevik government.[11] To the Bolshevik leadership, the central message of these crises was clear: efforts must be intensified not only to increase agricultural production, but also to ensure that enough grains were actually supplied to markets. Factors that contributed to the expansion of such twofold pressures on agriculture included an increase in overall population, rapidly increasing urbanization and industrial centers, tensions in ensuring marketable surpluses of agricultural goods, and the emphasis on planned development of the country. Although some in the Bolshevik leadership remained committed to gradual and orderly evolution of collective agriculture, a substantial segment of the party leadership came to support a more forceful collectivization drive. Rapid collectivization, they argued, could alleviate the dire need for grain to feed urban industrial workers as well as facilitate capital accumulation critically needed for industrialization.

The food crisis reached a critical stage in January 1928 when state purchases of grain stood at 300 million puds[12] compared to 428 million for the corresponding period in 1927. The exact causes of the drop in state collection of grains remains uncertain. Some scholars maintain that the reasons for this deficit lay with a bad harvest. But others argue that the 1927 harvest was a normal and average one. To them, government measures, such as, reduction of grain prices by as much as 20 percent in 1926, banning the voting rights of kulaks in local soviet elections and excluding kulaks from the more powerful village assemblies, and, more important, raising tax rates on well-to-do peasants, were some of the main causes responsible for the grain crises. These measures created powerful incentives for peasants, especially relatively richer ones, not to produce and market their products. Marketed grain supplies received a further setback when peasants began to use more grain for cattle fodder because relatively higher meat prices promised greater profits.

Among the Soviet leadership, Stalin stood for coercive measures to rectify the grain crisis situation. Indeed, mainly at Stalin's personal initiative, emergency confiscatory measures were adopted. The Stalinist group conceived the grain crises as offshoots of structural or organic causes originating from the deficiencies of the NEP. For them, the grain crises demonstrated an unavoidable intensification of the class war waged by the peasants against the Bolshevik regime and the socialist project itself. Stalin's response was to reduce prices offered to the peasants for grain and raise the prices of the manufactured goods delivered to them.

Nikolai Bukharin's group, however, remained unconvinced that the solution to the grain crises required coercive measures. Bukharin denounced Stalin's uncompromising position and emphasized that, instead of the unwillingness of the peasantry, it was the unpreparedness of the state, inadequate planning, inflexible price policies, and the negligent conduct of local officials that were responsible for the grain crises (Cohen 1980).[13]

Table 4.1
Gap Between Free and Official Prices in the Soviet Union, 1926-1929
(1913=100)

Dates	Food		Manufactures	
	Private	Official	Private	Official
1926 (December)	198	181	251	208
1927 (December)	222	175	240	188
1928 (December)	293	184	253	190
1929 (June)	450	200	279	192

Source: Nove 1969, 147 (reprint 1990).

Stalin's confiscatory measures, however, succeeded in accomplishing their immediate goals. By June 1929, the situation was brought under control. Both grain procurement and exports increased. Whereas in 1928 the state was able to procure 10.8 million tons of grain, the amount increased to 16.1 million in 1929. Soviet grain exports increased from 0.03 million tons in 1928, to 0.18 million tons in 1929 (Nove 1969, 170).

But the measures undertaken to increase grain collections, that is, the confiscation of grains from unwilling peasants, denial of certain political rights, and increased tax burdens on the well-to-do peasants, soon exhausted themselves. Moreover, dramatic price movements and an alarming rate of discrepancy between official and private prices kept the whole situation volatile. As Table 4.1 indicates, the grain crisis found expression in violent price movements and wider discrepancies between official and private market prices. After 1926 both official and free market prices for agricultural and manufactured products rose steadily, always maintaining a considerable divergence between one another. In 1929, for example, while the official price index for food products was 200, the price index in private trade was more than double, and reached 450. Thus, food items were sold in private markets at more than twice the price set by the government.[14] In the manufacturing sector also private prices were much higher than official prices throughout the period from 1926 to 1929. In such a situation black markets thrived in many parts of the country. Significant amounts of grain escaped official collection and reached private markets at from two to three times the official price. Confiscation of grain, wide divergence of prices in official and private markets and resultant black markets, powerfully threatened the existing wage structure and the processes of industrial expansion. It therefore became clear to a substantial part of the Bolshevik leadership that continuation of the NEP through reliance on an unwilling peasantry, with occasional confiscatory measures, would take the country nowhere. The country needed stable prices and more reliable farm policies.[15]

The 1927 War Scare

Another factor that played a crucial role in the emergence of Stalin, and thereby Stalinism, in the Soviet Union was the 1927 war scare. In early 1927 Stalin began to publicize a threat of economic blockade or even potential war against the "socialist homeland" by hostile capitalist powers. A number of events contributed to this war scare. In 1926, following Soviet interventions in a general strike in Britain, Britain severed diplomatic relations with the Soviet Union. The breakup lasted more than two years, until 1929. In 1927 France demanded recall of the Soviet ambassador on the ground that he made remarks derogatory to France's national interest. About the same time, the Soviet ambassador to Warsaw was assassinated. Stalin took advantage of these apparently isolated events by presenting them as elements of a far-reaching conspiracy by international capitalist forces to overthrow the socialist government in the Soviet Union.

On March 10, 1928, the Soviet security police (OGPU) announced a counterrevolutionary conspiracy involving technical specialists and foreign powers at the Shakhty Mines in the Donbass industrial complex. The conspirators were accused of acting on behalf of German, French, and Polish intelligence agencies as well as the former mine and factory owners. The security police accused fifty-five people of sabotage and treason, and some of the accused were forced to make public confessions to that effect. The trial, known as the Shakhty trial, implicated three German engineers, imprisoned thirty-eight defendants, and sentenced eleven people to death, of whom five were actually executed (Bailes 1978, 74-94).

Although the credibility of a foreign-based conspiracy still remains doubtful, Stalin transformed the Shakty trial into a national crisis. He proclaimed that the conspiracy demonstrated open resistance of both internal and external enemies to the progress of the socialist project in the Soviet Union.[16] Along with a sharp deterioration in the international situation, one of the most far-reaching offshoots of the Shakhty trial was a dramatic shift in the nation's industrial policy objectives. Suddenly, the need for a stronger defense against "imperialist powers" began to be meshed with the processes of industrial expansion. Both local and national congresses of the Communist party of the Soviet Union (CPSU) began to demand further strengthening of the country's capacity for defense to counter the designs of the imperialist powers. Accordingly, following the 1927 war scare, capital investments were concentrated in the chemical and metal industries, efforts were made to engage defense factories in civilian production in order to retain their capacity, and civilian factories were designed to meet defense needs. Moreover, military viewpoints were given serious consideration in the First Five Year Plan, especially in selecting capital investment plans for the location of many major new construction projects.

Another far-reaching side effect of the war scare was that it was played up as a part of factional fights. Stalin carefully directed it against both the Trotskyist and Bukharinist campaigns for party leadership. Stalin blamed the Trotskyists for provoking conflict in the party leadership at a time of severe international tension. At the same time, the Stalinist group used the Shakhty trial to discredit Bukharin's policy of collaboration and civil peace, Aleksie Rykov's credibility as manager of the state apparatus, which employed non-Bolshevik and non-Soviet specialists; and Mikhail Tomsky's leadership of the labor unions, which had a responsibility to oversee domestic as well as foreign workers.[17]

Struggle For Succession

An important reason for the emergence of Stalinism was Stalin's success in the struggle to succeed V. I. Lenin as the next leader of the country. While all the factors mentioned above had been instrumental in his success, the intraparty struggle for succession had added its own dynamics to the process. At the time of Lenin's death in 1924, the Politburo of the CPSU consisted of four factional groups, and until the end of 1925, the Soviet Union was led by a collective leadership.

Stalin, who became general secretary of the CPSU in 1922, headed a faction that enjoyed strong support among party apparatchiks. The Stalinist faction argued that socialism could be built in one country, that is, in the Soviet Union, without foreign assistance. Stalin used the party secretariat as an organizational weapon and astutely maneuvered factional politics for his eventual success in the struggle for Lenin's succession. Leon Trotsky, Lenin's apparent successor,[18] headed the leftist opposition. His platform propounded rapid industrialization, if necessary at the peasants' expense. Like Lenin, he believed that the Bolshevik Revolution was successful because of the political maturity of the Russian proletariat, despite Russia's economic and social underdevelopment. Trotsky held that ultimate success in establishing a socialist society in the Soviet Union, however, depended on working-class revolutions in Western industrialized capitalist societies, which then presumably would come to the fraternal assistance of Soviet socialist development. Thus, the project of building socialism could begin in the Soviet Union, but it needed the aid of world revolution for its successful completion.

A third faction of the CPSU consisted of the trio of Politburo moderates who constituted the "trivariate opposition." Bukharin, editor of *Pravda* and party theoretician; Aleksei Rykov, who succeeded Lenin as chairman of the Council of People's Commissars; and Tomsky, head of the labor union organization, provided joint leadership to this faction. This group had support among younger party intellectuals as well as the government bureaucracy and unions. The trivariate advocated moderate, peaceful, peasant-oriented transformation of the Soviet Union following a doctrine of socialism in one country. A final faction was represented by Gregory Zinoviev and Lev Kamenev, dual leaders whose main organizational base was the Leningrad Party over which Zinoviev presided. At the time of Lenin's death, both had a close relationship with Stalin, and both opposed Trotskyists. Supporters of Zinoviev and Kamenev and Bukharin had antagonistic relationships with Trotskyists. At earlier stages of the succession struggle, both of the former groups allied with Stalin to fight against his chief rival, Trotsky. This concerted attack on Trotsky in 1924 and early 1925, Tucker (1973, 299) remarks, "marked the beginning of the end for Trotsky and his political cause."

At the Fourteenth Party Congress, held in December 1925, Kamenev directly challenged Stalin's position as general secretary of the party. This open opposition to Stalin, however, met defeat in the congress, and eventually Kamenev was demoted to candidate status in the Politburo. In 1926 Zinoviev, Trotsky, and Kamenev were removed from the politburo. Zinoviev and Kamenev, forced out of their posts, formed an alliance with their old enemy, Trotsky. The United Opposition of these two groups criticized Stalin in 1926-1927 for making concessions to kulaks, refusing to industrialize the country, and bureaucratizing the state apparatus.

Party succession struggle boiled down to two key personalities: Stalin and Trotsky. Several factors contributed to Stalin's eventual victory. Stalin's opponents were not united, and they had an unshakable belief in the theory that the Soviet Union must go through a prolonged period of mixed economy as a proxy for capitalism before the country could move to full-scale socialist reconstruction. Stalin, an astute and pragmatic politician, continued to defend the NEP's *smychka*, the alliance between the peasants and workers. Such a position earned him crucial support from the Bukharinists, who stood for "civil peace," a developmental program based on an alliance with peasants. At the same time, Stalin warned against potential war and bloodshed that would ensue from a principle of permanent world revolution as propagated by the Trotskyists. Such a policy helped him in ensuring a kind of popular support as ordinary people were weary of further war and bloodshed in the country.

Stalin emphasized his commitment to the Russian proletariat for the success of the socialist project. He stood for "creative Marxism," meaning that Russia would lead the socialist revolution, whereas Trotskyists stood for "orthodox Marxism," meaning that socialist revolution would be led by Europe. At the Fourteenth Party Congress, held in December 1925, Stalin ruled out the necessity of class struggle in a proletariat state and approved initiatives to let peasants increase their productivity, organize cooperatives, and develop forms of exchange.[19] These strategies helped Stalin to eliminate Trotskyist opposition by late 1927, as he was able to expel many left leaders along with a large number of their followers from the party.[20] With the left opposition in disgrace and disarray, Stalin turned to the right opposition led by Bukharin. Bukharin was primarily a theoretician and a less formidable candidate for the succession of Lenin. By late 1929 Stalin was able to inflict crushing political defeats upon Bukharin and his followers. Thus Stalin, by defeating both the Left and the right opposition in succession, consolidated his supreme control over the CPSU.

Stalin's success was attributable not only to his adeptness at outmaneuvering other contenders to Lenin's mantle, but also to his single-minded focus and skill in consolidating his grip over the party and state apparatus. Stalin's Old Bolshevik rivals, notably, Bukharin, Trotsky, Zinoviev, Kamenev, Rykov, and Tomsky, "concentrated their attention on what they thought was a leadership struggle over economic and international policies," that is, the pace of industrialization, the NEP and the kulaks, the danger of war, world revolution versus "socialism in one country,"[21] and so on. These issues, however, important though they were, "were subordinate to the question of who, what group of people, actually exercised power in the USSR." Stalin, by contrast, was fundamentally focused not on this or that policy perspective, but on the "exercise of total power inside the Party, with the unity and integrity of its full-time apparatus as the number one priority" (Mandel 1992, 132). It was precisely because the Stalinist faction and its associated party bureaucracy had consolidated its power over the state that it was able to implement rapidly its policy priorities once that consolidation was completed.

All these factors played crucial roles in bringing an end to the NEP era. Historians disagree on exactly when the NEP ended, but few doubt that it had begun to die by late 1926.[22] Although the official end of the NEP was announced by Stalin in December 1929, the Fifteenth Party Congress, held in December 1927, brought a decisive end to the NEP, settled the issue of the succession of Lenin, and ushered in the era of Stalinism.[23]

INSTITUTIONS, PROGRAMS, AND POLICIES

The Stalinist solution to the dilemmas posed by the Great Industrialization Debate of the 1920s constituted an abrupt break with the NEP and a commitment to
radical reconstruction of Russian institutions, politico-economic life, and social values. Stalin's "revolution from above"[24] applied centralized methods of political control to the industrialization process. It presupposed that rapid, large-scale
industrialization, incorporating vast magnitudes of savings and investment (even larger
than those envisaged by the Leftist participants in the industrialization debate), was
essential for the survival and progress of the Soviet Union. The focus on industrialization, as well as its radical institutional form (notably, forced collectivization) and
unusually rapid pace, was based on several factors. These included the relatively
underdeveloped and dominantly agricultural character of the economy; the desire to
eliminate the independence of the peasantry and the actual or perceived potential
capacity of its middle and upper layers to thwart industrialization plans through with-
drawing or redirecting surplus agricultural output; traditional, nationalist aspirations;
a desire to extend the revolution beyond the achievements of the 1917-1921 period
and to "build socialism in one country"; a fear of encirclement by hostile capitalist
powers;[25] and power struggles for leadership within the Communist party itself as
well as in the party's relation to society.

The Stalinist revolution from above contained several major elements: (1) collectivization of agriculture or "rural revolution", (2) large-scale and rapid industrialization or "industrial revolution", (3) state ownership and control of the means of
production, (4) centralized, state-directed institutions for economic planning and
management, (5) social transformation or "proletarian cultural revolution", (6) comprehensive rule by a single dictator over society, party and the state, often called "totalitarianism", and (7) a Stalinist variant of Marxist socialist ideology.

Collectivization

The early stages of the Stalinist era were marked by one of the most dramatic and
far-reaching institutional changes in Soviet history: collectivization of agriculture.
Factors that contributed to an all-out collectivization drive in agriculture included
the following: (1) visions of gradual and orderly transformation of agriculture into
collectivization were repeatedly frustrated by persistent crises in grain collections;
(2) the urgency for grain to feed towns and factories demanded more aggressive and
more effective governmental measures; (3) it became almost impossible to continue
the policy of private agriculture combined with periodic governmental coercion;
confiscation of stocks, tax pressure on the well-to-do peasants, and such other means
met temporary grain collection objectives but were not viable in the long run; (4)
many party activists had long criticized the NEP's mixed economy and wanted to
turn to the great tasks of "socialist construction"; and (5) large increases in private
market food prices threatened the whole wage structure and the planned process of
industrial expansion. Moreover, the First Five Year Plan, which was being prepared
at this time, linked the prospect of industrial development to massive capital accumulation and economies of large-scale production in agriculture. Also, the relatively

weaker position of the Communist party in the countryside, the prejudices against the market and the NEP-men in general, and the overall political atmosphere, that is, the so-called "leap forward" psychology in the country, played significant roles in adopting a strategy for state-controlled collectivization of agriculture.

At least in the initial stages, collectivization was conceived as a cautious long-term strategy. In the late 1920s, "nobody was yet thinking in terms of an immediate policy of mass collectivization or of the liquidation of the kulaks" (Carr and Davies 1969, 264). But by 1929-1930, a shift to such a strategy became evident. On December 27, 1929, Stalin declared that the problem the Soviet Union faced was "Either we go backward to capitalism or forward to socialism." "It means," he explained, "that after a policy that consisted in limiting the exploitative tendencies of the kulaks, we have switched to a policy of eliminating the kulaks as a class... the path forward is the path of complete collectivization" (cited in Heller and Nekrich 1986, 232). Although such a decision was "neither preconceived nor premeditated," it led to a stronger offensive against the kulaks and a more intensive campaign for the extension of the collectivization (kolkhozy).

The collectivization drive moved into high gear with a central committee decree on February 4, 1930. The decree divided kulaks[26] into three categories: (1) actively hostile kulaks were arrested by the OGPU and sent to concentration camps, and their families were deported to the north, Siberia, and the far east; (2) the most economically potent kulak households were to be deported outside of the region of their residence; and (3) the least noxious kulaks were allowed to remain in the region but were given land of the worst kind. All the properties of the first two categories of kulaks were confiscated (Carr and Davies 1969, 161).

Deportations of kulaks in fact had begun in some regions by the end of 1929 and reached a peak in 1930-1931. One of the primary reasons for deportation was "to drive the middle peasants into collectivization not only by scaring them but also by slamming on their faces the door to their future advance qua individual peasants" (Lewin 1977, 131). Above all, dekulakization was considered necessary to provide the "material base" for the collective farms, and anybody opposed to collectivization was prosecuted. Between the end of 1929 and the middle of 1930, more than 320,000 kulak farmers were eliminated or expropriated.

Collectivization was carried out ruthlessly. Peasants outside collective farms were given inferior land and were loaded with extra taxes or delivery obligations. There were repeated instances in 1931-1932 of compulsory purchases of peasant livestock. Collectivization spread into more areas, more crops, and more peasants. After the kulaks had been eliminated by 1930, attacks were extended to better-off middle-level peasants to drive them into collective farms. Rapid and massive collectivization created extreme dislocation and disruption and nearly threatened, as the Rightists had predicted, the very survival of the Soviet system. Entire villages were deported to eliminate or absorb middle-class and rich kulak peasants. Collectivization was extended to farm animals as well as physical means of production, causing peasant resistance and large-scale slaughtering of livestock. Agricultural output and income plummeted. Several million persons died, largely from the famine that accompanied collectivization. The Russian peasant was subdued and agriculture was brought within the rubric of planned economy but only at a steep price, with adverse repercussions down to the present.

The collectivization of agriculture displaced millions of household farms that had been functioning on nationalized land and brought them under four new rural institutions: (1) state-owned farms (sovkhozy), reserved for very large or experimental farms; (2) collective farms (kolkhozy), the dominant form of property relations in the agricultural sector, combining nominally cooperative ownership with tight government control; (3) machine tractor stations (MTSs), owned by the state, which pooled farm machinery with a responsibility to conduct all heavy machine operations on nearby collective farms; and (4) private plots, approximately one acre of agricultural land that Stalinist policy allowed each household to work for its own needs and for sale in local markets (Dowlah 1992a, 73).

In principle, the kolkhozy, as producer cooperatives, were voluntary associations of workers, owning their means of production collectively, electing their own managers, and disposing of the cooperative's income.[27] In practice, peasants were forced into collective farms in the 1930s, exit required permission, tractors (provided by the MTS) were owned by the state, managers were appointed by the state bureaucracy, minimum obligatory workdays were imposed, and disposition of the income of the farms was subject to regulations and interventions from above.[28] Thus, there was little tangible difference between the kolkhozy and sovkhozy, except that kolkhozy members were permitted to own some farm animals and maintain small plots of land, on which they typically grew fruits and vegetables.[29]

These policies brought dramatic shifts to Soviet agriculture. Table 4.2 shows different stages of collectivization. Whereas in 1928 only 1.7 percent of total cultivated land was in the collectivized sector, the percentage rose to 93 percent by 1937. And whereas the state-owned or state-controlled agricultural sector contributed 3.3 percent to the gross agricultural product in 1928, the share rose to 98.5 percent in 1937.

Table 4.2
Stages of Collectivization and Contribution of Socialized Sector to Soviet Economy, 1927-1937

a. Stages of Soviet Collectivization, 1927-1937			
Year	Number of kolkhozy farms	Collectivized farms as percentage of total	Percentage of total Cultivated Area Occupied
1927	14,800	0.8	---
1928	33,300	1.7	2.3
1929	57,000	3.9	4.9
1930	85,950	23.6	33.6
1931	----	52.7	67.8
1932	211,100	61.5	77.7
1937	240,000	93.0	---

b. The Socialized Sector as a Proportion of the Soviet Economy (%), 1924-1937			
	1924	1928	1937
Of the national income	35.0	44.0	99.1
Of the gross national product	76.3	82.4	99.8
Of the gross agri. product	1.5	3.3	98.5
Of retail trade turnover	47.3	76.4	100.0

Source: Lavigne (1974, 17).

Collectivization provided the basic institutional means for eliminating the economic power and independence of the peasantry, for ejecting peasant labor from agriculture, and for organizing production and distribution within the agricultural sector to keep peasant consumption at minimum levels. Politically, collectivization was a brilliant success. Stalin wanted full monopolization of political and economic power, and although he had political power, the rural areas were virtually in the hands of private traders. Collectivization was instrumental in establishing comprehensive economic control not only over agriculture, but over the entire country.[30] Whether collectivization successfully resolved the NEP's alleged main economic problem—provisioning of surpluses of food, raw materials, labor, and exports for nonagricultural sectors—remains controversial. There is some "evidence that collectivization, far from enabling agriculture to contribute a surplus to the state during the First Five-year Plan, actually drained resources from the nonagricultural sector through the need to supply agricultural machinery." In any event, the "chief aim of collectivization was probably to break the power of the peasantry, the power of a social force independent of the state to determine what grain to produce and what to sell. Stalin was prepared to incur loss of production to gain state power over agriculture" (Cox 1991, 191).

Stalin's statement (1945, 305) that the collectivization revolution was accomplished *from above* and initiated by the state was immediately followed by the rather idealized claim that collectivization was "directly supported from below by millions of peasants, who were fighting to throw off kulak bondage and to live in freedom in the collective farms." In fact, not only the kulaks, but the vast majority of the middle, and even poor, peasants, probably were opposed to the collectivization drive, and "they joined the kolkhozy only under duress or because of fear" (Tucker 1977, 82-83). The claim in Stalin's time that collectivization was based on Lenin's "cooperative plan" is also misleading. First, the material base for collectivization that Lenin emphasized did not exist in the late 1920s. Lenin's collectivization hinged on a cooperative movement, but by 1927 only 10 million peasant households were members of cooperatives. Although Lenin envisaged 100,000 tractors in 1919 for collectivization, the Soviet Union possessed only 28,000 tractors in 1927. Another precondition that Lenin emphasized for collectivization was a cultural revolution. But in 1927 from 70 to 85 percent of the rural poor were still illiterate. Second, economic differentiation of the NEP period did not create sharp polarization between prosperous and poor peasants. Rather, it increased the proportion of small and middle peasants. Whereas only 20 percent of the peasants were middle peasants before the revolution, in 1927 their proportion had increased to 62.7 percent. Third, despite some growth of the kulaks during the NEP, their number in 1927 was 1 million or only 3.9 percent, whereas the share was 15 percent before the revolution. The kulaks of the late 1920s were in no position to become an economically and politically dominant force in rural areas. Therefore, Stalin's conclusion that breaking the backbone of the kulaks was a necessary condition for laying the foundation for a modern, productive, and collectivized agriculture remains controversial. Fourth, even Trotsky and Evgeniee Preobrazhensky, who propounded the theory of "primitive socialist accumulation" (in a largely agrarian economy like the Soviet Union, the expansion of state sector producers' goods can be attained only at the expense of the peasantry), condemned forced collectivization and liquidation of the kulaks. Collectivization was achieved at enormous human cost and misery.

Prominent Western Marxist economist Paul Baran (1957, 228) provided a more sympathetic account of the role of agricultural collectivization in economic planning and development. According to him, the potential economic surplus or excess of national income above essential consumption is often surprisingly large in underdeveloped economics. In pre-World War I Russia, for example, large surpluses of grain were extracted from the peasantry by the landholding aristocracy for export. Very little of the incomes from these exports found their way into productive investment because of luxurious upper class consumption, hoarding, "unproductive bureaucracies" and "expensive and no less redundant military establishments," and withdrawal of income by foreign capitalists. The first step in an efficacious strategy of planned development, therefore, is "mobilization" of the potential economic surplus.

This task is typically thwarted, however, by serious obstacles, not the least of which is the substantial, though transitory, "upheaval and disorganization" accompanying the revolutionary transformation out of the ancien regime. Once the immediate revolutionary crisis is over and prerevolutionary output levels are restored, as occurred in Russia through the NEP by the late 1920s, a second, more fundamental, obstacle appears. Though the "social revolution" generally will transfer control over large industry to the revolutionary government, the "agrarian revolution," which typically and probably unavoidably accompanies it, destroys the "social foundations" of the economic surplus (through the elimination of rent and interest payments and the division of large landed estates) and thus increases peasant incomes and mass consumption. Especially in countries where most of the output and economic surplus was generated in agriculture, the potential surplus "absorbed" by the peasant population must be "recaptured." Until it is, the actual economic surplus will fall far short of its potential, and transition to a centrally planned economic surplus, which is the key to centrally planned development, is delayed (Baran 1957, 263-67).

As long as the peasantry remains economically independent, it will remain "inaccessible to planning by the socialist government." An independent peasantry, ideologically and industrially undisciplined, holding recollections of prerevolutionary exploitation, and being the recipients, through an agrarian revolution, of the benefits of expanding income and consumption, is unlikely to cooperate in "mobilizing and recapturing an economic surplus" when this places the sacrifices of the industrialization process squarely on its shoulders. The only way to incorporate agriculture in a strategy of centralized economic development, concluded Baran,

> is by liquidating subsistence farming as the principal form of agricultural activity and transforming agriculture into a specializing, labor dividing, and market-oriented industry in which the structure of output as well as its distribution between the consumption of those who work in it and the surplus accruing to society as a whole can be determined by the planning authority, as in the case of other industries. Under conditions of socialism this transformation cannot be accomplished except by means of productive cooperation of the peasants, through collectivization of peasant farming. (267-68)

By transferring the disposal of agricultural output from individual peasants to government supervised collective farm managements, collectivization destroy(s) the basis for the peasants' resistance to the accumulation policy. (395)

With collectivization of agriculture, the portion of agricultural output consumed by the peasant population can be fixed by government allotment to collective farmers, while peasant consumption of nonagricultural products can be controlled by government regulation of agricultural and industrial prices.

Rapid Industrialization

Along with mass collectivization, Stalin initiated a state-directed industrialization drive or "industrial revolution" of unprecedented rapidity and magnitude.[31] Major elements of the Stalinist industrialization strategy can be summarized as follows. Soviet industrialization was based on *extensive* methods of production; it focused on mobilizing resources and manipulating savings and investment. This strategy involved two major facets: first, transfer of peasant labor to cities and factories and their transformation into a disciplined force of industrial labor; second, transformation of the industrial labor force thus created into capital goods. Transfer of the savings-investment process from the private sector to the government permitted savings and investment to be set at levels substantially above those that presumably would have been forthcoming if businesses, workers, and households had had an effective voice in production decisions. For the two major sectors of the economy, the strategy involved maximization of the transfer of labor, food, and raw materials from agriculture to industry, combined with minimization of investment of human and capital resources in agriculture and minimization of provision of food and other consumer goods, especially to the peasantry. For the system as a whole, the strategy maximized production of capital goods and thus minimized the production of consumption goods.

The following constituted the major bases for capital accumulation in the Stalinist industrialization drive: (1) the reduction in rental, interest, and royalty charges on industry and state, (2) the profits of state industry and banks, (3) taxation, (4) public borrowing, (5) increases in retail prices, (6) streamlining administration agencies and staff, (7) strong measures against stealing of public property and corrupt practices, (8) crackdowns on absenteeism, and (9) mass participation in industrial production, based on shop-floor "production conferences" (Bideleux 1985, 117).

The state-directed industrial revolution doubled investment as a percent of GNP (from about 13 to 26 percent).[32] A high investment strategy produced two outcomes. It increased net investment and expanded the stock of capital, and thereby raised productive capacity. In turn, and in the absence of offsetting factors, this increased national output. Offsetting factors include falling productivity of capital, if the labor force fails to keep pace with the expanding capital stock, and increases in the ratio of capital to output. Soviet planners minimized the first possibility by mobilizing large amounts of labor to accompany expansions in capital stock notably by transferring peasant labor to urban factories, increasing the labor participation rate (especially among women), fully employing labor, and expanding education and training. They also economized on capital by operating multiple shifts of plants, running obsolescent plants beyond limits that would be perceived as profitable in a capitalist environment, and minimizing investment in major areas of social overhead capital, such as transportation (notably, railroads) and housing, by more intensive utilization of equipment and structures and by drawing on the social overhead capital existing prior to commencement of industrialization programs.

Industry was treated as the leading sector in Soviet development. Stalin considered agriculture to be a "backward" sector, whose function was essentially to provide the surpluses of food, raw materials, exports, and labor needed for industry. Accordingly, the share of agriculture in total gross investment fell from about 16 percent to 11.4 percent in the decade beginning in 1928. Agriculture's share in national output had fallen to 31 percent by 1937.

Collectivization of agriculture and the virtual elimination of private trade in agricultural products, which had characterized the NEP period, enabled Soviet planners through the administrative hierarchy and selection of collective farm managers, to establish obligatory peasant labor on the collectives and mandatory deliveries; peasant income from their own output emerged as a (constrained) residual. Agricultural procurement prices were set by the state at low levels (and prices of industrial goods used in agriculture set at high levels) so as to depress rural living standards and thereby transfer "forced saving" to the state for investment in industry. Per capita income of the farm population fell by roughly half during the First Five Year Plan and did not regain the preplanning period level during the 1930s (Jasny 1951, 107). The consequent depression in rural living standards created a gap between rural and urban incomes. This, combined with vigorous recruitment programs among younger peasants, encouraged the transfer of labor from farm to factory.

Soviet planners followed an "unbalanced growth strategy." They focused scarce capital, managerial talent, and skilled labor on a small number of key areas. For example, the First Five Year Plan's main target was heavy industry, notably machine building. During the next two plans, heavy industry retained a high priority, but the focus was placed on metallurgy, fuel, and chemicals as well as machinery. Average annual rates of growth in these key areas were often between 15 and 20 percent in the 1930s. Other sectors, relatively neglected, grew at a slower rate.

The unbalanced growth strategy was based on several considerations: (1) it was presupposed that an attempt to advance on all fronts simultaneously would dissipate limited resources and yield meager results; by contrast, focus on a few key targets could achieve narrow but spectacular results in advancement, organizational change, and possibly technological improvement; (2) because of complementarities (technologically, temporally, and spatially) among different investments, maximum effectiveness from investment required a "bunching" and concentration of efforts; (3) the rapid tempo of growth in the key targeted areas tended to create strains and bottlenecks; these, in turn, became the new targets for the next plan; (4) especially in the early years, this strategy economized on scarce talent in planning and administration and simplified tasks of information gathering, assessment, and coordination.

Stalinist industrialization strategy largely relied on borrowed technology. Soviet planners adopted foreign technology in capital-intensive projects in the central processes of some technologies, such as blast furnaces or modern oil well drilling rigs. But they left less important auxiliary processes, such as materials handling and intraplant transport, unmodernized and unmechanized so that the overall process was not especially capital intensive. Such a "dual technology" enabled them to obtain the advantages of advanced technology in heavy industry, conserve scarce capital in areas that did not constrain output significantly, and use the relatively abundant unskilled labor of the country.

Soviet economic development under Stalin also emphasized heavy investment in human capital: (1) formal education, which was both broadened and intensified, emphasized the subjects and skills most important for economic development; as a result, for example, more medical doctors, agricultural specialists, and engineers were produced than graduates in social sciences and humanities; and (2) most of the initial training of skilled labor through apprenticeship programs and the teaching of new skills and specialties was accomplished on the job in factories and factory-run evening schools.

The significant commitment to the training of professionals, technicians, and skilled workers helped create a skilled labor force. It also complemented the high investment, proindustry, and dual-technology strategies. Skilled labor was especially important in heavy industry and in those industrial activities using capital-intensive technologies. Unskilled labor, especially recruits from the countryside, could be used in sectors and industrial processes with labor-intensive technologies.

The Soviet strategy for industrialization was characterized by import substitution and an aversion to foreign trade. This was based on several considerations, including the perception by Soviet leaders of being surrounded by hostile capitalist powers, the low levels of loans and credits from Western countries, the deterioration in the terms of trade during the 1930s (prices of Soviet exports fell more rapidly than prices of Soviet imports), the depression in the capitalist economies and a desire to be free from the vicissitudes of capitalist economic fluctuations, the commitment to rapid construction of heavy industry and fear that an open trading policy would interfere with domestic policies, and ideological opposition to bourgeois theories of comparative advantage.

The Soviet government, through its planning and administrative hierarchies and foreign trade corporations, maintained a monopoly of foreign trade. The domestic economy was thereby insulated from foreign trade. Foreign trade, however, was used to some degree as a "balancing" item for internal planning. Imports could supplement "deficit" products, and exports could serve an analogous function for "surplus" products. From a dynamic perspective, the import substitution policy contributed to Soviet economic growth. At least it was consistent with the focus on heavy industry because the import substituting industries were precisely the heavy industry and capital goods sectors, whereas export-oriented industries were in agricultural products, raw materials, and nondurable consumer goods.

The Stalinist industrialization strategy incorporated a policy of inequality in wage income. In the early 1930s, Stalin denounced the goal of income equality (*uravnilovka*) as "petty bourgeois" and indeed declared that "Marxism is an enemy of equalization" (cited in Moore 1951, 238). Thus, the ratio of lowest to highest wages increased from 1:1.8 shortly after the revolution to 1:40 in 1950 (Ossowski 1963, 116). For the highest positions, according to Medvedev (1976, 540), the differential, including various privileges, increased to 1:100. Such inequality was pursued with the rationale that a large-scale industrialization process required specialists, managers, and government officials whose talents and contributions surpassed those of the general body of peasants and industrial laborers and whose support and loyalty were necessary for the maintenance of the regime. It also required incentives to entice workers to work longer and harder, to encourage movement of labor to those sectors or areas of the economy given a high priority by the central planners, to stimulate the development of skills, and so forth. In part also, wage inequality served the function of responding to working-class discontent concerning the sacrifices of industrialization by providing greater relative rewards and opportunities for advancement for the more ambitious and talented and thereby also stratifying and dividing the working class, thus reducing its solidarity and potential for expressing its grievances.

A new system of wage scales was introduced, with payment depending on output (piece rates) as well as on one's job category. To accelerate the pace of the work, a shock workers' movement and the system of "socialist emulation" were utilized. In August 1929, a "continuous workweek" was introduced: the seven-day workweek was replaced by four days of work followed by one day of rest. The continuous week lasted until 1940, when government granted the workers Sunday as a day of rest. Stalinist antiegalitarian policy also resulted in material incentives, wage inequality, and special perquisites and privileges for managerial and technical workers and for party and government officials. The small size of the postrevolutionary Soviet working class, its inexperience, and its dispersal and decimation during the civil war made it virtually inevitable that "management and technical direction of labor would come to be undertaken solely by full-time administrators and technical specialists, i.e., not by ordinary workers" (Gelb 1981, 56). Industrialization strategies of the 1930s increased the role of managers and experts and stimulated commitment to hierarchy and managerial authority within the Soviet enterprise. "One man management," Stalin declared in 1931, based on mastery of "techniques" and the "business of industrial management," is essential to the "ability to direct" enterprises and thereby to achieve plan targets (cited in Daniels 1965, 125-27).[33] Stalinist measures also emasculated the labor unions' role in collective bargaining and wage setting and declared strikes to be improper.[34]

The Soviet industrialization process consisted of several stages with quite different rates of growth. The periods can be divided as 1929-1937, 1938-1940, 1940-1950, and 1951-1955. The period 1928/1929-1937 was that of the operation of the first two five year plans (FYPs), while the period from 1938-1940 was the time in which the third FYP operated (the third FYP was discontinued after World War II started). The fourth FYP was in force in 1946-1950. The period from 1950 to 1955 was that of the so-called fifth FYP, which ended with Stalin's death in 1953. The industrialization drive began with a short period of less than two years, designated as a warming up period (1928-1930). This period was characterized primarily by ideological shifts, which fundamentally replaced the NEP economy and permitted the Great Industrialization Drive to get into full stride. During this period, agricultural output stagnated as a result of the grain crises, and private trade fell rapidly. The warming up period ended with the start of an all-out collectivization drive in the autumn of 1929. Ideologically, the period ended with the acceptance of the 1933 annual plan early in January 1933. The catastrophe brought about by the all-out drive lasted throughout the winter of 1932-1933. Several millions of peasants perished from starvation between 1932 and 1934. This was followed by a period of rapid expansion lasting until the end of 1936. The four years from 1937 to 1940 constitute the purge era (more on this below). While the purges were over by the middle of 1938, their paralyzing effects on the economy lasted until the end of 1940. The next period, from 1946 to 1950, was characterized by a very rapid growth of industry, construction, transportation, and national income. Favorable growth and industrialization continued until 1955, although there was a temporary retardation in the rate of economic growth in 1953, the year Stalin died.

Transformation of State Ownership

Apparently, Stalin and other Soviet leaders came to believe that implementation of this ambitious strategy, especially in a short period of time, would require substantial institutional innovations. These innovations, which emerged in the late 1920s and early 1930s, were essentially completed by 1937. Taken together, they transformed the Soviet Union from the mixed NEP economy to one characterized by comprehensive governmental direction and control of the economic system. With adaptations, the Soviet political economy sustained the basic form established during the 1930s down to the 1980s.

One paramount, and foundational, institutional innovation was nationalization, or state ownership and control of the means of production. What was especially remarkable was the unusually rapid pace with which nationalization was accomplished and its comprehensivity throughout the economy. As noted in preceding chapters, land and the "commanding heights" of banking, transportation, communication, and heavy industry had been nationalized through the expropriation of the assets of the propertied classes of the ancien régime at the time of the Bolshevik Revolution. During the NEP period, as indicated in Table 4.2B, the share of the state-owned sector expanded significantly, notably in trade and industry. This process was carried through to completion during the 1930s. By 1937 the state owned virtually all productive assets, and state-owned and/or (as in the case of collective farms) state-controlled enterprises accounted for nearly 100 percent of Soviet national income, gross industrial output, gross agricultural output, and retail trade. In the Stalinist era, even such activities as barber shops, taxi cabs, and small grocery stores came under the domain of state ownership and control.

Western economists typically give greater priority to social processes for economic coordination (for example, the blend of planning and market economy) than to ownership per se in defining and classifying an economic system. Most Marxist and socialist economists reverse this argument. Polish economist Wlodzimierz Brus (1973, 86), for example, designates "ownership as the fundamental category which determines all other aspects of production relations." Nationalization is the primary means to expropriate the productive assets of the old propertied classes and thereby to control politics, and to direct the allocation of resources, the distribution of income, and the processes of economic growth. State ownership, according to Stalin and his successors down to the 1980s, provides the institutional foundation or "economic basis" for (1) the secure retention of political power by the dictatorship of the proletariat, under the guidance of its leading element or vanguard, the Communist party, and thereby the capability of carrying out "further socialist changes"; and (2) the establishment and extension of the scope and efficacy of national economic planning, thereby enhancing the capability of the state to direct and control employment and the allocation of resources, income distribution, and economic growth in accord with its purposes, and to eliminate the cyclical economic fluctuations associated with capitalist market economy (Koslov 1977, 26; Brus 1975, 12; Brus 1973, 74-76).

Although production thus came to be conducted comprehensively by state-owned and state-controlled enterprises, the state enterprise "belongs to the state" and "*owns* none of its assets" (Nove 1977, 26). Thus, "property rights" came to be exercised by the state, that is, by the political leadership and the bureaucracy, through the party and the state economic ministries and other associations intermediate between ministries and enterprises.

First, the state in such a system has the right to control enterprise residual income, which "flows into the central budget" (Kornai 1992, 71). "If one views the whole economy as a giant firm," USSR Inc., then "it finances the bulk of its operations out of profits," together with turnover taxes (Nove 1977, 30). However, "no individual member of the bureaucracy has a total right of disposal over the residual income. The right of disposal is restricted by a web of restrictions and prohibitions" (Kornai 1992, 73). Consequently, although high-level functionaries came to acquire status and numerous privileges in a stratified politico-economic order, they were not able to solidify their control over residual income as individual owners of productive assets or to provide intergenerational continuity in wealth and power comparable to that which capitalist families often succeed in accomplishing through inheritance.

Second, the state exercises the right to control enterprises. Because enterprise managers do not own state enterprises, their (formal) powers are those delegated to them by the state. The economic ministries appoint (and remove) enterprise managers and issue detailed plan instructions concerning many dimensions of enterprise decision making. Day-to-day management is conducted by intraenterprise bureaucracy, the lowest level in the societywide hierarchy of decision making.

Third, in a capitalist market economy, private owners of productive assets have the right of alienation, that is, they may rent, sell, give away, or bequeath their physical means of production to others. Because state enterprises are owned by the state, not enterprises, neither enterprise managers nor individual members of the state bureaucracy exercise alienation rights. However, "it is within the power of state organs to take away any of the enterprise's assets, if they think fit, without financial compensation" (Nove 1977, 25).

The stated task of the party, both during the NEP years and in the early years of collectivization and industrialization, was "building socialism in one country." In 1936, with the announcement of a new Soviet constitution, Stalin proclaimed that "the total victory of the socialist system in all spheres of the national economy has now been accomplished" through the firm and widespread establishment of "socialist ownership" of the instruments and means of production. Consequently, the working class, instead of being deprived of the means of production, "possesses them in common with all the people" (cited in Bettelhein and Chavance 1981, 800-1).

With the establishment of socialism in the 1930s, according to Soviet doctrine, class conflict and antagonism was said to have ceased. Soviet society was described as comprising two classes: workers and peasants. In addition, the intelligentsia, described as a layer or "stratum" (rather than a class), recruiting its members from workers and peasants, consisted of persons with high status in Soviet society, such as managers, scientists and technicians, planners and administrators, political leaders, and so forth, and constituted about 15 percent of the total population. Relations among these groups were said to be friendly and nonantagonistic. "Since they jointly own social property and jointly participate in the social production process, all peoples are equal and their relations are based on the principles of comradely cooperation and mutual assistance" (Kuusinen 1961, 695). According to Soviet doctrine, the elimination of class antagonisms does not resolve all individual conflicts. With the termination of class conflicts, however, and the establishment of socialism, the state "loses the character of an instrument of class suppression" (734). Instead, the Soviet perspective implies, the state mediates nonclass conflict by synthesizing individual and "immediate" interests into policy decisions genuinely reflective of the best long-run interests of society as a whole, as determined by state and party leaders.

Central Planning and Management

Another major element in Stalin's institutional transformation was a shift to overall economic planning through the state bureaucracy as the dominant social process for economic coordination and implementation of development strategies. In 1927 Soviet economists began drafting the first five-year plan, a comprehensive plan providing for the development and industrialization of the country. The plan was approved by the Sixteenth Party Conference held in April 1929. By the end of the 1920s, the *teleologists,* who favored unbalanced growth and "directive planning," had triumphed over the *geneticists,* who had advocated balanced growth and a kind of "indicative planning," based on market forecasts. During the early 1930s, Soviet planning was characterized by a "great leap forward" psychology and a belief in "politics over economics."[35]

Soviet Marxism associated national planning with various "economic laws of social ism." These "laws," such as the "law of planned proportional development of national economy," represented a blend of subjective and objective factors. According to Stalin's reinterpretation of historical materialism, the Bolshevik Revolution brought economic base and political superstructure into "agreement." Economic laws, notably pertaining to the development of society's "productive forces," continue to operate. But state ownership and planning permit centralized guidance and direction of the national economy. Thus, the party and state are in a position to comprehend economic laws and, consciously and according to plan, apply them to the development process. Under capitalism's blind laws, the economic base controls the political superstructure; under socialism, in the Soviet view, harmony between the economic base and political superstructure enables the state to become the "directing force" of the national economy.

Soviet central planning and management involved the elimination or emasculation of market exchange relations. This antimarket bias, although partly reflecting traditional Marxist and socialist critiques (notably the perceived anarchy of the market and its tendencies toward crises under capitalism), was undoubtedly reinforced by the view, nurtured by the experiences of the NEP period, that market forces were an obstacle to the Soviet leadership's aspiration of rapid, large-scale industrialization guided from above. The domain of market exchange was restricted to relations between government and collective farms and between government enterprises and households (as consumers and workers), supplemented by sales by peasants from their private garden plots and by a very small amount of exchange activities by private craftsman or professionals. Moreover, prices were assigned to inputs and outputs of state enterprises but, in most instances, were set by government agencies, based on non-market criteria, and used to pursue collective purposes designed by Soviet leaders and planners.[36] In the industrial sector, prices served essentially modest accounting purposes, assisting in plan formulation and in testing consistency of plans, rather than as information signals to guide resource allocation decisions.

The central planning apparatus of the Stalinist command economy worked as follows. The CPSU leadership, through its central committee or Politburo, determined general policy objectives and key targets for economic development. The state planning commission *(Gosplan)* and its associated supply planning agency *(Gossnab)* analyzed economic conditions and, in interaction with units of economic administration and management, formulated plans. First, general goals of political leaders were translated by *Gosplan* and economic ministries, through a complex process of bar gaining with lower level administrations and enterprises, into planning targets for investment and consumption. These took the form of long-term statements of aspirations (the famous five-year plans) and short-term "operational plans" (notably, annual plans). Second, the high priority placed on investment was reflected in plan revision and adjustment. If, toward the end of a planning period, achievement of both investment and consumption targets was not possible, scarce materials and other resources were concentrated on investment goods industries. Although the investment ratio "has rarely conformed closely to the planned amount," it has tended to surpass rather than fall short of the goal, and this outcome "is not inconsistent with the policy on investment" (Bergson 1964, 320).

Third, planners' preferences, under the supervision of the CPSU and through the planning and administrative hierarchy, replaced consumers' preferences. Through physical allocations and state control of the banking system, the investment ratio emerged from the planned choices and allocations concerning the composition of output. Fourth, financial planning complemented physical planning. Workers received wages in both consumption goods and investment goods industries, but they spent their incomes only on consumption goods. That resulted, in the absence of counteracting forces, in excess demand for consumption goods. To combat this, Soviet planners introduced the "turnover tax," an indirect tax added to the prices of products at the wholesale level. The turnover tax conveniently suctioned income away from consumption goods industries.[37]

Another component of central planning was the establishment of tight government controls over the monetary, fiscal, and pricing systems. These controls enabled Soviet planners and administrators to establish a financial mechanism to supplement and complement their physical and labor plans and allocations. The Soviet state budget

Table 4.3
Major Components of Soviet GNP: 1928, 1937, and 1940
(in billions of adjusted rubles at 1937 prices)

Sectors	1928	1937	1940
Household Consumption	105.7	113.2	129.5
Gross Investment	16.6	55.9	50.1
Defense	1.7	17.0	45.2
Government Services	8.9	29.5	37.1
Gross National Product	132.9	215.6	261.9

Source: Bergson (1961, 128)

encompassed republic and local as well as national, all-Union budgets, and constituted nearly 50 percent of the country's GNP. Government revenues were derived from sales (turnover) taxes, deductions from profits, social insurance contributions, direct taxes (for example, income taxes), and other sources. The first two sources together contributed more than 60 percent of the government revenues from the 1930s onward. The major categories of government expenditures were for investment, collective consumption, defense, government administration, and other expenditures. As Table 4.3 shows, over the years between 1928 and 1940, defense expenditures increased from 1.7 billion rubles to 45.2 billion rubles (adjusted at 1937 prices), while gross investment increased from 16.6 billion rubles to 55.9 billion in 1937 and then fell to 50.1 billion in 1940.

The planning agencies, however, were separate from the apparatus of economic administration and management and had no control over individual enterprises. The Soviet economy was managed by a hierarchy, with information moving upward from individual enterprises through intermediate, divisional *glavkis,* to republic and national ministries and, ultimately, to the Council of Ministers and the Politburo. Ministries then issued instructions and administrative orders back down the hierarchy to subordinate units. Plan instructions typically included specifications of what to produce, quantities and compositions of outputs and inputs, to whom to deliver output, and delivery dates, as well as productivity, investment, finance, labor, and wage plans.[38]

Institutions, and the methodologies for executing plans, that is, "for ensuring that the decisions of the economic authorities are correctly applied," supplemented those for plan formulation (Lavigne 1974, 25). To a considerable degree, the administrative apparatus itself supervised the execution of the orders it transmitted down through the management hierarchy. But the administrative hierarchy was complemented by a control hierarchy to reinforce its work, to provide an independent process of checking on plan implementation, and to involve mass participation (for example, through consumer complaints to newspapers about the quality of products or worker complaints concerning cheating by enterprise managers).

The most important control hierarchy was provided by the party. First, the party determined overall planning objectives and targets. The duty of the economic ministries was to carry out party policy. Second, the party was dominant in the appointment process. Key positions were staffed by party members. Through the *nomenklatura* system, the party also appointed ministers and labor union officials and filled other posts of significance. Third, local party officials were expected to keep an eye on plan fulfillment and to mobilize, through labor unions and educational programs, worker enthusiasm and productivity.

Sociocultural Revolution

Along with collectivization of agriculture, large-scale industrialization under state ownership, and a centrally planned command economy, Soviet society underwent a dramatic and profound social and cultural transformation during the Stalinist era, which is often called the "proletarian cultural revolution." Under the guidance and control of the party and state, remnants of the prerevolutionary social and cultural fabric were destroyed in breathtaking speed. Indeed, the period from 1929 to 1933 witnessed one of the most momentous periods of sociocultural transformation in Soviet history. Comparing those transformations to "the birth pangs of a world," Robert Tucker observes:

> A massive cadre formation process was launched, bringing in its wake a hectic restructuring of society, a growing industrial working class, sprawling bureaucracies and offices, managements, scientific establishments, a new hierarchy of status, privilege, and power, and an ominously growing security and coercion establishment that tried to match the energy of the builders by furiously ferreting out and destroying numerous social categories of the past as well as many of the newly formed groups. In the countryside, it was an upheaval as elemental as a hurricane— the old rural structures and ways of life were shattered to their very roots, with uncountable consequences for society and state alike. (1990, 52)

The social and cultural revolution occurring between 1928 and 1931 encompassed all spheres of life: education, culture, science, technology, arts, and literature. The entire Soviet society and culture came under direct state control through a political party and its indoctrination programs, government media propaganda and secret police, industrialization and collectivization drives, and dramatic progress in urbanization.[39]

This sociocultural revolution proceeded on all fronts. Societal transformation was facilitated by rapid industrialization and consequent displacement of the rural population and increased urbanization. The urban sector comprised only 18 percent of the Soviet population prior to the October Revolution. By 1939, with industrialization and urbanization, the urban population had grown to 24 percent; and in 1940, out of a total population of 173.6 million, 58.6 million lived in urban areas (Hunter and Szyrmer 1992, 47). Moreover, thousands of urban workers were sent to rural areas to help along the process of collectivization.

Under Stalin the whole Soviet higher educational system was revamped to meet industrial needs, its capacity was tremendously expanded, and preference in admissions went to those of working-class background. Education thereby became a primary tool for "proletarian advancement" and consequent social transformation. A vast majority of the working-class population received education in vocational lines to foster gainful employment in an ever-expanding industrial sector. The educational system produced impressive results. Total enrollment in higher education registered a threefold growth in a matter of from three to four years. Enrollment rose from 160,000 in 1927-1928 to 470,000 in 1932-1933. At the same time, the proportion of students of working-class origin increased from a fourth to a half.[40]

Table 4.4

Transformation in Education and Employment in the Soviet Union from 1928 to 1955

Year	Blue-collar Employment (in millions)	White-Collar Employment	Graduate Employment	Other Specialist Employment	Literacy Among 9-49 year-olds (Percentage)
1928	8.7	2.7	0.23	0.28	58
1940	23.7	10.2	0.91	1.49	87
1955	36.8	13.5	2.18	2.95	98

Source: Reconstructed from Bideleux (1985, 125).

Table 4.4 shows the dramatic transformation in blue-collar, white-collar, and other employment during the Stalinist period.

The Bolshevik party itself was transformed under Stalin's leadership. In 1929 the Communist party almost completely renewed itself; most of its members added in the 1920s were expelled (except, of course, the higher leadership in change of renewal). Newcomers were, in many cases, of low intellectual caliber and had little political experience. But they had the most important qualification needed: blind obedience to the party's, that is Stalin's, authority. Moreover, most of Lenin's party members came from urban areas. Even in 1927, 73 percent of the Communists were concentrated in the towns and only 27 percent in the countryside. Out of all party members, only 58 percent were workers, of which 36.8 percent were manual workers. Stalin broadened the worker (and peasant or former peasant) base of the party substantially. In 1928 alone, for example, he recruited from 200,000 to 250,000 workers into the rank and file of the party. Stalin mounted a nationwide literacy campaign. The Komsomols, subunits of the Communist Youth League, took to the campaign with great enthusiasm. The literacy campaign also achieved a monumental success. As Table 4.4 shows, the rate of literacy among the population, age nine to forty-nine, rose from 58 percent in 1928 to almost 100 percent by the year 1955.

Soviet sociocultural reforms undertaken during the 1930s brought a sweeping transformation in the peasantry. The essence of the NEP peasantry consisted of (1) the family farm as the basic socioeconomic unit, (2) small-scale farm operations, and (3) village life, with its communal institutions, as the basic environment (Lewin 1977, 121). Collectivization swept away small farms, and the sociocultural revolution repressed the values, norms, and institutions of the peasantry. Their popular religious beliefs, folklore, ceremonies, and communal life came under all-out attack from the Stalinist regime. "Most churches and mosques were desecrated, their clergy were often arrested, and lay believers, especially children, were persecuted" (Bideleux 1985, 124). The old intelligentsia was increasingly supplanted by newly trained graduates of the expanding system of technical education. A new service class rose by government design through the revolution from above. Organizations such as the Russian Association of Proletarian Writers (RAPP) were devoted to creating "proletarian culture," that is, a culture that would be proletarian in spirit and content.

Intense "social purges" were carried out in government offices. Nonproletarian officials, in particular, were subject to witch-hunts. Newcomers, presumably of proletarian origin, dominated the lower echelons of the economic, political, and administrative bureaucracy. The newcomers, in most cases, were poorly educated and badly prepared for their new positions, and all too often they combined greed with incompetence. Along with the atmosphere of terror, purges, and the general climate of witch-hunts and the search for enemies, such a mass of culturally low-key lower officialdom, as Lewin (1977, 119-20) remarks, provided "a proper milieu or even a social basis, to some extent for the flourishing of the personality cult and other irrational trends" of the Stalinist period. The sociocultural revolution also prompted purges in the higher education and intellectual spheres. Thousands of dissidents were sent to labor camps, and many in the intelligentsia and students, considered to be "socially alien" elements, came under attack. Many professors as well as engineers in the "bourgeois specialist" category underwent harassment and persecution at the hands of "proletarians" who, as enthusiasts of the cultural revolution, enjoyed hegemony over media, art, and political power.[41] Like the Shakhty trial and the subsequent show trials of the "Industrial Party" (1930), the Mensheviks (1931), and other groups, the Stalinist sociocultural revolution, as Fitzpatrick (1984, 840) observes, can be considered as a mobilization strategy aimed at creating an atmosphere of crisis so that the regime's demands for sacrifices and extraordinary efforts in the cause of industrialization could be justified. The sociocultural revolution succeeded in channeling enthusiasm and energy for defending the country and working for its advancement against all kinds of enemies. Also, Stalin used the sociocultural revolution to generate such organizations as Komsomols, labor unions, writers' unions, and so on to overturn "reactionary" and "bureaucratic" forces and to discredit his opposition within the party.

Totalitarian State Economy

The Stalinist politico-economic system has often been characterized by Western observers as "totalitarian." This concept emerged as a "novel political phenomenon" in the 1930s and 1940s, having "principal and indubtible manifestations" in Hitler's Germany and Stalin's Russia (Tucker 1971, 20-22; Arendt 1966; Friedrich and Brezezinski 1956). Some writers, Jacob Talmon (1981) for example, contend that, in principle, a democratic variant of totalitarianism is conceivable. But most analyses focus on a version incorporating (or requiring): (1) a single ruler or dictator, who exerts nearly absolute power and serves as the system's moving spirit,[42] and (2) absence of such procedural institutions of Western style democracy as popular election of legislative and executive leaders based on competition by candidates for public offices based on citizens' votes, and such associated civil liberties as the right to criticize and dissent from the positions and programs of the government and its leadership. Traditional dictatorships, however, also place limitations on political democracy and civil liberties. What differentiates totalitarianism, the Stalinist variant in particular, from personal tyranny by an all-powerful ruler in general is the comprehensive direction and control of society and its constituent groups by a monopoly party and party-dominated state.[43]

Austrian Marxist Rudolf Hilferding (1971, 511-17) emphasizes that Stalin's "totalitarian state-economy" embodied several interlocking elements. First, Soviet state power was essentially independent of the economy. Although economic circles have some influence on the ruling power, such influence "is conditional, has limits and is not decisive in the relation to the essence of policy." Second, political decision-making power was concentrated and centralized in the hands of a very small number of top leaders, who changed and directed the state apparatus "to suit their needs as rulers," ultimately taking the form in the later years of the Stalinist era of an "unlimited personal dictatorship." The "bureaucracy," though receiving some "modest crumbs" from the political leaders, was "not an independent bearer of power [but] only an instrument in the hands of real rulers." It was organized as a hierarchy and subordinated to the commanding power. Third, this dictatorial and essentially independent state power exercised its enormous strength and directed society's vast resources "according to its own laws." The economy, far from controlling the totalitarian system, was "determined by the policy of the ruling power and subjected to the aims and purposes of this power." Consequently, the economy was "deprived of its own laws" and became a "controlled economy," whose goals, strategies, and allocational priorities were determined primarily by a central political leadership. Moreover, such control, "once initiated in a totalitarian state, spreads rapidly and tends to become all embracing."

All Stalinist programs—collectivization, industrialization, state ownership, command economy, and the sociocultural revolution—strengthened the role of the state and party vis-à-vis the Soviet society and population. Each of these programs contributed to the proliferation of government and party bureaucracies and structures and to the subordination of the ordinary mass of people to the will of the state and party, ultimately, to Stalin himself. Major elements that contributed to Stalinist totalitarianism can be summarized as follows.

Stalin established what T. H. Rigby (1977, 53) calls a "mono-organizational society." All social, economic, and political activities of the country were run by "hierarchies of appointed officials under the direction of a single overall command." All sectors of Soviet society were integrated organizationally into a single, vast, pyramidal bureaucratic structure, in which goals were formulated at the apex, and each participant carried out his or her assignments as specified by an elaborate and all-encompassing division of labor. The Stalinist bureaucracy, however, was not a replica of the mechanistic "classical" model of bureaucracy suited for stable conditions and routine programs. Rather, the Stalinist bureaucracy was organic in character and dynamic in behavior, and participants constantly faced changing conditions, fresh problems, and unforeseen challenges. Such a bureaucracy adopted new programs and policies and had to adapt to the nonroutine and often unpredictable instructions of its supreme leader, Stalin.

Stalin blended the bureaucratic organizational culture with political legitimation and socialization of individuals. In the Stalinist mono-organizational society, all these elements were integrated under the auspices of an official ideology having monopolistic claims over the society and its destination. The state's claim to legitimacy, ideology, and instruments of repression became so intertwined that individuals who grew up in such a society "must not only acquire the technical skills necessary for their future work roles but also the values, attitudes, and behavior patterns enabling the society to cohere and operate effectively as a system" (57). Stalin established a personal dictatorship over the party and the state. During the Stalinist era, the state and society were subordinated to the party, and, in turn, the society, the state, and the party were brought under the direct control of the dictator. The unquestioned authority and untrammeled power that the dictator enjoyed enabled him to personally decide virtually anything he wanted to decide. His power and decisions were unconstrained by the power of "any individual, group, institution, or law... he was the final arbiter in matters of faith, truth, and public taste and morals" (60-61). In the absence of market forces in the economy and pluralist opinions and forces in political, social, and cultural spheres, the dictator succeeded in establishing his supreme command in all spheres of Soviet society.

Stalinist totalitarianism was complemented by an elaborate network of secret police who had arbitrary powers to eliminate any opposition, inhibit any unwanted discussion, and prohibit any movement against the regime.[44] The Stalinist regime relied to an extraordinary degree, compared both to the repressive tsarist autocracy and to other revolutionary regimes, upon administratively organized coercion and terror as techniques for ruling its citizens and for controlling its own party cadres. Stalin achieved collectivization of agriculture by using unbridled state power and by applying unlimited coercion against recalcitrant peasants. Several million peasants were expropriated and deported in the process. Similarly, rapid, large-scale industrialization was achieved by the force of the state; it was a state-directed and state-controlled industrial revolution. Soviet citizens at all levels and spheres of the society, economy, administration, and party were subjected to intense secret police surveillance. Many of them were sentenced to forced labor camps for indeterminate periods (Skocpol 1979, 230).

Stalin significantly expanded both the size of state machineries and state power. Whereas total employment of the tsarist regime was 260,000 in the nondefense sector in 1897, the Soviet government, in a smaller administrative territory than in 1897, employed 390,000 personnel in the same sector in 1929. Moreover, whereas tsarist Russia had only 105,000 of those personnel in the police force, the Stalinist police force totaled 142,000. Stalin's rationale for such explosive growth of the centralized state power and structure was apparently based on his dialectical formula that highest development of state power would eventually prepare conditions for the withering away of state power (Edeen 1958, 274-91). Moreover, objective forces in the country contributed to such bureaucratic expansion. The industrialization drive and nationalization, both of formerly private enterprises and new state-owned industrial ventures, brought thousands of industrial enterprises under state control. Most came under administrative subordination to great bureaucratic conglomerates. As industrial production units and plant capacities expanded, so did the industrial bureaucracy. According to Tucker, "as the state owned, state administered industrial economy mushroomed, the Moscow bureaucracy swelled proportionately" (1990, 106). Among others, expansion of the governmental structures was caused by increases in defense establishments. Whereas in 1927 the Soviet armed forces contained 686,000 men, by 1937 their number had increased to 1,433,000. Also, the governmental apparatus in Moscow expanded as the areas of autonomy of the constituent republics contracted (106).

The key to understanding the Stalinist politico-economic system is thus its structure of power. The "fundamental institution in the power structure" was the party and its associated bureaucracy. The party was interwoven with the state and was the "dominant force in their common activity." Its various bodies decided on all major appointments, promotions, and dismissals in the state bureaucracy; made fundamental decisions before the associated state bodies made theirs; and supervised the state bureaucratic apparatus. The resulting party/state bureaucracy exercised a monopoly of power and was bound together by its "resolve to retain power" and to rule collectively over "other citizens, deciding their destinies and disposing of the country's resources," its common ideology, its prestige and (substantial) privileges, and its coercion of the bureaucratic hierarchy itself and of the secret police apparatus that monitored it (Kornai 1992, 33-43). This power system was more "fundamental" than specific institutions or policies, such as, for example, central planning. Thus, it was "not the intrinsic nature of planning" that produced the "hypertrophy of the Soviet bureaucracy" under Stalin and his successors, but rather the "power of the bureaucracy" that produced "the specific forms of planning in the USSR and similar societies" (Mandel 1992, 37).

Like the Soviet state bureaucracy, the Communist party also grew, and changed dramatically in composition. In 1917 the party had 24,000 members; by 1924 the number had increased to 472,000 (350,000 full members and 122,000 candidate members). By 1925 the number of party members had risen to 801,804 (440,365 full members and 361,439 candidates members). By 1929 the Communist party membership had skyrocketed to 1,535,362 members (1,090,508 full members and 444,854 candidates members). Thus, since Lenin's death, the party membership had trebled. The whole process of party recruitment was dominated by Stalin, who enjoyed absolute authority over the party apparatus through the secretariats. Although in 1929, 75 percent of the secretaries of the large party organizations had joined before the revolution, at the primary organization level, 65 percent of the secretaries had joined the party after 1921.

Stalin also brought qualitative changes in the composition of the party. As Table 4.5 shows, workers and peasants constituted 60.2 and 7.2 percent respectively, of the Bolshevik party in 1917; their shares had changed to 55.1 and 27.3 percent, respectively, by 1927. Whereas in 1917 white-collar persons constituted 32.2 percent of the Communist party membership, that share dropped to 17.6 percent in 1927. Such reconstruction of the party in favor of workers and peasants significantly helped Stalin to consolidate power in the country. The majority of the new members of the party directly owed their positions and prestige to Stalin. Also, lack of education and experience on their part made them more loyal to Stalin, than, for example, could have been possible from the party members of 1917 who were Lenin's companions in the revolution or during the civil war.

Stalin consolidated his control over the party apparatus by conducting several purges. The purges from 1933 to 1938 can be divided into three phases: the purges

Table 4.5
Composition of Bolshevik Party in 1917 and 1927 (in percent)

| | By Social Class | | By Occupation | |
	1917	1927	1917	1927
Workers	60.2	55.1	----	39.4
Peasants	7.2	27.3	----	13.7
White Collar	32.2	17.6	----	46.9

Source: Reconstructed from Rigby (1968b, 85, 86)

Table 4.6
Casualty Figures of the Stalinist Regime, 1937-1938

In jail or labor camp already in January 1937	c. 5 million
Arrested January 1937 to December 1938	c. 7 million
	Total = c. 12 million
of which executed	c. 1 million
died in labor camp 1937-38	c. 2 million
	Subtotal = c. 3 million
In captivity in late 1938	c. 9 million
of which in prison	c. 1 million
in camps	c. 8 million

Source: Conquest (1968, 706-7)

of 1933, those of 1934-1935, and the great trials of 1936-1938. Each wave of purges brought repression nearer to the center of power. The purge of 1933 struck at the level of rank-and-file; mostly unpoliticized members were affected. The purges of 1934-1935 concerned mid-level cadres, or politically active party members. The third and final purge was unleashed against the ruling cadres and the intelligentsia of the party, which until then had shared power with Stalin. These purges threw the country into permanent terror, with repercussions in all spheres of life. Overall, the number of casualties from the purges is still unknown.[45] Also, although the purges ended in 1938, concentration camps, expropriation and deportation, and other kinds of punishment and terror continued throughout Stalin's regime. It is estimated that the total casualties of the Stalinist era amounted to at least 20 million people. Table 4.6 enumerates the number of people who were killed, sent to labor camps, imprisoned, or died in labor camps because of the Stalinist terror and purges. Total casualties of the Stalinist era probably were larger than the table stipulates because an estimated 7 million people or more perished during collectivization and the consequent famine and deportations.

Another powerful component of Stalinist totalitarianism was the personality cult that was erected around the leader. The personality cult began in 1929, on the occasion of Stalin's fiftieth birthday, with glowing tributes paid to Stalin by Karl Radek, a member of the CPSU Politburo who later was executed by Stalin. By the time of the Seventeenth Party Congress held in January 1934, the cult had reached its climax. Stalin became not only the "undisputed leader of the Soviet Union, but of all progressive mankind, the greatest man who had ever lived" (Laqueur 1990, 15). Stalin was everywhere—in newspaper editorials, public meetings and speeches, the arts and literature. As Rigby (1977, 61) remarks, "His spoken and written utterances were accorded the reverence of received truth, and ritually repeated in season and out." All these factors helped to consolidate the Stalinist totalitarian regime over the Soviet Union.

Stalinist Variant of Marxist-Socialist Ideology

Stalinist ideology was an amalgam of prerevolutionary Marxist and socialist thought, Bolshevik theory and practice after the revolution, and the experiences confronted in the process of engaging in the heroic tasks of collectivization, industrialization, and institution building associated with the challenges of "revolution from above." Ideology, together with the power monopoly of the political leadership, served as a major "superstructural" factor guiding the institutional innovations and programs for building the "economic base" during the Stalinist era.[46] Stalinist ideology also served as a tool by which the top political leadership could guide and educate subordinates in the party and state hierarchy and the Soviet citizenry in general. In a capitalist economy, the threat of unemployment serves as the paramount sanction to enforce labor discipline. In the Stalinist era, the commitment to full employment, which was perceived as strategic in mobilizing human resources for industrialization, had the effect of relegating economic sanctions to the bottom of the hierarchy of social control processes and thereby increasing the role of political coercion. Because of the negative consequences of undue reliance on terror, however, ideology became the paramount mode of persuasion and social control.[47]

The Bolsheviks who came to power through the 1917 revolution had long claimed to be inspired by Marxian doctrine. Considered as a Marx-inspired program, the Soviet experience with economic development and social change was filled with paradox. The Bolshevik Revolution took place in a country that hardly had fulfilled the prerequisites Marx had assumed normally requisite for socialist revolution. Russia in 1917 had a better start on modernization and economic development than many of the countries regarded as underdeveloped today, but she scarcely fit the Marxian image of a developed country where capitalism has already prepared the way for the creation of a socialist society.

The problems facing Bolshevik leaders were radically divergent from those envisaged by Karl Marx. It is not surprising, then, that the institutions, strategies, and methods that evolved in relation to these circumstances also came to diverge in significant ways from the classic Marxian vision of socialist economy. At the least, Soviet communism represented a very special variant of Marxian socialism, embodying a combination of applied Marxism, economic underdevelopment, and Russian history and politics. In economic terms, Soviet communism was not a successor to capitalism in the economically developed countries; it is better described as a substitute for industrializing capitalism in certain relatively underdeveloped countries.[48]

The response of Soviet leaders to their anomalous situation was to recast Marxism in the light of their situation and to place strategic emphasis on those dimensions of Marxian thought that seemed most applicable to their experiences, denigrating other aspects and interpretations and presenting their own interpretations as "true" Marxism. The reformulation of a classic social philosophy to fit altered conditions is not unique to Communist experience. What is special in the Soviet situation is the intense degree to which the official ideology pervaded all public discussion, and the extent to which divergences from the classic Marxian vision were reconstituted as illustrations of the true "Marxist-Leninist" position. Over time, ideology in the Soviet system thus "degenerated" as a means to explain social practice and became increasingly an integral part of the monopoly power structure. By the time of the Stalinist period, there was "no open competition between alternative ideologies for the hearts and minds of the population." The party and state bureaucracy, led by Stalin as dictator, exercised "an almost full ideological monopoly" (Kornai 1992, 49). The major substantive elements of the Soviet variant of

Marxist ideology, discussion of which has been dispersed throughout earlier sections of this chapter, can be recapitulated as follows:

1. An imperative need for rapid, large-scale industrialization, with focus on investment over consumption and heavy industry over light industry.

2. A similarly imperative need for rapid, comprehensive collectivization to eliminate the kulak class and bring the peasantry under the rubric of state control and to achieve economies of large-scale production and modernization in agriculture.

3. The superiority of (rapidly established, comprehensive) state ownership and control of the means of production over private, capitalist property relations, as a means to abolish class exploitation of labor and to secure state direction of the economy.

4. The superiority of (rapidly established, comprehensive) national economic planning and bureaucratic coordination over the market economy as a means of fostering a unified and optimal character and pace of economic development, directing the allocation of resources and distribution of income in accord with the social purposes of the political leadership, and avoiding the wasteful economic fluctuations, depressions, and unemployment of capitalist market economics.

5. The need for a comprehensive sociocultural revolution, directed by the top leadership and its party and state bureaucracy, designed to abolish illiteracy, expand education and acquisition of industrial skills, transcend traditional prerevolutionary attitudes, and create a new intelligentsia of administrators, party members, and managers.

6. The need for a monopoly of power by the political leadership and for a centralized and enlarged state as the single most decisive factor in "socialist construction" and as the key agency for combating residual "capitalist elements"; defending against external attack; providing the intelligence for economic planning and management; constraining, educating, and disciplining workers, peasants, and lower level members of the bureaucracy; and molding social attitudes and enforcing respect for socioeconomic roles and duties.[49]

7. The need to retain certain capitalist elements of economic organization and management, as a means to foster rapid economic development of the forces of production, namely, the industrial hierarchy; one-man management; inequality in status, income, and privileges; firm labor discipline; and division of labor, notably between manual and nonmanual labor.

8. Designation of a politico-economic system embodying these aforementioned features as socialist[50] and democratic,[51] based partly on the confluence of interests of state and society and on the capability of party and state leaders to discern the real long-run interests of society, even if these conflict with the "immediately" perceived interests of workers, peasants, and consumers.[52]

NOTES

1. Stalin was born Josef Dzhugashvili on December 20, 1879, in Gori, a small town in Georgia. He joined underground Bolshevik party activities in his teens and became a close associate of Lenin prior to the October Revolution. Despite having little formal education and lacking mastery of the Russian language, he struggled up the ladder of the Communist

party to become its longest serving general secretary. Stalin died in office on March 6, 1953, at the age of seventy four.

2. Whether Stalin or Stalinism was necessary for Soviet economic and military progress remains controversial. See, for example, Nove (1990) and Hunter and Szyrmer (1992).

3. Stalin himself described his measures for collectivization as a "revolution from above" in the *Short Course*, which he edited in 1938. Comparing these measures to the October Revolution, Stalin described his program as a "profound revolution, a leap from an old qualitative state of society to a new qualitative state... the distinguishing feature of this revolution is that it was accomplished *from above*, on the initiative of the state" (cited in Tucker 1977, 83).

4. The Stalinist version of socialism and its relationships to Marxism and Lenin's views are examined by Dowlah and Elliott (1991) and Dowlah (1992b).

5. Several points should be noted in this context. First, whether Stalin replaced or continued the Bolshevik tradition remains a controversial issue. The authors discuss contending viewpoints on this issue elsewhere. See Dowlah and Elliott (1991); Dowlah (1992a, 116-24); Elliott (1984); Rigby (1977, 53-76); and Tucker (1977). Second, Stalinism evolved over time; its final triumph was not achieved until 1936-1939 (Cohen 1977, 24-25). Third, throughout his lifetime, Stalin fostered the idea that he was a true Leninist Bolshevik. On the other hand, it was under his leadership that in 1952 the All Union Communist (Bolshevik) party was renamed as the Communist party of the Soviet Union (CPSU). It has often been argued that elimination of "Bolshevik" from the party's name symbolized Stalin's eventual disassociation with the Bolshevik tradition.

6. While the richest 10 percent of the peasantry owned between 35 and 45 percent of the agricultural means of production the bottom 30 percent owned between 4 and 7 percent.

7. Often kulaks were blamed for the deficiency in the marketable agricultural surplus. But in the late 1920s, middle and poor peasants produced as much as 85 percent of total grain production in the Soviet Union as opposed to some 50 percent before the war.

8. In fact, the improvement of agricultural productivity and the mechanization of agriculture became increasingly important themes of CPSU policy during the second half of the 1920s. As a result, the proportions of machines sold on credit increased from 30.7 percent in 1925-1926 to 47 percent in 1926-1927 and 81.1 percent in 1927-1928. Between 1926 and 1929, substantial progress was made in the supply of implements, machinery, and tractors to the countryside. Domestic production of agricultural implements doubled in the period from 1925-1926 to 1928-1929. Consequently, the use of wooden ploughs in the countryside fell from 46.5 percent in 1924 to 28.5 percent in 1929. The number of tractors rose from 2,560 in 1924 to 34,943 in 1929 (see Carr and Davies 1969, 217).

9. Some scholars, however, believe that the NEP had the potential to expand industrial capacity. They note that investment in *Vesenkha* planned industry amounted to 1,304 million rubles in 1927-1928, an increase of 21 percent over 1926-1927. Also, the same year, industrial output increased by 26.3 percent in terms of 1926-1927 prices. It not only outstripped the rate of 16 percent as proposed by *Vesenkha* in July 1927, it also exceeded the rate of growth in the previous year. Therefore, speculations that the NEP industries would cause a slowdown in future economic growth remains controversial (see Carr and Davies 1969, 311 and Shmelev and Popov 1989).

10. The experience of 1925-1926 seemed to give credence to the thesis of agriculture's potential as a basis for industrial expansion. In that year capital investment in *Vesenkha* planned industries was equal to or greater than the average annual investment of the prewar years. In 1926-1927 producer goods industries received 71 percent of investment as compared with 64 percent in 1925-1926, and the fixed capital and property of producer goods industries amounted to more than half of the total capital of *Vesenkha* planned industries. Greater concentration of investment funds can also be gauged from the fact that in 1926-1927 industrial

production in *Vesenkha* planned industries increased by nearly 20 percent, while the total output of all industry expanded by 17 percent. Such achievement, "the first fruit of the control already exercised by the state over the peasant," was made possible, in the absence of foreign assistance, largely by an agricultural surplus (see Carr and Davies 1969, 171, 275, 291-92).

11. Indeed, noncooperation of the peasants with the Soviet government remained a powerful factor throughout Soviet history. Agriculture constrained the Soviet economy from the beginning to the end. It never was able to supply adequate food even though almost 22 percent of the Soviet population remained employed in the agricultural sector and as much as 20 percent of investment resources was allocated to the agricultural sector.

12. Pud was a unit of Soviet measure of weights that equaled 36 pounds.

13. Bukharin denounced confiscatory measures for creating very tense situations in the countryside. In July 1928 he cautioned the closed Central Committee plenum that such measures could lead to "war communism" without a war (Tucker 1990, 83).

14. According to Carr and Davies (1969, 269), at the end of 1928 free market prices of wheat varied in different regions between 119 and 314 percent of official prices; prices of rye ranged between 119 and 384 percent; prices of oats varied between 127 and 307 percent, and in early 1929, private prices of agricultural products soared out of all relation to official prices.

15. As Nove (1969, 149) observes, "The price policies, in industry and agriculture, which developed in 1926 and were obstinately continued,... could of *themselves* have destroyed the NEP, even if no other complications had ensued." Similarly Carr and Davies (1969, 269) remark, "Never since the winter which preceded the introduction of the NEP had the prospect been so grim. A situation so completely out of hand bred a mood in which desperate remedies may well have seemed the only way out."

16. Stressing the need for ever greater vigilance and state repression, Stalin declared in *Pravda* in July 1927: "It is hardly open to doubt that the basic question of the present is the threat of a new imperialist war. It is not a matter of some undefined and intangible 'danger' of a new war. It is a matter of a real and genuine threat of a new war in general and a war against the USSR in particular" (cited in Tucker 1990, 75).

17. Bukharin, Rykov, and Tomsky constituted a united opposition to Stalin's campaign for Lenin's succession. More on their positions will follow below.

18. At the time of Lenin's death, Trotsky and Stalin were the main two contenders to succeed Lenin for the highest office in the Soviet Union. In his *Last Testament,* Lenin opposed Stalin's candidacy to be his successor, and he asked the Communist party to "devise a way of shifting Stalin from this position (general secretary) and appointing to it another man who in all other respects falls on the other side of the scale from Comrade Stalin, namely, more tolerant, more loyal, more polite and more considerate of comrades, less capricious, etc." (cited in Tucker 1973, 271). Apparently, many believe, Lenin was referring to Trotsky as his potential successor.

19. Stalin, however, disassociated himself from Bukharin's earlier call on April 25, 1925, to the peasants to "enrich yourselves," in other words, to pursue the path of private trade and commerce.

20. Stalin deported Trotsky to Turkey in February 1929, after having him forcibly removed from Moscow on January 17, 1928, and confined to Alma-Ata in Central Asia for a year.

21. This doctrine held that the Soviet Union could industrialize and modernize on its own, without the necessity of prior world revolution or substantial foreign economic assistance.

22. The grain procurement crises of 1927 and 1928—sharp reductions in peasant deliveries of grain to the state—were the visible symptoms of the NEP's coming demise.

23. The congress, held in December, 1927, known as the "Industrialization Congress," authorized the first Five Year Plan, an ambitious projection of industrial advance. On the agricultural front, it called for a 12 to 15 percent increase in the collectivization of peasant households. The congress also instructed the Central Committee "to continue without respite the development of socialist industrialization and the further attack on capitalist elements, with a

view to their liquidation." Scholars generally trace the end of the NEP to the decisions of this congress. It should be mentioned, however, that in his address to the congress, Stalin maintained that collectivization would be entirely voluntary, and he did not specifically mention any termination of the NEP. Even at the Sixteenth Congress, held in 1928, Stalin asserted that the NEP was not discarded, and it would be continued as long as it was useful for the socialist reconstruction of the Soviet Union. But he insisted that, by saying that the NEP would be needed for an "indefinite period," Lenin did not mean "the NEP for ever." See Lange (1943, 16) and Jasny 1972.

24. Although this expression referred specifically to collectivization, it aptly describes the entire Stalinist industrialization strategy and its accompanying institutional transformation.

25. "We are 50-100 years behind the advanced countries," Stalin stated in 1931. "We have to traverse this distance in ten years. We will either accomplish it or else we will be crushed." (Cited in Baran [1952, 392]).

26. In 1926-1927, 108 million people in rural areas were engaged in agriculture, of whom about 6 million, or approximately 1 million households, were considered to be kulaks. This one million "capitalist peasants," however, produced 9 percent of all agricultural output and 14 percent of marketed output in the country.

27. Nove (1977, 122) usefully summarizes these, and other, significant differences between kolkhozy and sovkhozy.

28. The deprivation of internal passports after 1932 "attached the peasant to the soil of the kolkhoz or sovkhoz as securely as his serf ancestor had been attached to the soil of the landed estate." This, together with minimum obligatory workdays, explains the "common [unofficial] peasant practice" of referring to collectivization as a "second serfdom" (Tucker 1977, 96-97).

29. The private garden plot was "vitally important as a producer of potatoes, vegetables, eggs, fruit, [and] meat and dairy produce," contributed significantly to the total agricultural output (45 percent during World War II, 25 percent as late as the mid-1970s), and, through free kolkhoz markets, provided the peasantry with cash income (Nove 1977, 123).

30. As Cohen (1980, 27) remarks, "under the NEP most citizens, particularly the immense peasant majority which still constituted over 80 percent of the population, lived and worked remote from party or state control."

31. Stalin became preoccupied with rapid industrialization as soon as he was able to defeat the "super-industrializers" including Preobrazhensky and Trotsky. In fact, as early as December 1925, Stalin told the Fourteenth Party Congress, "We must make every effort to make our country an economically self-reliant, independent country... a center of attraction for all other countries which gradually drop out of capitalism and enter the channel of socialist economy... (which would entail) utmost expansion of our industry... without converting our country into an appendage of the world capitalist system" (quoted in Bideleux 1985, 117).

32. As Jasny (1961, 2) remarks,

The principle that the share of investment in national income should grow more rapidly than the national income itself became so characteristic of the Stalinist industrialization strategy that the years and periods when this was not achieved were definitely marked down as unfavorable, indeed, as times of great disturbance. Also, the disproportionately rapid expansion of heavy industry remained the basic principle of the Soviet economy, one of its basic 'laws' until the death of Stalin.

33. One-man management (yedinonachaliye), as defined by one Soviet writer, means that "the leadership of each production unit... is assigned to a single executive who is endowed by the state with the necessary rights to manage and who bears full responsibility for the work of the given unit. All individuals working in the unit are obliged to fulfill the instructions of the executive" (cited in Yanowitch 1977, 137).

34. The emasculation of labor unions' rights to negotiate wages and working conditions and to strike was justified on ideological grounds. Workers were perceived to be owners of the means of production; therefore, it was argued, collective bargaining and striking would constitute bargaining with and striking against themselves, which would be an impropriety by definition.

35. The triumph of politics over economics resulted in extremely ambitious and unrealistic plans, especially in the early stages of the Stalinist era. For example, the optimal plan provided for coal production to double, from 35 million tons to 75 million tons by 1932. Stalin sought to increase the figure to 105 million tons. Similar leaps were made in all control figures for the First Five Year Plan. In December 1929, a gathering of "shock workers" (*udarniki*) called for the fulfillment of the First Five Year Plan in four years. On February 4, 1931, Stalin replaced the "Five in Four" plan by fulfilling the plan in the decisive sectors of industry in three years. Even with a return to relatively more sober planning after World War II, plan formulation remained a constant tug of war between *Gosplan*, which strived to set high targets and low allocations of resources, and ministries and enterprise managers, who attempted to negotiate for higher resource allotments and lower targets.

36. For example, prices of certain necessities, such as bread, butter, and other food items, were set below cost, while prices of luxuries including automobiles, refrigerators, and air conditioners, were set at levels substantially above cost.

37. For example, suppose that wage income is 65 billion rubles in the consumption goods industry and 35 billion rubles in investment goods industries. Abstracting from personal saving, other forms of taxes and transfers, and nonwage costs, workers receive 100 billion rubles income. If turnover taxes equal to 35 billion rubles are imposed on consumption goods, workers as consumers can spend their entire income on consumption, and receipts from the sale of consumption goods will be sufficient to cover the costs of production and, via turnover taxes, provide an arrangement for financing investment, which is both convenient and essentially invisible to consumers.

38. The actual system of planning and management, however, was never as thoroughly centralized or tightly administered as the above discussion might imply. First, because of the separation of planning and administration, as Nove (1977, 60) points out, central planners did not in fact make the bulk of detailed decisions. Second, central planners and administrators focused on major commodities and categories, leaving the details to be filled in by planning and administrative agencies at lower levels, for example, by one or more of the fifteen republics or eighteen economic regions. Third, although orders moved down through the administrative hierarchy, information, on which orders were based, originated at the enterprise level and moved up. Because of the delegation, negotiation, and empire building inherent in these factors, some Western observers have described the Stalinist system as a kind of "centralized pluralism" (Nove 1977, 63) or even "poly-centrism" (Roberts 1971, 197).

39. Stalin inaugurated the Proletarian Cultural Revolution by declaring, "There are no fortresses that workers, Bolsheviks cannot conquer... the working class cannot become the real master of this country if it does not succeed in overcoming its lack of culture, in creating its own intelligentsia" (quoted in Bideleux 1985, 124). On another occasion, in June 1931, Stalin told a gathering of industrialists; "The working class must create for itself its own productive technical intelligentsia... not a single ruling class has managed without its own intelligentsia" (quoted in Tucker 1990, 102).

40. In 1930 one of the students of such working-class origins was Leonid Brezhnev, who later became general secretary of the CPSU.

41. Cohen (1977, 27-28) observes that Stalin's "revolution from above" had "enthusiastic agents below, even if only a small minority, from the cultural to the industrial and rural fronts." This "substantial popular support for Stalinism" was based on two main factors. First, expansion of the state and its social and cultural functions during the 1930s brought a "great proliferation of official jobs and privileges. While many were victimized, many people also profited from Stalinism, and identified with it." Subsequent wartime patriotism also engendered additional support for the "increasingly nationalistic, and victorious, Stalinist system." Second, popular support had deep social and cultural roots. Stalinist bureaucratic elites created in the 1930s were "akin to the traditional tsarist *soslovie*, an official privileged

class that served the state." The new intelligentsia, like the new working class, was largely recruited from the "petty bourgeois majority" which flooded into the cities in response to the opportunities for upward mobility and material advancement provided by industrialization (see also Lewin 1974, 1977).

42. Unlike traditional authoritarian rule, however, totalitarianism is a dictatorship with a mass social base and substantial popular support. In the Soviet Union, according to Soviet analyses in the Stalinist era and after, this was manifested by the working-class installation, with the tacit support of the peasantry, of the Bolsheviks in power during the revolution. Thereafter, elimination of the capitalist and propertied rich, rapid economic development, and generous programs fostering social welfare established a revolutionary new system during the Stalinist years, the leading beneficiaries of which were the working masses of the country. This, Soviet Marxists have contended, constituted substantive democracy, whatever the procedural forms of governmental and industrial organization were (Shahnazarov 1974).

43. Kornai (1992, 46-47) usefully explicates three main dimensions of a totalitarian power system, although he refers to the "bureaucracy," whereas we would identify the locus of totalitarian power in the party leadership (that is, in the 1930s, Stalin) and its party and state bureaucracy or "politocracy" (Horvat 1982, 81-82). First, totalitarian power is comprehensive in the sense that it, in principle, "extends to every sphere of life," thus blurring (though not abolishing) distinctions between state and civil society, between public and private spheres of life. Second, the power of the politocracy is totalitarian in the sense that it "permeates the whole of society and influences every citizen." For example, a worker's residence and place of work is recorded on his or her internal passport or identification, and that information, supplemented by other data (e.g., a record of a job dismissal), is kept on file by party, police, and personnel authorities. Third, power is totalitarian when politocracy "is not subordinate to any stable legal system." Because laws may be ignored, transgressed, or easily adjusted, "the formal system of law is subordinate to the current endeavors of the [political leadership and its] bureaucracy." A totalitarian system, in short, is not subject to the "rule of law."

44. Khrushchev's address at Twentieth Congress in 1956 remains a classic critique in this regard. See Chapter 6.

45. According to Andrei Sakharov, between 1936-1938 alone, more than 1.2 million party members, half the total membership, were arrested. Most were shot or died in camps (cited in Conquest 1968, 713).

46. Horvat (1982, 21-22) uses the evocative phrase "etatism" to describe an ideology and politico-economic system that combines certain traditional socialist features, such as, the abolition of capitalist property relations and the "emancipation of the exploited classes" and the commitment to a "strong, centralized, authoritarian state" as the "main pivot" of society, wherein "the ruling political organization openly claims the monopoly of political power."

47. In both capitalism and etatism, leaders manipulate incentives of subordinates as means of social control (Dahl and Lindblom, 1953). Both also exercise coercion, but differently. "In governing the society, the capitalist ruling class uses primarily economic coercion, followed by pressure to force minds into conformity and, finally, by political coercion. In etatism ideological coercion is followed by political coercion, with economic coercion occupying last place in the sequence" (Horvat 1982, 82).

48. Soviet-style "socialism is not a stage beyond capitalism but a substitute for it, a means by which the nations which did not share in the Industrial Revolution can imitate its technical achievements, a means of achieving rapid accumulation under a different set of rules of the game" (Robinson 1960, 15).

49. "The destruction of classes is not achieved by extinguishing the class struggle but by intensifying it. The withering away of the state happens not through the weakening of state power, but through its maximal strengthening" (Stalin, cited in Horvat 1982, 22).

50. According to the Stalinist variant of Marxism, the state and society through these institutional innovations become essentially congruent. Consequently, Soviet practice is fundamentally consistent with the major classical Marxian aspirations: (1) "national [state] ownership of the means of production is the most highly developed, highest and basic form of socialist property" and constitutes "their social, joint ownership by the working people themselves"; (2) socialist ownership "reunites labor power and the means of production," thereby dissolving their capability of functioning "as instruments of exploitation"; (3) labor power "ceases to be a commodity" because the producers themselves now collectively own and control the productive means and output and because all members of society have equal access to the means of production and thereby an equal right to work and to be compensated according to their individual labor contribution; (4) the "antagonistic contradiction between necessary and surplus labor" disappears because both necessary and surplus product "is used exclusively for the benefit of the working people," in the forms of current individual consumers' goods, collective consumption, or development of productive capacity which enables "improvement of the workers' well-being" in the future; (5) under socialism, the "fundamental interests" of workers, peasants, and the intelligentsia are "the same," that is, all social groups have a "common interest" of "increasing and developing the property belonging to all," causing "bourgeois individualism" to give way to "socialist collectivism," whereby relations of "comradely cooperation and mutual assistance... serve the interests of society as a whole" (Koslov 1977, 62-65, 74-75).

51. "What would have happened to the Party, to our revolution, to Marxism," asked Stalin (1939, 356-57), "if Lenin had been overawed by the letter of Marxism" and had been constrained by such "old propositions of Marxism" as Friedreich Engels's dictum that "the working class can only come to power under the form of the democratic republic [which thereby] is the specific form for the dictatorship of the proletariat?" For the quotation from Engels's 1891 comment, see Marx and Engels (1936, 486). On the Soviet conception of "socialist democracy" and its superiority to "bourgeois democracy," see Shahnazarov (1974) and footnote 43, above.

52. As stated by a Soviet writer a bit more than a decade after Stalin's death, the "difference in the official position of leaders and the toiling masses in fulfilling the production function does not generate contradictions between them because, in keeping with their objective position and vocation, the leaders take care of social interests and fight for the welfare of the people" (cited in Horvat 1982, 184). However, because the "unity of fundamental interests" of workers and peasants "does not imply their full coincidence," party and state leaders must "subordinate the collective and personal interests of workers and collective farmers to the interests of society as a whole and so to ensure planned cooperation between them" (Koslov 1977, 76).

Chapter 5

Stalin and Totalitarian State-Directed Economy: Consequences and Contradictions

CONSEQUENCES

The Stalinist revolution was comprehensive in magnitude and scope. It encompassed every aspect of Soviet society, economy, education, culture, administration, and politics. From the day-to-day life of ordinary citizens to the giant institutions of economy and polity, little of the old survived unchanged. Virtually everything changed—dramatically, fundamentally, and (presumably) permanently. Roles, responsibilities, and interrelationships of individuals, institutions, government, economy, society, and Party were thoroughly redefined and reconstituted. A dominant agrarian society was transformed into one of the greatest economic and military powers of the world. Isaac Deutscher (1967, 566-68) aptly states that another contemporary totalitarian leader, Adolf Hitler, who inherited Germany as the wealthiest nation of Europe, left it impoverished and savaged at the end. Joseph Stalin, who took over an impoverished country inferior to any medium-sized European nation in the 1930s, transformed it into the first industrial power in Europe and the second in the world in a matter of a decade.[1]

On its own terms, the Stalinist revolution was highly successful. The aim of industrialization was readily achieved. As Table 5.1 shows, the Soviet economy grew at an annual rate of 4.8 percent between 1928 and 1937.[2] In the same period, Soviet industrial production grew at a phenomenal annual rate of 11.3 percent. Inasmuch as the entire capitalist bloc was experiencing a prolonged economic depression during the same period, the extraordinary success of the Stalinist model stunned the world. Soviet industrial expansion continued after World War II. According to Naum Jasny (1961), between 1928 and 1950, the gross industrial output of the Soviet economy expanded almost 4 times in size at U.S. prices and about 4.7 times at Soviet 1926-1927 prices.

Table 5.1

Outcome of the Soviet Industrialization Drive of 1928-1937

	1928	1937
A. CHANGE IN MANUFACTURING		
1. Heavy manufacturing share in overall manufacturing		
Net product share (1928 prices)	31	63
Labor force share	28	43 (1933)
2. Light manufacturing share in overall manufacturing		
Net product share (1928 prices)	68	36
Labor force share	71	56 (1933)
B. CHANGES IN MAJOR ECONOMIC SECTORS, STRUCTURE OF OUTPUT		
1. Share in net national product (1937 prices)		
Agriculture	49	31
Industry	28	45
Services	23	24
2. Share in labor force		
Agriculture	71	51 (1940)
Industry	18	29 (1940)
Services	12	20 (1940)
C. RATES OF GROWTH (1928-37) AND CAPITAL STOCK		
1. GNP (1937 prices)		4.8%
2. Labor force		
Nonagricultural		8.7%
Agriculture		-2.5%
3. Industrial production (1937 prices)		11.3%
4. Agriculture production (1958 prices)		1.1%
Livestock		-1.2%
5. Gross industrial capital stock		
(1937 prices, billion rubles)	34.8	119
D. CHANGES IN THE STRUCTURE OF GNP BY END USE (1937 PRICES)		
1. Household consumption - GNP	80	53
Annual growth rate (1928-37)		0.8%
2. Communal services - GNP	5	11
Annual growth rate (1928-37)		15.7%
3. Government administration and defense - GNP	3	11
Annual growth rate (1928-37)		15.6%
4. Gross capital investment - GNP	13	26
Annual growth rate (1928-37)		14.4%
E. FOREIGN TRADE PROPORTIONS		
1. Exports + imports - GNP	6%	1%
F. PRICES		
1. Consumer goods prices		
(state and cooperative stores, 1928 = 100)	100	700
2. Average realized prices of farm products		
(1928 = 100)	100	539
G. URBANIZATION		
1. Rural population (mill.)	147.0 (1926)	114.4 (1939)
Percent of total	82%	67%
2. Urban population (mill.)	26.3 (1939)	56.1 (1939)
Percent of total	18%	33%

Source: Sections A-F: Gregory and Stuart (1981, 84-85); section G: Nove (1977, 267).

Under Stalinist economic strategy, agriculture was relegated to a secondary position. It registered an annual growth rate of only 1.1 percent during the period from 1928 to 1937, compared to more than 11 percent annual growth in the industrial sector during the same period. Such overwhelming emphasis on the industrial sector led to a decline in the agricultural labor force, while the industrial labor force increased rapidly leading to a structural transformation of the economy from an agrarian to an industrial stage of economic development. As a consequence, the share of the agricultural sector in Soviet net national product declined from 49 percent in 1928 to 31 percent in 1937, while that of industry rose from 28 percent to 45 percent over the same time period. Moreover, because of emphasis on heavy industry, the share of heavy industry in the total manufacturing sector jumped from 31 percent in 1928 to 63 percent in 1937. On the other hand, because of the deemphasis on light industry, its share fell from 68 percent in 1928 to 36 percent in 1937. Overall, industrial production, the labor force, and capital stock grew at unusually high rates. As the industrialization strategy emphasized building "socialism in one country," that is, without foreign assistance or successful socialist revolution elsewhere, foreign trade (exports plus imports) contracted significantly. As Table 5.1 shows, whereas foreign trade constituted 6 percent of the Soviet GNP in 1928, its share had dropped to a mere 1 percent by 1937.[3]

Stalinist industrialization was achieved at a steep price in terms of private consumption. Private consumption as a percent of GNP fell significantly, from 80 percent to 53 percent between 1928 and 1937. Also, the prices of consumption goods rose more rapidly than the prices of farm products, turning the internal terms of trade against agriculture and providing vivid empirical testimony to the policy of subduing the peasantry and bringing agriculture within the bounds of national planning. On the other hand, as Table 5.1 shows, the shares of collective consumption or communal services, government administration and defense, and gross capital investment expanded to a total of nearly half the GNP. By 1937 the state economy controlled almost 100 percent of national capital stock, industry, agriculture, and foreign trade.[4]

As well as remarkable economic growth, the Stalinist model showed considerable success in terms of other macroeconomic goals, such as employment and inflation. It succeeded in eliminating cyclical unemployment, which has historically plagued market capitalist economies. The high priority placed on employment was evidenced by the constitutional duty and right of the Soviet citizen to work. Indeed, unemployment became so rare a phenomenon that the Soviet Union stopped maintaining unemployment statistics in the 1930s. Conditions of full employment prevailed throughout the Stalin years.[5]

Factors that contributed to the success of the Stalinist economy in achieving substantially full employment included (1) very ambitious "taut" planning, which generally created excess demand for labor; (2) the centralized apparatus of planning, notably control over the state budget and banking and monetary systems, which gave the government coordinated control over aggregate demand; (3) the state foreign trade monopoly, which insulated the internal economy from the shock of external fluctuations; (4) programs of education, training, and recruitment, which created desired labor skills and guided workers toward desired sectors and locations; and (5) a dual-technology strategy, which encouraged a strong demand for unskilled labor as well as skilled workers.

Soviet planners made deliberate use of inflation to shift resources from consumer goods into investment goods and sustain labor incentives. Inflationary pressures during the 1930s included reductions in the supply of consumer goods attendant to the shift of resources to heavy industry, increases in wage incomes because of higher money wages and expanded employment, and increases in the money supply. Although industrial wages rose substantially, more than 400 percent, between 1928 and 1937, retail prices rose even more rapidly, 700 percent, largely because of the unusually rapid expansion in nonconsumption government expenditures (Holzman 1955, 168-73). In the post-Stalin period, price indexes were remarkably stable (Nove 1977, 246-51).

Prior to World War II, the Soviet economy experienced two major periods of economic disruption and dislocation, involving substantial reductions in real output, namely the civil war and the collectivization drive of the early 1930s. The policies and processes adopted by Soviet leaders no doubt contributed to the dislocation. If the war and postwar experiences of 1941-1945 and after are added, three great waves of contraction and expansion can be identified: war communism-NEP, early collectivization-planned industrialization, and war-postwar. Compared with Western capitalist countries, however, Soviet growth was less unstable as a result of the institutions of centrally directed economy, notably the factors mentioned earlier concerning employment. Through the banking system and the state budget, planners sustained high levels of aggregate demand. Indeed, rapid industrialization and taut planning generally were characterized by excess demand in many sectors. Enterprises continued production even if their output was temporarily unsold. Workers retained jobs even if they were underemployed. In an essentially fully employed economy, expansion of the labor force and positive net investment virtually ensure expansion in real output. Real output falls only in the possible, but rare, event that productivity falls more than employment of labor, capital, and raw materials rises.

If economic growth and stability were strong points in Soviet planning, resource allocation was an area of relative weakness. Planning processes were slow, cumbersome, expensive, and dysfunctional. However, what Soviet planning lacked in consistency and allocative efficiency it often made up for in effectiveness, from the perspective of Soviet leaders and planners. The priority planning system permitted focus on high priority areas and thereby encouraged rapid growth of a selective sort. Taut planning provided discipline and inspiration for concerted developmental effort. Thus, central planning and market processes

> are not alternative roads to the same destination. Planning is advocated by those who wish to achieve a very different distribution of goods among the population than would have been achieved by the market, and to allocate resources, in a dynamic economy, in a direction which the market, left to itself, would not have chosen. (Ellman 1979, 50-51)

Because Soviet institutions and planning processes were concerned primarily with fostering rapid industrialization and growth, they must be assessed in that context. From this perspective, Soviet planning "worked" in the sense of rough consistency, enabled the kind of priority decision making conducive to desired industrialization strategies, and perhaps encouraged the sort of dynamic efficiency that contributed to the rapid and comprehensive transformation of Soviet economic society. Soviet labor policy, for example, was an area in which the Soviet economy in the Stalin years attained a high degree of "goal achievement efficiency" if not "allocative efficiency" as that latter expression is understood by Western economists. The goal of rapid industrialization required (1) a rapid increase in the industrial labor force, (2) an improvement in the quality of the industrial labor force, and (3) a reallocation of labor from light industry to heavy industry. "Soviet labor policy seems to have performed these functions reasonably well" (Gregory and Stuart, 1981, 99).

Whereas the population during the Stalinist era grew at an average annual rate of about 1 percent, the labor force grew at the remarkably high rate of 2.5 percent (Moorsteen and Powell 1966, 643, 648). Soviet policies in this period contributed significantly to this outcome. First, the commitment to full employment encouraged a larger number of people to enter the labor force and helped ensure their employment (albeit not always efficiently). Second, rapid growth in the labor force was stimulated also by measures that increased the "participation rate," that is, the ratio of the labor force to the population. These included legal and moral pressures for all able-bodied people to work, reductions in sexual discrimination in employment and entry into the labor force of large numbers of women, organized recruitment of urban labor from the countryside, coordination of education and industrial needs, and organized systems of job placement for students and graduates.

As mentioned earlier, Soviet educational and manpower policy during the Stalin era brought dramatic qualitative improvements in the labor force. Rapid reductions in illiteracy through general education, massive acquisitions in labor skills through vocational education and on-the-job training, and creation of a new intelligentsia of technical, administrative, and managerial labor through higher education and other measures were hallmarks of a revolutionary transformation of the human resource base of economic development. Over time, increasing numbers of the new intelligentsia were products of technical institutes and universities, whose preparation focused principally on engineering and other technical subjects germane to production in the setting of rapid industrialization through the auspices of centralized planning.

Not only were Soviet managers well trained, they were well remunerated and fairly tightly controlled. Incentives for Soviet managers were material and moral, monetary and nonmonetary, positive and negative. Base pay for managers was substantially higher than for average workers and was supplemented significantly by bonuses for plan fulfillment and over fulfillment. Managers were also rewarded by automobiles, housing, recognition in news stories promotion, and the power and prestige of managerial status. These positive rewards might be supplemented by negative sanctions for failure, including loss of bonus, demotion or dismissal, and, during the Stalinist era, even imprisonment or execution.

Soviet labor allocation was accomplished by a blend of central planning and market forces. In the Stalinist era, labor supply was fairly tightly controlled by nonmarket means. In the 1930s, organized recruitment was instrumental in moving peasant labor from farm to urban factory. Constraints were placed on labor mobility to reduce worker turnover—including an internal passport system and a requirement that workers obtain permission to change jobs. Forced labor, finally abolished in the late 1950s, accounted for 10 percent or more of the labor force during World War II.

In many instances, however, some freedom in the choice of occupation and work-place was honored, and the allocation of labor resources depended on the quasi-market forces of interaction between planned demand and worker supply. Appealing to work-ers by material incentives was reinforced by full employment, the high-pressure economy, and taut planning. Also, wages were set (and readjusted) by central admin-istrative decision, and workers did not confront a monolithic, monopsonistic em-ployer. Ministries, industries, and enterprises competed for scarce labor in a high-pressure, sellers' market environment.

Wages were differentiated by region, industry, enterprise, skill, working condi-tions, and length of work. For example, wages were higher in Siberia than in the Black Sea region, in heavy than in light industry, in large than in small enterprises, in mining and other riskier circumstances, and for overtime work. Central authorities encouraged movement of workers among industries by altering the base wage and stimulating acquisition of skills or occupational mobility by adjusting the differen-tial between the wage for a particular category and the base wage. In the Stalin pe-riod, the intense demand for skilled labor and technicians was manifested by large wage dispersion between skilled and unskilled labor. Whereas prior to the industrial-ization drive, wage levels in light industry were generally higher than those in heavy industry, the reverse occurred during the 1930s, a pattern that continued after 1953.

In short, under the Stalinist model, the Soviet Union, albeit with heroic sacrifice, heavy cost, and severe dislocation, was propelled from the position of a relatively undeveloped economy to one of the world's two superpowers. Moreover, industrial-ization was achieved through the hard work of the Soviet people. Development pro-grams were self-financed by a society whose political leaders diverted the savings generated by the state from its own population to investment instead of consump-tion. The population was obliged to work more, longer, and harder for a proportion-ally smaller reward (Millar 1981, 273-92).[6]

From a social perspective, Stalin also literally rebuilt Soviet society. The percent-age of the Soviet population living in cities nearly doubled between 1928 and 1939. Whereas in 1928 only 29.8 million people, or 18 percent of the total population, lived in urban areas, their number swelled to 39.7 million, or 33 percent of the total popu-lation, by 1933. By 1940, 58.6 million people, out of a total population of 173.6 mil-lion, were living in urban areas. Within a period of twelve years, from 1928 to 1940, the urban population in the Soviet Union grew by 30 million, and scores of new cities and towns sprang up and old ones expanded.

Along with a rapid urbanization program, Stalin energetically promoted educa-tional opportunities, especially avenues for scientific and technological studies. The literacy rate, which among nine- to forty-nine-year-olds, was 58 percent in 1928, was raised to 87 percent by 1940. Thus, a largely uneducated rural nation was con-verted into an educated, urban, and skilled nation.[7] Unlike the political system, which was totalitarian in character, and the command economy, which emphasized isola-tionism, the Stalinist educational system remained relatively open to world knowl-edge.[8] Most important, the Stalinist education system opened doors of opportunities to better jobs and careers to millions of young men and women. By providing such advancement in their personal lives, Stalin was able to create an obedient and loyal workforce in the country, which remained rather indifferent to Stalinist terrors, purges, and other repressive measures.[9] The Stalinist system was especially geared to women's rights and equal opportunities, a commitment far ahead of its time. Women were increasingly integrated into the ever-expanding processes of industrialization.

TENSIONS AND CONTRADICTIONS

Although few doubt Stalinism's main contribution—the rapid transformation of a backward agricultural country into a mighty military and industrial power[10]—many Western and Soviet observers contend that this monumental feat was associated with many negative consequences, tensions, and contradictions with far-reaching repercussions in Soviet economy, polity, and society. Some question whether such a model was "necessary" in the first place,[11] while others hold Stalinism ultimately responsible for the systemic problems that led to the eventual disintegration of the Soviet Union itself.[12] The major contradictions and tensions associated with the institutions and programs of the Stalinist model may be summarized as follows.

Collectivization

First, forced collectivization was based on the presupposition that a "primitive socialist accumulation" was needed for industrialization. Because the peasantry was believed to be unwilling to cooperate with the Soviet regime, an agricultural surplus was diverted by force for industrialization. But the so-called agricultural surplus was achieved by imposing extreme suffering on the peasantry, by seriously undermining rural consumption needs, and creating devastating dislocation in rural social, economic, and religious life. Moreover, lowered agricultural output, reduced capital stock and livestock, and drastic cuts in rural consumption brought not only serious distress to the urban population, but also had negative effects on other segments of Soviet society, for example, reductions in per capita output of such agricultural commodities as meat, milk, and dairy products.

As Holland Hunter and Janusz Szyrmer (1992, 11) remark, "The political tensions associated with agricultural collectivization and the drive to offset its negative impact through industrial expansion led in turn to Party purges, show trials, and general terror that cast a pall over the whole decade." Furthermore, it has been argued by some that the continuation of the NEP policies "would have permitted at least as rapid a rate of industrialization with less cost to the urban as well as to the rural population of the Soviet Union" (Millar 1974, 766).[13] More recent studies contend that, without resorting to massive and forced collectivization, the Soviet agricultural sector could have maintained 1928 food consumption standards for a growing population and that, without the loss of animal tractive power caused by collectivization, traditional peasant agriculture could have contributed positively to the Soviet drive for industrial development (Hunter and Szyrmer 1992, 121). Above all, the human cost of Stalinist collectivization was millions of lives. The Soviet Union never fully recovered from the Stalinist excesses committed during the collectivization drive.

Industrialization

The Stalinist industrialization strategy was based on extensive methods of production; that is, more and more inputs led to more and more output. Besides squandering the human and natural resources of the Soviet Union at an unprecedented scale, such a strategy neglected technological infusion in production processes. Moreover, Stalinist "success indicators" emphasized target fulfillment in terms of quantity, not in terms of cost, quality, or technical change, thus discriminating against innovation. Another striking contradiction of the Stalinist industrialization strategy was that the Soviet government accomplished its task without a concomitant increase in the living standards of its population. During the 1930s, prices rose more rapidly than money wages and, consequently, real wages fell. Throughout the Stalinist era, the working class was called upon to make Draconian sacrifices of consumption in favor of investment, and institutional processes were established to enforce them. Also, Stalinist industrialization strategy emphasized "socialism in one country," which denied Soviet development the advantages of international division of labor and technological advancements.

Another striking aspect of the Stalinist industrialization strategy was that it resulted in a great increase in inequality. The state exploited the ordinary citizenry in the name of rapid and large-scale industrialization in order to catch up with the Western countries. The consumption sector was suppressed and forced savings were diverted, in the form of investment, to heavy industries in order to foster rapid industrial growth and to defend against the potential attacks of capitalist countries.[14] Inequality had its manifestations in material incentives, wage differentials, and special perquisites and privileges for party and government officials; an emphasis on hierarchy, authority, and discipline in industrial management; and the undermining of the role of labor unions and workers' self-governance. Indeed, open antagonism toward egalitarian principles resulted in a degree of wage inequality in Soviet society that exceeded that of several capitalist countries at that period of time. Also, Stalinist industrialization caused wastage, abuse, and misuse of human resources. Many trained and skilled persons were imprisoned in labor camps to work on manual jobs,[15] and many people were weeded out simply because of their political beliefs.[16] Also, millions of rural people were brought to urban areas on an unprecedented scale, without creating adequate housing facilities. Between 1928 and 1939, the urban population rose by 102 percent, at a rate of 4.4 percent per year, while the urban housing stock increased by only 45 percent, registering a growth rate of only 2.2 percent annually. In 1939 only 4.0 square meters of urban housing was available per capita in the Soviet Union as opposed to 4.7 square meters in 1928.

Institutional Transformation

The creation of new institutions, such as state ownership, centralized planning, and bureaucratic coordination, was instrumental in strengthening state control over the economy and thereby in imposing the aspirations of party and state leaders on the industrialization process. At the same time, these institutions had negative consequences, derived from both general deficiencies and qualities specific to Stalinism.

Planned, bureaucratic coordination of economic life generates problems pertaining to both formulation and execution of plans. One major limitation of centralized plan formulation is the absence of an indigenous social process for calculating consumer preferences. The "basic needs" perceived to constitute minimum living standards can perhaps be assessed directly by political leaders without great loss in consumer welfare. But beyond basic needs and "collective wants," bureaucratic coordination and centralized planning have no indigenous mechanisms for recording and communicating consumer preferences and thus for calculating, from the consumer's viewpoint, the desirability of alternative choices concerning resource allocation.

This general problem of centralized planning was compounded by factors specific to Soviet experiences, especially during the Stalin years, notably, the high priority for investment over consumption and heavy industry over light industry, and the proclivity to impose very demanding or taut plans as a means of inspiring heroic efforts. Consequently, shortages in many consumer goods (accompanied by surpluses in some) were common, accompanied by queues, indicating imbalances and inefficiencies from the perspective of consumer demands. Moreover, although consumers more or less exercised "freedom of consumers' choice" in the Stalin years, "planners' sovereignty" (within the framework of the overall goals set by the politocracy) carried the corollary that resources would not necessarily be shifted to permit expansion of the desired commodities. Thus, allocative efficiency, based on the assumption of "consumers' sovereignty," presumably was sacrificed to patterns of planned development desired by the party and state bureaucracy. Because the consumer sector was used as a buffer in the event of discrepancies between plan resources and requirements, plan fulfillment departed substantially from plan targets, with detrimental effects on personal incentives and productivity.

Efficiency in plan formulation also requires accurate calculations of the costs of alternative levels and combinations of outputs. According to Western economists, this requires quantification in comparable values and an institutional process for making such comparisons (as is provided, for example, by economic systems that utilize market pricing systems). A major limitation of centralized, bureaucratic allocational systems, such as those that were established in the Stalin years, is that they lack indigenous institutional mechanisms, that is, market pricing systems, for calculating costs.

Of course, the Stalinist state bureaucracy set prices. But, as noted earlier, such prices were primarily for accounting purposes, not for guiding resource allocations. There were two main obstacles to incorporation and the efficacious use of pricing systems in Soviet planning. First, there were major ideological biases against doing this. Market price systems were associated by Soviet Marxists with the "anarchy" of capitalist market exchange and were perceived as a barrier to ex ante, planned decisions. Moreover, traditionally, Soviet planners were reluctant to extend recognition of the role of prices in economic calculation to capital and land, and they attempted to formulate criteria for the allocation of investment funds, for example, in terms of a simplistic variant of the labor theory of value.

Second, the institutional structure and behavioral principles of centralized planning made successful incorporation of price systems difficult. Centrally set prices involve considerable subjective bureaucratic guesswork. Once set, prices were not changed except at periodic intervals, and thus, were unlikely to record accurately changes in demand and supply. For simplification, prices also were apt to be set for general categories of goods and therefore were unlikely to reflect accurately special considerations of quality and product differentiation. Finally, time lags occurred between the communication of data from decentralized data gatherers to centralized decision makers, often making the information obsolete or misleading by the time it arrived.

There were also important shortcomings in Soviet systems of plan execution and control. First, because of the determination by Stalin and other top political leaders to establish and maintain a monopoly of party-state control over the economic system, the planning and control bureaucracies were unusually centralized. Consequently, the disadvantages of centralized decision-making were magnified. The Stalinist model, with its hierarchically structured vertical information channels and chains of command, tended to maximize responsiveness of lower level administrators and managers to directives of political leaders and planners and to minimize responsiveness to laterally related enterprises, sectors, regions, or consumers. Such a strategy created bottlenecks and inefficiencies. The centralization of decisions tended to overlook concretized knowledge of "time and place" of local administrators and managers. Big, overall decisions applied indiscriminately to wide areas of the economy tended to neglect special features of particular cases and microeconomic interdependencies. Infrequent revision of strategic decisions created an institutional mechanism insufficiently flexible and adaptable to changing circumstances.

Second, there was a conflict between "political" and "realistic" elements of planning targets. The input-output figures in central plans were often a mixture of political goals and statistical data. Planning data served the important political purpose of guidance and exhortation, of urging subordinates to greater achievement than that which would have been likely if the data represented merely reasonable expectations of output possibilities and input requirements. Output targets and input allocations resting upon expectations of actual performance provide no basis for penalizing or prodding inefficient producers and can conceivably lead to progressive deterioration of efficiency. However, if planning targets are mere hopeful anticipations, not generally realized or realizable, planners and managers will soon discover that, as realistic statistical data, plans are unreliable. Each manager then will have to make his or her own best-guess judgment as to how and to what extent he or she should attempt to adhere to planning targets. Multiply this several thousandfold, and rigorous ex ante coordination, so important to centralized planning, evaporates. Coordination by a pricing system does not raise this conflict because there are no physical targets to be met. Physical output quotas and input assignments are not necessary.

Third, successful execution of economic plans requires both a centralized overview of the whole economic system and decentralized concern with the concrete circumstances of time and place. These two principles conflict, and even the most efficiently organized centralized economy will be a best-guess mixture between them. Again, the price system as a process for social coordination avoids this conflict by abstaining from the necessity of centralized decisions.

Fourth, the more successful the political leadership was in establishing systems of economic incentives, and the more vigorously individuals were convinced that their own rewards would best be maximized by attaining planning goals, the greater were the pressures to simulate such attainment through informal techniques of industrial management. Taking advantage of their specialized knowledge of particular conditions, managers understated output possibilities and overstated requirements to provide a margin of safety (*strakhovka*) for unforeseen contingencies and for general inefficiency and the "quiet life." Simulation of plan achievement also included producing the wrong assortment of goods, sacrificing quality for quantity, misappropriating funds, using influence to work up deals not recognized in official plans, and even outright falsification of accounts (Berliner 1952). Fifth, a centrally planned economic system has no one simple criterion of success equivalent to, say, profit maximization in a capitalist economy. A central plan consists of a large variety of targets and expectations in regard to output levels, input combinations, labor force requirements, product varieties and assortments, and so on.

No plan ever will be met perfectly. When it is not, central planners must establish priorities to relate underfulfillment of one goal to overfulfillment of another. But once managers have learned what the priorities are, they will adjust their behavior. "Whenever controllers give high priority to one particular goal in their evaluation of plan fulfillment, and make that priority effective through bonuses, enterprise managers will violate other parts of the plan in order to fulfill the high priority indicator" (Campbell 1960, 130). A classic illustration is the sacrifice of quality for quantity when high priority is placed upon meeting quantitative targets.

In short, although Stalinist institutional transformation contributed to "goal achievement efficiency" (state control, rapid industrialization), the new institutions also exhibited serious departures from both static and dynamic efficiency in resource use and allocation. Some of the sources of inefficiency no doubt reflected limitations of state enterprise and bureaucratic coordination in general. But most problems confronting institutional change during the Stalinist era were also rooted in the unusual rapidity, magnitude, and comprehensivity with which those changes were imposed. Soviet-style central planning was not content with providing overall macroeconomic guidance. Instead, a highly overcentralized system was created by Stalin and, despite proposals for reforms, continued by his successors, in which virtually everything was "planned" from Moscow. State ownership, from a Western socialist perspective, also went far beyond reasonable bounds. Socialist writers, from the "Golden Age of Marxism" (1883-1914) (Kolakowski 1978, Vol. 2) to Alec Nove (1991), have contended that social ownership of the "commanding heights" of corporate capitalism may serve a useful purpose in a sensible socialist program. But socialization of small farm and business proprietary economy, as in agriculture and trade, to say nothing of nationalized barbershops and taxicabs, was surely counterproductive. This institutional extremism, which constituted a "put all your eggs in one basket" strategy, had powerfully negative consequences. By giving state economy monopoly power, it virtually eradicated small business and proprietary economy and lost the benefits of competition. By enmeshing enterprise and collective farm managers in an extensive web of control from above, it concentrated the dynamic energy, enthusiasm, and commitment of the system in top political and administrative leadership, leaving a vast morass of lethargy and potential stagnation waiting beneath if the leadership ever faltered or if the underlying population ever came to question the leadership's authority or sagacity.

Sociocultural Revolution

Socially and politically, the Stalinist revolution created what Robert Tucker (1971, 121-42) calls a "dual Russia." On the one hand, there was a "Russian State," or "official Russia," that embodied centralized autocratic state power which operated through a hierarchy of bureaucratic institutions and their local agents. On the other hand, there was the population at large, the "Russian society," or "popular Russia"—"a separate and distinct Russia with a life and truth of its own." The relation between the "Russian State" and the "Russian society" was that "between conqueror and conquered"; their common denominator was the "apprehension of the autocratic state power as an alien power in the Russian land." The people were not assimilated into the state; they lived independently of the state authorities. Stalinist institutions and policies subdued the people to the will of the state, but they failed to integrate them into the state; the state remained an alien body to the common people.

This is especially true in the case of the rural people. The state's clear preference for industrial production and the policy of forced collectivization isolated the rural population from the developing sectors of the economy, and the rural economy and population became even more backward relative to the urban industrial sector than had been the case in 1928. The Soviet Union never succeeded in overcoming the social, educational, and technical backwardness of both the people and the enterprises in the Soviet rural sector that Stalinism created (Millar 1981, 292). Therefore, claims that Stalinism achieved modernization in the Soviet Union are also misleading. Stalinism achieved industrialization, not modernization. Whereas modernization implies an integration of a whole society, Stalin ended up with a dual society.

Totalitarian State Economy and Ideology

Finally, the Stalinist version of socialism, in both theory and practice, was based on an extremely centralized strand of Marxist thought that envisaged not only virtually complete nationalization of the means of production and bureaucratic planning and control, but also a (totalitarian) state of unprecedented scope and intensity.[17] Indeed, one may reasonably argue that the "prime factor that brings the other system-specific phenomena," such as state ownership, bureaucratic coordination, collectivization, and rapid industrialization, "is the undivided power of the Communist party imbued with its specific ideology" (Kornai 1992, 361); that is, the political structure dominates over economic institutions and strategies. Many of the problematic features of the Soviet economy during the Stalin years were thus rooted in the drive for a monopoly of political power by the top leadership.[18]

This "main line of causality" (Kornai 1992, 391) from political structure, including ideology, to economic institutions and strategies, needs to be understood flexibly. First, we must avoid the circularity of reasoning embodied in "deducing theory from practice and then ascribing practice to the theory." For example, although ideological hostility toward the kulaks and the petty bourgeoisie in general was "undeniably one element" in Stalinist agricultural strategy, it would be "much too simple to assert that forcible collectivization followed inexorably from Marxist or communist ideology" (Nove 1991, 123-24). Second, it is ahistorical to think of the Stalinist system as an "unchanging phenomenon." On the contrary, as Stephen Cohen (1977, 24) asserts, Stalinism evolved over time, from the "truly revolutionary events of the early 1930s to the rigidly conservative sociopolitical order of 1946-53." The 1930s themselves were characterized by several stages, Cohen continues, culminating in "the final triumph of Stalinism over the Bolshevik tradition and the political completion of revolution from above." In this evolutionary process, the political power monopoly, Stalinist ideology, and economic strategies and institutions changed and mutually interacted on one another.[19] In this process, however, Stalinism's totalitarian political structure played a compelling, some would say dominant, role.

This drive for absolute power from the center was based on an open distrust, not only of the underlying population, but of the party and state bureaucracy as well. To secure his autocratic rule, Stalin in effect emasculated the party and struck an alliance with the secret police. No opposition was tolerated, as evidenced by the successive waves of purges that reached their apogee in the late 1930s. Not only party members, but people in all spheres of life—doctors, engineers, artisans, artists, writers, and poets—were subject to the unbridled power and unchallengeable will of the dictator. As discussed above, Stalin was above the law of the land, and he could do, and indeed did, virtually anything he wanted. Stalin was also responsible for bringing a political integration of diverse national, ethnic, and cultural groups into Soviet society. Such an amalgamation of nations, cultures, and ethnic and religious groups was typically carried out by denying these groups their historic territories and supplanting their group-specific identities and aspirations. This systematic employment of terror as an instrument of power generated social chaos and economic disruption, a massive squandering of human resources, and such institutional excesses as overcentralization, overcollectivization, and overnationalization. Finally, to many Soviet observers, including, one suspects, a majority of the Soviet people, the Stalinist model came to be regarded as a travesty of the socialist project, as envisioned, for example, by Karl Marx, Friedreich Engels or even V. I. Lenin. As Tucker observes,

> Stalinism as revolution from above was a state-building process, the construction of a powerful, highly centralized, bureaucratic, military-industrial Soviet Russian state. Although it was proclaimed "socialist" in the mid 1930's, it differed in various vital ways from what most socialist thinkers—Marx, Engels, and Lenin among them—had understood socialism to mean. Stalinist "socialism" was a socialism of mass poverty rather than plenty; of sharp social stratification rather than relative equality; of universal, constant fear rather than emancipation of personality; of national chauvinism rather than brotherhood of man; and of a monstrously hypertrophied state power rather than the decreasingly statified commune-state delineated by Marx in *The Civil War in France* and by Lenin in *The State and Revolution*.[20] (1977, 95).

In sum, there were many negative consequences of Stalinist policies that went far to offset the positive aspects. However, it is also true that the successes of the Stalinist model altered key conditions in the country, which, in turn, dialectically contributed to a growing obsolescence of the model itself.

NOTES

1. The magnitude, speed, and far-reaching character of the socio-political and economic transformation that was accomplished warrants its characterization as a revolution ("from above") or a "revolution-within-a (Bolshevik)-revolution." See Tucker (1977, 79-81); Elliott (1984); Dowlah (1992b); Dowlah and Elliott (1991).

2. It should be pointed out, however, that divergent claims exist concerning growth of Soviet GNP during the Stalinist era. Official Soviet statistics of growth of Soviet industry and national income during the Stalinist era have often been claimed to be exaggerated. On the other hand, estimates of Soviet national income conducted by Western experts and agencies also remain disputed. But by all estimates, Soviet GNP growth during the Stalinist period remains respectable compared to that of Western economies. According to Bergson, the average annual growth rate of Soviet GNP was 5.8 percent during the 1928-40 period. Hunter and Szyrmer (1992, 161) give an estimated 6.6 percent growth for the same period. For details of different sources see Gregory and Stuart (1990, 95); Hunter and Szyrmer (1992, 35-36); Bergson and Kuznets (1963, 342-60).

3. For details on official and non-official estimates of Soviet exports and imports for the period of 1928-1940, see Dohan and Hewett (1973, 24-27).

4. Even private trade was virtually eliminated. Official prohibition of private trade came in 1931. Very limited private trade was allowed in a few handicrafts, but it was heavily taxed. Tax rates in such permitted trade ranged between 50 percent and 81 percent. For example, a person engaged in private trade, not employing any hired labor, had to pay 1,596 rubles on the first 8,401 rubles of annual income, plus 37.5 percent on the balance up to 12,000 rubles of private income.

5. One of the remarkable features of the Stalinist full employment strategy was that people were put on "payrolls, not on the dole, with positive consequences for their sense of self-worth," as "wage payments rather than some form of public assistance was the basis for incomes" (Hunter and Szyrmer 1992, 160). It should be noted, however, that Soviet workers were often inefficiently employed, both during and after the Stalin era, because (a) complementary equipment and raw materials were often lacking, (b) "taut" planning encouraged hoarding of reserve pools of underutilized labor in anticipation of future needs, and (c) legal or customary constraints prevented firing workers.

6. The Stalinist industrialization strategy approximated Preobrazhensky's industrialization program, which Stalin strongly denounced during the Great Industrialization Debate of the mid 1920s. As the above discussion shows, heavy industry was emphasized, growth of agriculture and consumption sectors were de-emphasized, resources were diverted to the industrial sector, and, finally, the share of foreign trade sector in GNP declined. But one should not conclude that Stalin simply carried out the programs enunciated by Preobrazhensky and other Left opposition leaders. As Tucker (1971, 112) reminds us, "The use of coercion to effect a swift total collectivization had never, for example, been a part of the Left opposition's program, nor did it envisage the pace of industrialization that Stalin sought to enforce."

7. As Deutscher (1966, 568) writes:

The whole nation has been sent to school. Its mind has been so awakened that it can hardly be put back to sleep again. Its avidity for knowledge, for the sciences and the arts, has been stimulated by Stalin's government to the point where it has become insatiable and embarrassing. It should be remarked that, although Stalin has kept Russia isolated from the contemporary influences of the west, he has encouraged and fostered every interest in what he calls the "cultural heritage" of the west. Perhaps in no country have the young been imbued with so great a respect and love for the classical literature and art of other nations as in Russia.

8. Deutscher (1966, 568-69) notes that up to World War II, the total editions of foreign classics sold in the USSR were as follows: Byron's works half a million copies, Balzac nearly two million, Dickens two million, Goethe half a million, Heine one million, Victor Hugo three million, Maupassant more than three million, Shakespeare more than one million, and Zola two million.

9. Many Soviet young men and women "were proud of their advancements beyond what had been possible for their parents and grateful to the system that opened doors for them. The new opportunities made it easier to bear the sacrifices required by the rigors of the 1930s" (Hunter and Szyrmer 1992, 161).

10. Characterization of the Stalinist model as a success, however, remains controversial. Some suggest that Stalinism was indeed successful, although they admit that the model became inappropriate for the subsequent stages of Soviet development. Opponents argue that the economic successes of the Stalinist model were less than those claimed. According to them, Stalinist economic growth was attained by appropriating private wealth and by depressing living standards, and such growth, based on extensive methods of production, did not create real productive capacity upon which sustained future growth could be built. For contending perspectives on this issue see Goldman (1983); Szeleneyi (1989); Elliott (1989); Dowlah and Elliott (1991); Dowlah (1992a, 119-120).

11. For details on the debate on whether Stalinism was "necessary," see Nove 1964; Hunter and Szyrmer 1992; Conquest 1968; and Tucker 1977.

12. Such viewpoints have been expressed by many Soviet and Western observers. For discussion of systemic problems created by Stalinism, see Tucker (1977); Drewnowski (1982); Aganbegyan (1988a); Dowlah (1992a, 183-195); Kagarlitsky (1990).

13. For a discussion of "what-might-have-beens," see Tucker (1977, 88); Katz (1971); Hunter and Szyrmer (1992). Soviet economists Shmelev and Popov (1989) go further than this. They claim that Soviet economic growth was highest during the NEP period, not during the Stalinist period as many tend to believe.

14. According to Jasny (1961, 2), while the total personal income (calculated at constant prices) of the expanded population increased by about one-third from 1928 to 1952, the real value of the funds in the hands of the state for investment, military and other expenses grew almost eightfold during the same period.

15. Between 1928 and 1953, gulag labor, comprised 5 to 10 percent of the Soviet population. Although "the state did seek to derive economic benefit from forced labor," its costs—in high death rates and loss of population, low productivity of gulag labor, lower overall output because of the diversion of resources to the gulags and expenses of incarceration, and the alienation of inmates and their families—"were immense." It is believed that the gulags had a net negative effect on Soviet economic development. They may be best characterized as "the product of an irrational Stalin and his associates and not... as being consciously designed for economic purposes" (Gregory and Stuart 1981, 197). Also see Rosefielde 1981; Dallin and Nicolevsky 1947; Swianiewicz 1965.

16. Khrushchev's remarks at the Twentieth Congress of the CPSU in 1956 are worth mentioning in this context. Along with denouncing Stalinism for "rude violations of internal party and Soviet democracy, sterile administration, deviations of all sorts, covering up the shortcomings and vanishing of reality," Khrushchev also condemned Stalin for giving "birth to many flatterers and specialists in false optimism and deceit." Indeed, many believe Stalinist terror, purges, and network of secret police eliminated many creative and courageous minds, and opened opportunities for conformists to survive and succeed.

17. For contending centralized and decentralized perspectives on socialist political economy, see Elliott (1976); Selucky (1979); Dowlah (1992b).

18. Kornai (1992, 365) summarizes the dominant role of the political "superstructure" in the process of institutional change in such countries as the USSR as follows: "The new superstructure crushes the base that is alien to it and rearranges it entirely. It nationalizes and collectivizes; it steadily eliminates private property and squeezes the market into a smaller and smaller space. The bureaucratic apparatus of economic control springs up and spreads in all directions. As this process goes on, the property relations, coordination mechanism, and economic processes alter according to the new system, these changes react continually on the political forms and bring a transformation of the ideology in their train."

19. Many of the practical and ideological features of Stalinist totalitarian rule "took shape as makeshift solutions to the social chaos, the 'quicksand society,' generated by the destruction of NEP institutions and processes during the initial wave of revolution from above." The Stalinist system was thus "less a product of Bolshevik programs or planning than of desperate attempts to cope with the social pandemonium and crises created by the Stalinist leadership itself in 1929-33" (Cohen 1977, 25; Lewin 1977).

20. See, among others, Tarasulo (1989); Zemtsov and Farrar (1989); Winiecki (1989); Nee and Stark (1989).

Chapter 6

Khrushchev and Authoritarian Reform Economy

INTRODUCTION

This chapter examines Nikita Sergeivich Khrushchev[1] and his period of leadership in the Soviet Union as an exemplar of an authoritarian reform model of socialist political economy. Khrushchev emerged as the supreme leader of the Soviet Union in 1957, after a five-year-long power struggle following Joseph Stalin's death.[2] Khrushchev's assumption of power coincided with one of the most optimistic chapters in Soviet history. The Soviet Union was developing faster than many advanced capitalist countries, the gap in her level of economic and social development with the United States was rapidly decreasing, and the Soviets had demonstrated a spectacular success in nuclear and rocket strength.[3] Overall, the Soviet Union appeared to be stronger, wealthier, and more influential than ever before.[4]

Khrushchev extended the nation's optimistic mood further by orchestrating the sharpest break with the Stalinist model in the Soviet Union prior to Mikhail Gorbachev. He initiated far-reaching reorganization of the country's economic, social, and political structures. Politically, Khrushchev brought an end to the era of Stalinist personal dictatorship, personality cult, and rule of secret police terror. Although the Stalinist tradition of one-party rule was continued, Khrushchev reintroduced "Leninist legality" in the party; that is, discussion and dissent were allowed within it. Beyond that, by promoting intellectual deliberations outside the party, fostering the rule of law in government and society, and overseeing the dwindling role of the state's coercive organs and instruments, Khrushchev made a transition from Stalinist totalitarianism to an authoritarian form of state. Economically, Khrushchev made significant efforts to revitalize the consumer sector, which was disproportionately penalized during the Stalinist period in favor of rapid and large-scale industrialization. Khrushchev also significantly reversed economic inequality and did away with the harsh methods of labor management that characterized the Stalinist Soviet Union. Socially, he eliminated Stalinist repressive measures and adopted a persuasive and conciliatory approach toward the population. He encouraged more openness, which resulted in greater participation, especially by members of the intelligentsia, in governmental programs and processes. The socio-politico-economic model that emerged out of this movement away from Stalinism can be described as an authoritarian socialist reform model.

Essential similarities and differences between the Soviet politico-economic system under Stalin and Khrushchev may be clarified by using T. H. Rigby's (1977) concept of the "mono-organizational society," discussed briefly in Chapter 5. This concept addresses relationships between top political leaders and the bureaucracy. Rigby describes Soviet society as one in which "most activities are directly managed by innumerable organizations of bureaucracies, all of which are linked up in a single organizational system" and command apparatus, in which the party plays a crucial participative, supervisory, and coordinative role (59-60). As such, Soviet society was a "bureaucratic" system but one that departed from the "classical" model of bureaucracy (characterized by clear hierarchical structure and elaborate division of labor) by incorporating overlapping jurisdictions and blurred division of labor through parallel party and governmental hierarchies and methods, including exhortation and heroic demands placed on Soviet managers, designed to mobilize energies for innovation, growth, and change. These features, common to both Stalinist and post-Stalinist periods, "constitute a system qualitatively new in human experience" (61). If to these we add such traditional tyrannical elements as police terror and personal dictatorship, we have a reasonably accurate description of the Stalinist era. Debate continues on whether the more tyrannical features of Soviet communism were "historically necessary" for Soviet industrialization. But by the time of Stalin's death, after a generation of socialization to the system, they were increasingly regarded as unnecessary. Moreover, police repression and personal dictatorship by the leader, like Stalin's heroic strategies, "were increasingly found to be inconsistent with oligarchical rule as well as costly to societal performance, while the defense of those features that constituted the mono-organizational system became the common ground on which the oligarchical consensus rested" (25). The main features of the Khrushchev period are described below using the four criteria developed earlier.

UNDERLYING CAUSES

The origins of Khrushchev's authoritarian reforms can be traced to the following interrelated and interdependent factors.

Khrushchev's Consolidation of Power

Since the Soviet Union lacked constitutional or other institutional procedures for leadership succession,[5] Khrushchev had to defeat his political opponents to emerge as the dominant leader of the country. Like the succession of his predecessor, Stalin, Khrushchev's assumption of the top leadership involved a multiyear struggle of coalition politics, shifting positions, and the eventual consolidation of power. Besides his personality cult and the instrument of secret police terror, Stalin's power and authority was built around two official positions: chairman of the USSR Council of Ministers, which made Stalin the official head of the Soviet government, and secretary of the CPSU Central Committee, which conferred upon him the leadership of the party.[6] To succeed Stalin, therefore, one had to be the Premier as well as the head of the party; that is, leadership of the Communist Party and the Soviet government were combined in one person. The man who succeeded in doing so immediately after the death of Stalin was Georgy Malenkov, who was typically acknowledged as being the heir presumptive of Stalin.[7] Malenkov was appointed the chairman of the Soviet Union Council of Ministers on the day Stalin died. The next day, the Malenkov-Beria leadership placed Malenkov's name at the top of the five-member list of the CPSU Central Committee secretaries. Malenkov, by acquiring the premiership of the Soviet government and the first secretary position of the CPSU, emerged as the new leader of the Soviet Union.

But Malenkov's leadership marked an interregnum in Soviet history.[8] Indeed, none in the Soviet leadership was able to fill the void created by Stalin's death. Malenkov's emergence as the new leader demonstrated the need for an orderly succession of power and continuation of Communist leadership. The issue of Stalin's succession, however, was not resolved; instead, a succession struggle ensued almost immediately among the main contenders for Soviet power.

The struggle for power centered around Malenkov, Lavrenty Beria (head of the secret police), and Khrushchev—"Stalin's three most powerful subordinates during his last years, essentially supervising the state, police, and party apparatuses respectively" (Hough and Fainsod 1979, 198). On March 6, 1953, Malenkov, Beria and Vyacheslav Molotov were appointed chairman and first deputy chairmen of the Soviet Union Council of Ministers, respectively. Khrushchev, still a member of the Presidium, was placed last in the list of five Central Committee secretaries of the party. The eventual triumph of Khrushchev, a distant contender for Stalin's succession, was facilitated by several major developments.

Khrushchev's prospects as a potential leader were heightened within weeks of Stalin's death. On March 14, 1953, Malenkov was forced to relinquish his position as first secretary of the CPSU Central Committee. This development, which many believe Khrushchev himself had organized, confined Malenkov's power to that of the head of government and passed on the party leadership to Khrushchev. In the immediate aftermath, Khrushchev seized the opportunity to deliver the inaugural address at the Central Committee Plenum of September 1953, which not only earned him formal title of the first secretary of the party but also established him as the coequal of Malenkov in Soviet leadership. As de facto head of the CPSU, Khrushchev was now in a position to strengthen his power base in the party by putting his own people in key positions and by transforming the party into the centerpiece of power in the country. Both of Khrushchev's predecessors, Lenin and Stalin, had based their power on the party bureaucracy. The first secretary position provided Khrushchev with the historic route to outmaneuver his rivals and to consolidate his power. The execution of Beria, Stalin's interior minister, in December 1953,[9] within months of Stalin's death, further enhanced Khrushchev's chance for power. Beria's execution eliminated one of the three main contenders of power. Moreover, the fact that Beria, a close lieutenant of Stalin, also belonged to Malenkov's group enhanced Khrushchev's position in the Party.

Khrushchev's position was further strengthened in February 1955 when, following policy differences involving the role of agriculture and light industry in the post-Stalinist Soviet economy, Malenkov resigned from the premiership and Nikolai Bulganin, a Khrushchev nominee and a deputy chairman of the Council of Ministers, was elevated to the position of Premier. Malenkov was demoted to a position of deputy chairman. With Malenkov, Beria, and Molotov outmaneuvered and defeated, Khrushchev emerged as the de facto head of the party and the government. His final triumph came, however, with his speech at the Twentieth Congress of the CPSU in 1956.[10] Khrushchev's calculated attack on Stalin and his excesses ushered in an era of de-Stalinization and made him a familiar figure both inside and outside the country almost instantaneously.[11] The speech also enabled Khrushchev to deal a final blow to his main rivals—Malenkov and Molotov—by associating them with Stalinist excesses and crimes. In addition, by 1957, he had masterfully undermined the power of the government bureaucracy by instituting the Council of National Economy or *sovnarkhozy* (discussed below). The government had long been regarded as the leading political institution in the Soviet Union. Khrushchev's victory in the power struggle elevated the party to that position, a place it retained thereafter.

Obsolescence of the Stalinist Economy

Stalinist totalitarian state economy was successful in its own terms. But the very success of the Stalinist development strategy altered key conditions in the country, which contributed to inconsistency with the highly centralized processes and institutions emphasized by the Stalinist model. First, whatever the suitability of the Stalinist industrialization strategy for transformation from an underdeveloped, dominantly agricultural society to a significantly higher level of economic development, that task had already been largely accomplished. Second, the greater size and complexity of the post-Stalinist economic organization required more sophisticated and finely tuned instruments and methods, which made a command model increasingly obsolete. Third, Draconian sacrifices of consumption in favor of investment, and accompanying institutional processes to enforce them, had a logic and rationale in the 1920s and 1930s that no longer existed. Increased emphasis upon consumption and an increased quality and variety of consumer goods accelerated the obsolescence of Stalinist planning from the center and increased the need for institutional mechanisms to relate production decisions more closely to consumer preferences. Fourth, the lack of a skilled and loyal managerial corps and the need for creating a disciplined labor force could no longer be credibly used as rationales for concentrating and centralizing power and authority for planning and administrative decisions, for these needs had been largely attained. Fifth, revolution, war, civil war, radical institutional transformation, and the danger of counterrevolution no longer credibly justified the maintenance of highly centralized planning structures. With the passage of time, new generations had emerged for whom the revolution was but history, who more or less accepted the basic institutional structure of the society, but who were willing to support reforms or changes.

Sixth, Stalinist industrialization strategy, which was based on extensive methods of production, began to show increasing signs of exhaustiveness. By the end of the Stalinist era, opportunities for substantial economic growth merely by expanding the capital stock (capital widening) were distinctly limited. Growth now required the injection of technological improvements (intensive methods) and careful choices among alternative investments (capital deepening), which in turn required creativity of labor—a feat a highly centralized economy was less equipped to accomplish. Seventh, Stalinist development strategy based on autarky denied Soviet economic development the advantages of international division of labor. Continuation of this policy became increasingly counter-productive in the post-World War II era of global competition. Eighth, with increasing size and complexity, the informational problem of accounting for production plans and performance mounted steadily. The centralization of decisions tended to overlook the particularized knowledge of "time and place" of local administrators and managers. Big, overall decisions applied indiscriminately to wide areas of the economy tended to neglect special features of particular cases and microeconomic interdependencies. Infrequent revision of strategic decisions created an institutional mechanism insufficiently flexible and adaptable to changing circumstances. Therefore, problems of coordination, flexibility, and efficiency of Stalinist planning methodology were increasingly questioned. Finally, the success indicators of the Stalinist system were also criticized for their distorted impacts on incentives. "Success indicators" emphasized target fulfillment in terms of weight or quantity, not in terms of quality. In general, the Stalinist model lacked an integrating, synthesizing success indicator (such as profitability) to enable planners and administrators to evaluate economic performance in a comprehensive way that would not distort local decision making. Therefore, post-Stalinist leaders came under increasing economic, technological, domestic, and global pressures to discontinue or reform the Stalinist model of political economy.

Societal Pressure for Change

Stalin was the linchpin of the whole Soviet system. All powers of the party, society, and state were concentrated in his person, and for decades the dictator single-handedly wielded power so extensively and intensively that his death left a void in all key institutions in the country. With Stalin dead, suppressed aspirations of the people began to surface. It soon became evident that in the Soviet Union of altered conditions and changed circumstances a dictator of the Stalinist variant was neither available nor desirable. The party, state, and society, indeed leaders of all major institutions of the post-Stalinist Soviet Union, demanded new directions and leadership modes, and mass consciousness and optimism fueled the reformist mood to such a scale that only a different kind of personality or set of personalities was viable.

First of all, Soviet society had long been yearning for liberation from systematic use of terror, the state secret police, the threat of concentration camps, and, in general, from a coercive state that used unbridled power to subdue its own population. Stalin's death raised expectations among the masses that new leadership would bring an end to these practices that had crippled society throughout the Stalinist era. Accordingly, the post-Stalinist CPSU felt impelled to abandon its policy of terror-imposed discipline and single-man dictatorship and shift its focus to rule of law and collective leadership. Second, now that industrialization had been achieved, a great majority of the Soviet people aspired to higher standards of living. This, in turn, was translated into greater demand for consumer goods, such as housing, transportation, and health care. Therefore, the source of legitimacy of the state and party shifted to the satisfaction of consumer demands requiring improvement in the standard of living and a shift of emphasis away from heavy to light industries, especially to agriculture.

Third, Stalin bequeathed institutional and policy arrangements in which the exigencies of his personal power had undermined a bureaucratic, rule-based system. With Stalin's death, the single directing center disappeared, and state machineries began to demonstrate an inability to function without personalized guidance and direction. Stalin's successors, therefore, were left with two options: replacement of Stalin with another directing center, that is, continuation of the tradition of a supreme leader; or institutionalization of the state, that is, a streamlining of various bureaucratic structures and hierarchies to formulate and implement necessary policies. Institutionalization of bureaucracy required policy making as an interaction between institutions with less interference from political leadership. Both the post-Stalinist society and the bureaucratic structures exerted considerable pressure for the latter option. Advocates of such a change argued that removal of personal or external interference would help foster professionalization of bureaucracy, and a professional, and therefore impersonal, bureaucracy would promote the rule of law in society. Members of the bureaucracy favored such a change because, in addition to their own job security, it would facilitate professional decision making based on concerns for quality and efficiency (Gill 1987).

Fourth, Stalin's death signified a lessening of the fear of party-government reprisals to creative or nonconformist thinking and actions. In other words, greater freedom in thought and action and the freer use of talents and capacities seemed possible to many in Soviet society. Demand for greater freedom was especially triggered by Khrushchev's address at the Twentieth Congress, which aroused considerable hope and expectation among members of the public. In fact, this speech began the liberation of the Soviet people from Stalinist totalitarianism. As personal safety began to receive legal protection and the penalty for failure was no longer loss of one's life, fuller expression of thoughts, popular desires and grievances began to surface. Moreover, the post-Stalinist leadership, even before the emergence of Khrushchev as the dominant leader, furthered rising expectations of the people by backing the leadership's promises with significant accomplishments. The zeal for reform and change in sensitive and important areas of Soviet life was apparent throughout the Soviet economy in this period. Attention was also directed to comparisons of Soviet technology with that of other countries, and scores of delegations and technicians were sent to Western countries to study new developments in world science and technology.

INSTITUTIONS, PROGRAMS, AND POLICIES

Although Khrushchev was the paramount leader of the Soviet Union for seven years, from 1957 to 1964, he was a key player at the apex of Soviet leadership from Stalin's death in 1953. Many of the measures undertaken during Malenkov's interregnum had Khrushchev's input and support. Indeed, many policies and programs of the Khrushchev era were actually initiated between 1953 and 1957. These measures succeeded in making a transition from totalitarianism to authoritarianism in the Soviet system.

Establishment of the Rule of Law

Khrushchev's period signified a distinctive qualitative change in terms of law and order that marked a sharp discontinuity with the Stalinist rule of terror. Even before Khrushchev opened the floodgates of anti-Stalinism in 1956, the use of secret police terror largely had come to an end following the unconditional release of the Kremlin doctors in April 1953.[12] Release of these doctors came with a governmental promise that henceforth all cases of official "highhandedness and lawlessness" would be severely punished, and the legal rights of Soviet citizens would be safeguarded. The arrest and subsequent execution of Beria and his close associates signified a death blow to the unbridled power of the secret police in Soviet society and the dawn of a law-based society (Hough and Fainsod 1979, 207).

Khrushchev's efforts to establish a law-based society received definitive momentum with his speech given at the Twentieth CPSU Congress. In this speech, Khrushchev dramatically revealed the extent of the Stalinist purges and the costs of Stalin's repression. He accused Stalin of "rude violations of internal party and Soviet democracy, sterile administration, deviations of all sorts, covering up the shortcomings and vanishing of reality." He condemned those who were "blinded and hopelessly hypnotized by the cult of [Stalin's] personality" for not understanding "the essence of the Revolution and of the Soviet state," "the role of the Party and of the people in the development of Soviet society," "in a Leninist manner."[13]

Khrushchev's bold assault on the Stalinist personality cult and totalitarianism in general opened an energetic era of fresh thinking and great optimism in Soviet society.[14] By eliminating the extensive use of terror, he was able to provide a more congenial environment for relatively unconstrained surfacing of new thoughts and ideas. The manifestation of such ideas, especially concerning economic issues, was particularly significant in his period.[15] In the same speech, he also conceded that capitalist countries might attain socialism peacefully, without civil war and even through democratic parliamentary means. Therefore, by rejecting Leninist and Stalinist notions of an inevitable world war between capitalism and socialism, he shifted the Cold War to the economic front and repudiated the logic of accumulation of unlimited power in the hands of the state to defend socialism. His relaxation of foreign policy tensions also signified a diversion of funds from military purposes to expansion of the consumer sector.

Emphasis on Consumer Goods

Khrushchev significantly moderated the Stalinist priority of heavy industries over light industries by emphasizing higher growth rates in the production of consumer goods. Responding to popular desires and grievances in the post-Stalin era, he greatly expanded investment in housing construction, food production, and other consumer goods.[16] He reversed Stalin's policy of building expensive administrative buildings, stadiums, palaces of culture, and so on and allocated more resources to building houses, schools, hospitals and children's institutions in order to reap the benefits of a quarter of a century of rapid industrialization. During this period, both the overall Soviet population and its urban population grew rapidly, and the need for new housing concomitantly expanded. A typical four-room apartment in a Soviet city housed four families. Khrushchev sharply accelerated housing construction. Whereas urban housing completed in 1950 was 24.2 million square meters, in 1958 it had almost tripled, to 70.1 million, and in 1960 it jumped to 82.8 million square meters. Private housing increased by more than 300 percent between 1953 to 1957 (Schwartz 1985, 81-84).

Soviet economy experienced a similar transformation in the areas of health care, education, and social security benefits during this period. The Soviet heath care budget rose to 44.0 billion rubles in 1959 from 21.4 billions rubles in 1950. The budget for education also almost doubled—from 56.9 billion rubles to 94.3 billion rubles in 1959. Social security benefits quadrupled during the same period, from 22 billion rubles in 1950 to 88.2 billion rubles in 1959. In 1959 there were 4.4 million old-age pensioners out of a total of 25.3 million of pensionable age, whereas in 1950 there were fewer than 1 million pensioners. Spectacular progress was also made in respect to durable consumer goods. Whereas in 1958 fewer than 1 million television sets were produced, in 1964 the number had increased threefold—to 3 million sets. Production of other durable consumer goods, such as refrigerators, sewing machines, and washing machines, also increased remarkably. Production of nondurable consumer goods, such as clothing, hosiery, wool, textiles, shoes, and so on, also increased, although less spectacularly.[17]

Reforms in Industrial Management

Khrushchev extensively reorganized the Stalinist system of industrial organization. Besides a political motivation to curb his principal rival Malenkov's power base in the state bureaucracy, his attempt at a sweeping reorganization of the industrial sector was based on two dominant economic considerations: (1) a slowdown of industrial production in the mid-1950s as shown in Table 6.1, and (2) the capital investment crisis of late 1956, which indicated that ambitious targets set forth in the Sixth Five Year Plan might not be attainable. He initiated the so-called *sovnarkhozy* reforms in 1957 by blaming the central ministries for overemphasizing narrow departmental interests, fostering inefficient production and investment decisions, and thereby contributing to waste of scarce resources, overcentralization, and the neglect of regional considerations.

Khrushchev's *sovnarkhozy* reform replaced twenty five major economic ministries of the Soviet central government with 105 regional economic units *(sovnarkhozy)* to be coordinated by newly created Councils of the National Economy. In most cases, a separate *sovnarkhozy* was created for each province and was made subordinate to the republic's Council of Ministers. These measures stripped power from central ministries and transferred responsibility for economic coordination to regional or local bodies (as almost all of these regional economic councils coincided with the boundaries of oblasts or republics). He justified such a sweeping restructuring of industrial organization by arguing that (1) such decentralization would bring the "center of gravity" of public administration "closer to production"; (2) it would make possible the tapping of "reserves that are latent in the socialist economy"; and finally (3) such regional devolution would foster interregional coordination and bring an end to

Table 6.1
Slowdown in Soviet Industrial Production, 1952-1955

Sector	1952 (actual)	1955 (plan)	1955 (actual)
Cotton Textiles*	5,044.0	6,267	5,905.0
Wool Textiles*	190.5	271	252.3
Silk Textiles*	224.6	573	525.8
Knitted Underwear**	234.9	382	346.5
Knitted Outerwear**	63.5	88	85.1
Hosiery***	584.9	777	772.2
Leather Footwear***	237.7	318	274.3
Sewing Machines****	804.5	2,615	1,610.9
Bicycles****	1,650.4	3,445	2,883.8
Motorcycles****	104.4	225	244.5
Watches/Clocks****	10,486.0	22,000	19,705.0
Radios/TVs****	1,331.9	4,527	4,024.6
Refrigerators****	----	330	151.4

*Million meters. ** Million units. ***Million pairs. **** thousand units.

Source: Nove (1969, 325).

functional biases and blinders built into the national ministerial system (Breslauer 1982, 74).

Agricultural Reforms

Khrushchev's preoccupation with agriculture dates back to the Stalinist days. Indeed, one of the major criticisms of Stalinism that he raised in his so-called secret speech of 1956 was Stalin's vehement opposition to increased investment in agriculture. Khrushchev replaced the Stalinist strategy based on extraction of surpluses from agriculture for industrialization, by a policy of expansion of the agricultural sector itself. Immediately after Stalin's death, the tax burden and delivery quotas for peasants were lowered, and procurement prices for both compulsory deliveries and above-quota agricultural products were raised. As a result, compared to 1952, state procurement prices for agricultural goods increased 2.6 times in 1957. Kolkhoz revenue and wages in the agricultural sector experienced similar increases.

In 1954 Khrushchev launched a grandiose agricultural campaign, the so-called Virgin Lands Program, to bring millions of square acres of unused land in Kazakhstan, Siberia, the northern Caucasus, the Volga, and the eastern regions of the Soviet Union under grain cultivation. Denouncing the plans of others, Malenkov for example, who emphasized importing food from abroad and shifts in resources from heavy industry to expansion of consumer goods, Khrushchev called for increased domestic production of foodstuffs by bringing vast unused lands under cultivation and without requiring deep cuts in the heavy-industrial sector or increased imports from abroad. He vastly increased the supply of agricultural machinery by almost doubling the productive investment in agriculture. Capital stock in agriculture increased at an average annual rate of 11.3 percent from 1953 to 1958. The share of agriculture in total Soviet investment expenditures rose from 13.7 percent in 1952 to 17.6 percent in 1956.

Table 6.2
Indexes of Farm Prices Paid by the Soviet Government, 1954-1958 (1952=100)

Product	1954	1956	1958
All farm products	207	251	296
All crops	171	207	203
Wheat	752	647	621
Rye	730	625	1047
Corn	564	572	819
Rice	243	887	957
Cotton	102	114	106
Flax fiber	166	213	239
Sugar beers	111	229	219
Sunflower	626	928	774
Potatoes	369	814	789
All livestock	307	371	546
Cattle	476	508	1147
Hogs	786	976	1156
Milk/milk products	289	334	404
Eggs	135	155	297
Wool	146	246	352

Source: Schwartz (1965, 120).

Subsequently, it fell to 14.2 percent in 1960 and then again increased to 17.4 percent in 1964. Originally designed for 32 million acres of land in 1953, the Virgin Lands Program had expanded to 101 million acres by 1960. Overall, the Virgin Lands Program contributed to a dramatic success in the agricultural sector. Agricultural performance improved both in terms of total output and marketed output of grain. The average annual output of grain increased from 80.9 million tons in 1949-1953 to 110.3 million tons in 1954-1958 to 124.7 million tons in 1959-1963. State grain procurement increased from an annual average of 32.8 million tons in 1949-1953 to 46.5 million tons in 1954-1963. The number of cattle increased from 56.6 million in 1953 to 66.8 million in 1958; gross output of meat increased from 5.8 million tons in 1953 to 7.7 million tons in 1958; and milk production increased from 36.5 million tons in 1953 to 58.7 million tons in 1958.

In March 1955, kolkhozy were allowed, within certain constraints, to decide their own production targets, and the planners' authority was restricted to specifying the delivery obligations of the kolkhozy. Kolkhozy were amalgamated into larger state farms, and over 20 thousand specialists and party workers were transferred to the countryside to help boost agricultural production. As a result, the number of kolkhozy dropped to 67,700 in 1958 from 91,200 in 1953. The number of state farms, on the other hand, grew from 4,857 in 1953 to 6,002 in 1958. Whereas in 1953 only 18.2 million hectares of land were sown, the area was increased to 97.43 million hectares in 1965. In 1965 the state and collective farms employed 8.6 million people; in 1953 the number stood at 2.6 million.

Khrushchev sought to eliminate arbitrary bureaucratic control and stressed scientific calculation of costs for agricultural production and economic incentives for farmers. He proposed a wage system that would permit collective farmers to receive monthly monetary payments. Previously, the same agricultural product could have three different prices: one for selling it to the state as a part of the compulsory delivery quota, another if it was an above-quota sale, and still another if it was delivered to the machine tractor station (MTS) as a payment in kind. Khrushchev replaced this system by the principle of the same price for the same product grown in the same area. Thus different agricultural products in different zones had different prices. Table 6.2 shows the indexes of average state prices paid for procurement from collective farms, collective farmers, and other workers and employees. Khrushchev instituted the same wholesale prices for both state and collective farms for purchasing farm machinery and other production essentials. Previously kolkhozy had been charged much higher prices than state farms for essentials of agricultural production.

Another notable institutional change in agriculture that occurred during Khrushchev's era was the eventual elimination of the MTSs in 1958. Previously, government-owned MTSs, one of the basic features of the Stalinist system, controlled services of tractors, grain combines, and similar heavy equipment on which kolkhozy depended. With the merger of kolkhozy, larger state farms were now capable of making efficient use of power-driven machinery. At the same time, improved financial strength of the state farms made a separate existence of MTSs redundant.[18]

Reforms in Wages, Incentives, and Prices

Some of the most daunting economic problems that Khrushchev faced in the post-Stalin Soviet Union were low morale, widespread absenteeism, deliberate squandering of time by workers, and above all, unsatisfactory performance of the industrial workforce. All these were offshoots of the Stalinist industrial management that suppressed any genuine possibility of collective bargaining by workers. Stalin criminalized job changing and truancy, introduced compulsory labor service for youth, and directed skilled workers and specialists to jobs anywhere in the country. As a consequence, the only power workers had to compensate for their grievances was passive restriction in the supply of their labor. Liberalization of Stalinist society thus demanded fundamental reforms in labor policy so that productivity could be raised, workers' motivation could be improved, and legitimacy of the government could be restored to the working population.

Given these objectives, in 1956, Khrushchev revoked the 1941 law that provided criminal penalties for labor turnover, that is, changing jobs or quitting jobs voluntarily. Workers' use of the new-found freedom of mobility could be gauged from the fact that, following Khrushchev's April 1956 decree, industrial turnover rose sharply, from 15 percent of the workforce in 1950 to 38 percent in 1958. He also raised wages and shortened the workweek. As a result, whereas the industrial worker's average annual income was 925 rubles in 1950, it stood at 1,240 rubles in 1961. This increase in workers' wages and salaries resulted in a significant reduction in the inequality of income characteristic of the Stalinist command economy. Although the basic six-day workweek was retained, during 1957-1958 a seven-hour workday was introduced generally and a six-hour day was introduced primarily for underground or especially hazardous occupations. Khrushchev also replaced the Stalinist industrial wage system—with its thousands of pay scales that were differentially applied in factories, industries, ministries, and departments—by a nationally applicable wage structure with a small number of simplified scales. As a result, workers of a given occupation could receive the same wages regardless of their location of employment.

As we have seen in preceding chapters, the Bolshevik Revolution and its aftermath had egalitarian effects on income distribution through the confiscation of property and virtual abolition of property income (interest, land rents, dividends). These were partially offset by increased wage differentials under the NEP, so that by 1928 the spread between high and low wages was nearly equivalent to that in the United States at the same time (Wiles 1977, 438). Under Stalin, wage inequality grew, stimulated largely by a desire to encourage the acquisition of labor skills perceived to be strategic for industrialization. Peasant incomes also differed significantly, based on differential labor and skills, and were substantially lower than those of industrial workers, perpetuating and extending labor income inequalities. After Stalin's death, notably in the Khrushchev years, Soviet wage inequality decreased dramatically, stimulated apparently by the successful achievement of a larger supply of skilled labor and by an undersupply of unskilled labor. Wage differentials between skilled and unskilled labor were decreased, basic wages were raised, piecework was reduced, and prices paid to collective farms were increased.[19]

Khrushchev initiated a number of measures to increase industrial efficiency, reduce production costs, and make more efficient use of productive resources. He set up Communist party control commissions in industrial and trade enterprises to check on the punctual fulfillment of delivery schedules and production quotas by enterprises. Success indicators used to determine managerial bonuses in nonpriority industries were changed. Instead of focusing on reaching or exceeding output targets, bonuses were made dependent primarily upon a manager's ability to produce at lower costs. Managers were asked to turn out high-quality goods, to deliver commodities on time, and to emphasize qualitative aspects of work.

Khrushchev also enhanced labor unions' prestige by empowering them to establish a permanent production conference in each enterprise. The factory union committees had the power to review and, if necessary, to revoke or change decisions on disputes between individual workers and management. Enterprise management was prohibited from firing any worker or appointing any new worker without the union's consent. Labor unions were consulted over a wide range of other matters, from distribution of bonuses to establishment of wage categories for different jobs. Unions had the right to call for the removal or punishment of production executives who failed to carry out obligations under collective agreements. At the national level, all important decisions of the State Committee on Labor and Wages, which was responsible for basic labor policy, had to be approved by the national labor union leadership.[20]

In addition, labor unions came to play a larger role in helping to administer enterprise funds for incentives, sociocultural activities, welfare, and housing; supervising the maintenance of facilities and safety devices for workers; and representing individual workers in grievances against management. As a result of the Khrushchev reforms, according to Alec Nove, unions "do in fact have powers to protect members against arbitrary acts of neglect on the part of the management. Indeed, the powers are there and are impressive" (1977, 225). The role of Soviet workers in industrial policy decisions from the late 1950s onward was smaller than that envisaged in the classic Marxian images of a future socialist economy and than that apparently achieved under "workers' self-management" in Yugoslavia. But, especially during the Khrushchev era, "workers' participation in industrial management goes considerably beyond that found in American firms and... workers have a real say in enterprise decision making" (Szymanski 1979, 53; Conquest 1967).

Wages in the Soviet Union, between 1960 and 1977, rose at an annual average rate of 3.9 percent (Gregory and Stuart 1981, 364). The course of real wages, therefore, depended on the extent of price inflation. Whereas American businesses operate in a "relatively unplanned, low-pressure economy" characterized much of the time by excess supply and "buyers' markets," Soviet managers functioned in a "rigorously planned, high pressure economy" with accompanying excess demands and "sellers' markets" (Gruchy 1977, 471). We would expect, therefore, that the former economy would tend toward unemployment and the latter toward inflation. Concerning the Soviet Union, this expectation is fulfilled for the periods from 1928 to 1937 and from 1941 to 1947, when the annual inflation rates indicated by official Soviet data were 20.5 and 18.1 percent, respectively (Nuti 1986, 333-53).

In the Khrushchev and early Brezhnev years (1958-1971), some of the inflationary pressures of the 1930s and 1940s continued, although in moderated form, for example, wage increases, high government demand, taut planning, shortages of particular products because of microeconomic imbalances, and increases in the money supply. However, inflation rates in official Soviet price indexes in the post-Stalin years were essentially zero (Nuti 1986). Western analysts typically have been skeptical about Soviet price statistics, citing indicators of both "repressed inflation" (queues, waiting lists, increases in the magnitudes of saving accounts) and "hidden inflation" (higher prices in free Kolkhoz markets and the practice of claiming minor quality changes as a basis to raise prices) (Kornai 1992, 255). Several Western studies (for example, Schroeder and Severin 1976, 631) estimate an adjusted average annual inflation rate in the Soviet Union at about 1.5 percent in the 1960s and early 1970s. This compares quite favorably with the higher inflation rates both of the Stalin era and of Western capitalist economies in the postwar years, and yields an average annual rate of growth in real wages of about 2.4 percent.

It seems reasonable to attribute this result to the institutions and processes of the Soviet economic system, notably, the insulation of the domestic economy from perturbations of international price changes through the state monopoly of foreign trade, and state direct controls of prices and wages as well as physical allocations, and to Khrushchev's policies of expanding living standards, reduced income inequality, and material incentives.

CONSEQUENCES

Khrushchev's period was marked by a remarkable improvement in the household sector, increased availability of all sorts of consumer goods, an increase in housing

Table 6.3
Selected Macroeconomic Growth Rates of the Soviet Union, 1955-1962

Year	Growth in National Income Produced	Growth in Labor Productivity	Growth in Real Per capita Income
1955	11.9	9.5	0.9
1956	11.3	7.0	5.9
1957	7.0	6.6	8.7
1958	12.4	6.2	5.9
1959	7.5	7.4	1.8
1960	7.7	5.4	6.4
1961	6.8	4.4	1.6
1962	5.7	5.5	3.2

Source: Hewett (1988, 226)

construction, extension of educational and medical facilities, and a substantial decrease in income inequality. Soviet national income registered an average annual growth rate of 8.8 percent during the period from 1955 to 1962.[21] As Table 6.3 shows, Soviet labor productivity increased at an annual rate of 6.5 percent, and real per capita income grew at an annual rate of 4.3 percent during the same period. The overall growth rate of the economy, however, slowed down after 1958, following significant growth between 1955 and 1958. A similar tendency can be noticed in labor productivity and real per capita income.

Growth in housing construction exceeded the growth of the urban population. As discussed before, housing construction increased from 24.2 million square meters in 1950 to 75.1 million square meters in 1964. Overall performance in the consumption sector was very strong during Khrushchev's period. As Table 6.4 shows, the rate of growth in the production of consumer goods ranged from 8 to 13 percent from 1954 to 1959. In the 1960s, the growth rate fell, however, to 7 percent, then to only 2 percent. The rate of growth in heavy industry remained double digit throughout the Khrushchev years, although it dropped a bit in the late 1950s and early 1960s compared to the reference year of 1954. The all-industry growth rate, which combines performance in both heavy industry and consumption, was 10 percent or above between 1954 and 1960, and ranged between 7.5 percent and 10 percent in the early

Table 6.4
Annual Growth Rates of Soviet Industrial Production, 1954 and 1958-1964

Year	All Industry	Heavy Industry	Consumer Goods
1954	13	14	13
1958	10	11	8
1959	11	12	10
1960	10	11	7
1961	9	10	7
1962	9.5	11	7
1963	8.5	10	5
1964 (first half)	7.5	10	2

Source: Schwartz (1965, 124).

Table 6.5
Soviet Grain Production, 1953-1962 (millions of metric tons)

Year	Total Grain Harvest	Basic Virgin Areas*	Rest of the Country
1953	82.5	26.9	55.6
1954	85.6	37.3	48.3
1955	106.8	27.7	79.1
1956	127.6	63.3	64.3
1957	105.0	38.1	66.9
1958	141.2	58.4	82.8
1959	125.9	55.3	70.6
1960	134.4	59.2	75.2
1961	138.0	51.3	86.7
1962	148.2	56.4	91.8

* Includes Kazakhstan, the Urals, Siberia, and part of the Volga region.

Source: Reconstructed from Schwartz (1965, 107 and 131).

1960s. Overall, during the period from 1956 to 1960, production of consumer durable goods grew at 10.4 percent annually. Annual industrial production increased more than 50 percent between 1958 and 1963. The growth rate, however, was higher in the heavy industry sector compared to the consumer goods sector. The consumer goods sector grew only 36 percent during the same period.

Agricultural production experienced sharp ups and downs during Khrushchev's era. As Table 6.5 shows, whereas the total grain harvest was 82.5 million metric tons in 1953, Soviet grain production had increased to 148.2 million metric tons by 1962. Overall, the growth rate of agricultural output was more than 7 percent between 1954 and 1959. It then fell to from 1.5 to 2 percent from 1960 to 1964. Indeed, in 1963, Khrushchev himself was forced to acknowledge that the policy of developing an extensive agriculture, represented by the Virgins Land Program, ultimately had failed.

Measures undertaken by Khrushchev substantially improved living standards. Average wages rose significantly. In 1950 the average wage of state employees was 64 rubles per month; by 1964, it had increased to 96 rubles, registering an annual increase of from 2.8 to 2.9 percent during this period. Also, in 1953, there was no legal minimum wage in the Soviet Union. In 1956 a minimum wage was adopted, which became universalized by 1965 (McAuley 1987, 138-55). As already noted, decreases in wage differentials between skilled and unskilled labor substantially reduced income inequality in the Soviet Union in the Khrushchev years. Between 1956 and 1964, the ratio of average wages for the top 10 percent of workers to the bottom 10 percent fell, from 4.4 to 3.3, a reduction of one-third (Yanowitch 1977, 25). Comparatively, the distribution of money income after taxes in the Soviet Union in the late 1960s "was more unequal than in the other planned socialist economies of Eastern Europe, was about equal to the distribution of income in the capitalist welfare states (the United Kingdom and Sweden), and was more equal than in the capitalist nonwelfare states (the United States, Canada, and Italy)" (Gregory and Stuart 1981, 353).[22]

Khrushchev's emphasis on the consumption sector also resulted in a large expansion in health care and educational opportunities. The number of medical doctors

Table 6.6
Differential Annual Growth Rates in Soviet Consumption and Investment, 1928-1978

	Household Consumption	Gross Investment	1/2
1928-1937	0.7	14.5	0.05
1950-1955	8.7	8.7	1.00
1958-1964	4.8	7.4	0.65
1965-1969	6.2	6.8	0.91
1970-1978	3.4	5.7	0.35

Source: Gregory and Stuart (1981, 337).

increased from 347,600 in 1958 to 484,000 in 1965, and the number of hospital beds increased from 1,533,000 to 2,224,000 during the same period. The number of teachers, which was 1,733,000 in 1955, had increased to 2,497,000 by 1965. The number of students increased from 30,070,000 to 48,245,000 during the same period (Nove 1969, 343-45). The heightened focus on consumption in the Khrushchev period may be shown also by comparative data on the rates of growth in both aggregate consumption and investment and per capita consumption. Table 6.6 shows that the rate of growth in Soviet investment in the 1930s (14.5 percent) was twenty times as high as the growth rate in its consumption (0.7 percent). In the postwar period, both the late Stalin-Makenkov years and the Khrushchev era, the rate of growth in investment fell and the rate of growth in consumption rose. It is notable, however, that investment under Khrushchev continued to grow more rapidly than did consumption.

A broadly similar pattern may be seen in per capita consumption. Table 6.7 shows two main points of interest. First, the rapid growth rate in per capita consumption in the 1950s and 1960s (which includes the Khrushchev years), of 4.5 percent, contrasts starkly with the negligible growth rate, of 1.1 percent, during the Stalin period from 1928 to 1937. Second, the robust growth rate in Soviet per capita consumption from 1950 to 1969 significantly exceeded that in the United States and other Western capitalist countries. Table 6.8 indicates four main points. First, because of the faster growth rates in the Soviet Union during the Khrushchev (and early Brezhnev) years, the gap between per capita consumption (and per capita GNP) in the Soviet Union and Western capitalist countries fell. Second, although the relative gap was thus reduced, the absolute gaps remaining by 1970 were still fairly large. Third, the gap was greater in per capita consumption than in per capita GNP, indicating in another way the heavier priority placed on investment relative to consumption in the Soviet Union as compared to capitalist economics. Fourth, the gaps were greater between the Soviet

Table 6.7
Growth of Per Capita Consumption in the Soviet Union and the United States, 1928-1978

	Soviet Union		United States
1928-1978	2.8	1869-73 to 1927-29	2.4
1928-1937	1.1	1929-1978	1.7
1950-1969	4.5	1950-1969	2.3
1970-1978	2.5	1970-1978	2.7

Source: Gregory and Stuart (1981, 360).

Table 6.8
Per Capita Consumption and GNP of Soviet Union as Percentage of the United States and Other Countries, 1955 and 1970 (valued in United States Prices)

USSR as a Percent of:	1955		1970	
	Total Per Capita Consumption	GNP Per Capita	Total Per Capita Consumption	GNP Per Capita
United States	27	36	47	60
United Kingdom	41	53	67	88
France	47	59	61	73
West Germany	48	57	69	75
Italy	79	94	86	109
Japan	--	--	84	88

Source: Gregory and Stuart (1981, 357).

Union and the United States than other capitalist countries. For example, by 1970, Soviet per capita consumption was 84 percent of Japan's and Soviet per capita GNP had surpassed that of Italy.

Politically, the most significant contribution of the Khrushchev era was a transition from the Stalinist totalitarian state based on secret police terror to a more law-based authoritarian system of government. Khrushchev's emphasis on socialist legality, the relative openness of society, and social and economic equality contributed to a sense of "personal safety among the top elite," the rise of certain informal "constitutional restraints" on the actions of the leader, and an increase in the "degree of consultation on top policy decisions" (Hough and Fainsod 1979, 236). Finally, by accepting his abrupt dismissal from leadership in 1964, Khrushchev demonstrated that Soviet leaders could retire and still remain alive.

TENSIONS AND CONTRADICTIONS

Khrushchev's seven years of leadership covered a momentous period in Soviet history marked by dramatic changes in the Soviet people's hopes and expectations, bold policy and program initiatives and tumultuous reversals, and climactic national and international events. He not only repudiated the Stalinist cult, he also rocked the economic, political, and ideological foundations of Soviet society and thereby created not only powerful enemies, but also far-reaching tensions and contradictions in the Soviet Union. First of all, he consolidated his leadership with a bold speech that attacked Stalin and his personality cult. He criticized Stalin for "administrative violence, mass repressions, and terror" and the "moral and physical annihilation" of the Soviet people. In the same speech, he praised Stalin for his "heroic" contributions to the collectivization and industrialization programs conducted during the 1930s, which were accomplished partly through the repressive measures that he denounced. His radical attacks on Stalin succeeded in opening a floodgate of anti-Stalinism from the reformist segment of Soviet society and intimidated the conservatives who feared that anti-Stalinism could get out of control and inflame discontents in Soviet society at large. Indeed, it was the conservatives who orchestrated Khrushchev's eventual ouster from power in 1964.[23]

As noted earlier, the easing of repression and the substitution of oligarchic, collective leadership (with Khrushchev as chief executive) for Stalin's secret police terror and personal dictatorship marked a shift from totalitarian to authoritarian rule. It also indicated certain internal tensions or contradictions and served as a harbinger of a process of disintegration of the Soviet system which came to fruition thirty years later during the rule of Mikhail Gorbachev.

One major contradiction was that the easing of repression had "mixed effects." Stalin's use of terror contained powerful elements of irrationality and disfunctionality. Many innocent persons were imprisoned or executed, causing intense stress, alienation, and feelings of injustice. The reassurance that loyal service would not lead to coercive punishment in the interest of a higher rationality reduced the "tension in the bureaucracy, so helping to stabilize the reform." However, this left "greater scope for criticism and opposing views within the bureaucracy, so weakening one of the classical Stalinist system's basic cohesive forces: iron discipline extorted by fear" (Kornai 1992, 412). Thus, one of the crucial pillars of the party-state's monopoly of power and control was eroded.

Khrushchev's condemnation of Stalin's use of terror, in his 1956 "secret speech," solidified his claim to power and justified the easing of repression, the release of political prisoners, and movement toward a "rule of law." But it also brought about a "moral crisis" among the intelligentsia and the bureaucracy, many of whom presumably felt duped and betrayed by their leaders. A politically directed system requires a ruling and bureaucratic elite that is "dedicated and disciplined in a common belief" (Solo 1967, 59) or widely shared ideology, and is devoted to an ideal transcending their own self-seeking interests, in effect, to a "religious structure of consciousness" (Horvat 1982, 28) based on authority and faith. In this context, the revelation of crimes against the faith by (former) leading authority engenders a deep sense of disappointment, with profound spillover effects, such as commitment to reform and questioning the sagacity of all, including new, leadership. Under these circumstances, "revision of the earlier official ideology is inevitable." Ideology in a period of reform, such as that exemplified by Khrushchev, is "far less consistent" than the earlier Stalinist faith and "contains many more internal contradictions." Moreover, because modifications of an original ideological edifice based on critique of its excesses stimulates additional critique and further modifications, the dynamic result is likely to be a process of "steady disintegration" (Kornai 1992, 414-18), thereby causing a breach in a second pillar of monopoly state power and party control.

Although Khrushchev criticized or abandoned certain elements of Stalinism, he retained others, notably the aspiration of continued industrialization and economic development and a belief in the superiority of the Soviet brand of socialism, as embodied in such institutions as state ownership, collective farms, bureaucratic coordination, centralized planning, and, above all, the dominant position and leadership role of the party in guiding the nation's development. Consequently, a high participation rate by the able-bodied, working-age population in the labor force (about 92 percent during Khrushchev's tenure) and the full employment of everyone willing and able to work continued to be essential ingredients of Soviet development strategy and continued to militate against such negative economic sanctions as dismissal and unemployment as means of imposing labor discipline. With political repression and ideology diminished as motivators, and discipline through negative economic sanction continuing to occupy a position in the basement of the Soviet incentives system, Khrushchev turned to the remaining logical alternative: material incentives.[24]

The expanded use of material incentives contained both advantages and disadvantages. Stalin, too, had used material incentives as a component of his industrial strategy. But, given the intense pace of industrialization and unusually strong emphasis on investment over consumption, industry over agriculture, and heavy industry over light industry, the corollary of material benefits for the few was deprivation for the many, especially the peasantry. Khrushchev had the advantage of a much higher level of output and resources than did Stalin at the outset of the industrialization process in the late 1920s. This, combined with a revision of planning priorities so as to give greater attention to consumption, agriculture, and light industry, enabled him to provide material inducements to a much larger fraction of the underlying population and to structure the material incentive system in an egalitarian, rather than inegalitarian, manner. One may suppose that such a "goulash communism," as Khrushchev's strategy was quickly christened by the Western press, was widely popular.

On the other hand, this intense focus on material incentives contained significant limitations for the long-run institutional stability of the Soviet system. Khrushchev's strategy presupposed the very optimistic assumptions that (1) the Soviet growth rate(s) would continue to exceed the growth rates(s) of the Western capitalist countries indefinitely and (2) the Soviet Union would catch up with and surpass the capitalist countries in a relatively short period of time. Thus, the perceived superiority of the Soviet version of socialism over Western-style capitalism came to hinge primarily on economic performance (rather on such lofty socialist ideals as overturning exploitation, emancipating human labor, and ending tyrannical subordination to the division of labor), indeed, economic performance of a particular sort, that is, achievement of higher levels of individual consumer goods. This ideological reconceptualization, however brash and aggressive ("your grandchildren will live under socialism," "we shall bury you"), both put all of Khrushchev's "eggs in one basket" and was extremely fragile in the sense that Soviet socialism's superiority over capitalism now came to be perceived as depending on a particular and optimistic pattern and pace of economic performance. If Soviet economic growth were to falter or Western economic growth were to improve, or if external circumstances were to require major shifts in priorities toward military spending, Khrushchev's optimistic expectations could become a chimera and, as a corollary, the much vaunted Soviet superiority and, with it, the basis for the perceived sense of legitimacy of the post-Stalinist system among the underlying population as well as lower level bureaucrats and managers could be severely threatened.

Khrushchev's reforms sought to dismantle only certain selected aspects of Stalinist totalitarianism, leaving others, notably the leading position of unified party and state control, unchanged. This turned out to be unrealistic. Although elements of pluralism and decentralization were not dominant during the Khrushchev era, they became stronger and served as forerunners of centrifugal forces that ultimately dissolved the Soviet system. These openings toward pluralism included increased bargaining among such contending power blocs as the party, the industrial administration, the army, and the secret police; increased strength of regional, local, national, and ethnic groups; a diminished role of labor unions as mere transmitters of the goals of the politocracy and their corollary increased independence and influence on industrial management, as noted earlier; and reestablishment of liberal (reform) and conservative factions within the party, analogous to the Bolshevik experience in the 1920s (Kornai 1992, 418-23).

Khrushchev sought to combine retention of centralized planning with economic reforms to improve overall efficiency and growth. But several of the policies and programs designed to accomplish this difficult blend were inconsistent, self-contradictory, and insufficiently thought out. He often announced bold policy innovations from which he later retreated. For example, his much celebrated decentralization of economic administration, the *sovnarkhozy* reform of 1957, was abandoned in 1961. The *sovnarkhozy* reform was initially justified on the grounds that it would eliminate central bureaucratic control, ensure decentralization, and improve productivity and output with the support of local party activism. But soon it was discovered that the *sovnarkhozy* were too small for efficient operation of the economy. Accordingly, the former 100 or so *sovnarkhozy* were merged into fewer than 50 in 1961. Khrushchev set up seventeen Councils of Coordination and Planning, each with wide powers over a large economic region consisting on an average of six or seven former *sovnarkhozy*. Thus, beginning with a plan for decentralization, he ended up with recentralization and consequent sustenance of power by the centralized bureaucracy.

More fundamentally, regional organization of economic planning, in principle, reduces some of the problems of organization by industries (the pre-*sovnarkhozy* mode), for example, the proclivity toward industrial empire building and neglect of interconnections among industries. Regional organization of decision making fostered closer attention to interindustry connections within industries, but exhibited an analogous problem of its own, namely, a tendency toward regional empire building and neglect of interrelationships among regions. Ultimately, the only solution was to recentralize, and, as a corollary, return to the original set of problems. As long as managers and administrators were judged by achievement of planning targets, they tended to try to please superiors in the vertical, hierarchical chain of authority; consequently, they tended to neglect customers, whether enterprises or consumers (although different ones), in either mode of organization.

Several of Khrushchev's reforms were abandoned because of conservative opposition. For example, he initiated a dramatic educational reform in 1958 to provide a comprehensive boarding school system so that, among others, working-class and peasant children would receive greater access to education. At the same time, to combine education with work, he sought to replace the existing universal ten-year secondary education for all (ages seven to seventeen or eighteen), with universal education through the eighth grade (seven to fifteen). Completion of the eighth grade would allow students to receive additional polytechnic education while at work. Higher education was to be preceded by at least two year of employment. Facing opposition, he reversed the decision in 1964.

Khrushchev also initiated sweeping political reforms. His 1962 reforms divided the whole Communist party at all levels—local, provincial and republican—into two separate sections: an industrial party, exclusively dealing with industry; and an agricultural party, concerned with agricultural issues. Such a bifurcation was intimately connected with his long-term effort to shift the focus of party policy to agriculture and the consumer, and away from steel and defense. Along with the *sovnarkhozy* reforms, such party bifurcation was expected to shift power of operational guidance of the economy from the state to the party. But soon, facing an uphill challenge by the bureaucracy and widespread criticism from the party itself, Khrushchev had to eliminate the bifurcation of the CPSU.

Another troublesome inconsistency of Khrushchev's regime arose from his commitment to the consumer sector. In the immediate aftermath of Stalin's death, mainly to combat his principal rival Malenkov, Khrushchev insisted on the continuation of the priority of heavy industry over consumer industry. Later on, he reversed the policy by officially proclaiming priority to light over heavy industry. Yet the actual economic indicators demonstrated an unmistakable priority given to the producers' goods sector. In 1963 heavy industry accounted for almost 75 percent of all Soviet industrial production, while in 1952 the corresponding share of heavy industry was less than 70 percent. Also, the seven-year plan for 1959-1965 was much less consumer oriented than the Sixth Five Year Plan. Capital investment in agriculture also lagged much behind that in heavy industry.

Khrushchev's policy of openness encouraged wider public participation in debate over government programs. Such participation was spectacular among economists. With his blessings, Soviet economists enjoyed wider latitude in expressing their views on reforming the economic system. In the late 1950s and early 1960s, a powerful reform movement sprang up that demanded adoption of "profit" criteria in the operation of Soviet industrial enterprises, as illustrated by the work of Evsey G. Liberman, discussed in Chapter 7. This movement identified two powerful sources of inefficiency in Soviet planning: (1) enterprises demonstrated a tendency to construct modest plans because bonuses were based on plan fulfillment or over fulfillment and (2) central planning directives to enterprises inhibited managers' freedom of action and hindered their ability to make the best use of the resources at their disposal. The critics of centralized planning called for substantial economic reform of the planning system, including use of the rate of profit earned on total capital invested in an enterprise as the basis for incentive payments. Discussion of reform proposals, presumably with the blessings of government, not only exposed many problems in Soviet economy and society, it also undercut the theoretical foundations of traditional economic policy and created powerful political grounds in favor of change.

Despite tentative steps in the direction of economic reform, however, Khrushchev did not definitively embrace or implement programs to decentralize economic planning or seriously extend the role of market economy. Partly, no doubt, this is explained by his own misgivings about decentralizing and marketizing reforms. But, more fundamentally, radical economic reforms would have ruptured the consensus among leaders of the party, state, and administrative hierarchies. That consensus featured a rejection of such prominent elements of Stalinist totalitarianism as the personal tyranny of one-man rule and secret police terror, but essentially it retained intact a commitment to a hierarchically structured, centralized planning system. A thoroughgoing incorporation of profitability criteria, for example, as proposed by Liberman and others, could very well require systemic reforms in the entire economic mechanism of central planning, for instance, increased use of markets and market prices, and possible changes in the accountability and financial autonomy of enterprises. Because such radical change was discordant with commitment to the perceived party/state direction of the national economy through the central planning system, especially by its conservative adherents, the potential extent of feasible reform in that system was limited.

Khrushchev's de-Stalinization policy also backfired internationally. It fed Eastern European unrest which culminated in revolts in Poland and Hungary (and, later, in Czechoslovakia). The conservatives used the revolts to press their demands for moderation of the de-Stalinization campaign and to curb Khrushchev's power. His programs and policies, therefore, created powerful enemies in the government and in the party, both inside and outside the Soviet Union. Especially with the declining performance of the Soviet economy in the early 1960s, his rivals succeeded in accumulating enough strength to oust him from power in October 1964.

NOTES

1. Khrushchev was born in Kalinovka, a village at the Russian and Ukraine borders, on April 17, 1894. Son of a peasant-turned-miner, Khrushchev joined the Communist party in 1918 at the age of twenty four. He was appointed a member of the CPSU Central Committee in 1934 and, as a supporter of Stalin, thrived during the Stalinist regime. In 1949 Khrushchev became a secretary of the CPSU Central Committee and a member of the Politburo charged with the agricultural sector. After Stalin's death, Khrushchev, at the age of fifty nine, launched his campaign to succeed Stalin from this position.

2. The Soviet Union was ruled by a "collective leadership" during the interval. Georgy Malenkov, who was considered to be Stalin's successor, was the leader of the collective leadership until 1955. But the leadership issue remained unsettled as Khrushchev, considered to be a distant contender for power at the time of Stalin's death, mounted a formidable challenge to Malenkov's leadership.

3. The Soviet Union acquired the thermonuclear device in August 1953, the second nation to do so after the United States. In 1957 the Soviet Union launched the first Sputnik, demonstrating its intercontinental ballistic missile (ICBM) capabilities. By 1959 Khrushchev claimed that nuclear parity with the United States had been achieved.

4. Referring to this period's optimism thirty years later, Mikhail Gorbachev (1988a, 418) made the following statement at the Seventieth Anniversary of the Bolshevik Revolution: "A wind of change swept the country, the people's spirit rose, they took heart, became bolder and more confident."

5. Neither the Communist party statutes nor the Soviet constitution recognized the problem of leadership succession in the Soviet Union. Soviet society was conceived as a harmonious body requiring unified leadership. Political office bearers were considered only as the agents of the CPSU, which, in turn, was considered an organic part of the Soviet population, governed by collective leadership.

6. At the time of Stalin's death, there was no position called general secretary of the CPSU. In his last days, Stalin came to be known as the first secretary. This tradition was continued until 1966.

7. Malenkov became a member of the Communist party Central Committee in 1934. Made a secretary of the Central Committee in 1939, he was elevated to candidate membership in the Politburo in 1941 and became a full member in 1946. Fifty one years old in 1953, Malenkov had worked closely with Stalin since 1941. Stalin began to confer significant powers on to

Malenkov in 1948 when Malenkov's principal rival for Stalin's succession, Zhdanov, died. At the Nineteenth Party Congress held in 1952, Stalin allowed Malenkov to deliver the major report of the Central Committee, providing a clear indication that Malenkov was Stalin's heir apparent.

8. Malenkov's interregnum was known for the "New Course," that he introduced in March 1953, emphasizing higher standards of living and increased supplies of consumer goods. He intended to reverse the Stalinist strategy of building heavy industry at the expense of the consumer sector, and he announced a comprehensive series of price cuts in consumer goods and food. Malenkov's initiatives bolstered the purchasing power of Soviet consumers, but, ironically, the situation in the consumer market worsened further as the supply of goods available for sale failed to match increased consumer demand. Malenkov also spelled out major changes in the government's agricultural policy: decreasing the agricultural tax, increasing procurement prices for agricultural goods, and substantially reducing quotas for compulsory deliveries of garden produce to the state. Malenkov publicly acknowledged the disparity between the goods produced and the demands of the population and officially substantiated the fact that the economy was producing many unwanted goods.

9. Beria was accused of using the Ministry of Internal Affairs, which he headed, for the interests of foreign powers, sabotaging the government's agricultural policy, and undermining the friendship of the peoples of the Soviet Union. The Presidium removed him from power on June 26, 1953, and ordered his and his coconspirators' immediate executions on December 24, 1953.

10. This so-called secret speech of Khrushchev was made to 1,400 delegates in a closed-door meeting of the Central Committee of the CPSU. The delegates were asked to keep it "secret," and the press was barred from printing the speech. But the contents of the speech were leaked out immediately in the international press. Even within the Soviet Union, thousands of copies of the speech were read "secretly" by local party members, youth groups, and others throughout the country. In the wake of Khrushchev's speech, tens of thousands of meetings took place in the Soviet Union, which were attended by more than 40 million people (Kellen 1961, 173-74).

11. It should, however, be pointed out that Khrushchev's 1956 address was rather cautiously worded. Khrushchev did not fail to praise Stalin for his "services during the revolution and Civil War, his struggles against Trotskyists, Bukharinites, and bourgeois nationalists, and his contribution to industrialization and collectivization" (Hough and Fainsod 1979, 213).

12. These doctors were arrested in January 1953, just weeks before Stalin's death. They were accused of conspiracy (the so-called doctors' plot) against the Soviet leadership, primarily Stalin.

13. These excerpts of Khrushchev's address are quoted from Kellen (1961, 167); Schwartz (1965, 75-76); Degras (1962).

14. Thirty years later, Gorbachev (1988a, 418) appreciated the moment by declaring at the Seventieth anniversary of the Bolshevik Revolution, "It required no small courage of the party and its leadership, headed by Khrushchev, to criticize the personality cult and its consequences, and to reestablish socialist legality."

15. By the late 1950s and 1960s, thanks to Khrushchev's liberalization, a considerable revival of economics had occurred in the Soviet Union under the guise of mathematical economics. Although the theories and proposals were presented in Marxian terms, they were embedded in a conceptual apparatus essentially comparable to mainstream Western economics and emphasized such notions as opportunity cost, productivity of capital and other resources, marginalist analysis, "optimum" resource allocation, rent and capital charges, and so on. At least for a time, the new economists had a strong influence on economic policy and a potent role in determining the direction of teaching and research in economics (Elliott 1985, 400).

16. Indeed, emphasis on consumer goods began immediately after Stalin's death, with Malenkov's leadership. Whereas Malenkov emphasized an immediate shift in national development strategy in favor of consumer goods, Khrushchev opposed that idea by arguing that

both heavy industries and consumer industries must go hand in hand. He argued that claiming that "at some stage of socialist construction the development of heavy industry ceases to be the main task and the light industry can and should overtake all other branches of industry" is a "profoundly incorrect reasoning, alien to the spirit of Marxism-Leninism." Khrushchev argued that production of consumer goods could be increased without a cutback in the heavy industry sector. See Hough and Fainsod (1979, 208).

17. For details on Khrushchev's emphasis on the consumer sector, see Schwartz (1965, 81-84, 121-88) and McAuley (1987, 138-55).

18. The discussion on Khrushchev's agricultural reforms is based on Smith (1987, 95-117) and Nove (1969, 326-32).

19. According to Bergson (1989, 79), inequality in wages and salaries had been "extraordinarily great" in 1946, and by 1956 had "markedly decreased." This reduction in wage inequality, which continued throughout the Khrushchev period, has been characterized by Yanowitch (1977) as a "Soviet income revolution."

20. For details on Khrushchev's reforms in wages, incentives, and prices see Schwartz (1965, 99-103); Filtzer (1987, 118-35); McAuley (1979).

21. According to estimates of the U. S. Congress (1982), the average annual growth rate of the Soviet Union was 5.4 percent from 1955 to 1965. The same source indicates a 7.5 percent annual growth rate in industry and a 3.5 percent annual growth rate in agriculture during the same period.

22. Wiles (1977, 443) has made the following estimates of the ratios between the top and bottom 10 percent of per capita income after income taxes for the mid-1960s to the early 1970s: the United Kingdom 3.4; the United States 6.7; Italy, 5.9; Canada, 6.0; Sweden, 3.5; Hungary, 3.0; Czechoslovakia, 3.1; Bulgaria, 2.7; and the Soviet Union, 3.5.

23. After the fall of Khrushchev, a *Pravda* editorial on October 16, 1964, described Khrushchev's policies and programs as: "harebrained scheming, immature conclusions and hasty decisions and actions divorced from reality...unwillingness to take into account the achievements of science and practical experience."

24. In principle, there was another alternative, namely, the abolition of constraints on civil liberties and the adoption of the principles of political equality, full-scale democratization (including the possibility of alternative political movements and parties), and self-governance and self-management in factories, offices, and collective and state farms. But such a (revolutionary) strategy would have conflicted with both Khrushchev's own position and the post-Stalin party's consensus on authoritarian rule and could have jeopardized the sustenance of such crucial elements of that consensus as the oligarchic power structure, state ownership, bureaucratic coordination, and centralized planning.

Chapter 7

Brezhnev and Oligarchic Collectivist Economy

INTRODUCTION

This chapter examines Leonid Ilyich Brezhnev's[1] period (1964-1982) of Soviet development as an exemplar of an oligarchic collectivist model of Soviet political economy. The hallmarks of Brezhnev's two-decade rule over the former Soviet Union were institutional continuity, political stability, economic stagnation, policy incrementalism, and collectivity of leadership. During Brezhnev's period, the processes of administration and politics were highly bureaucratized, the CPSU's traditional prerogatives over national economy were revitalized, the locus of power was shifted to a collective leadership consisting of the main interest groups in the country, and some of the de-Stalinization processes initiated by Nikita Khrushchev were restrained or revoked.[2] The politico-economic model that emerged in the Soviet Union out of these characteristics of Brezhnev's regime can be described as "oligarchic collectivism" (Miliband 1983). The oligarchic collectivist model will be analyzed below following the four criteria developed in earlier chapters.

UNDERLYING CAUSES

Several factors that caused the collapse of the Khrushchev regime concurrently contributed to the emergence of the oligarchic collectivism model. Besides powerful international factors, such as the Cuban fiasco of 1961, the split in the world Communist movement as exemplified by the escalating conflict with China, and dissensions in Rumania and Albania, the economic, political, and social factors that contributed to the fundamental character of the Brezhnev version of Soviet-style socialism can be categorized as follows: (1) the October coup and collective leadership, (2) unification and strengthening of the CPSU, (3) slowdown in economic growth in the early 1960s, and (4) pressures for economic reforms.

Consolidation of Collective Leadership

Much to the surprise of many outside and inside the Soviet Union, Khrushchev was ousted from power by a political coup carefully orchestrated by his close colleagues: Leonid Brezhnev, Aleksei Kosygin, Nikolai Podgorny, and Mikhail Suslov—all members of the CPSU Presidium.[3] Khrushchev was replaced by a collective leader ship that represented key interests in the country, namely, the party apparatus, the economic and military bureaucracies, the KGB (State Security Committee) and the police forces. Brezhnev, heir apparent of Khrushchev and the most acceptable personality among the plotters, replaced Khrushchev as the new leader of the CPSU, while Kosygin, a deputy premier of Khrushchev's government, was appointed chairman of the Council of Ministers. Besides rejecting the highly personalized leadership style exemplified by Khrushchev, such a division of party and government leadership also demonstrated a commitment to collective leadership.

Although a well-represented collective leadership under Brezhnev initially succeeded in shifting emphasis from conflict to cooperation as envisaged by the political slogans of "trust in cadres" and "collectivity of leadership," the members of the coalition were soon immersed in a prolonged power struggle. But, unlike previous struggles of succession in Soviet history, this one was played out beneath the surface and on an individual basis; that is, rival personalities neither were organized jointly nor represented factional politics.

The main challenge to Brezhnev's leadership came from Kosygin.[4] As head of the government under the new leadership, Kosygin openly embraced economic reforms by emphasizing consumer satisfaction and living standards. Although in 1965 the Central Committee of the CPSU approved Kosygin's reforms in modified forms, the party under Brezhnev's leadership remained less enthusiastic about their implementation. As a result, Kosygin's reform initiatives, primarily directed to the mechanics of enterprise management and operations, as explained below, eventually failed.[5] This failure also eliminated Kosygin's prospects to succeed Khrushchev.[6]

The next challenge to Brezhnev's position came from Podgorny, whose emphasis on consumer demands and economic reforms brought him closer to Kosygin's position. To minimize his potential as a rival to party leadership, Brezhnev promoted Podgorny to the presidency of the Soviet Union in December 1965.[7] Brezhnev's position was also challenged by Alexander Shelepin,[8] a former KGB chief and a deputy premier of the current government. In December 1965 Brezhnev eliminated his deputy premiership and abolished the Party-State Committee which he headed. In May 1975 Brezhnev removed Shelepin from the politburo, thus eliminating the last major rival to his power.

In the meantime, the Twenty-third Party Congress held in 1966 appointed Brezhnev general secretary of the party, approving his superior power and thus making him the "first among equals." The same congress also renamed the CPSU Presidium as the Politburo. The Twenty-fourth Party Congress held in 1971 confirmed Brezhnev's supremacy more decisively as he was able to induct new members of his choice into the enlarged Politburo. By 1973 Brezhnev was able to put his own team in power. Leading representatives of important interest groups, including Marshall Grechko (defense minister), Yuri Andropov (KGB chief), and Andrei Gromyko (foreign minister)—all Brezhnev's cronies—entered the Politburo. In 1976 the Twenty-fifth Congress further affirmed Brezhnev's supremacy as ten of the sixteen Politburo members by then were his appointees. Brezhnev's consolidation of supreme leadership culminated as he combined party and state leadership in his person by assuming the presidency of the Soviet Union in 1977 under a new constitution.

It should be pointed out, however, that although by 1971 Brezhnev was able to remove or isolate most of his leading rivals, and by 1977 most of the expanded Politburo and Central Committee members were his clients, Brezhnev had to emphasize the institutionalization of collective rule and utilize the Central Committee. In short, "the relationship between the general secretary and the central committee remained mutually vulnerable and mutually dependent" (Volten 1982, 33-34). That also explains why, during the whole period of Brezhnev's consolidation of power, the overall party hierarchy and leadership remained remarkably stable (more on this below).

Strengthening of the Party

The collective leadership under Brezhnev eliminated Khrushchev's bifurcation of the CPSU and regained traditional prerogatives of the party by demanding continuation of party control and supervision of economy and society. As a result, the party's control, both in terms of day-to-day intervention and overall direction, intensified. The party apparatus, especially the central secretariat, controlled all leadership positions at all levels of society. A unified and strengthened party hierarchy assumed responsibilities to coordinate the activities of state institutions at local, regional, republican, and central levels.

Brezhnev's "party activism," however, differed significantly from Khrushchev's interventionist strategies. Whereas Khrushchev exhibited a personalized and confrontational leadership style that was bent on "efforts to change institutions and policies," Brezhnev was committed to "primarily serving the continuity of Soviet institutions and in gradual adjustments of policies" (Bialer 1980, 71). Brezhnev's interventionist strategy, therefore, demonstrated qualitative differences from Khrushchev's. Brezhnev's party activism, as George Breslauer (1982, 156-163) points out, was rooted in technological and managerial sophistication and in the ability of the party to reconcile narrow departmental interests with a broader perspective. Brezhnev emphasized reconceptualization of the role of the party in governance so that it could play a more balanced role with other institutional players within the society.

The Brezhnev collective leadership also emphasized continuity and stability in the Party leadership. Party cadres received greater tenure and security. Compared to a 62.4 percent and 49.6 percent survival ratio of the full members of the Central Committee at the Twentieth and Twenty-second Party Congresses, the survival ratio of the full members of the Central Committee gradually increased throughout the Brezhnev period: 79.4 percent at the Twenty-third Congress, 76.5 percent at the Twenty-fourth Congress, 83.4 percent at the Twenty-fifth Congress, and 89.0 percent at the Twenty-sixth Congress. In fact, the Brezhnev period experienced the lowest turnover rate of party leadership in Soviet history. The inner circle of the party hierarchy remained remarkably stable.[9]

Leading members of the collective leadership, especially in the initial periods, displayed remarkable concern for the collective character of the regime.[10] The collective leadership made sure that all major group interests were represented in the leadership and that no group or personality dominated the government or the party. Subsequent consolidation of power by Brezhnev as the supreme party leader, which, among other things, involved demotion of some personalities, such as Podgorny and Shelepin, and promotion of others, including Gromyko and Ustinov, did not cause a major change in the distribution of power either in the party or government because all major specialized hierarchies were represented in the Politburo. The oligarchical leadership emphasized frequent meetings of the collective policy-making bodies[11] and relied on such strategies as consensus building, bargaining, and continuity, instead of reforms, policy changes, or new programs.

Thus, strengthening of the CPSU during the Brezhnev period was associated with stability and job tenure for the members of its Central Committee and Politburo. All aspects of Soviet politics—from promotion to the balance of function and prestige— were systematized. Such continuity or job tenure, however, did not mean that a fixed leadership group held office throughout. In fact, Brezhnev's period experienced an enormous increase in the CPSU's membership: a total of 17.4 million people, almost 10 percent of the Soviet population, were members in 1983. Thanks in part to the steady expansion of the Central Committee, new members in 1971, 1976, and 1981 constituted 37 percent, 30 percent, and 28 percent of the respective memberships. The size of the Central Committee was expanded from 125 in 1952 to 195 in 1966, 241 in 1971, 287 in 1976, and 319 in 1981. As a result of such expansions and replacements, the Central Committee always had a majority of members who were only in their first or second terms (Daniels 1988, 94).

Consumer Frustrations and Economic Slowdown

One of the main factors that played a crucial role in Khrushchev's downfall and the emergence of the collective leadership was the relatively poor performance of the Soviet economy in the early 1960s. Whereas the Soviet GNP grew by 6 percent between 1951 and 1955, the growth rate dropped to 5.8 percent between 1956 and 1960 and to 5 percent between 1961 and 1965. Slowdown of the economy was pronounced in almost every sector of the Soviet economy. Labor productivity, which had grown at an annual average rate of 4.7 percent between 1950 and 1962 (Gregory and Stuart 1981, 341), dropped to 4 percent in the early 1960s. Among others, factors such as workers' discontent, ineffective use of new capital investment, and poor worker morale contributed to low productivity. There was a steady fall in the growth of factor inputs over the years, as well as combined factor productivity, particularly from the early 1960s. The annual rate of growth of labor factor input was 1.9 percent between 1951 and 1955, 0.6 percent between 1956 and 1960, and 1.6 percent between 1961 and 1965. In terms of capital, growth rates were 9 percent between 1951 and 1955, 9.8 percent between 1956 and 1970, and 8.7 percent between 1961 and 1965 (Goldman 1983, 47).

Problems were further compounded as people contrasted Khrushchev's glowing promises of economic advance with the reality of economic slowdown. Therefore, one of the toughest problems that the collective leadership faced immediately after assuming power was to confront the growing disillusionment of consumers who had long been promised a higher standard of living. Besides overtaking the United States in production of many material goods and the transition to a Communist economy based on material abundance, Khrushchev's promises included higher real wages for industrial as well as agricultural workers, increased minimum wages, reduced work hours, and elimination of income taxes. Several of these promises remained unmaterialized when Khrushchev was deposed (Schwartz 1965, 175-79).

Along with a more realistic evaluation of the capacity of the system, the collective leadership toned down people's expectations, abandoned comparisons of Soviet agricultural and consumer goods output with those of the United States, and instead gradually shifted to comparison of achievements with their own past performance such as the records of 1913, 1940, or 1955. The collective leadership realized that the center of gravity of global competition had shifted from ideology to economics and, accordingly, intensified emphasis on scientific and technological innovation as the potent force of national economic progress.[12]

Moreover, the collective leadership in the Brezhnev era abandoned (or postponed the timetable for) Khrushchev's optimistic promises of near-term material abundance and what Karl Marx (1935) had called the "higher phase" of communism. Instead, at the Twenty-fourth Party Congress held in 1971, Brezhnev introduced the concept of "developed socialism." Its connotation was that, by the late 1960s, Soviet society had reached a stage in which industrialization and capital accumulation had achieved an advanced development of the forces of production, and social relations of production were solidly based on socialist principles, thereby indicating that Soviet society was moving in the right direction towards "natural" and gradual transition from socialism to communism.

The Communist party, in its program of 1962 under Khrushchev's leadership, had optimistically promised to "catch up" with capitalist countries within a decade or two, to achieve material affluence, and thereby to implement the Communist distributive principle of "from each according to his ability, to each according to his needs" (to replace the socialist principle of "to each according to his work"), and the lofty socialist aspiration of "a society in which labor for the good of society will become the prime vital requirement of everyone" (cited in Koslov 1977, 396).

The concept of "developed socialism" was elaborated at the Twenty-fifth Party Congress in the mid-1970s. At this congress, Brezhnev stated that the achievement of developed socialism presented the party and the Soviet people with a "new historical task, that of preparing the material and social conditions for the transition of society to communism." The material and technical bases for developed socialism to meet this challenge were identified essentially as those of modernization and intensive development, characterized as "combining the advantages of socialism with the achievements of the scientific and technological revolution." This would require such conditions as "automated systems of machines," large-scale production, comprehensive electrification, mechanization, application of chemistry, fuller development and utilization of human and natural resources, and rapid scientific and technological progress (Koslov 1977, 396-401). One major social basis for transition, Soviet Marxists argued, was convergence of farm property into state farms and supersession of individual peasant garden plots. Another prerequisite was to perfect "comradely cooperation and mutual assistance" among workers, peasants, and the intelligentsia, and to convert labor into a "prime necessity of life." This, in turn, required the abolition of "arduous and onerous types of work," "essential differences between mental and physical work," and, differences between town and country; the achievement of a shorter working day and greater leisure time; and the development of "socialist competition" and "communist education of the people." Until these tasks had been accomplished, a "full and final victory" of socialism had occurred, and the socialist phase of development had been completed, "there can be no transition to communism" (Koslov 1977, 396, 411).

By thus backing away from the immediate establishment of communism, and by emphasizing instead a gradual movement toward it, based on modernization and technological progressivity, the collective leadership was able to accommodate policies that would promise material prosperity for the whole society in the long run as well as permit private trade and individualistic economic pursuits in the short run. Also, responding to the declining rate of growth in per capita consumption since 1955, the collective leadership agreed to skew resource allocation toward meeting consumers' demands for higher standards of living.[13] In making such ideological and material compromises, Soviet authorities abandoned the grand expectations propounded by Khrushchev in the late 1950s and early 1960s.

Pressures for Reforms

Although the Brezhnev regime was primarily preoccupied with institutional continuity and political stability, it came under increasing pressures for economic reforms. Thanks to the unprecedented liberation of intellectuals during Khrushchev's period, many economists proposed serious reform plans, especially in the early 1960s, aimed at improving the efficiency and effectiveness of central planning in a nonmarket Soviet economy. Especially prominent among the new ideas was Professor Evsey Liberman's proposals, which called for reforming the planning system. Liberman's proposals raised tantalizing possibilities, although he emphasized the moderate character of his proposed reforms and their contribution to improving the efficiency of central planning within the framework of the Soviet system.

Liberman's proposals contained three major dimensions: the role of the central authorities (the centralized dimension); freedom and flexibility of individual enterprises (the decentralized dimension), and the role of profitability (within the framework of the central plan) as a generalizing and unifying "success indicator" and incentive system. Under Liberman's proposal, central authorities would continue to make the basic macroeconomic decisions affecting the character and pace of economic growth and would retain control of all of the major levers of central planning. Within this framework, and given centrally fixed targets for output, product assortment, and delivery dates, enterprises would have discretionary control over several subordinate areas—labor productivity, the number of workers, wages, production costs, accumulations (savings), capital investment, and new technology—and would be instructed to maximize their rates of profit (Elliott 1985, 400-401).

Liberman's proposals received the initial acceptance of Khrushchev, who ordered some experimental implementation of those proposals in August 1964, shortly before his ouster.[14] But demand for the extension of such experiments intensified with the advent of collective leadership as evidenced by Kosygin's preoccupation (discussed below) with enterprise reforms.

Serious discussion of the Liberman proposals, however, exposed some associated problems of a centrally planned economy. For example, if profitability were to be the guide for rational conduct of enterprises, than profits had to be based on prices that reflected actual supply and demand conditions for different commodities in the economy. Such considerations brought to surface alternative proposals to improve the procedures for centralized decision making advanced by mathematical economist Leonid Kantorovich back in 1939. In his pioneer work on linear programming, Kantorovich formulated solutions to the problems of allocation and price under central planning. The mathematical economists, following Kantorovich's model, proposed to reform the economy by establishing optimal pricing and resource allocation, based on the techniques of linear programming and input-output analysis, and using computers, so that the absence of "free market" operations could be compensated for by a centrally planned Soviet economy.

INSTITUTIONS, PROGRAMS, AND POLICIES

The ruling oligarchy of the Brezhnev era stressed political stability and pragmatic plans for economic growth in sharp contrast to Khrushchev's more optimistic schemes. Based on a more realistic assessment of the actual capacity of the economy, the Brezhnev leadership projected GNP growth targets for the eighth (1966-1970) and the ninth (1971-1975) plans below 7 percent. Soviet planners also projected a less than 5 percent annual growth rate for the tenth plan (1976-80).[15] The Brezhnev regime was disturbed by many of the consequences of the Khrushchev reforms, including declining economic growth, a near-stagnation situation in the agricultural sector, weakening central control over the economy, and scattering of planning activities among regional authorities. The new leadership, therefore, reversed some of Khrushchev's institutional changes. By October 1965, bifurcation of the CPSU and the *sovnarkhozy* reforms, two of Khrushchev's most sweeping reforms were reversed, and controls by central ministries and the unified CPSU were reestablished throughout the nation. In order to reestablish the primacy of central planning and management, the Soviet party-state was revamped, authority was centralized, traditional administrative control was reinforced, and the Party-state apparatuses were strengthened. Brezhnev's period, which primarily symbolized continuity and stability, brought forth few institutional or other major changes as explained below.[16]

Reforms in Enterprise Management.

In the early days of the Brezhnev regime, Kosygin initiated economic reforms, focusing primarily on planning and management aspects of state enterprises. Kosygin sought to enhance the power and responsibilities of enterprise management relative to higher administrative authorities to improve enterprise performance. He granted enterprise managers greater latitude in the utilization of resources, including labor, redesigned incentive systems to bolster enterprise performance, and reduced the number of success indicators. Enterprise managers were permitted to use either time rates or piece rates depending on their enterprise needs (Katz 1972, 136).

Kosygin designated two main success indicators for the determination of enterprise performance:[17] profitability (defined as the ratio of profits to fixed and working capital) and sales revenues. Whereas the sales revenue indicator was expected to prevent profitability from rising at the expense of the quality of products, the profitability indicator guarded against production at any cost. Enterprise profits, in turn, were divided into three funds: a material incentive fund meant for the payment of bonuses; a development fund, which the enterprise could invest at its own discretion; and a sociocultural fund targeted for housing and welfare of enterprise workers. For distribution of the funds, first of all, all the claims on enterprise profits—such as payment of the capital charge, differential rent, and interest on bank credits—were made, and the remaining profits were to be allocated into the three funds mentioned above in accordance with the norms set by higher authorities.

Kosygin also attempted to initiate cost accountability *(khozraschet)* in enterprise management by introducing rent charges in some branches of the extractive industry, levying a 6 percent interest charge on the undepreciated value of assets and linking enterprise bonuses to the achievement of targeted profits. The use of sales and profits as success indicators, along with the emphasis on reduction or elimination of subsidies, forced enterprises to be more responsible in terms of financial accountability. To make possible these various funds and to accommodate interest and rent charges, prices were revised to eliminate losses generally and to achieve the necessary margin of profit.

All of these were important reforms, but they fell short of serious decentralization or transition to the market principle. The autonomy of enterprises was still restricted in two crucial ways. Decisions about output mix and input mix (that is, what to produce and how to produce) still were basically subject to methods of centralized oversight, which remained virtually unchanged, and prices still remained poor guides to decision making because they were set administratively and were based on the traditional cost of production approach.

During the 1970s, many of the modest Soviet economic reforms of the 1960s were modified or reversed. The size and distribution of enterprise incentive funds became more tightly regulated by central planning authorities and ministries. The manager's discretionary control over investment funds was also restricted. The number of enterprise targets was expanded, and once again included indicators for productivity, quantity and quality of output, delivery dates, and so forth.

In contrast to more comprehensive economic reforms in Eastern Europe, notably Hungary, Soviet reforms were quite conservative from the outset. Their purpose was to improve the quality of economic policy and performance within the framework of an essentially unaltered system of centralized planning, administration, and allocation. Moreover, many of the reform proposals were unimplemented or, as noted, reversed. Some attempts were made at improved planning and tighter control over enterprise management through automated information and management systems and computerization. Because of the lack of, or underutilization of, computer hardware and computer systems, however, sophisticated mathematical modeling and optimization analysis remained secondary to traditional planning methods. After a relatively brief period of reform, Soviet leaders returned to an essentially centralized system of planning and political direction of economic life.

Mergers and Reorganizations

Brezhnev sought to reorganize the central administrative apparatus by streamlining the decision-making hierarchy in the ministries and by promoting mergers of enterprises into production associations. In March 1973 Brezhnev issued decrees to merge industrial enterprises under one decision-making authority apparently to promote administrative efficiency and to redirect resources from the least productive enterprises to the most productive ones. These decrees replaced the *glavki*, the organizations that supervised all enterprises involved in closely related products within each ministry, with all-union industrial associations (VPOs), whose authority generally covered similar enterprises throughout the country. Newly created VPOs, which also included research and design organizations and technical institutes, were expected to function on a *khozraschet* basis.

By the mid-1970s the merger movement had gathered momentum. The VPOs accounted for 6.7 percent of total industrial output in 1970, and the share was increased to almost a quarter (24.4 percent) of total industrial output of the economy by 1975. The VPOs' share continued to climb in the second half of the 1970s, and by the early 1980s it represented almost one-half of total industrial output in the Soviet economy (Hewett 1988, 245). The VPOs, however, were criticized for lack of authority and incentive systems for effective management of enterprises, and for ending up with exercising administrative control over the enterprises as the *glavki* did before.[18] The VPOs were also criticized for representing the tendency of the Soviet leaders to look to supply-side solutions, instead of the demand-side consequences of the nation's economic problems.[19]

Reforms in the Economic Mechanisms

The Brezhnev administration initiated another reform program to improve the efficiency and effectiveness of state enterprises in 1979. Known as the Program to Improve the Economic Mechanism (PIEM), these reforms came in response to the dismal performance of the Soviet economy and focused on relationships between enterprises and central planning mechanisms.[20] The PIEM was expected to retard increasingly deteriorating economic conditions in the country, such as the slowdown in economic growth, low levels of labor productivity, and shortages of inputs. It sought improvement in the economic mechanism by focusing on planning and supply elements and on performance indicators of enterprises. Emphasis was given to collection of more accurate information on factor inputs; application of a larger number of more precise input-output norms; closer approximation to "optimal tautness" in the planning of supply, production, and investment; better coordination of plans across time and space; and a greater role for enterprise contracts (Bornstein 1985, 2-8).

The PIEM sought efficiency in investment and promotion of self-financing and financial responsibility among the ministries and enterprises. It called for improvement in product quality and timely delivery of products. Every enterprise was asked to prepare an annual report providing detailed information on its production capacity and financial flows. Enterprises were instructed to utilize their full productive potential by efficient use of raw materials, manpower, and other resources. It designated labor productivity, calculated as net rather than gross output per worker, as a key indicator for enterprise performance. Application of technology and related skills to improve product quality or to produce new products was recognized as another important performance indicator. Others included fulfillment of contract delivery obligations (covering volume, assortment, quality, and timeliness), total cost of production, earned profit, and gross or marketable output.

Brezhnev's 1979 reforms also emphasized transition from extensive to intensive methods of production. By introducing the concept of Normative Net Output (NNO),[21] the Brezhnev regime sought to replace traditional gross or marketable output as an indicator of enterprise performance. Traditional or extensive methods of production involved greater use of factor inputs and thereby contributed to gross or marketable output, but not necessarily to net output. The NNO was expected to discourage enterprises from using greater inputs of material, fuels and energy, and other resources.[22]

The PIEM also sought to revise enterprise material incentive funds and form workers' "brigades" in enterprises. To strengthen enterprise incentives, the PIEM tied the increase in labor productivity to the share of highest quality output in total output. The size of the enterprise's material incentive fund was tied to personal bonuses; therefore, a direct linkage was emphasized between the growth of labor productivity and the growth of output. The PIEM also introduced the brigade system in enterprises, which, as a form of work organization was expected to provide greater incentives to production workers. The brigade system attained a moderate level of success for a short period of time. By the beginning of 1983, the share of workers organized in brigades reached 75.1 percent in construction and 59 percent in industry (Bornstein 1985).

Agricultural Reforms

Brezhnev sought to establish himself as an agrarian reformer. In fact, out of the eight Central Committee plenary sessions of the CPSU devoted to specific economic issues after 1965, six were concerned with agricultural problems (Dowlah 1992a, 82). Brezhnev's focus on agriculture was also qualitatively different from that of his predecessor, Khrushchev. As early as the March 1965 Central Committee Plenum, Brezhnev announced a new deal for the Soviet peasantry. Denouncing Khrushchev's expansionist agricultural campaigns, which emphasized corn or grain production on formerly uncultivated lands as illustrated by the Virgin Lands Program, Brezhnev shifted emphasis to greater farm autonomy, adopting locally suitable methods of agricultural production, and restricting central control to a bare minimum.

Also, following Khrushchev, the Brezhnev administration raised purchasing prices for agricultural products including above-quota deliveries, lowered tax obligations upon collective farmers, broadened the scope of farming on family plots, and reduced prices that kolkhozy had to pay for agricultural machinery and impediments. Efforts were made to reduce urban-rural income gaps. Brezhnev extended regular monthly payments and provided better pension benefits to the kolkhozniki. Old age pensions, minimum monthly income, and reduced taxes on private plots and private livestock holdings were guaranteed. Such measures resulted in tangible improvements in the living standards of kolkhozniki although they still earned less than salaried agricultural workers on sovkhozy (state farms) or industrial blue-collar workers. But such measures contributed to substantial increases in food supplies in the urban areas.[23]

The Brezhnev regime also initiated a number of capital-intensive strategies for revitalization of the agricultural sector. Investment in the agricultural sector steadily increased. From 19.6 percent of total investment between 1961 and 1965, investment in agriculture increased to 23.2 percent of total investment between 1966 and 1970 and to 26.2 percent between 1971 and 1975 (Nove 1969, 363). The share of agriculture in Soviet national investment rose to 27 percent in 1976-1980, and it could even have been over 33 percent if investment in related industrial fields had also been taken into consideration (Johnson and Brooks 1983, 196). This huge influx of capital allowed the Brezhnev regime to pursue massive programs aimed at upgrading agricultural production and mending previously neglected infrastructures. Ambitious programs were undertaken to increase the supply of fertilizers, tractors, electricity, and water to rural areas.

Brezhnev's agricultural reforms, however, were criticized for ignoring needed substantive structural modifications. Indeed, they made no effort to revamp significantly an overcentralized and truncated agricultural administration, or to do away with huge food subsidies. The Brezhnev regime also failed to stop the serious "rural exodus," the drain of badly needed youth and talent from the rural areas to the urban centers, which further aggravated agricultural problems.[24]

Consistency and Efficiency in Soviet Planning

Consistency and efficiency are two important dimensions in centralized planning. Both aspects became increasingly problematic during the Brezhnev period. By consistency, we mean coordination among different parts of the plan. The demand for labor must equal its supply. The output of coal must be sufficient to produce the planned targets for steel production. Steel must be available in proper quantities and varieties to achieve plans for tractor output. Financial equilibrium must accompany and accommodate physical coordination: the monetary value of input must be consistent with the monetary value of output; money income must be equal to planned consumption (and saving) and so on.

According to Gregory Grossman, maintaining physical balance or consistency is the "chief daily task and chore" of an economy in which decisions are made on the basis of "directives from above." Before an economy can turn to the more exacting requirements of allocational or developmental efficiency, it must attain at least minimal balance between supplies and demands of particular goods. "It is this task that in fact constitutes by far the largest part of the so-called planning in the command economy, not what we in the West usually understand by this term, namely, the delineation of economic goals and the selection of strategies and instruments of their realization." Much of the planning activity in a command economy "is devoted to an arduous activity that substitutes for the most elementary accomplishment of the market mechanism." This explains why physical planning is so important in the context of the command economy. "To attain and preserve balance, a command economy must collate the physical availabilities and requirements of very many commodities, and this in turn necessitates physical targets for production and input utilization" (1965, 142-44).

Consistency poses a special challenge for centralized planning for two major reasons: mutual interdependence and the general substitution of bureaucratic coordination for market price systems. In economic affairs, all variables are interwoven, often in complex ways. For example, an increase in the production of steel requires expansion of such steel inputs as coal and iron. But coal and iron mining and smelting requires machinery made, among other things, from steel. Moreover, a centrally planned economy has no built-in social processes, such as market price systems, that work spontaneously to promote consistent connecting linkages among interdependent production processes or to foster movement toward a balance between demands and supplies of goods, labor, other resources, and investment funds. Central planners must consciously identify and measure mutual interdependencies and formulate plans accordingly because an increase in aggregate economic performance depends on a balance among constituent parts. Bottlenecks (for example, the undersupply of skilled labor, the lack of spare parts for trucks) can disrupt economic development.

Maintaining consistency became more problematic during the Brezhnev years for three main reasons. First, the economy became more complex, and with growing complexity, the challenges and costs of constructing consistent plans multiplied. Second, maintaining balance in consumption goods output was thwarted in numerous (and growing) instances by the tendency toward "sellers' markets" and shortages of particular goods. Meanwhile, Khrushchev's promises of material abundance had raised the expectations of an increasingly urban, educated, and sophisticated population. These trends argued in favor of a revision of planning methodology wherein central planners would concentrate on determining the overall level of consumption, leaving the allocation of resources to the production of specific consumption goods to be guided by consumers' preferences through market processes. But, partly because of the interdependencies between the production of consumption and investment goods, the Brezhnev politocracy was unwilling to relinquish its central direction of consumption. Third, growth rates diminished over time, that is, growth rates were lower in the early 1980s than in the 1970s, and in the 1970s than in the 1960s. This made the inefficiencies associated with imbalances (too many trucks, too few fuel pumps, or vice versa) more, rather than less compelling.

If consistency or balance is one grand theme of centralized planning, efficiency or optimality is thus the other. Soviet leaders and planners, however, attached a different meaning to the concept of "efficiency" than do many economists in industrialized capitalist countries. In mainstream economics, efficiency presupposes "consumers' sovereignty"; that is, an efficient use and allocation of resources are roughly definable as the least costly mode of satisfying a given pattern of individual consumers' wants with a given body of scarce resources. Alternatively expressed, an optimal position is one from which it is not possible by any reallocation of factors to make anyone better off without making at least one person worse off. This principle (known as "Pareto Optimality") attempts to judge economic efficiency independently from issues of distributive equity. It also presupposes that resources are fully employed somewhere in the economy and that the "waste" of (involuntary) unemployment does not exist. Although it may be given a dynamic interpretation, its dominant application is to the "static" issue of squeezing greater benefits, in production and consumption, out of a given set of resources and under a given technology. Some illustrations of allocational efficiency issues are determining the least-cost combination of inputs, the most efficient level of output and scale and location of plant, the optimal allocation of investment funds among different sectors and projects, and so on.

The Soviet conceptualization of efficiency differed concerning most components of this Western perspective. First, Soviet leaders presupposed a politically directed efficiency, that is, the substitution of the directives and preferences of the political leaders for those of consumers. Second, instead of focusing on how to obtain better resource allocation with a given (capitalist) pattern of wealth distribution and employment, Soviet Marxists claimed that a revolutionary overturning of capitalist wealth and privilege, the elimination of (capitalist-style) depressions and cyclical fluctuations, and the establishment of full employment provide a framework for a fuller, more equitable, and thereby more efficient use of resources. Third, in the traditional Soviet view, "molding" the preferences of consumers and workers in more collective directions was seen as contributing to efficiency. For example, if consumers could be persuaded, through education and the mass communications media, to place a high priority on subways relative to automobiles, large amounts of steel and other products could be saved and allocated outside of the automobile industry. If workers' tastes could be nudged in more socially oriented directions, labor productivity might be enhanced, perhaps substantially. Fourth, Soviet leaders regarded rapid growth, notably in certain high priority directions (heavy industry, investment, the military, space research) as the paramount test for efficiency in practice. As Maurice Dobb (1966, 244-45) puts it, "Securing an optimum allocation of resources between alternative uses, with both resources and uses treated as given" may well be less important for social well-being than fostering rapid social and economic change. Conversely, "successful development from one situation, with its given combination of resources and configuration of demand to another might be a more crucial test of the contribution by an economic system to human welfare than the attainment of perfect equilibrium in any given situation."

Yet, efficiency is an important criterion for centralized planning. The promotion of high rates of growth over the passage of time requires reasonably close attention to the "minimization of the sacrifice of alternatives" in any given period of time. It is true that the strategy of centralized development in a developing economy places static allocational efficiency at a lower level of priority than the more dynamic criteria of economic growth and development. Still, an underdeveloped economy with fewer resources, a lower standard of living, and lower reserves of plant, equipment, and stocks of goods can ill afford waste and a cavalier attitude toward efficiency in the use of the meager resources it does have.

Central planners proposed various techniques for reducing the problems of consistency and efficiency. First, the "ability to build on the past and to change things around if plans are out of line enormously simplifies the task of planning" (Oxenfeldt 1965, 97). Even comprehensive plans do not begin completely from scratch; they typically represent modifications of previous plans. With the passage of time, plans may be changed in the process of execution. Second, flexibility in plan reformulation is related to priorities in planning goals. Given the primary objective of rapid, large-scale industrialization, and the lower emphasis upon consumer sovereignty and consumer welfare, it is possible to shift resources from consumer goods industries to the production of investment goods if, toward the end of the planning period, it becomes apparent that initial planning targets were excessively optimistic and the joint attainment of investment and consumer goods goals is unlikely. This way, consistency can be maintained in the crucial investment goods sector by sacrificing, if necessary, the production of consumer goods.

Third, the scope of centralized planning can be restricted to a relatively small number of "key links" and basic commodities. Detailed plans can be left to lower levels and to local planners more familiar with local conditions and needs. Fourth, once financial balances are coordinated with physical balance sheets of the quantities of resources required to attain output targets, "planned costs" can be determined by adding the products of input quantities and prices. A "planned profit" may be added to determine the selling price of each commodity. Under such a system, profit will vary inversely with the relation of actual cost to planned cost. If enterprises meet output targets with smaller quantities of inputs than those designated in the plan, actual costs will be lower than planned costs, and actual profits will be higher than planned profits. If plant managers are permitted to retain a portion of this "unplanned profit" and use it for managerial bonuses, welfare benefits, and investment, it can serve as a "collective incentive" to increase efficiency and "beat the plan." With both output and price set by the production and financial plans,

> the enterprise can do nothing to improve its financial position by restricting output: on the contrary, to restrict output will reduce its receipts and hence any profit to be left in its hands. Here the enterprise is harnessed firmly within the shafts of the Plan. The sole way in which it can improve its financial position, and hence the sole direction in which profit can operate as an incentive, is by an economy in its consumption of productive resources. (Dobb 1966, 355)

The dominant methodology in Soviet planning during the Brezhnev era continued to be "balances planning," notably for materials or intermediate products, labor, and finance. We shall focus here on material balances. A material balance for a particular product, for example, steel, is an accounting statement akin to a balance sheet, which lists resources, for example, production (X), stocks (S), and imports (M), on one side and allocation to interindustry (1 through n) and final (Y) users on the other. Thus, a "balance" for product 1 would exist when $X1 + S1 + M1 = X11 + X12 + \ldots + X1n + Y1$. What happened when the demand for a particular material exceeded supply? If planning targets for high-priority items were reduced, the resulting "loose" plan would fail to apply the pressure perceived to be necessary to urge on high achievement. A very "taut" plan, however, tends to create inconsistencies and bottlenecks. Essentially, planners strived for a reasonably high-level balance, and attempted to achieve this balance primarily by making adjustments. First, attempts were made to expand supply, partly by reducing stocks a bit or expanding imports slightly, but primarily by expanding production. Of course, this could create additional imbalances if enlarged production required additional inputs, which in turn, required expanded production in those areas, and so on. Consequently, enterprises were urged to increase efficiency, or to make better or more intensive use of equipment. Second, attempts were made to reduce demands, both interindustry demands, by improving efficiency in the use of the particular inputs and/or substituting another input in more plentiful supply, and final demands, especially by shifting resources from low-priority (consumption) to high-priority uses.

Material balance planning was slow and cumbersome; certain of its features stimulated dysfunctional results. "Taut" plans encouraged *strakhovka*, or safety margins, wherein enterprise managers overstated needs, understated capacities, and hoarded scarce materials. Excess demands stemming from taut planning also permitted managers to get rid of their outputs more or less regardless of quality. Focus on output targets caused ministry administrators as well as enterprise managers to direct their energies to the "vertical" relationships within their respective ministries to the neglect of "horizontal" relationships with other sectors or environmental considerations. Consistency was achieved "on paper" but violated in practice. Plan adjustments with complex input-output ramifications were rarely calculated beyond a few iterations. Optimality was generally beyond the scope of material balances planning because, among other reasons, alternative variants were not typically compared and assessed. Because the consumer sector was used as a buffer in the event of discrepancies between plan resources and requirements, plan fulfillment departed substantially from plan targets, with detrimental effects on personal incentives and productivity.

What material balances planning lacked in consistency and allocational efficiency, however, it made up in effectiveness or what we earlier called "goal-achievement efficiency," at least from the perspective of Brezhnev era political leaders, planners, and administrators. The priority planning system permitted focus on high-priority sectors and thereby encouraged rapid growth of a selective sort, even spectacular achievements in some areas (for example, space technology). Taut planning provided discipline and inspiration for concerted developmental effort. Continued devotion to comprehensive state ownership permitted direct imposition of party and state preferences on economic development. Thus, centralized planning, despite its inefficiencies and despite lagging growth rates, growing complexity, increasing disaffection among the intelligentsia, and restiveness among the underlying population, was retained more or less intact during the Brezhnev period.

Oligarchic Collectivism

Collective leadership, embodying a firm commitment to institutional continuity, crystallized into an unprecedented bureaucratic stability in the Soviet Union. Inheriting Khrushchev's authoritarian system, Brezhnev transformed it into a bureaucratic collectivism in which all powerful interest groups were represented more or less on an equal basis, and major decisions were reached on the basis of consensus among the major participants. Efforts were even made to revive some elements of Stalinism that had previously been scrapped by Khrushchev, for example, tightening the top party and state command and control systems, thereby, gaining greater centralization in political and administrative direction of economic life, and firmer disciplining of dissenters. Seweryn Bialer (1980, 69-80) identifies six "most distinctive and significant traits" of the "oligarchic pattern" of bureaucratic collectivism.

First, unlike Khrushchev, who emphasized the formation of a new consensus, Brezhnev's leadership was primarily concerned with maintaining a consensus. Second, a core of senior leaders below Brezhnev were afforded more respect and exposure and carried more weight in decision making across a broad spectrum of policy issues and had primary responsibility for a number of policy areas. Third, conflicts over power and policy were not accompanied (until the last few years) by expulsion or disgrace of the losers. Fourth, all major specialized hierarchies of the Soviet party-state had their chief executives represented in the Politburo, a situation that existed during Stalin's last Politburo but never in Khrushchev's Presidium. Fifth, among the full membership of the Politburo there was greater representation of leaders who were not associated directly with the central Moscow establishments. Sixth, in the Brezhnev period neither of the two major institutions of the top leadership, the party's central secretariat or the Presidium of the Council of Ministers, had enough of its members in the Politburo even to approach a majority.

The development and persistence of this oligarchic leadership pattern had its origins in the determination to dismantle Khrushchev's "harebrained schemes." Subsequently, the coalition survived because the personal power positions of the probable contenders were at the beginning apparently more evenly balanced than in the past and their personal following was much less crystallized. Moreover, the divisions of opinion among the leaders were less polarized and the distance between divergent opinions was narrower. Elite fluidity and the commonly recognized need to stabilize the regime played their parts too. As discussed above, under Brezhnev, the leadership turnover rate was the lowest in Soviet history. Bialer (1980, 97-126) remarks that the new generation that came to maturity during Brezhnev's regime was scarcely touched by the traditions of populism and egalitarianism that had characterized earlier generations. Instead, the new generation demonstrated materialistic wants and expectations, highly developed career orientations, professionalism, and elitism.

Through its policies the bureaucratic leadership, however, succeeded in replacing inspiring hopes for reforms and visions of the future as propounded by Khrushchev with conservative defense of bureaucratic positions of power against all liberalizing influences from within the country and from without (Brown 1989, 6). Bureaucratic power and politics were committed to "all-national interests, as counter-opposed to particularistic interests," expounded by the offices of the central Secretariat or the general secretary (Bialer 1983, 3). The bureaucratic-oligarchic leadership maintained a delicate balance of power and consensus among functional bureaucratic interests, several levels of political leaderships, and a circular flow of power which, according to Daniels (1988, 93), constituted a "participatory bureaucracy."

CONSEQUENCES

The Brezhnev period was characterized by severe economic stagnation. Overall economic growth slowed down remarkably. As Table 7.1 shows, the average annual growth rate for the Soviet GNP, by Western estimates, rose slightly in the late 1960s (to 5 percent), and then fell rather precipitously thereafter, reaching a low of 2 percent for the period from 1981 to 1985. The growth rate in national income utilized (national income produced minus losses and net exports) followed a similar pattern, falling from 7.1 percent in the period from 1966 to 1970 to 2.7 percent in the period from 1981 to 1985. The growth rate in real per capita income also fell during this

Table 7.1
Soviet Economic Performance Indicators, 1961-1985
(Average annual growth rate, percent)

Items	1961-65 FYP7	Act.	1966-70 FYP8	Act.	1971-75 FYP9	Act.	1976-80 FYP10	Act.	1981-85 FYP11	Act.
Macroeconomic activity										
National income produced	n.a	6.5	n.a	7.8	n.a.	5.7	n.a.	4.4	n.a.	3.5
National income utilized	7.3	6.0	6.9	7.1	6.7	5.1	4.7	3.9	3.4	2.7
GNP (Western estimate)	n.a.	4.7	n.a.	5.0	n.a.	3.0	n.a.	2.3	n.a.	2.0
Sectoral output										
Industrial production	8.6	8.8	8.2	8.3	8.0	7.4	6.3	4.5	4.7	3.7
Machine building & metalworking	n.a.	12.4	n.a.	11.8	11.4	11.6	n.a.	8.2	7.0	6.2
Agricultural production	7.9	2.4	4.6	4.3	4.0	0.6	3.0	1.5	2.5	2.1
Labor productivity										
In all material	n.a.	5.5	n.a.	6.8	n.a.	4.6	n.a.	3.3	n.a.	3.1
production in industry	5.7	4.5	6.0	5.6	6.8	6.0	5.5	3.1	3.6	3.2
In agriculture	n.a.	3.3	7.3	6.2	6.7	1.4	n.a.	2.8	n.a.	2.7
In construction	n.a.	5.2	n.a	4.1	6.5	5.2	n.a.	1.5	n.a.	2.7
Capital formation										
Gross total investment	n.a.	6.3	8.0	7.5	6.7	7.0	n.a.	3.3	n.a.	3.5
Gross state investment	8.8	7.3	n.a	7.2	6.2	7.1	2.8	3.7	1.1	3.5
Real per capita income	4.9	3.9	5.4	5.9	5.5	4.4	3.9	3.3	3.1	2.1

Source: Hewett (1988, 52).

period, from 5.9 percent between 1966 and 1970 to 2.1 percent between 1981 and 1985. As Tables 7.1 and 7.2 indicate, roughly parallel patterns of reductions in growth occurred in the various sectors of the economy. Indeed, the "slowdown in the growth of industrial output was somewhat more pronounced than for national income as a whole." Investment growth rates also decreased, but, given the leadership's desire to sustain consumption growth, "not by as much as planners had hoped" (Hewett 1988, 54-55).

Labor productivity growth rates dropped markedly, from 6.8 percent per year in the late 1960s to 3.1 percent in the early 1980s, vivid testimony to the failure to shift from an extensive growth strategy, based on expansion in resource inputs, to an intensive

Table 7.2
Soviet Economic Performance by Sector, 1966-1980
(Average annual rate of growth)

Sector	1966-70	1970-75	1975-80
Construction	5.4	5.6	2.5
Transportation	7.1	6.5	3.6
Communication	8.6	6.4	4.7
Trade	7.1	4.7	2.7
Services	4.3	3.4	2.7
Others	3.6	2.1	1.7

Source: Adapted from CIA (1985).

Table 7.3
Soviet Economic Growth under Brezhnev: Planned versus Actual, 1976-1980
(in percentage)

	Planned (1976-80)	Actual (1976-79)
Gross National Income	5.0	3.1
Coal	3.0	0.6
Steel	3.6	1.2
Consumer Products	4.6	1.8
Agriculture	4.9	2.3
Oil	5.5	4.5
Gas	8.5	8.9
Chemicals	10.3	3.0

Source: Adapted from MacKenzie and Curran (1991, 435).

growth strategy, based on technological progressivity, innovation, and improvements in resource use and allocation. As is evident from Tables 7.1 and 7.3, actual economic performance generally fell below planned goals from the early 1970s onward, despite the downward revisions in goals in the light of the deteriorating economic performance. No doubt, declining growth rates were especially disappointing because, during the earlier years of the Brezhnev regime, the Soviet economy's growth performance was superior to the performance of the whole period.

Agricultural production, for example, initially demonstrated promising signs. Thanks partly to Kosygin's agricultural reforms, the rate of growth in agricultural output almost doubled. Between 1966 and 1970, the volume of agricultural output increased at an annual rate of 3.4 percent, substantially above the rate of the previous five-year period. Grain production showed continued progress as output increased from 167.7 million tons in 1966 to 1970 to 181.6 million tons in 1971 to 1975 and to 205 million tons in 1976 to 1980. Similar progress was made in terms of other agricultural goods, such as cotton, sugar beets, potatoes, meat, and milk (Nove 1969, 363-64). This accelerated growth in agricultural production facilitated a substantial increase in the rate of growth of production in light industries based on agricultural raw materials.

At a later stage of the Brezhnev era, the agricultural sector also lost its momentum and instead began to show signs of slow growth or stagnation. Overall agricultural output, as Table 7.1 shows, grew by an average annual rate of 4.3 percent from 1996 to 1970, then experienced a very low growth rate of 0.6 percent from 1971 to 1975, followed by low growth rates of 1.5 and 2.1 percent from 1976 to 1980 and 1981 to 1985, respectively. The industrial sector registered growth rates of 8.3 percent from 1966 to 1970, 7.4 percent from 1971 to 1975, 4.5 percent from 1976 to 1980, and 3.7 percent from 1981 to 1985. As shown in Table 7.2, transportation and communication, which grew at annual rates of 7.1 and 8.6 percent during the period from 1966 to 1970, dropped to 3.6 percent and 4.7 percent, respectively, from 1976 to 1980. Between 1965 and 1977, the Soviet Union ranked first in the world, among other industrial goods, in oil, coal, pig iron, steel, iron ore, tractors, and cement production (Bialer 1980, 150). However, at the later stage of the Brezhnev period, as Table 7.3 shows, key goals of the ninth and tenth plans, although deliberately set below the levels of previous plans, remained unfulfilled.

Table 7.4
Selected Durable Consumer Goods in the Soviet Union, 1965 to 1977
(per thousand population)

Items	1965	1970	1975	1977
Watches, clocks	885	1,193	1,319	1,408
TV sets	68	143	215	229
Refrigerators	29	89	178	210
Washing machines	59	141	189	200

Source: Kelley (1980, 116).

Soviet living standards increased briskly in the early Brezhnev period. As Table 7.4 shows, in terms of durable consumer goods, the nation was significantly better off in 1977 compared to 1965. As indicated in Table 7.5, consumer durables increased at an annual rate of 8.5 percent during the period from 1966 to 1975. Soviet health services grew at an annual rate of 4.6 percent during the same period. But, again, during the later part of the Brezhnev era, consumer goods production did not sustain its earlier momentum. Therefore, compared to other industrial nations, the Soviet status remained the lowest. Also, the traditional high standard of health care that had distinguished the Soviet system from other industrial nations declined in the later part of the Brezhnev years.

The lackluster economic performance in the later Brezhnev years is evidenced also in lower growth rates in the overall levels of consumption and per capita consumption. A comparison of Tables 7.4 and 6.6 indicates that the average annual rate of growth in household consumption in the early Brezhnev period at first rose (6.2 percent, from 1965 to 1969), but then fell progressively, to 3.9 percent (1965-1975), then to 3.4 percent (1970-1978). As indicated in Table 6.7, annual average growth rates in per capita consumption also fell, from 4.5 percent (1950-1959) to 2.5 percent (1970-1978), despite a reduction in the rate of growth in investment.

In short, the adverse consequences of conservatism, bureaucratic management, and commitment to proceduralism and inherited institutions began mounting in the later days of Brezhnev's rule. The most visible manifestation was the economic stagnation of the late 1970s and early 1980s. Accompanying the weaker economic performance were accelerating social problems, such as rampant alcoholism, high infant mortality rates, and declining life expectancy. Interwoven with these indicators were increasing signs of disintegration in party-state institutions and control over the economy: increasing dissent, bureaucratic corruption, black markets, and expansion in the illegal

Table 7.5
Growth of Consumption in the Soviet Union, 1961-1975
(in percentage; average annual rates of growth)

Year	Total	Food	Consumer Durables	Health & Education
1961-65	2.6	2.1	8.3	4.2
1966-75	3.9	3.3	8.5	4.6

Source: Bialer (1980, 150).

activities of the underground economy. The last of these requires some comment in closing this section. Some of the most common forms of illicit activities were theft of socialist property, using company time for gainful private activity, cheating of customers (for example, by giving short measure or adulteration of goods), "speculation" (that is, purchase and resale of goods for private gain), illegal production, and corruption (Grossman 1976, 835-42).

Illicit production took many forms, for example, engaging in prohibited trades (making or repairing weapons, operating gambling houses or bathhouses, making candles or other religious articles), using government tools and materials in moonlighting activities, underground production of blue jeans and other products associated with Western youth culture, engaging in private production on the job or under the cover of a state enterprise or collective farm, or employing others in underground manufacturing. Theft, cheating, and corruption are hardly unique to a centrally directed economy. However, several institutional and policy aspects of the Soviet system appear to have given the underground economy special stimulus. Price controls, combined with repressed inflation, made shortages of consumer goods and hence black markets likely. Much private activity was prohibited. Much that was permitted required a license and payment of a high fee. Certain kinds of products, such as blue jeans or rock and roll music, were underproduced relative to market demand. These and other factors encouraged underground economic activity and informal market exchanges (Grossman 1976, 842-47). The apparent increasing prevalence and magnitude of the underground economy in the later days of the Brezhnev regime provide partial testimony to the greater boldness and restiveness of the Soviet population combined with a practical, conservative reluctance by the politocracy to clamp down on deviations from the institutions and policies of centralized planning.

TENSIONS AND CONTRADICTIONS

Along with other systemic traits that the Soviet system inherited from the Stalinist era, Brezhnev's eighteen-year rule had been responsible for far-reaching tensions and contradictions which contributed to the eventual disintegration of the Soviet Union itself. We shall focus on those factors in greater detail in the next chapter; therefore, the discussion here will be brief.

By emphasizing institutional continuity and political stability, the Brezhnev regime ended up with an oligarchic, bureaucratic, collectivist rule that plunged the country from Khrushchevian instability into moribund immobility. First of all, emphasis on personnel stability skewed leadership authority and power in favor of the Stalinist generation. Thanks to the emphasis given to personnel stability, the leadership turnover rate fell to less than 10 percent by the end of the Brezhnev era. Whereas the age of full members of the Soviet Politburo averaged 55.4 years in 1952, in 1980 the average age was 70.1 years, and more than 50 percent of those were over 70 years old. The average age of candidate members of the Politburo was 50.9 years in 1952; in 1980 it had increased to 62.5, and 22.2 percent of them were more than 70 years old (Bialer 1980, 82-83).

Moreover, Soviet leadership in the Brezhnev regime demonstrated contradictory features shared with late-Stalin or post-Stalin generations. The Stalinist generation of leadership began political careers early, usually away from great metropolitan centers, and advanced very rapidly through party ladders mainly by demonstrating generalist expertise. The late-Stalin generation, on the other hand, having lower-class origins, spent longer periods at their learned occupations in low or mid-level positions before moving into the bureaucracy, and therefore gradually moved into higher positions. The post-Stalin leaders were distinguished by overwhelming emphasis on technical skills and education as the dominant avenue of mobility. They also demonstrated a structural change of Soviet society as they came primarily from the industrial base as opposed to the agriculture-cum-industrial base of their predecessors (Bialer 1980, 114-15). Therefore, as consensus building, the hallmark of the Brezhnev system, became increasingly difficult, the younger generation became more and more frustrated with the existing politico-economic system. Also, the post-Stalin generation demonstrated greater sensitivity to material progress than the other components of Brezhnev's leadership, and their disillusionment with the system mounted as the economy failed to meet those needs.

Third, the main "priority of the Soviet ruling elite in the 1960s and 1970s was stability and the preservation of the status quo, and they struggled to prevent social change from breaking out of the straight-jacket of existing political and economic institutions." But tranquility and the "quiet life" were purchased at a high price, namely, an economic and social "stagnation" that eventually brought the Soviet Union "to the brink of economic collapse and civil war" (Rutland 1993, xi).

The leadership's strong preference for stability was based on certain shared values. One such shared value was that a "hierarchy of power was the normal, acceptable way to run the society." Specifically, leading politicians and bureaucrats saw no serious alternative to centralized economic planning and management. "None of them," for example, "imagined that a market economy was an option." This unwillingness to contemplate systemic change fostered a rigid and unyielding attitude toward reforms which might have improved economic performance or otherwise contributed to the longevity of the regime. Another stagnation-inducing shared value was the presupposition of the need to maintain a "united front" among the leadership and to "regulate the flow of information so as to steer society along the correct lines" and preserve the party's monopoly of political power. This practice, by excluding the overwhelming majority of the population from participation in public life and by preventing "a rational discourse about policy goals and the means to realize them," caused communication to atrophy, not only in society at large but within the leadership itself. The consequence was a "disturbing lack of feedback" about "real social and economic trends" and thereby a deterioration in the quality and relevance of decisions. A third set of shared values embodied the dual presuppositions that the Soviet Union must be preserved as a unified multinational state and must be a world superpower. These two assumptions were connected because superpower status "gave force to Moscow's claims on the outlying regions and republics" and dissolution of the multinational state would "undermine their [Moscow's] own authority." But the presumed imperative of superpower status "plunged the country into ever more-costly rounds of arms spending and Third World adventurism, until reality finally broke through" and forced Soviet leaders to reconsider "the pretense of global superpower status" (Rutland 1993, 12-16).

Fourth, by emphasizing continuity and thereby neglecting reforms and change, Soviet leaders in the Brezhnev era committed an irreversible mistake—they bypassed the scientific and technological revolution that had been the foundation of economic prosperity for the rest of the industrial world at that period of time. Also, by emphasizing self-sufficiency, Soviet leaders deprived the economy of the advantages of the international division of labor. As a result, the Soviet production process remained largely extensive or traditional and depended on increased infusion of raw materials, labor, and investment which the country was less and less able to do, and enterprises and machineries grew increasingly outdated technologically.

Fifth, technological backwardness, combined with low productivity, widespread alcoholism, and overall frustration in society, contributed to a major slowdown in the Soviet economy. Moreover, the generational changes in the Soviet population that demonstrated greater sophistication in terms of skills, education, training, and urbanization were hardly addressed by the Soviet leadership. As explained in detail in the next chapter, these tensions and contradictions not only demanded abandonment of the stereotyped Brezhnev regime, but also helped to elicit the transformation of Soviet society as a whole.

NOTES

1. Son of a Russian metallurgical worker, Brezhnev was born on December 19, 1906 in the Ukraine. He joined the Komsomol (Young Communist League) in 1923 and became a member of the Communist party at the age of twenty four. Brezhnev graduated from Dneprodzerzhinsk Metallurgical Institute as an engineer in 1935. He came in touch with Khrushchev in 1946 while working for the Fourth Ukrainian Front of the Soviet Army. Brezhnev was appointed the first secretary of the Communist party of Moldavia in 1950. He was elected to the Central Committee and became a candidate member of the Presidium in 1952. In 1953, immediately after Stalin's death, he was removed from both positions. Khrushchev brought him back to the political limelight with the Virgin Lands program in 1954 and inducted him into the Presidium in 1957. He was appointed chairman of the Presidium of the Supreme Soviet in 1960 and made a secretary of the Central Committee in 1963. Brezhnev succeeded Khrushchev at the age of fifty eight.

2. Brezhnev's abrupt interruption of de-Stalinization processes and adoption of dissimilar policies within a few weeks of Khrushchev's ouster, according to some observers, constituted "creeping re-Stalinization" (Dornberg 1974, 195). As discussed below, under Brezhnev, the forces of centralization and bureaucratization became resurgent. Also see Goldman (1983); Bialer (1980).

3. Among the plotters, Suslov, the chief ideologist of the CPSU, was considered to be the mastermind of the conspiracy. The plotters demanded and obtained Khrushchev's resignation "in view of his advanced age and deterioration in the state of his health" at a meeting of the Party Presidium on October 13, 1964. Khrushchev's resignation was made public on October 16, and *Pravda* accused him of "Wild schemes, half-baked conclusions and hasty decisions and actions divorced from reality; bragging and bluster; attraction to rule by fiat; unwillingness to take into account what science and practical experience have already worked out.... armchair methods, one-man decisions, or disregard for the practical experience of the masses" (cited in Dornberg 1974, 184).

4. Born on February 18, 1903, in the Ukraine, Aleksei Kosygin graduated as an engineer from Kiev Technological Institute for the Food Industry in 1931. In 1938 he became first secretary of the Communist party of the Ukraine. He became a deputy premier of the Soviet government at the age of thirty-six, premier at the age of thirty-nine, and a full member of the Soviet Politburo at the age of forty-two.

5. For details on the failure of Kosygin's reforms see Dowlah (1992a, 43-47); Hewett (1988, 230-33); Bialer (1980); Aganbegyan (1988b, 57-59); Katz (1972).

6. The failure, however, did not cost Kosygin his position. Thanks to the collectivity of leadership, Kosygin continued as the premier of the Soviet government until October 1980, when he resigned for health reasons. He died within two months of his resignation. Kosygin was replaced by Nikolai Tikhonov.

7. The presidency of the Soviet Union had thus far been a ceremonial position. Brezhnev himself had held this position immediately before he became the secretary of the Party Central Committee in 1963.

8. Shelepin joined the party at the age of twenty-two in 1940 and was made the chief of the KGB in 1958 by Khrushchev. Widely considered to be a leader in the October coup that deposed Khrushchev, Shelepin was made a party secretary in 1961, a deputy premier in 1962, and a member of the Presidium in 1964.

9. Bialer (1980, 91) describes the leadership and elite turnover rates during the Brezhnev period succinctly: "If Khrushchev brought the Soviet elite the gift of security of life, Brezhnev assured it security of office. Soviet high officials do not fade away; they die in office."

10. Indeed, the initial emphasis on collective leadership was so earnest that it baffled many scholars. Schapiro (1971, 628), for example, remarks, "Perhaps the single most important question in Soviet politics in the next few years will be the survival of collective rule, or the reemergence of a single supreme leader who has been a characteristic feature throughout Soviet history."

11. Brown (1980, 141-43) notes that, during Brezhnev's period, the Central Committee spent on average fewer days per year in plenary session than in Khrushchev's time, but the Politburo met at least as frequently, and party congresses were held more regularly.

12. Kosygin's remark in this regard is worth quoting: "The center of gravity of world economic competition between socialism and capitalism is shifting precisely to these [material prosperity] aspects of production" (cited in Breslauer 1982, 139).

13. The average annual Soviet growth rates in per capita consumption were 5.3 percent in 1951-1955; they dropped to 4.2 percent in 1956-1960 and to 2.5 percent during 1961-1965 (Goldman 1983, 47).

14. Dornberg (1974, 193) states that Khrushchev had approved the experimental implementation of the Liberman system in two textile plants, named Bolshevika and Mayak.

15. Khrushchev had projected annual growth rates above 7 percent for the seventh plan.

16. It should be pointed out, however, that during the initial periods of the Brezhnev regime, especially under Kosygin's leadership, some economic reform programs were initiated on the basis of Liberman's proposals. Subsequently, however, the regime lost interest in any serious transformation of the Soviet economy or society due to factors to be explained below.

17. According to Hewett (1988, 231), while previously enterprises were given thirty-five to forty obligatory targets, Kosygin's reforms lowered the targets to the following eight: output of principal products (in physical units), sales volume, total profits and the rate of profit on capital, total wage fund, the level of payments into the state budget, capital investments from centrally provided funds, specific tasks linked to introduction of new technology, and allocation for the most important material supplies.

18. According to Goldman (1987, 57), the VPOs turned out to be "nothing more than a disguised version of the old, pre-reform administrative units," and in most cases, "the change involved nothing more than calling in a painter to put a new title on the old door."

19. Hewett (1988, 245) observes that, the mergers initiated by Brezhnev's 1973 decrees were actually a faulty attempt to imitate financially successful mergers in the United States.

20. It should be noted that, because the initiatives lacked commitment and support from the political leadership, many of them remained unimplemented.

21. The NNO of an enterprise was calculated as the product of the quantity of output and the net output normative per unit of each item.

22. The NNO was criticized on several grounds. According to Bornstein (1985), the NNO was calculated in net output normatives (NONs) constructed from planned branch average costs (per unit of output) of labor and social insurance plus a profit related to total costs minus direct material expenses. But the calculations of labor costs were deficient because the NNO began in 1982 whereas the NONs were based on 1980 labor costs. Also, enterprises and ministries often overstated their labor costs in order to get higher NONs and industrial wholesale prices. Goldman (1987, 57) points out that, in the absence of meaningful prices, the NNO hardly stimulated product innovation in the enterprises, as managers had little reason to risk the production of new or improved goods.

23. According to Dornberg (1974, 189-91), in the early 1970s, private peasant plots accounted for only 3 percent of all the cultivable land in the Soviet Union, and privately owned animals represented only 25 percent of the Soviet Union's total livestock population. Yet, Soviet consumers obtained more than 60 percent of their potatoes and eggs; 40 percent of their fruits, vegetables, meat, and dairy products; and even 30 percent of the wool they used from the private agricultural sector. According to Wadekin (1982), in 1977 about 15 million private plots, averaging about one acre, produced 27 percent of all Soviet agricultural products, 34 percent of livestock outputs, and almost half of all vegetables and potatoes.

24. During the Brezhnev period, there was a considerable outflow of labor from rural areas, especially in the "non-black-earth" regions of central and northern Russia (Nove 1969, 365).

Chapter 8

Gorbachev and Democratizing Socialist Economy: Origins, Institutions, and Policies

INTRODUCTION

This chapter and the next examine Mikhail Sergeyevich Gorbachev's[1] (1985-1991) period of Soviet development as an exemplar of a self-declared movement toward a more democratic and humane socialism. Gorbachev's appointment as general secretary of the CPSU, in March 1985,[2] ushered in a revolutionary epoch in the Soviet Union and around the globe. In sharp contrast to previous models of Soviet society, Gorbachev's program for moving toward a more democratized socialism, known as perestroika, envisaged a fundamental structural and technological renovation of the Soviet economy, a reactivation of Soviet persons and attitudes, and an overall redirection of the nation's economic, political, and social priorities. Economically, Gorbachev sought to transform an overly centralized command system of management into a more decentralized one based on economic methods and on an optimal combination of centralism and self-management. Politically, Gorbachev initiated programs of glasnost (openness) and *demokratizatsiya* (democratization) in order to reenergize the nation's political and ideological underpinnings and elicit support for perestroika. Socially, perestroika emphasized the awakening of a crippled and dormant Soviet society.

Beginning in 1985 and culminating in a "Programmatic Declaration" adopted by the Twenty-eighth Party Congress held in July 1990, Gorbachev propounded an (evolving) "new image" of a "humane, democratic socialism." Although this version of Soviet socialism was described as an "important stage in the advance to communism" through "accelerated socio-economic development," it abandoned the optimistic expectations of Nikita Khrushchev's 1961 programmatic statement (i.e., imminent material abundance, substantial expansion of collective goods including free goods, and the withering away of the state). Gorbachev also substituted the expression "developing socialism" for Leonid Brezhnev's "developed socialism." This suggested that the Soviet Union was at the outset of a "lengthy stage in the historical development of socialism" and at an earlier stage of both economic and social development than had hitherto been asserted by Brezhnev. Therefore, specification of the details of "full communism" were premature, and attempts to advance too rapidly toward it "might cause both political and economic damage" (cited in White 1992, 223-29).

Moreover, "socialism" itself was subject to further development. On the one hand, the "qualitatively new state of society" envisaged under his leadership, Gorbachev held, "renounced everything that deformed socialism in the 1930s and that led to its stagnation in the 1970s." On the other hand, it inherited the "best elements" of its founding fathers and the constructive achievements of other societies and systems. It would be a "society of free people, a society of and for the working people, built on the principles of humanism, socialist democracy, and social justice." It would be based on a variety of modes of ownership, including local, cooperative, and individual as well as state forms; would substantially enhance the role of democratic self-management in industry and agriculture; would make a "stage-by-stage transition to a market system"; and would retain a significant role for central planning but abandon the "command-administrative" methods of the past. The Communist party itself would become much more democratized and would shift from a dominating to a guiding role in pursuing "historically progressive aims." Such a society would be characterized by "profound and consistent democracy" and "the full range of rights." It would be "open to the world and to cooperation in the interests of building new international relations" based on "universal values" (223-29).

Questions of the internal coherence and feasibility of this new image of a Soviet socialist future will be examined in later sections of this and the following chapter. What is striking about the Gorbachev era is the great diversity of opinion, both inside and outside the Communist party, concerning the reconstruction of Soviet economy, polity, and society. Gorbachev's elucidation and, to some extent, implementation of the various elements of his program stimulated ferment and debate at least as great as that of the great industrialization debate of the 1920s.

Six tumultuous years of perestroika ended with radical reform from above and a democratic revolution from below—characterized by a significant replacement of the centrally planned economy by market-oriented processes and institutions, heavier orientation toward consumer satisfaction and social needs, a significant reduction in the military industrial establishment, unprecedented openness of Soviet polity and society, and widespread democratization and decentralization of politico-administrative processes in the former Soviet Union. Perestroika was substantially responsible for the liberation of the Eastern European countries and the dissolution of the Soviet Union, that is, for the independence of the former Soviet republics. Gorbachev's model of democratizing socialism will be analyzed around the four themes developed in previous chapters. The first two topics will be examined in this chapter, the latter two will be considered in Chapter 9.

UNDERLYING CAUSES

Gorbachev inherited a Soviet Union in a profound and all-pervasive "near" or "pre-crisis." Rapidly worsening economic and political conditions in the country demanded

Table 8.1
The Soviet Union: Growth of GNP by Sector of Origin, 1961-1985*
(Average annual rates in percent)

Sectors	1961-65	1966-70	1971-75	1976-80	1981-85
Industry	6.5	6.4	5.5	2.7	1.9
Construction	4.7	5.4	4.5	2.9	2.9
Agriculture	2.8	3.4	-2.3	0.2	1.2
Transportation	10.2	7.2	6.6	3.6	2.3
Communication	7.3	8.6	6.4	4.7	3.8
Trade	5.0	7.3	4.5	2.7	1.6
Services**	4.4	4.3	3.5	2.7	2.2
Military Personnel***	2.0	3.7	2.0	1.5	0.3

* Based on estimate of value added at 1982 factor cost. ** Includes consumer services like housing and utilities. *** Includes military wages.

Source: Kurtzweg (1987, 138).

an immediate and radical overhaul in nearly every sphere of society. The Soviet leadership and the citizenry alike realized that existing economic and political structures and processes failed to meet the needs of a mature, industrialized, and urbanized society, or those of a viable Soviet future.[3]

Economically, the stagnation of the years from 1979 to 1982 shattered the Soviet dream of surpassing the capitalist countries as had long been promised and questioned the legitimacy of the Soviet version of socialism.[4] Such factors as slow or negative economic growth, low productivity, low morale, technological backwardness, and paradoxes of labor shortages and overemployment and large inventories and shortages had become so counterproductive that fundamental economic reforms could no longer be postponed. Politically, bureaucratic indifference suffused the whole nation as the government and party fell into inaction and immobility. Any new program demanded opening up of the human mind and rejuvenation of social energy. Major factors responsible for disappointing economic, political, and social conditions of the pre-Gorbachev Soviet Union that contributed to the emergence of perestroika can be designated as follows.

Grand Economic Slowdown

The slowdown in the economic growth of the Soviet Union was significantly pronounced in the latter part of the 1970s and in the early 1980s when average growth fell to 2.3 percent per year.[5] By some estimates, growth of the agricultural sector, as Table 8.1 shows, was negative from 1971 to 1975, 0.2 percent from 1976 to 1980, 1.2 percent from 1981 to 1985. In fact, this sector showed no growth at all in 1984 and 1985. Growth of Soviet national income used in consumption and accumulation declined from an annual rate of 5.1 percent from 1971 to 1975 to 3.1 percent in 1985 (David Miller 1989, 115; Dowlah 1992a, 96). Soviet industrial production experienced a continued decline after the 1960s—from a 6.5 percent annual growth from 1961 to 1965, it fell to 1.9 percent from 1981 to 1985. However, as Tables 8.2 and 8.3 indicate, the industrialized capitalist countries also experienced reductions in growth rates in the 1970s and 1980s. Although Soviet growth during the later Brezhnev years worsened, so too did that of the capitalist countries.[6]

Table 8.2

Comparison of GNP Growth in the Soviet Union and Western Countries, 1961-1985
(Average annual growth in percent)

	USSR	US	FRG	Fran	Italy	UK
1961-65	4.8	4.6	4.8	5.8	5.2	3.2
1966-70	5.1	3.0	4.2	5.4	6.2	2.5
1971-75	3.0	2.2	2.1	4.0	2.4	2.2
1976-80	2.3	3.4	3.3	3.3	3.8	1.6
1981-85	1.9	2.4	1.3	1.1	0.9	1.9

US GNP calculated in 1982 prices. GNP growths of FRG, France, Italy and UK are calculated from GDP in 1980 prices.

Source: Kurtzweg (1987, 136).

The more or less steady decline in Soviet growth rates from the 1950s onward to the unusually low rates of the early 1980s is portrayed vividly in Table 8.4. Even official Soviet data indicate that between 1951 and 1955 and 1981 and 1985, average annual growth rates fell as follows: in national income, from 11.4 to 3.6; in industrial production, from 13.2 to 3.7; in agricultural production, from 4.2 to 1.0; in labor productivity, from 8.2 to 3.4; and in per capita real income, from 7.3 to 2.1. The first four sets of figures need to be adjusted for population increases, which were a bit

Table 8.3

Comparison of Soviet and Western Real Gross Product, Factor Inputs, and Productivities, 1960-1978

(Average annual percentage rates of change)

Countries	GNP	Factor Inputs			Factor Productivities		
		Total	Labor	Capital	Total	Labor	Capital
US							
1960-73	4.4	2.3	1.3	4.1	2.1	3.1	0.3
1973-78	2.9	2.3	1.5	3.6	.6	1.4	-.7
Japan							
1960-73	10.8	4.7	.9	12.2	6.1	9.9	-1.4
1973-78	3.8	2.5	.2	7.2	1.3	3.6	-3.4
UK							
1960-73	2.9	.8	-.9	3.9	2.1	3.8	-1.0
1973-78	0.4	.1	-.0	4.7	1.8	4.0	-1.7
France							
1960-73	5.8	1.9	-.1	5.1	3.9	5.9	.7
1973-78	3.0	1.2	-1.0	4.7	1.8	4.0	-1.7
USSR							
1960-73	5.2	3.6	1.4	8.8	1.5	3.7	-3.2
1973-78	3.6	3.3	1.3	8.1	.3	2.3	-4.5

Source: Cohn (1987, 12).

Table 8.4
Soviet Economic Growth, 1951-1985
(Average annual rates of growth, official data, percentage)

Years	Produced national income	Gross indust. prodn.	Gross agric. prodn.	Labour prod'y in ind.	Real incomes per head
1951-55	11.4	13.2	4.2	8.2	7.3
1956-60	9.2	10.4	6.0	6.5	5.7
1961-65	6.5	8.6	7.2	4.6	3.6
1966-70	7.8	8.5	3.9	5.8	5.9
1971-75	5.7	7.4	2.5	6.8	4.4
1976-80	4.3	4.4	1.7	4.4	3.4
1981-85	3.6	3.7	1.0	3.4	2.1

Source: White (1992, 106).

under 1 percent annually during these years, and increases in prices. If the rising social costs from exhaustion of natural resources and pollution, continuing deterioration in the quality of products, and increases in over-reporting are also factored in, net growth rates in national income and industrial output in the later Brezhnev years would probably be close to zero, and growth rates in agricultural output would be negative.

Falling growth rates reduced the maneuverability of the Soviet leadership in responding to competing claims from different sectors of the Soviet society. To stay abreast of the United States as a military power at a time when American military provisioning was expanding dramatically, to provide the bases for further economic development in a context of falling growth rates both in resource inputs and productivity, and to satisfy ever-rising pressures for higher living standards by an increasingly restive population, the sustenance of high growth rates was indispensable. The status of the Soviet Union as a world power, the "social contract" between the political leadership and the population, even political stability, were thus all at stake. Indeed, the reduction in growth rates in the Brezhnev years had proceeded to an extent that virtually signified the onset of economic stagnation, that is, no growth or even an absolute contraction in production and income.

As Gorbachev put it at the Twenty-seventh Party Congress, held in 1986, the "acceleration of socio-economic development of the country is the key to all of our problems: near-term and long-term, economic and social, political and ideological, internal and foreign. Only by such a path is it possible and desirable to attain a qualitatively new situation in Soviet society" (cited in Hewett 1988, 50). In "calling for a reversal in the downward decline in growth rates," Gorbachev was "doing no more than expressing the general leadership view" that overcoming stagnation and fostering high growth were "essential for the future of the system" (51). Improvement of economic performance, particularly growth rates, was both the highest priority of the Gorbachev leadership and the most difficult of all the tasks it confronted.

The success of the Soviet industrialization strategy was based on the Soviet Union's rich resource endowments as well as on its collectivist institutions. These comprised not only abundant natural and demographic resources, but "moral and motivational resources" as well, including "social patience," that is, the willingness to accept

Table 8.5
Soviet Factor Productivity, 1961-1984
(Average annual growth rate, percent)

Item	1961-65	1966-70	1971-75	1976-80	1981-84	Weights
GNP	5.0	5.3	3.7	2.6	2.7	--
Total productive inputs	4.5	4.1	4.2	3.5	3.0	--
Man-hours	1.6	2.0	1.7	1.1	0.8	0.56
Capital	8.8	7.4	8.0	6.9	6.3	0.41
Land	0.6	-0.6	0.8	-0.1	-0.2	0.03
Total Factor productivity	3.4	1.2	-0.5	-0.9	-0.3	--
Man-hours	3.4	3.3	2.0	1.5	1.9	--
Capital	-3.5	-2.0	-4.0	-4.0	-3.4	--
Land	4.4	5.6	2.9	2.7	2.8	--
Intensive/extensive	0.10	0.23	-0.14	-0.35	-0.11	--

Source: CIA (1985, 68).

low living standards in exchange for security, stability, full employment, and minimal pressures to increase efficiency and productivity. None of these resources, according to many Soviet scholars, "was renewable. All of them were depleted over the decades," culminating in the "stagnation" of the early 1980s (Levada 1992, 60). Until the 1960s, for example, the Soviet economy was able to draw on an unusually large pool of underemployed agricultural labor, allowing industrial employment to expand easily by transferring former peasants to urban factories. In addition, a high rate of growth of capital stock was made possible by mobilizing unusually high rates of national savings, reinforced by an investment policy that favored heavy industry over light industry and production of consumer goods[7] and which stretched investment resources by using inherited capital (for example, railroads and urban housing) intensively, repairing and continuing to use older equipment, and ignoring the adverse environmental effects of industrialization.

This strategy began to unravel, especially in the later years of the Brezhnev administration. On the one hand, diminishing returns began to set in increasingly, as indicated, for example, by the rising costs of the extraction of raw materials and fuels, falling productivity, and greater environmental degradation. On the other hand, growth rates in the supplies of productive inputs themselves dropped precipitously in the late 1970s and early 1980s, as is indicated by the data in Tables 8.3 and 8.5. By the late 1970s, reserves of agricultural labor had been exhausted: industrialization had transformed traditional labor surpluses into labor shortages. Birthrates declined significantly, and the population was increasingly aging, indicators of a slower rise in the supply of labor in the future. The slowdown in the rate of growth of investment (recall Table 6.1), designed to enable faster expansion of consumption, was accompanied by reductions in the pace of accumulation of new plants and equipment, despite increases in investment as a percent of GNP, from 28.2 percent in 1970 to 34 percent in 1983 (Cohn 1987, 16). Expansions in the supply of land, for example through irrigation and land reclamation, were increasingly offset or, in some instances, more than offset by such things as greater salination and environmental destruction. Thus, the extensive development strategy, based on infusion of ever-larger amounts of labor, capital, and material inputs, became less and less viable over time as the rates of growth in inputs declined. In addition, the skewed composition of Soviet economic growth, that is, the traditional preference for heavy industry over the light and consumption goods industries, continued (though to a lesser extent) during the Brezhnev period, which resulted in an increasing criticism of the overproduction of iron and steel and other similar commodities and the underproduction of consumer goods and services the Soviet citizenry presumably would have preferred.[8]

The vulnerability of Soviet economic performance, stemming from its unusually heavy reliance on extensive development, was compounded by a "hyper-trophic" priority given to the military sector (Mandel 1991, 202). As noted earlier, from the outset, the fledgling Bolshevik state was opposed, indeed invaded, by armies from the Western capitalist powers. Joseph Stalin subsequently rationalized the intense pace of development and the priority given to heavy industry in the 1930s by the prospect of imminent invasion and destruction from the West and the subsequent postwar Sovietization of Eastern Europe by the imperative need to protect Soviet western frontiers through the creation of a set of subservient buffer states. The ensuing Cold War pitted the industrializing East against the industrialized and modernized West in a game of massive military procurement and provisioning.

This was a game that the Soviet economy could continue to support viably only as long as (1) its extensive development strategy was successful in generating continued high growth, (2) the Soviet population was willing to continue to forego rising living standards in favor of continued military prowess, (3) the magnitude of the military provisioning was moderate. Having commented on the disintegration of the Soviet extensive development strategy, and deferring discussion of Soviet living standards to the next section of this chapter, we turn to the third of these three factors.

The Cold War was an unusually taxing game for the Soviet Union. With a GNP of about half that of the United States in the post World War II period, it was necessary to devote roughly twice the proportion of Soviet resources to military provisioning as the United States to achieve and retain parity. CIA estimates suggest that, in the early 1980s, for example, the Soviet Union allocated from 15 to 17 percent of its GNP to the military (excluding the space program and security forces) as compared to about a 7 percent share of GNP in the United States (Hewett 1988, 67). Moreover, because technology was much less advanced in the Soviet Union than in the United States, a substantially larger share of Soviet scientific and technological talents and energies were devoted to military uses. Because scarce Soviet technological capabilities were thus allocated to the military, the technology in many areas of the nonmilitary economy was primitive, rendering a shift to an intensive development strategy virtually impossible. Some Western observers have reasoned that these considerations underlay the Soviet military slowdown between 1976 and 1985, whereby the rate of growth in military expenditures was reduced from about 4 percent annually to about 2 percent (Hewett 1988, 68), although, partly because of the slowdown in growth rates, military spending as a percent of GNP rose during the late 1970s to early 1980s (Aslund 1989b, 15).

These problems were compounded by the escalation of military spending by the Reagan administration during the 1980s, vividly manifested by an 85 percent increase in such expenditures between 1981 and 1984. It is reasonable to suppose that this fact, together with a lack of success in shifting to an intensive development strategy in the early 1980s, despite reductions in the priorities given to investment, heavy industry, and the military, underlay Gorbachev's decision to withdraw from Eastern Europe and begin the process of the dismantling of the Soviet nuclear war machine. Indeed, it has been argued that the "initial stimulus to domestic economic restructuring was largely external." Many military leaders in the mid-1980s supported perestroika "as a means to strengthen the economic and technological base on which military power depends" (Bova 1992, 43, 48). "Only an intensive economy, developing on the basis of the latest scientific and technological achievement," Gorbachev stated in 1984, "can... ensure the strengthening of the country's position on the international stage and allow her to enter the new millennium with dignity as a great and flourishing power" (47).

The need to shift from an extensive to an intensive development strategy was demonstrated also by external developments occurring in the capitalist world market. During the 1930s, Stalin's initial industrialization drive was based almost exclusively on an internal mobilization of resources. The Soviet Union lost the benefits of international division of labor but was protected from the vicissitudes of volatile capitalist economic fluctuations and depressions. By the 1970s, however, Soviet economic isolation had thawed, at least to the extent of greater reliance on exports of petroleum, a leading source of strategic hard currencies needed to finance imports of machinery embodying new Western technologies. This increased Soviet vulnerability to the impact of fluctuations in world oil prices. When the Soviet system "started to shudder violently in the 1970s, international oil prices soared unexpectedly, and the Soviet Union, as the world's largest oil producer, was able to buy abroad the food, consumers' goods and industrial machinery that it could not produce." As in the 1960s, serious economic reforms were put off. "But when oil prices fell in the 1980s, the Soviet Union's economic disintegration began" (Parks 1991a, H8). As Gorbachev explained to the Party's Central Committee in 1988, if sales of petroleum (and such alcoholic beverages as vodka) were omitted from the statistical calculations, the actual economic growth over the preceding twenty years "dropped to zero and in the early 1980s there had been an actual decline" (White 1992, 113).

Agriculture was the most disappointing sector in the Soviet economy, despite having received more than one-fifth of the total national investment during the Brezhnev years. Even in the 1920s, the Soviet Union was one of the world's largest grain exporters. But by the post-Stalinist period, it had been transformed into the world's largest grain importer. In the early 1980s, more than 20 percent of the Soviet labor force was still employed in agriculture, as compared to from 3 to 5 percent in the United States. Yet, grain imports continued to expand, though with fluctuations, during the 1970s. In the last four years of the Brezhnev regime, grain imports had reached the unusually high level of from 25 to 43 million metric tons (up from 7.3 million tons in 1964 and 0.6 million tons in the bumper crop year of 1969) and constituted up to 25 percent of total Soviet grain requirements. An annual average of 300 million tons of meat was also imported during the 1970s, although

Soviet grazing lands were among the world's largest (Goldman 1983, 65-66). Total Soviet agricultural imports grew from $5.1 billion in 1974 to $20.9 billion in 1982 (Cook 1992, 196).

Besides an unfavorable northern climate, characterized by a short growing season and periodic drought, the disappointing performance of Soviet agriculture, especially during the late 1970s and early 1980s, had its roots in, among other things, low investment in rural infrastructure, an adverse composition of labor, and faulty procurement prices for agricultural goods. Soviet agriculture, relative to the United States and relative to the specified output targets for the sector, remained undercapitalized. The Soviet agricultural labor force was composed mainly of nonworking-age persons, and their productivity level was low—output per worker per day on Soviet farms was only from 5 to 10 percent of the U.S. level. Procurement prices for agricultural goods that did not reflect true economic trade-offs, the Stalinist legacy of overcentralization of decision making and planning processes, and restrictions on private initiatives in agriculture were substantially responsible for the systemic failure of Soviet agriculture.[9] For example, in a speech given in November 1981, Brezhnev in effect admitted that the whole pattern of Soviet agricultural investment had been counter-productive. A "disproportionate share" of investment had gone to massive government projects, such as irrigation and drainage, and too little had been allocated to things that would directly benefit individual peasants, such as barns, decentrally located storage facilities, small-scale machinery, and roads and other marketing infrastructure. Among other adverse consequences, during the late 1970s and early 1980s, "approximately 20 percent of the grain, fruit, and vegetable harvest, and as much as 50 percent of the potato crop perished because of poor storage, transportation, and distribution" (Goldman 1983, 79, 81).

Weaknesses in Soviet agriculture had profound and widespread repercussions. First, increasing waste and inefficiency in and subsidization of agriculture carried the corollary of slower growth in consumers' living standards and thereby lessening support for the Soviet leadership. Second, large and accelerating grain and meat imports squandered hard currency earnings which could have been used to import investment goods embodying productivity-enhancing modern technologies. Alternatively, because hard currencies were earned primarily from petroleum exports, a by-product of rising food imports was the diversion of precious petroleum from domestic uses to exports. Third, misallocation of agricultural investment adversely affected the rate of growth in labor productivity and thereby the overall rate of GNP growth, at a time when productivity increases were becoming more important (and increases in the quantities of inputs less so). Fourth, because of the weakness of the agricultural sector, the Brezhnev regime believed it was necessary not only to invest in and subsidize agriculture, but also to cater to the peasantry, for example, by permitting enlargement of subsidiary garden plots and the time the kolkhozniki would be permitted to devote to them. This, in turn, encouraged peasants to neglect their collective duties, steal collective farm materials and equipment, and so forth, all indicators of the disintegration of the integrity of the inherited collectivist institutions and party-state control over agriculture.

Low Growth and Productivity

The Soviet development model essentially accomplished industrialization, a large GNP, and military prowess. But it did not achieve "modernization," that is, an advanced and technologically progressive economy. Throughout the post-Stalinist era down to the early 1980s, the ratio of national output to combined (capital + labor) input in the Soviet Union was less than 50 percent of that in the United States and about one-third less than that in such West European countries as France and the United Kingdom. Productivity comparisons restricted to industry are less unfavorable (because of the relatively low productivity of Soviet agriculture, commerce, and services) but still reveal the Soviet Union as a laggard in productivity, about 30 percent below the United States and West Germany and slightly below Italy (Bergson 1987).

It is striking that whereas the market capitalist economies, especially since the 1950s, have heavily utilized modern technology to improve labor and capital productivity, the Soviet Union has lagged significantly behind. During the 1960s and early 1970s technological progress often accounted for more than 50 percent of the growth of output in industrialized capitalist countries, but in the late 1970s it invariably accounted for less than 50 percent and often averaged about one-third of the output growth in the Soviet economy (Aganbegyan 1988a, 73). The Soviet Union lagged behind the United States by as much as eight to ten years in advanced microcircuits, four to ten years in minicomputers, nine to fifteen years in mainframe computers, eleven to fifteen years in supercomputers, three to ten years in fiber-optic equipment, and five to nine years in computer-operated machine tools (CIA and DIA 1989).

Possible explanations of low economic efficiency in the Soviet Union, such as cumbersome and overcentralized planning and control processes, the lack of a unifying "success indicator" such as profitability and associated dysfunctional elements of managerial incentives, the lack of authentic market pricing systems, and the neglect of potential advantages from specialization and division of labor through international trade, have been identified in earlier chapters. We have also observed that, to some extent, Soviet leaders purposefully sacrificed efficiency to other objectives, such as military power, rapid growth, industrialization, and collectivist institutions. Several additional factors pertinent to the circumstances that Gorbachev inherited from the "period of stagnation" shall be noted here.

First, the Soviet economy, in both Stalinist and post-Stalinist periods, succeeded in achieving essentially full employment of labor, thus avoiding the waste or inefficiency of large-scale unemployment. Several features of Soviet bureaucratic coordination, however, contributed to the inefficient employment of resources and thereby to low productivity. Basing managerial bonuses on gross output, for example, stimulated excessive use of raw materials (which raised gross output). For example, the Soviet Union used 1.5 times more raw materials and 2.1 times more energy per unit of national income than the United States. Between 1960 and 1986, the Soviet national income rose by a factor of from 4 to 4.4 whereas material input increased almost five times.[10] When natural resources were abundant and cheap, their extravagant use was less of a burden. By the early 1980s, however, the growth rate in raw materials extraction had decreased threefold compared to the early 1970s, and rising costs in mining and consequent increasing prices of fuels and raw materials made greater efficiency in their use essential (Aganbegyan 1988a, 70-71).

Soviet managers also often employed more labor than was needed to produce any particular level of output. This practice was based on several considerations: a reluctance to lay off workers because of adverse political implications, a desire to hoard labor to permit output expansion in the future; and a pragmatic recognition that the wage fund allocation from higher administrative authorities was a function of the number of workers employed. In the early days of Soviet industrialization, the vast supplies of fresh workers from the countryside also encouraged their inefficient employment. But the decline in the growth rate of the labor force in the Brezhnev years, notably its virtual collapse (to an average annual rate of 0.4 percent) between 1981 and 1985, made more economical use of labor essential.

Low productivity was also attributable to the inefficient employment of capital. The disproportionate priority given to investment relative to consumption encouraged such a large increase in the ratios of capital investment to both output and labor that capital productivity growth rates were typically negative in the post-Stalinist period. Because of overly taut planning and a desire to minimize delivery delays from suppliers, managers hoarded equipment as well as labor. In the Brezhnev years, 20 percent of equipment in the construction sector and from 20 to 30 percent of equipment in the industrial sector remained unutilized. Because managers were typically rewarded on the basis of the gross value of their activity rather than on the completion of projects or the satisfaction of their customers, investment projects often went unfinished for many years. Because of the routinization of decision rules encouraging the extended use of capital investment, a large portion of Soviet plant and machinery, by the early 1980s, was either obsolete or in need of replacement.[11]

Second, because of party-state monopoly power relative to society and highly centralized decision processes in service of the party-state bureaucracy, post-Stalinist decision makers had an "almost phobic reaction to innovation" (Goldman 1983, 42). Technological innovation, for example, brought serious risks but provided weak incentives for industrial managers. On the one hand, new products and processes typically required interruption of normal, routine practices and carried the risk that things would not work out as hoped, causing plan underfulfilment and loss of bonuses. On the other hand, if innovations were successful, rewards were slim. Indeed, administrators would readjust targets and tighten plans for future production.

As for social and institutional innovation, the politicians and bureaucrats had strong vested interests in maintaining highly centralized planning processes as a means of sustaining their own power and privileges. Moreover, there was an unusual, and expanding, reluctance to tamper with the inherited centralized institutions. Writing toward the end of the pre-Gorbachev era of bureaucratic stability, Marshall Goldman characterized insightfully the dilemmas of reform in such a context:

> Even those who feel a change is long overdue are hesitant about moving too fast.... There is a realization, even among those who are not satisfied with the existing situation, that significant changes have been delayed for so long that a change, when it does come, is likely to be convulsive.... Too much reform too fast is likely to be destabilizing, especially for the bureaucracy. (1983, 54)

Third, the Brezhnev regime, by strengthening and recentralizing the party-state bureaucracy and stabilizing the positions of its leadership, enhanced the power, status, and thereby privileges of the *nomenklatura*. As economic growth slowed, inequalities increased, and members of the *nomenklatura* increasingly were able to provide better educations and connections for their children, thus extending inequalities intergenerationally and reducing upward economic mobility. The retreat from the relatively more egalitarian programs of the Khrushchev period and the widening gap between the official, relatively egalitarian ideology, which stressed "comradely cooperation" and solidarity of interests among workers, peasants, and the intelligentsia, and the brazenly inegalitarian practices of the Brezhnev regime and its increasingly conservative and self-protective bureaucracy, fostered alienation and political dissidence and had adverse effects on labor morale, discipline, and alcoholism, contributing to the "sharp drop in productivity" in the later Brezhnev period (Goldman 1983, 100). Because the beneficiaries of the increasingly inegalitarian consequences of Soviet institutions, policies, and economic performance in the late 1970s and early 1980s were often (or were perceived to be) Russian, growing tensions and frictions took the flavor of nationalist discontent by the non-Russian republics against the (Russian) center as well as greater alienation toward the politocracy by the underlying population.

Low productivity at a given moment in time, in principle, could be overcome by rapid productivity growth over time. In practice, as Table 8.3 suggests, the Soviet Union experienced the lowest rate of increase in labor and capital productivity among the industrialized countries between 1960 and 1978. Moreover, as the Brezhnev era proceeded, as shown in Tables 8.4 and 8.5, productivity growth rates deteriorated. Between 1966 and 1970, possibly associated with the early Kosygin reforms, total, labor, and capital productivity growth rates rose. All three measures of productivity growth fell dramatically in the early 1970s, followed by low or slightly lower productivity growth thereafter. Lagging labor productivity growth was the paramount cause of productivity growth reductions.

The Consumption Predicament

By Western standards, Soviet per capita consumption remained low and largely unsatisfactory throughout Soviet history. Soviet consumption was disproportionately low relative to the country's industrial, scientific, and educational achievements.12 Thanks to the so-called left-over principle, that is, the systematic allocation of large shares of national resources to heavy industry and defense and the corollary neglect of the consumer sector, the Soviet economy was handicapped by chronic shortages of consumer goods.

Soviet per capita consumption declined throughout the 1930s. It then marked an annual increase of 3.1 percent until 1955 and registered an annual increase of 4.1 percent from 1958 to 1964, during Khrushchev's period. A comparison of Tables 7.4 and 6.7 indicates that the average annual rate of growth in household consumption in the early Brezhnev period at first rose (6.2 percent in 1965-1969), but then fell, more or less progressively, to 3.9 percent (1965-1975), then to 3.4 percent (1970-1978), and finally to 3.1 percent (1983-1985). Annual average growth rates in per capita consumption also fell, from 4.2 percent in the 1950s, to 3.8 percent in the 1960s, to

2.4 percent in the 1970s, and finally to 0.9 percent in the early 1980s, despite a reduction in the rate of growth in investment (Schroeder 1992, 91).

By the early 1980s, consumer markets were in significant "disarray." Shortages, queues, and black markets "were normal features of everyday life for consumers." Although the Soviet system had succeeded in providing minimal levels of food, clothing, and shelter for its population, it displayed increasing difficulty in adjusting the composition of production to consumers' preferences and in meeting consumers' demands for "products of better quality, variety and design and for more and better services" (95). These problems eroded work effort and the efficacy of pecuniary incentives, contributed to a breakdown of labor discipline, worsened such social problems as excessive drinking, and helped to create a popular mood of discontent and pessimism (Schroeder 1987, 330-31).

Although the consumer sector accounted for 37 percent of the growth in national income, it received only 8 percent of the capital investment in the early 1980s. Outlays on housing construction dropped from 23 percent in 1960 to from 14 to 15 percent in the early 1980s; expenditures in the educational sector during the same period dropped from 10 to 7 percent; and national income allocated to medical services dropped to less than 4 percent. The low quality of goods, frequent unavailability of necessities, and poor delivery systems often compounded the situation.[13]

Soviet leaders in the later years of the Brezhnev era indicated increasing concern over the poor quality of many products and services. As intimated by a rising tide of critical letters to newspapers, it seems clear that, especially in the consumer sector, "many Soviet-manufactured goods" were "unreliable and incapable of operating at designed capacity." Others, although reliable enough, embodied "obsolete technologies" and were superseded by more technologically advanced goods in the West or even in many parts of the developing world. There is some evidence that this "widespread" and "chronic" problem, with adverse effects on both labor productivity and faith in the legitimacy of the political leadership and its institutions by the general body of the population, increased in the early 1980s. Despite excess demands, retail inventories grew more rapidly than the supplies of consumers' goods. Between 1981 and 1984, for example, retail sales growth fell to 2.8 percent per annum, while inventory growth averaged 8.7 percent per annum. As Yuri Andropov, Brezhnev's successor, observed in 1983, televisions, watches, refrigerators, and so on, in the six and seven figures and accounting for from "1.2 to 8.4 percent of the annual output of these various commodities," were sitting in warehouses because consumers, despite excess demands, refused to buy them (Hewett 1988, 78-81).

The paradox of shortages of consumption goods and surpluses of inventories had, however, been a systemic phenomenon in the Soviet economy for decades. In 1985, for example, the average inventory/sales ratio in the Soviet Union was 2.4 in industry and 3.6 in trade—which was much higher than in other industrialized countries. In the United States, for example, the average inventory/sales ratio was 1.73 in manufacturing industry and 1.24 in wholesale trade during the recession year of 1982.[14] The low quality of domestically produced goods and scarcity of imported goods had still other consequences. Because consumers had little they wanted to buy, they eventually ended up with huge savings. Total savings in the Soviet Union registered sustained increases of more than 10 percent annually from the mid-1970s. From 91.0 billion rubles in 1975, savings rose to 156.6 billion in 1980.[15] Such enormous savings in individual hands helped to promote a vigorous private illegal market (the "second" or "underground economy"), which, according to some estimates, reached up to 25 percent of the Soviet GNP.[16]

Several factors are responsible for the deteriorating growth rates in consumption levels and living standards during the Brezhnev administration era. First, in the 1930s and early 1940s, depression, fascism, and disruption of the world market, combined with unusually rapid industrialization and full employment in the Soviet Union, yielded very favorable assessments of Soviet achievements, despite the neglect of, indeed reduction in, the real wages and consumption of workers and peasants. As the post-Stalinist era progressed, "Soviet society could less and less free itself from the desire of at least tens of millions of consumers to imitate the consumption patterns of the richer capitalist countries" (Mandel 1991, 201). The postwar unification of the world market, the long wave of prosperity and expansion, including high rates of growth in consumption, and the continued large disparities between per capita consumption, despite the succeeding economic slowdown in the West in the 1970s and after, stimulated emulation of Western living standards by many Soviet citizens. The Soviet Union had long been engaged in what its leaders called "competition between the two systems." Its failure to catch up with the industrially advanced capitalist countries, in either living standards or technological modernization, undermined the legitimacy of the regime. "This was particularly marked among the elite who traveled abroad or were able to obtain imported consumer goods" (Ellman and Kontorovich 1992, 18).

Thus, the "pre-crisis" of the 1980s was as much comparative and international as it was absolute and internal. The slowdown in economic growth (and associated problems) culminating in the early 1980s posed a serious challenge to the policy makers. Weakening economic performance made the country increasingly vulnerable to unfavorable comparisons with the capitalist economies. Although the capitalist economies clearly had problems of their own, especially after the early 1970s, it was not clear that they had entered into a stage of final crisis and secular decline or that the Soviet economy could realistically regain the lost dynamic of its earlier years. Consequently, the notion of catching up with and surpassing the capitalist countries, especially in per capita income and consumption, had to be abandoned. It had become increasingly clear by the 1980s that the Soviet Union could not compete with the Western capitalist countries, militarily, politically, or economically.

Militarily, as mentioned above, matching the West was out of question. The Soviet Union failed to compete politically as well, as "its initial revolutionary successes failed to develop into functioning, alternative systems of democracy" and instead settled into varieties of dictatorial and authoritarian rule. Neither could it compete in the "new fields pioneered by capitalist advance: consumer culture [and] the third industrial revolution and the spread of information technology." Finally, the Soviet Union and its Eastern European allies "never constituted a dynamic trading bloc capable of rivaling the West. It always occupied a defensive, subaltern place in the international economy. It lagged behind, and was condemned to copy, in the field of technology." The Soviet bloc was simply too weak and its internal mechanisms were too rigid to allow such a development. Thus, adverse comparative and international considerations, as distinguished from absolute and internal factors, played very important roles in eliciting Soviet critique of the Brezhnev period and adopting perestroika in the mid-1980s (Halliday 1991, 94).

Second, low productivity growth and low per capita consumption growth became interconnected in a kind of cumulative "vicious circle" in the late 1970s and early 1980s. Slower productivity growth brought slower growth in per capita consumption, despite attempts to offset the productivity slowdown by reducing the growth rates of investment and military spending. But slower expansion in per capita consumption caused additional reductions in labor productivity. Workers who are at least minimally well fed, clothed, and housed, and provided with adequate medical care, demonstrate greater efficiency and productivity. Bereft of minimal levels and growth rates in these areas, labor productivity growth falls.

Demographic Decay

Soviet economic problems were further compounded by a sharp decline in the growth of the labor force in the 1980s.[17] Between 1971 and 1978, the annual increment of the working-age population (from sixteen to fifty-five for women and sixteen to sixty for men) increased by more than 2 million each year; however, that number fell to 0.4 million in 1985. The decline in the working-age population was caused by a falling birthrate and a sharp increase in the pension-age population. Also, the Soviet labor shortage was highly regionally specific. The shortage was acute in such traditionally industrialized regions as the Ukraine, Russia, Byelorussia, and the Baltic republics. The working-age population was expected to increase in the industrially less developed regions.[18] Moreover, expected growth in the overall working-age population during the fifteen year period from 1981 to 1995 was gloomy. To Gorbachev and his advisers, this condition indicated an end to the traditional abundance of industrial labor in the country and reinforced the perception of the dire need to move toward greater reliance on technological programs and more on efficient use, combination, and allocation of resources.[19]

Sociopolitical Factors

In contradistinction to pervasive degeneration in the economic sphere, Gorbachev inherited an educated and urbanized population with sophisticated demands and expectations. Less than one-fifth of the Soviet population lived in urban areas before the early 1930s. The urban population increased to 32 percent in 1939, 49 percent in 1960, 52 percent in 1972, and 65 percent in 1985. By the late 1970s and early 1980s a predominantly peasant population had been transformed into an industrial, urban, working-class population. Second, urban centers grew in size and complexity. By the early 1980s, 272 cities in the Soviet Union had more than 100,000 inhabitants, whereas the number of such cities was only 88 in 1959.[20] Such a proliferation of large cities facilitated an internal regrouping of urban populations, making them increasingly ungovernable under the existing sociopolitico-economic system. Third, until the 1960s the majority of the urban population were born in the countryside; but by the 1970s the majority of them were born in the cities. Thus, the peasant outlook and mentality gave way in the 1980s to a qualitatively different, new urban generation whose aspirations and needs were shaped increasingly by Western lifestyles. Indeed, a "cultural revolution," in such areas as standards of living, status, culture, and roles, began to surface. Therefore, pressures on the authorities for more effective articulation of citizen demands, such as differential access to education, professions, and social mobility, intensified.

The Gorbachev regime also inherited a highly skilled and educated workforce. As late as 1959, the overwhelming majority of the Soviet population (91.3 percent of workers and 98.2 percent of kolkhoz peasants) had completed only four years of elementary education. Just two decades later, in 1979, a substantial majority of both the urban (86.3 percent) and rural (69.3 percent) populations had completed secondary education.[21] Between 1959 and 1984, the number of specialists with secondary education rose from 7.9 million to 28.2 million. In 1939, only 1.2 million persons in the Soviet Union had completed higher education; by 1984, the number stood at 18.5 million. Those with higher degrees quintupled between 1960 and 1987 (from 0.3 million to 1.5 million). Expanding education was reflected also in the changing educational background of the political leadership. For example, the proportion of party members who had completed higher education rose from 11.6 percent in 1957, to 28 percent in 1981 to 34.3 percent in 1989. The proportion rises at the higher levels of party authority: In 1980-1981, 70 percent of the Central Committee members had completed higher education; by 1987, 99.9 percent of the local party and Central Committee secretaries had college or university degrees (Lane 1992, 163-64).

The urban employed population in the Soviet Union consisted of three groups: workers (about 60 percent), officials and specialists (about 40 percent), and kolkhoz peasants (from 1 to 5 percent). Among the workers from 10 to 12 percent were unskilled or poorly skilled, from 44 to 46 percent were physical workers, and 3 or 4 percent were highly skilled workers involved in physical and intellectual activities. In the second category, the officials and specialist group, 11 or 12 percent were poorly trained or untrained, 17 or 18 percent were in professional jobs (requiring secondary and specialized schools or university training), from 2.4 to 3 percent were in medium-rank managerial and professional positions (requiring university level and higher training),[22] and 2 percent were in upper rank leadership positions and performed largely intellectual functions. The professional classes and intellectuals directed all spheres of economic, political, and social life in the Soviet Union.

The Soviet educational system produced doctors, engineers, and other specialists in numbers greater than their demand in the economy. Between 1960 and 1986, the overall employed population in the Soviet Union increased by 155 percent, but the number of specialists grew fourfold. As a result, in 1969 alone, 28,000 engineers were employed as "industrial workers," and throughout the Brezhnev period many doctors were employed as "agricultural labor." In addition to sharpening consciousness among the urban working class, denial to the well-educated majority of the opportunity of realizing the fruits of their learning resulted in a decline in the growth rate and a deceleration in technical progress in the Soviet Union.

These undercurrents of transformation—urbanization, industrialization and education—in turn, resulted in profound changes in Soviet society.[23] First, the composition and structure of the working class and professionals dramatically changed. Second, patterns of occupational and job structures were transformed. Third, these transformations resulted in dramatic alterations in intergenerational attitudes and outlooks. The political and economic consequences of these changes were impelling. An educated and Westernized labor force constituted a distinct cultural shift in the development of Soviet society, which generated radically altered needs and demands. Economically, what was an unnecessary luxury for the older generation became an unavoidable shortage for the younger generation. Politically, raising wages or relaxing bureaucratic controls no longer satisfied a more informed and self-conscious working class. What was required was broadening the rights of workers qualitatively, to humanize and democratize production relations as a whole. Pressures for sweeping political and economic changes mounted because of social and economic transformations, which also brought about substantial changes in the psychological arena. Attention shifted from macro issues, such as economic development and the national education system, to micro issues, such as personal and human relations and small-scale community welfare. The new environment, coupled with the contemporary technical and scientific revolution, intensified demands for greater opportunities for autonomous activity, creativity, and individuality, which clashed with the existing authoritarian and overcentralized political-economic system.

One of the most important results of industrialization, urbanization, and expanding education was the creation of and disproportionate increase in a new middle class of skilled, technical, professional, and managerial labor. This group had "a higher level of expectations, a more sophisticated view of the world, and greater political awareness" (Lane 1992, 163). It aspired to greater political participation, to an improvement in living standards, and, especially, to a rectification of what it considered injustices in its treatment relative both to urban manual labor, on the one hand, and high level members of the party and state bureaucracy, on the other.

From the perspective of the emerging Soviet new middle class, income differentials were too small and did not justly reward differential skills, education, and motivation. Between 1932 and 1986, the ratio of wages of technical and managerial labor to manual labor fell, from 2.63 to 1.1. Wage ratios for office workers to manual labor also fell during this same period, from 1.5 to 0.78. The promanual labor and relatively egalitarian character of the Soviet wage distribution becomes clearer when one compares relative wages in the Soviet Union with those of Western, industrial capitalist economies. For example, in the early 1980s, the wage ratio of a chief doctor to an unskilled manual worker was 2.5 in the Soviet Union and 4.8 in the United Kingdom. For an underground coal miner, the respective wage ratios were 3.8 and 1.9 (170).

At the other end of the social spectrum, the Soviet new middle class was squeezed from above by high-level party and state bureaucrats. First, the Soviet political and administrative elite had privileges, such as access to special housing, stores, recreational facilities, and health care, which barely trickled down to those in the middle layers of Soviet society. Second, the new middle class, although often better educated than the politocracy, lacked access to political power and participation in the oligarchical, and relatively immobile and closed, environment of the Brezhnev era.

Thus, many managers, technical workers, and professionals (and students aspiring to these occupations), notably those who had access to foreign travel or other sources of information about relative wages and living standards in capitalist countries, came to believe that they could be absolutely and relatively better off under a "normal" Western-style politico-economic regime. The new middle class in general and the intelligentsia in particular constituted an increasingly active social stratum intent on improving their relative positions in Soviet society. These were natural allies for Gorbachev in the development of perestroika and a major force in shaping the policy proposals of the political elite under his leadership (165).

In short, a cluster of economic, social, and political factors contributed to the emergence of perestroika. The Gorbachev leadership realized that the extensive methods of production that had helped the Soviet economy achieve rapid industrialization had lost their potency. The Soviet economy of the 1980s had neither enormous raw materials, as it did during the Stalinist period, nor surplus agricultural labor to direct to industrial expansion. Moreover, the demographic slowdown made transition from extensive to intensive methods of production imperative for the Gorbachev regime. It was also realized that years of bureaucratic management of the economy had cost the Soviet Union the benefits of scientific and technological revolutions. Technologically, other than the defense sector, the Soviet Union was far behind even South Korea or Singapore.[24] Factors such as the need to reduce sharply the disproportionately high allocation of GNP to the military buildup, the indispensability of boosting Soviet consumption, the realization that reform of the economic environment was impossible without a reform of the economic system, and perhaps above all, the fact that nothing could be accomplished without opening up the minds of the Soviet people contributed to the emergence of perestroika in the mid 1980s.[25]

INSTITUTIONS, PROGRAMS, AND POLICIES

Redirection of the National Economy

Perestroika constituted a redirection of Soviet economic and social structures and priorities and a reactivation of its human and material resources. In sharp contrast to the piecemeal reforms of the past, its reforms were more comprehensive and foundational. It emphasized the substitution of intensive methods based on scientific and technological revolution for the traditional methods of production and the replacement of administrative management by a management based on economic methods. Three Russian words—*uskoreniye* (acceleration), *intensifiatsiya* (intensification), and perestroika (restructuring)—symbolized Gorbachev's economic goals.

At the initial stage, the Gorbachev leadership set forth ambitious growth rates for the economy—above 4 percent annually for the period from 1986 to 1990 and over 5 percent for the 1990s—which required doubling the growth rates of 1976 to 1985 and returning to those of the 1960s and early 1970s. Industrial growth for 1986 to 1990 was targeted to double that of the preceding decade and reach even higher rates during the 1990s. Agricultural production targets for 1986 to 1990 were expected to triple those of the preceding fifteen years. Labor productivity was set to grow at 4.6 percent annually, and real per capita income growth was targeted at 2.7 percent during the twelfth plan (1986-1990) and from 3.4 to 4.7 percent for the 1990s (Dowlah 1992a, 153-54).

Perestroika directed the bulk of the investment fund toward restructuring and re-equipping existing plants rather than building new ones. Emphasis was shifted to modernizing antiquated capital stock and upgrading the quality and technological level of machineries and other capital instruments. By 1990, 90 percent of all machinery was expected to meet world standards, compared to about 20 percent in 1985. Gorbachev, especially at a later stage, also sought to move to a "regulated market economy" by dismantling much of the centrally planned economy. Major reforms initiated by perestroika to accomplish these redefined national objectives will be discussed as follows.

State Enterprise Reforms

A key component in the economic restructuring of the Gorbachev era was the promulgation of the principle of the "autonomy of government enterprises." Although reality lagged behind rhetoric, the aspiration was to evolve toward a fairly radical decentralization in the authority to make production (and, to a lesser extent, investment) decisions by the transfer of decision-making power from ministries and intermediary administrative units to individual firms. Under the Law on State Enterprises, in 1988, this was to be accomplished in stages and through an evolutionary process. Enterprises producing half of the country's output were to implement the new system in 1988, and enterprises producing the remaining half were required to join the program in 1989.

Each ministry, in collaboration with *Gosplan,* would construct an aggregate plan for production in the area under its oversight (for example, the total output for various kinds of steel products). State authorities would also set key industrial prices, specify major inputs, determine the overall pattern of investment, provide enterprises with control indicators and productivity norms, and issue "state orders" (*goszakazy*), the provision of which enterprises would contract themselves to deliver.

Within this framework, enterprises were expected to exercise initiative in various ways. First, enterprises were to formulate their own production plans, established through negotiation with higher level administrative units. Second, because control indicators, economic normatives, and other devices lost their traditional directive character, enterprises were freed from day-to-day interference by the central apparatus and were to exercise considerable discretionary power over the means of achieving planned output targets, for example, product mix, wages, and employment. Third, state orders were to commence at levels less than 100 percent of planned output. If state orders for a particular year were set, for instance, at 80 percent of planned output, then the surplus above 80 percent would be available for the enterprise to sell at prices to be set through negotiation with prospective customers. These prices presumably would exceed the prices set by state authorities, and enterprises could obtain thereby (perhaps substantial) profits by such transactions.

Because enterprises were extended wide discretionary powers over the allocation of retained profits, it was expected that managers and workers would be motivated to cultivate assiduously both the means to enhance productivity, so as to increase production and surpluses above state orders, and the market transactions needed to realize the profits from such surpluses. Fourth, state orders were expected to decrease over time. Thus, central administrative direction could decrease and enterprise autonomy (and market economy) could increase gradually and organically, as enterprises acquired greater experience, skill, and contracts. Fifth, within certain limits, enterprises were expected to become independent, self-accounting, self-financing, and self-managing. State enterprises were expected to cover all their expenses, including wages and investments, from their own revenues. Enterprises were called upon to work in a competitive environment, to attract customers for their products, and to negotiate with suppliers for their own raw materials. The government relinquished its commitments to enterprises, and persistently loss-making enterprises faced liquidation or bankruptcy. Such a self-financing mechanism (*khozraschet*) was expected to enhance labor productivity and improve the quality of products by generating businesslike attitudes among enterprises, and by making them more responsive to market demand.

State enterprises were granted wider authority under three different models of economic accountability (*khozraschet*). The first model called for the distribution of residual profit into various funds after taxes and interest payments were paid. The state enterprise's income in this model was made up of the wage fund and residual profits. Central authorities were legally prohibited from confiscating the residual profits of enterprises. A second model distributed the income remaining after deduction of material costs. Under this model, taxes and interest payments were paid from income, and after-tax income remained at the disposal of the enterprise as collective income and then was divided into work remuneration, production development, and other funds that were formed according to guidelines provided by central authorities. The main difference between these models lay in the fact that, while the former more or less guaranteed wages, the latter provided no such guarantee. Under the second model, which stood for stricter self-accountability, the wage fund could go below or rise above the usual levels. This model emphasized "hard-budget constraint," as all expenses must be paid first, and only the remainder could be distributed in the form of wages and other incentives. Under a third model, employees rented the enterprises from the state, the state collected a fixed amount of rent from the employees as specified under the lease agreement, and the remaining income was distributed by the employees according to their own preferences. Another offspring of the *khozraschet* movement was interbranch state associations or socialist firms (MGO), in which producers joined in voluntary unions that were independent of ministerial control. At a later stage, in late 1990, the autonomy of state enterprises was further extended when enterprise managers were allowed to operate in the interests of their employees and "stockholder-owners" in determining the volume and structure of production conforming to market demand and supply conditions.

Workers' Participation in Enterprise Management

Our discussion of economic restructuring in the preceding section focused on decentralization in the sense of greater autonomy of enterprises relative to central planners and administrators. In principle, such reforms could be implemented in the context of maintained centralized and authoritarian patterns of decision making within enterprises, as under both traditional versions of Western capitalism and Stalinist and post-Stalinist Soviet economy. But perestroika, again more in aspiration than in practice, envisaged greater decentralization of decision making within enterprises as well as between enterprises and the economic bureaucracy. Through legislative changes of the late 1980s, groups of workers (brigades) working on particular projects or tasks were authorized to strike compacts with their enterprises. If a brigade overfulfilled its contracted output target, it was empowered to divide the revenues from the surplus output among its members. Brigades were also given some discretionary power in determining relative wages within the group and financial incentives to reorganize work so as to increase labor productivity and release labor for relocation elsewhere within or outside the enterprise. In these ways, in combination with greater enterprise autonomy, a closer linkage between performance and benefits, in the form of wages, bonuses, and expanded resources for social investment (for example, recreational facilities), was expected to stimulate increased workers' collective interest in productivity and job results.

Perestroika also incorporated more democratic modes of workers' participation in management. Under its enabling legislation, workers were empowered to elect workers' councils to supervise management and the managers themselves. The workers' councils were authorized to supervise overall performance of enterprises, the distribution of funds pertinent to long-term goals, such as investment and product innovation, and the housing and welfare needs of workers. Top enterprise managers were to be elected for five-year terms by a conference of workers in multicandidate elections. The goals of this extension of intraenterprise democracy were to inculcate in workers the feeling of coownership, to hold managers more effectively accountable, to provide an alternative or supplement to ministerial oversight, and to secure the working class as allies in perestroika's implementation. All of these goals, in turn, were expected to increase labor productivity and thereby contribute to perestroika's overall aim of modernization.

Reforms in Central Planning and Administration

As a corollary to greater decentralization and autonomy to and within enterprises, the range and detail of centralized planning and administration were reduced substantially. In place of detailed input-output plans, *Gosplan* began to emphasize overall, macroeconomic targets; strategic planning; nonbinding control indicators, such as net output, profit, and foreign currency receipts; and long-term norms, such as efficiency and productivity. Hence forward, ministries were expected to control enterprises in limited ways, such as fulfilling state orders; imposing ceilings on investments and materials allocations; determining overall rules regarding profits, profit distribution, and labor productivity; and exercising "indirect controls," such as centrally set prices, finance, and credit allocations (Gorbachev 1987, 90; Ericson 1988, 2). Eventually, state orders were expected to be limited to such matters as military defense, big investment projects, and nondefense collective consumption. In short, central planning was not to be abandoned; indeed, it was to be retained as "overriding and universal." But it was to take on new forms, some of which were to be realized "through the market."[26] Specifically, central planning was expected to provide the overall economic indicators and strategies within which government policies and enterprise decisions would be made. Central administrators were expected to oversee the allocation of "centralized state resources, the creation of new branches of production, major projects, transport infrastructure, reconstruction of towns, etc." (Aganbegyan 1988a, 120, 132).

Late in perestroika's evolution, the Gorbachev leadership proposed to shift emphasis from improving the centralized planning machinery to dismantling it and moving toward a "regulated market economy," as enunciated in the "500-day program," initially endorsed by Gorbachev and approved by the Supreme Soviet of the Russian Republic in 1990. The Supreme Soviet of the Soviet Union adopted a somewhat similar, but softer, program at a later point. This program, designed by S. S. Shatalin and other economists in the "radical" wing of the party, envisaged a switch to much greater reliance on market processes, market-based fiscal and monetary institutions to reduce budgetary deficits and subsidies, major alterations in the character and scope of economic planning to focus on broad trends and goals rather than on detailed microeconomic management, destatization of property relations, and greater decentralization of authority to the republics and local governments.

Although huge scientific and production enterprises remained under central control, medium and small enterprises that produced for local markets were transferred to the republican and local governments. Central ministries were expected to become the scientific, technical, planning, and economic headquarters of individual industries. Up to 1987, the high degree of centralization was demonstrated by the fact that industrial enterprises accounting for 61 percent of total output were directed by the Council of Ministers and ministries of the central government (all-union ministries), 33 percent were overseen jointly by the central and republican governments (union-republic ministries), and only 6 percent were under the exclusive jurisdiction of republics (republic ministries). By the late 1980s, substantially greater autonomy had devolved to the republics. First, the economic bureaucracy shrank dramatically. The number of staff in the apparatuses of ministries, committees, and departments had declined between 1985 and 1988 by 543,000, a decline of 33.5 percent. Second, in June 1989, Gorbachev's government announced that all union-republic ministries would be abolished and their activities would be transferred to the republics (Lane 1992, 40-41). Third, by 1990, the number of all-union ministries was reduced from fifty to thirty-two. Fourth, the role of all-union ministries was radically changed from the supervision of particular industries to the provision of overall control functions. An all-union law of April 1990 gave the central government jurisdiction over pricing; credit, finance, and the money supply; taxes and the budget; investment; science, technology, and communication and information systems; employment and minimum wages; health and public education; foreign economic policy, customs, and foreign loans; economic development; and such other functions as statistics and weights and measures.

Perestroika also revamped the economic organization and management structures in order to eliminate duplication and inefficiency and streamline responsibilities. *Gosagroprom* (State Committee for the Agro-Industrial Complex) was created in November 1985 to replace three union-republic food-processing ministries. The Bureau of Machine Building was created by integrating the functions of eleven former civilian machinery production ministries, and *Gosstroi* (State Committee for Construction) was created by merging four all-union ministries. The State Foreign

Economy Commission was founded as the coordinating supreme authority on international economic affairs. The State Committee for Computers and Information Sciences was established to coordinate the activities of intersectoral scientific and technical complexes. The number of ministries was reduced, and ministries were relieved of day-to-day responsibilities; sectoral subbranches (*glavki*) were replaced by several thousand large associations and enterprises directly accountable to all-union ministries. The State Committee for Work and Social Problems (*Goskomtrud*) was reorganized to handle labor replacement, released workers, and unemployment problems. By 1990 the 500-day program envisioned a "mutually beneficial" relationship based on equal partnership with the republics. It allowed the republics to determine the level of basic taxes and to form their own budgets. All these constituted a sharp decline in the authority of central management and major organizational and institutional changes in the republics.[27]

After the unsuccessful coup of August 1991, the apparatus of decision-making power was decentralized still further. The Communist party, in effect, was destroyed as an organized political force in the country. Its assets were seized, it was declared unconstitutional in some republics (for example, Russia), its groups in government and economy (in factories, the KGB, and the armed forces) were banned, and Gorbachev resigned as general secretary, hence losing a major political base. The Cabinet of Ministers (successor to the former Council of Ministers) was abolished, and its members were dismissed. In its place, a State Council was established, consisting of the leaders of the republics and chaired by the president. Except for foreign affairs, defense, and security, all union-level ministries were dissolved in favor of republic ministries, and their properties typically were nationalized. The Supreme Soviet was reorganized to include a Council of the Union, constituted by population and focused on the "rights and freedoms" of Soviet citizens, and a (new) Council of Republics, composed of members delegated from republican supreme soviets, was concerned with overseeing the work of republican legislative bodies. The power of the republics was further enhanced by their declarations of independence. Even the name of the country was changed, from the Union of Soviet Socialist Republics (USSR) to the Union of Sovereign States (USS).

Market and Price Reforms

One of perestroika's prominent tenets is that, as the role and scope of central planning and administration decrease, that of market and price processes should increase. Indeed, the matter can be put more strongly. If bureaucratic coordination of economic relationships is to diminish, then other social processes, such as market relations and democratization, must enlarge their roles. And if, as occurred in Soviet practice in the Gorbachev era, the actual or proposed diminution of centralized decision and coordination processes accelerates over time, the need for market processes (and their underlying institutional infrastructure) also accelerates.

Gorbachev and his associates anticipated that it would be feasible over time to incorporate an expanding role for market and pricing processes into the Soviet "mix of plan and the market," and that the result would be greater economic efficiency and improved economic performance. At the same time, however, they also perceived a danger of "throwing out the baby with the bathwater." They believed that central planning, within the context of public ownership and an egalitarian social welfare policy, yielded important social benefits, notably, social fairness, greater economic stability than in capitalist economies, full employment, generous social security and free or subsidized public services (housing, education, medical care, recreation, pensions), and minimal inequality (Galbraith and Menshikov 1988, 11-13). Conversely, market processes, notably under capitalist property relations, exhibit serious economic defects, such as unemployment, inflation, economic insecurity, and wealth and income inequality. Under conditions of significant shortages of many consumer goods, removal of governmental price controls would almost certainly cause prices to rise. Price inflation would cause reductions in real income for those whose money incomes failed to keep pace, for example, pensioners and the poor generally. In turn, an environment of rising prices creates uncertainty, demands for higher wages, and social unrest. To minimize these dangers, Gorbachev and his advisers believed that economic restructuring should strike a balance between plan and market. The enlarging role for market processes should be constrained in several ways.

First, in deeds as much as words, perestroika's proponents exemplified the view that the speed of movement toward a more market-oriented economy should be moderate, so as to minimize the extent of short-run dislocation and obtain needed political support. Second, although perestroika incorporated changes in property relations, which would move the Soviet Union in the direction of a "mixed economy," it was presupposed that a paramount role for public ownership of the means of production would be sustained. Consequently, emergent market processes would occur primarily in consumer goods. Land or factories could be leased to individuals or groups of workers, who then would be empowered to exercise such property rights as managerial control and distribution of benefits. But, because the property right of alienation over productive assets would not (generally) be extended to private citizens, a full land or capital market in the Western capitalist sense would not exist. The dominant position concerning the labor market was mixed. On the one hand, the role of market processes in the allocation and employment of labor was expected to expand under perestroika. Adjustments in production and productivity of labor were expected to generate changes in the demand for labor and thereby potential unemployment. On the other hand, Gorbachev was unwilling to accept the view that a more market-oriented economy required significant unemployment (beyond frictional unemployment) to impose economic coercion as a means of achieving labor discipline. The typical position was to expect unemployment to rise but to "set up a system capable of finding new jobs for the laid-off workers" (Hewett 1988, 293).

Finally, the newly emerging market economy was to be "regulated." For example, the minimization of unemployment would require an effective application of monetary and fiscal policy, education and job training, and assistance in job relocation. Curbing inflation might require not only budgetary discipline, but also wage-price guidelines, selective use of price controls, and policies to promote competition and reduce monopoly. Restraining inequality suggests the need for tax, budgetary, and other policies. The Gorbachev position, broadly put, was to endeavor to achieve a balance between high-priority reforms in the interest of efficiency and modernization and to retain, as fully as possible in that context, the traditional perceived advantages of Soviet-style socialism in the interest of equity. With or without market processes, it was widely believed by supporters of economic reform that, because of large-scale subsidies and price controls, Soviet prices diverged substantially from costs. To rectify this problem, prices often needed to rise.

Although perestroika proposed the most sweeping price reforms in Soviet history, time and again such reforms were postponed either temporarily or for an indefinite period. In the absence of market mechanisms, most prices in the Soviet Union were fixed by *Goskomtsen*—the State Committee on Prices. In an average year, *Goskomtsen* approved about 200,000 prices and rates on goods and services, kept track of 24 million prices, and directly set 42 percent of all wholesale prices in the economy. Procurement prices of agricultural goods and prices of such natural resources as fuel, energy, and other raw materials were traditionally kept low by ignoring the cost of rent and underestimating the cost of labor. As a result, state subsidies on wholesale and retail prices mounted. Between 1965 and 1988, for example, such state subsidies increased twenty times, from 3.6 billion to 73 billion rubles and eventually constituted 20 percent of the state budget. Also, prices of most essential goods and services remained unchanged for decades (Shmelev and Popov 1989, 155-171).

Therefore price reform became imperative for the successful implementation of perestroika. The main focus of Gorbachev's price reforms was to reduce or eliminate state subsidies and to create an economic environment for the promotion of the self-financing of state enterprises. The reforms were expected to encompass all forms of prices: wholesale prices, procurement prices for agriculture, retail prices, tariffs, rates, and fees for services. The share of centrally set prices was expected to fall sharply, and such prices were to be fixed on the basis of socially necessary expenses of production and sale, utility, quality, and effective demand. Contract prices, limit prices, and those set by enterprises were to become more common, and were to be set on the same basic principles. Also, procurement prices for agricultural goods were geared to create conditions favoring certain key areas of agricultural production and increasing the profitability of farms. A more flexible approach to the marketing of surplus agricultural produce was introduced so that state or collective farms could sell all produce harvested over and above their production targets. Also, in order to bring the level of domestic prices into line with world market prices, wholesale prices of fuel and raw materials were raised significantly.

By 1987 *Gosplan* reduced the number of centrally planned industrial products from 123 to 60, and that of centrally allocated resources from 256 to 23. As a result, about 20 percent of all industrial output was planned and distributed from the center, another 30 percent was administered by departments and local authorities, and the rest was not planned at all. In early 1990 decisions were made to eliminate state control on prices of such foodstuffs as bread, meat, and dairy products. These decisions envisaged direct state control over 60 percent of all prices and indirect state control over 25 percent, leaving 15 percent of all prices outside state control. These decisions were scheduled to go into effect by early 1991; however, in practice, prices continued to be controlled by the government.

Subsequently, the 500-day program envisaged the elimination of price controls on most goods, except for a narrow range of essential consumer goods, by 1992. The program, however, granted republics and local bodies the right to enforce price ceilings in instances of excessive increases in decontrolled prices. Full implementation of its provisions could have constituted a decisive break with former practice. In a somewhat milder form, the "Guidelines for the Stabilization of the Economy and the Transition to a Market Economy," adopted by the Supreme Soviet in October 1990, proposed a "gradual liberalization of prices" as one stage in the transition. In the spring of 1991, an "anti-crisis program" was announced that embodied three elements. (1) the prices of consumers' goods were raised, on the average, by 60 percent, to bring prices more closely into line with production costs; (2) thereafter, prices of about 30 percent of retail commodities would be determined through market processes, and the remainder, including essential foods, would be set by state authorities; and (3) "social compensation" measures were established for poorer citizens who were adversely affected by price increases (which typically exceeded increases in their incomes). From the perspective of Gorbachev's increasingly restive radical promarket critics, this cautious approach to economic liberalization represented too slow a movement toward price reform and market processes. To his conservative pro-central planning critics, the willingness to embrace even this degree of market economy was perceived as consorting too closely with the market and as being too insensitive to its potential inegalitarian distributive consequences.

Financial Reforms

Perestroika also initiated a transformation in the country's financial markets. Previously, the credit system in the Soviet economy was coordinated by central planning authorities through administrative means. In order to switch to market-oriented methods of credit, money, and finance, in July 1987, six specialized banks were founded: the *Gosbank* (State Bank), the *Promstroibank* (Industrial and Construction Bank), the *Agroprombank* (Agro-Industrial Bank), the *Zhilsotsbank* (Housing, Social, and Communal Bank), the *Sbirigatelnyibank* (Savings and Consumer Credit Bank), and the *Vneshneekonombank* (Bank of Foreign Economic Activity). Also, especially after 1988, other commercial and cooperative banks were set up. These banks were expected to function as commercial enterprises, compete for their own markets, promote commercialization of their services, grant credits cautiously, offer competitive interest rates, and build their own capital markets. State enterprises, on the other hand, were granted autonomy to choose their own banks. Eventually, especially at a later stage of perestroika, initiatives such as the introduction of checking accounts for individuals, a consumer credit system, stock exchanges, and the financing of joint enterprises with foreign companies received serious consideration.

Gorbachev's regime also tried (unsuccessfully) to bring growth in the money supply, which traditionally outstripped growth in national income in the Soviet economy, into balance with existing material resources. Imbalances between effective demand and supply of goods traditionally had been responsible for chronic shortages, which stimulated an underground economy. Gorbachev also attempted to enhance the purchasing power and convertibility of the ruble. Under the 500-day program, the *Gosbank* was to be transformed into a reserve system administered by a Central Council, whose chairman was to be appointed by the Supreme Soviet and the directors of the central banks of the republics. The *Gosbank*, like Western central reserve banks, was entrusted with a monopoly of the creation of money and coordination of banking policies.

Property Relations

Perestroika was responsible for the boldest effort in Soviet experience since the New Economic Policy (NEP) to promote private and cooperative economic activities and various hybrid forms of economic organization. These included the private garden plots of collective farmers, individual and family proprietorships, supplementary private undertakings by persons employed in the state sector, cooperative businesses of three or more individuals, small capitalist enterprises employing a minimal amount of hired labor, and various hybrid forms, notably, leasing of facilities and equipment from state enterprises, joint private-public enterprises (including joint ventures with foreign firms), and enterprises organized as joint stock or corporate businesses.

There were several inducements for the creation of private or nontraditional enterprises. First, such ventures were largely free (or freer) from state regulation than traditional enterprises. This created the opportunity to take advantage of market demand and cost conditions so as to generate substantial monetary reward. This was true, not only for entrepreneurs, but for cooperative members and hired workers, whose incomes as participants in private and cooperative activities were typically twice as high as (or higher than) those of employees engaged in traditional state enterprises. Second, private ownership (and to a lesser but significant extent other nontraditional ownership forms) provides the widest panoply of property rights as described in earlier chapters, that is, control, benefits, and alienation (right to dispose of productive assets). The private owner who is her or his own boss, obtains the considerable gratification of personal autonomy, mastery, and individual liberty. From the perspective of the political leadership, the creation and expansion of nontraditional forms of business also had significant advantages. It was hoped that such new business ventures would expand production and reduce shortages, especially in consumer goods and services. It was also expected that easing restrictions against private production would reduce "social tensions" by permitting active and enterprising people to engage themselves in business activity (and reduce the likelihood that they would emerge as critics of the political leadership) (Kornai 1992, 435).

A liberal policy toward the creation of nontraditional forms of enterprise, moreover, was a means to correct the extremism of the Stalinist years, carried over more or less intact into the post-Stalinist period. Stalin was not content with the NEP policy of placing large capitalist corporations (the so-called commanding heights of capitalist economy) under public ownership. Instead, by the end of the 1930s, public or (in agriculture) collective farm ownership accounted for nearly 100 percent of the output of industry, agriculture, and trade. The Stalinist regime thereby, and probably unnecessarily, alienated a substantial segment of the population and denied society the benefits of the productivity, adaptability, and creativity of small-scale private business. Economic liberalization in property relations could reduce such alienation and capture some of these benefits.

Finally, there is a natural "affinity" (Kornai 1992, 447) between private ownership and market processes. Private owners, seeking to foster profits and avoid or reduce losses, spontaneously turn to purchases and sales with each other and with households to mediate their social relationships. Therefore, expansion of private enterprises tends to the spread of market relations and, gradually, to the institutional infrastructure of market economy, for example, wholesalers, warehouses, telephone and delivery services, and so on. The spread of market economy, as Adam Smith noted, stimulates higher productivity and production through the greater division of labor. It was also hoped that it would provide an alternative to bureaucratic coordination for state-owned enterprises and an outlet for their surpluses above state orders. At the same time, at least until the early 1990s, the policy of the Gorbachev administration toward nontraditional forms of ownership emphasized the need for their compatibility with "socialist ownership." Because the major perceived potential incompatibility was that of medium and large-scale capitalist enterprise, however, the opportunity for movement toward a "mixed economy" characterized by a substantial increase in various nontraditional forms of ownership was considerable.

In perestroika's initial stages, the emphasis was on expansion of producer cooperatives and private individual enterprises, in which businesses in consumer services, food services, and the production of consumer goods received preponderant attention. Three or more individuals of state employees, pensioners, homemakers, and the handicapped were allowed to undertake private cooperative initiatives. The "Basic Principles for Development of Cooperative Forms of Production" in 1986 legalized producer cooperatives organized on a voluntary basis. Still, private activities remained restricted as the laws were designed to increase industrial outputs in selected sectors by encouraging individuals and members of small cooperative enterprises to devote their after-hours to working for additional income.

Economic liberalization received further impetus with the enactment of the Law on Self-Employment, in May 1987, which permitted private initiative wherever it was not explicitly prohibited and granted extensive rights to local authorities to regulate private and cooperative initiatives. Perestroika also abandoned the country's centralized material and technical supply system (*Gossnab*) in favor of a wholesale trade system so that businesses, including cooperatives and private enterprises, could obtain required goods and services from markets according to their choice. Perestroika's reforms contributed to a significant expansion in cooperative economic activities in the Soviet economy; for example, cooperative cafes, taxi cabs, medical care, teachers and tutors, and construction proliferated. Initially, such activity was limited to agriculture; it then spread to other sectors, such as light manufacturing and trade. But progress of private and cooperative initiatives remained circumscribed as these laws did not guarantee the rights of citizens to engage in self-employment activities. Private businesses were also subject to a very high rates of progressive income taxation that ranged up to 90 percent.

Subsequently, the cooperative laws of fall 1987 and spring 1988 extended cooperative activities to small shops, industry, and the processing of raw materials and semi-finished goods and the construction, trade, and service sectors of the economy. A new agricultural policy of March 1989 abolished district agro-industrial complexes and allowed individual, family, and cooperative forms of agricultural organization in land cultivation and animal husbandry on a long-term lease basis. Partly because of administrative and political limitations, private and cooperative activities did not constitute a large part of the Soviet GNP in the early years of perestroika. However, the absolute numbers of small and medium-size proprietary and cooperative businesses became significant, and their rates of growth were very large. For example, the number of individual private proprietors rose from 100,000 at the end of 1986 to 300,000 at the beginning of 1988, although this constituted only 0.2 percent of those employed in the Soviet Union. In 1987 about 200,000 people were employed in cooperatives, although such enterprises contributed only 0.1 percent to the GNP (Shmelev and Popov 1989, 270).

Cooperatives were seen as vehicles to expand production without dismantling state-owned enterprises, to absorb workers displaced by the introduction of new technologies, and to provide a "mixed" from of ownership in between state and private enterprises. The cooperatives, in principle, were excused from obligatory state plans and orders, could set their own prices, and could engage in foreign trade. Their taxes, set by republic authorities, were typically reduced below those of the Brezhnev years, enabling the creation of numerous "cooperative millionaires." By January 1991, there were more than 245,000 cooperatives, employing more than 6 million people, concentrated in domestic services, catering, consumer goods, and construction. The Law on Cooperatives of May 1988 has been widely described as "the most radical single economic measure to have been introduced in the first years of the Gorbachev leadership" (White 1992, 119).

At a later stage, perestroika initiated even more fundamental property reforms by revising ownership rights and promoting diversified ownership of the means of production. The Law on Property of 1990 radically altered property relations by providing legal, political, and economic steps in the direction of bolder private ownership and initiative, and allowing foreign companies the same rights as domestic enterprises to set up industries in the Soviet Union. The law permitted individuals, among other things, to own residential buildings (with their plots and lands), means of transportation, money, stocks and other securities, and means of production for peasant farming and other types of labor enterprises and business activities. The law allowed the hiring of workers other than family members and the inheritance of property. It thereby constituted a remarkable break with a central tenet of Soviet Marxism that rejected capitalist private ownership of means of production in socialist economy. The law also authorized a major change in state ownership of enterprises. It entrusted the enterprises to own, use, and dispose of property and perform operations that were not legally prohibited in the country. In May 1990 the government also approved the construction and sale of private housing.

Subsequently, the 500-day program proposed even greater privatization and liberalization of the economy. It called for the transfer of state property to citizens through destatization, the creation of special privatization agencies and land reform committees to facilitate individual ownership of property, and the launching of market-oriented motivational mechanisms and institutional arrangements to promote privatization. In addition to privately owned firms and cooperatives, the Gorbachev era was characterized by the development and expansion of various hybrid kinds of enterprises in between private ventures and old-style state operations. These included such forms as leasing arrangements, joint stock companies, and joint ventures. Under leasing, the state, through such institutions as ministries and local authorities, entered into contractual relationships with state enterprises, cooperatives, or workers' collectives. Upon payment of a fee, the leaseholder had the right to distribute all profits, after deductions, thus creating, in principle, substantially greater decentralization, enterprise autonomy, competition, and, hopefully, efficiency. Leased enterprises employed

3.8 million persons or 2.7 percent of total employment in the Soviet Union in 1990. In 1991 employment in leased enterprises grew to 9 million and accounted for 6.6 percent of total employment. Under legislation passed in December 1990 and in 1991, some state enterprises in Russia were transformed into joint stock companies and their capital was converted into stock (typically owned by state agencies), or they were simply transformed into corporations. Although such hybrid enterprises remained under general state oversight, they were delegated significantly greater financial independence.

By January 1, 1992, there were 8,902 joint stock companies in Russia, mostly in Moscow, St. Petersburg, and Western Siberia, and 539 corporations. Joint ventures, that is, enterprises jointly owned by state-owned firms and foreign firms, also expanded in the Gorbachev period, especially in Russia, which accounted for more than 60 percent of the total. Expected benefits were greater access to foreign capital, foreign technology, and global markets. The number of such ventures expanded dramatically, from 191 in 1989, to 1,274 in 1990, to 2,905 in 1991, although the number of joint enterprises actually in operation was less than half of those registered. Employment in all hybrid forms of enterprise expanded from 7.9 million or 5.7 percent, in 1990, to 14.1 million or 10.4 percent, in 1991. If private enterprises are added, total employment outside state enterprises, collective farms and consumer cooperatives, and social organizations expanded from 12.8 million or 9.3 percent, in 1990, to 20.6 million or 15.2 percent, in 1991 (Bim, Jones, and Weisskopf 1993).

Perestroika also sought to do away with traditional autarchic tendencies of the Soviet economy. The principle of "socialism in one country," founded by Stalin and pursued by pre-Gorbachev leaders, largely isolated the Soviet economy from the international market. Only 12 percent of Soviet national income in the mid-1980s came from the international sector as opposed to between 25 and 40 percent in other advanced countries. Also, Soviet exports failed to keep up with the changing structure of international trade. Although the share of raw materials and other traditional manufacturing products declined as the share of such high-tech products as electronics and aerospace rose rapidly in international trade, Soviet exports were dominated in the late 1980s by fuel and electricity (53 percent), raw materials (9 percent), and machines and equipment (14 percent) (Aganbegyan 1988a, 141).

Therefore, integration of the Soviet economy into the global economy was perceived as imperative by the Gorbachev regime, which desired to take advantage of the international division of labor and to improve foreign economic relations. As early as April 1985, the Ministry of Foreign Trade's monopoly over international trade was eliminated, and a number of ministries and institutions were granted rights to operate directly in international markets. Subsequently, the State Foreign Economic Committee and the Ministry of Foreign Economic Ties were created to oversee all facets of foreign economic activity.[28] Gorbachev's initial emphasis on foreign economic relations had two aspects: the attraction of international, primarily Western, capital for joint ventures; and building stronger ties with the Eastern European states to create an integrated socialist economy. Joint enterprises had to meet at least three prerequisites: (1) the share of foreign capital in the joint ventures could not exceed 49 percent, (2) joint ventures had to conform to Soviet labor laws, and (3) joint enterprises had to be headed by a Soviet citizen. Joint ventures were also subjected to a 30 percent tax on profits, and an additional 20 percent tax was imposed in case the profit was transferred to a foreign country. Subsequently, the drive toward greater integration with global economy and international division of labor was intensified. In December 1988, all enterprises and organizations with competitive products on the foreign market received international trading rights. The prerequisite of a 51 percent Soviet share in joint ventures was relaxed, differentiated hard currency coefficients were gradually phased out, and international companies were welcomed as efforts were made to attain ruble convertibility.[29]

Demokratizatsiya **and** *Glasnost*

Gorbachev came to believe that past economic reforms in the Soviet Union failed because they were not reinforced by broad-based public participation. He contended that transformation of the Soviet economy required a similar transformation in other spheres of society.[30] While perestroika stood for far-reaching economic reforms, glasnost and *democratizatsiya* signified a thorough reconstruction of the political and intellectual foundations of Soviet society. Moreover, to the Gorbachev regime, perestroika, glasnost, and *democratizatsiya* were inextricably interdependent.

Gorbachev and his supporters described glasnost and *democratizatsiya* as both ends and means—that is, as desirable features of a mature socialism, on the one hand, and as means for fostering perestroika, on the other. Thus, Stanislav Menshikov describes glasnost as both "an instrument of the economic reforms" and "another example of the conscious effort to expand democracy." One reason for the failure of the economic reform efforts of the 1950s and 1960s was that "those reforms weren't coupled with the spread of democracy. Democracy and economic reforms are necessary complements to one another" (Galbraith and Menshikov 1988, 76). Gorbachev similarly declared that "no radical change is possible without it [glasnost]" and that there is "no democracy, nor can there be, without glasnost. And there is no present-day socialism, nor can there be, without democracy" (Gorbachev 1987, 79).

Glasnost or "openness" embodied "two closely connected requirements. One [was] to put a stop to secretiveness," that is, to inform the public of government decisions and plans to implement them. "The other [was] that the truth must always be told; the publication of false statements must cease" (Kornai 1992, 425). Glasnost implies liberalization of the press and the mass media generally, the support of officials who issue true reports, and the tolerance of independent organizations that propagate their criticisms and dissent through written as well as spoken means. The Soviet intelligentsia, notably, writers, artists, and journalists, were among Gorbachev's most enthusiastic supporters of glasnost. And Gorbachev was singularly adroit in using glasnost as a means to foster perestroika by exposing the party and state apparatus of centralized planning and management to public scrutiny and critique. Gorbachev boldly used the press to forge an alliance with the urban intelligentsia against the "bureaucratic legions" of the "power hierarchy, the party apparatchiks" (Smith 1988, 2). He mobilized newspapers and magazines not only against the residual terror and tyranny of the post-Stalin regime, but against the waste and inefficiencies of the overcentralized system of planning and management as well. In addition, Gorbachev put pressure on the party and state hierarchy by unleashing popular protests and demonstrations. Finally, Gorbachev used Soviet television to provide "an object lesson in democratic politics." The 1988 Party Conference, for example, became a practical demonstration of how dissent and criticism can be used as weapons against encrusted authority and privilege (Gorbachev 1987, 75).

Evidently, Gorbachev concluded that, to succeed, economic restructuring had to penetrate the consciousness of society, from bottom to top. To do this, workers would have to accept perestroika as "theirs." Mass acceptance of perestroika was to be fostered by vigorous use of the media of mass communication to inspire the "new consciousness" and monitor perestroika's progress. Because Gorbachev lacked both the tyrannical powers of Stalin and a definitive consensus among the various factions of the party, he needed the active support and participation of the intelligentsia in the propagation of his ideology and program. Part of the price for the intelligentsia's contributions to perestroika's success was liberalization and openness in society at large, notably in cultural and literary matters.

Gorbachev similarly believed that perestroika required *democratizatsiya*. First, perestroika was expected to require a more or less lengthy process of "transition," during which the logic of the entire reform effort would not be evident. Second, it was expected that there would be costs and dislocations as well as benefits from perestroika, with costs probably dominating over benefits during the early years of restructuring. Third, the ministerial economic bureaucracy, indeed, the middle and lower levels of the party bureaucracy itself, had slipped out of the control of top political leadership. The industrial ministries, for example, had become "self-regulating bodies... inert and resistant of outside control." Democratization of the political apparatus was "intended to break up the control of these administrative elites and vested interests" (Lane 1992, 58) by legitimating and thereby enhancing the power of the legislature (and chief executive).

Under these circumstances, it was believed to be essential to enlist public support. This, in turn, implied *democratizatsiya*, that is, an extension of liberty, power, and participation (or reasonable approximations thereof) in exchange for acceptance of the travails of a new era of transition and adjustment. Thus, at the July 1988 Conference of the CPSU, Gorbachev stated that socialism "will die unless we reform the political system." Such reforms opened the way to a "democratic image of socialism" (*Time*, July 11, 1988, 25). Workers' councils and elections of managers were considered an integral part of this process. So, too, was the expanded role of labor unions in elaborating the social components of economic plans, monitoring managers' compliance with labor contracts, and critically evaluating managers (indeed, demanding their resignation when they behaved discordantly with workers' interests). Another strategic element in *democratizatsiya* was the provision of legislation guaranteeing enterprise autonomy and workers' rights in self-management, as well as civil and political liberties, for example, laws to facilitate citizens' appeals in court against unlawful actions of government bodies and officials (Gorbachev 1987, 108, 114).

A high point in the process of *democratizatsiya* was reached at the July 1988 CPSU Conference. The most dramatic moment of the conference was the decision, urged by Gorbachev, to reorganize the governmental system by transferring day-to-day responsibilities for economic and political management from the party to the state. First, in accord with Gorbachev's vision of the restoration of the soviets or local communal organs of government "as bodies of political power and as the foundation of socialist democracy" (Gorbachev 1987, 112), the soviets (presided over by the party's regional secretaries) were to have greater authority to oversee enterprises in their localities. Second, a popularly elected 2,250-member Congress of People's Deputies was to be established, which, inter alia, would elect a smaller Supreme Soviet with real legislative powers and a president with real executive power (*Time* July 11, 1988, 29). Third, the party was to retain ultimate power—without "official opposition"—and to exercise an ideological role and provide guidance concerning collective decisions. But the party was itself to be democratized. This was to be accomplished partly by establishing a strict demarcation between functions of party and state and partly by the "development of intra-Party democracy, the strengthening of the principles of collective leadership in work, and broader openness in the Party" (Gorbachev 1987, 123), notably, through the nomination of more candidates than party offices and secret-ballot elections (Lane 1992, 74).

If all of this were implemented, it would not add up to a full-blown democracy; however, it would constitute, as claimed, democratization, that is, a process of movement toward more democratic and participatory patterns of rule. Similarly, it would not achieve Western-style competing political parties as a means of organizing and adjudicating propertied, working-class, and other interests, but it would contribute to making the Soviet Union a significantly less monolithic and more pluralistic society. Whereas Khrushchev shifted from Stalinism to a milder authoritarianism, Gorbachev reached the anticlimax of Soviet totalitarianism by embarking on a process of movement toward a democratic state and society, based on an aspiration of "democratic humane socialism."

Reduction in Military Spending

The Gorbachev regime proposed to trade guns for bread. Soviet defense expenditure was unreasonably disproportionate to its economic capacity—thanks partly to competition with the United States, which had a much larger GNP and also had substantially increased defense expenditures during the Reagan era. The share of Soviet GNP devoted to military activities increased from between 12 and 14 percent in the early 1970s to between 15 and 17 percent in the early 1980s (CIA and DIA 1989), despite reductions in the rates of growth of military procurement after 1976. Combined with slow overall economic growth in the late 1970s and early 1980s, it therefore became increasingly difficult for the Soviet leadership to sustain any growth in nonmilitary economic development. If higher economic growth rates were to be rekindled, downsizing of the military sector was essential.

Also, Gorbachev radically redefined the ideological perspective of the Soviet Union. His "new thinking" emphasized discontinuance of traditional rivalry with the capitalist bloc, use of military forces for more purely defensive objectives, exclusion of nuclear arms and other weapons of mass destruction from military arsenals, use of resources freed as a result of disarmament for the development of civilian priorities, and promotion of general human moral and ethical norms as the basis of international relations. Thanks to a foreign policy that emphasized peaceful coexistence of capitalism and socialism, under Gorbachev's leadership the Eastern European countries were freed from Soviet military control, and eventually the Cold War came to a peaceful end.[31]

Gorbachev was thus able to reduce expenditures on armaments and to divert resources from defense to the consumption sector. Defense spending cuts were carried out primarily in military research, development, testing, and evaluation. Gorbachev initiated processes of conversion of military plants into civilian production. At the Nineteenth party Conference, the Soviet leadership acknowledged that the threat from the West was declining and emphasized less need for defense expenditure. In December 1988, Gorbachev made specific promises at the United Nations for unilateral cuts in Soviet military manpower and equipment. The Twenty-eighth Congress of the CPSU (July 1990) called for conversion of defense production to facilitate the integration of the Soviet economy into the global economy. Indeed, Gorbachev's Draconian defense cuts fueled dissatisfaction among the military forces. The failed coup of August 1991 might be considered in part a manifestation of disapproval of Gorbachev's policies by the Soviet military-industrial complex.

NOTES

1. Gorbachev was born into a peasant family of Stavropol Krai in the Russian Republic on March 2, 1931. Gorbachev became a member of the Communist party in 1953 and graduated from Moscow State University in law in 1955. He became a central committee secretary in charge of agriculture in 1978, a candidate member of the Politburo in 1979, and a full member of the Politburo in 1980, and he served as the chairman of the Legislative Proposals Commission of the Supreme Soviet from 1979 to 1984. During Andropov's period, Gorbachev was responsible for overseeing the Soviet economy. Under Chernenko's regime, Gorbachev chaired the Foreign Affairs Commission and was the top ideologist of the Communist party. Gorbachev, fifty-four, was appointed general secretary of the Communist Party on March 11, 1985, only five hours after the announcement of Chernenko's death. Gorbachev was the last general secretary of the CPSU.

2. During the two-and-a-half years between the death of Brezhnev in November 1982 and the appointment of Gorbachev as general secretary of the CPSU in March 1985, the Soviet Union had two interim leaders: Yuri Andropov, sixty eight (November 12, 1982- June 16, 1983), and Konstantin Chernenko, seventy three (February 13, 1984-March 10, 1985). Both leaders were older than average when they assumed power, and they both died in office. Andropov, born in 1914, was chief of the KGB from 1967 to 1982. He was appointed party ideologist in May 1982 and chairman of the Presidium of the Supreme Soviet in June the same year. Chernenko, born in 1911, became a full member of the Politburo in 1978 and succeeded Andropov. The periods of Andropov and Chernenko signified little changes in Soviet economy or society.

3. Gorbachev (1987, 24) observed in his book *Perestroika* that there was "a growing awareness" in the public consciousness that things could not go on as they were indefinitely and any delay in comprehensive reforms "could have led to [an] exacerbated internal situation."

4. As Hohmann (1987, 29) writes, "The economic potential of the Soviet Union came under pressure from all sides of the polygon of economic policy goals—the assurance of adequate capital formation, the stabilization of progress in the standard of living, the guaranteed ability to maintain the aspired military capacities, the provision of an economic basis for Soviet hegemony policy, the restoration of legitimacy to the Soviet system."

5. Soviet economic performance, however, was fairly strong from 1960 to 1975, when annual GNP growth rates averaged over 4 percent. Scholars differ in respect to the actual beginning of the slowdown in Soviet economy. Aganbegyan (1988a, 2-3), for example, argues that the rate of growth of Soviet GNP (based on Soviet official statistical data), actually fell nearly 2.5 times during 1971 and 1985. For details see Aganbegyan (1988a, 81-83); Hohmann (1987); Hanson (1987); and Miller (1987).

6. For example, from 1981 to 1985, the Soviet economic growth equaled that of the United Kingdom: each registered a 1.9 percent annual growth. For details see Dowlah (1992a, 95-97).

7. Aganbegyan (1988a, 7) points out that, in any typical postwar planning period, capital investment increased 1.5 times, the extraction of fuel and raw materials rose by 25 to 30 percent, and the labor force expanded by 10 or 11 million people.

8. As Goldman (1983, 33) observes, the continued emphasis on heavy industry actually enabled the Soviet Union to win the "wrong race." The Soviet economy kept overproducing steel, machine tools, petroleum, and other industrial products, thereby enabling the Soviet Union to overtake and surpass the United States in such items by 1980, as Khrushchev had promised in 1961, when what was increasingly desired was a shift to the manufacturing of consumers goods "for the ultimate enjoyment of the population."

9. For details on Soviet agricultural performance, see Bornstein (1981), Millar (1981), Goldman (1983), Johnson and Brooks (1983).

10. For a fuller discussion of the relationships between Soviet productivity and technological progress, see Berliner (1976); Dowlah (1992a); CIA and DIA (1989).

11. Based on a survey conducted by the Soviet Institution of World Economy and International Relations. For details, see Shmelev and Popov (1989, 128-30).

12. Gorbachev, in his book *Perestroika* (1987, 5), puts it more vividly: "Our rockets can find Halley's comet and fly to Venus with amazing accuracy, but side by side with these scientific and technological triumphs is an obvious lack of efficiency in using scientific achievements for economic needs, and many Soviet household appliances are of poor quality."

13. Based on Aganbegyan (1988a, 75-88); Dowlah (1992a, 96-103; 1990a).

14. For details on inventory/sales ratio in Soviet and other industrialized economies, see Shmelev and Popov (1989, 145-46).

15. For details on savings rates and bank deposits in the late 1970s and early 1980s, see Goldman (1983, 55-56) and Dowlah (1990a, 176-183).

16. For the growth of the second economy in the Soviet Union see Grossman (1977, 1979). See also Chapter 7.

17. The process of demographic slump in the Soviet Union in the early 1970s occurred as a direct consequence of massive population losses during World War II. Also see Kostakov (1987, 22) and Campbell (1983).

18. Between 1980 and 1990, the working-age population in the Soviet Union was expected to increase by less than 6 million in contrast to an annual growth of 10 or 11 million during the 1960s. Also, most of this increase was expected to take place in the relatively less industrialized Central Asia and Kazakhstan regions. For details see Campbell (1983, 69).

19. Some scholars, for example Kostakov (1987, 21), reject this interpretation as a "superficial explanation without foundation." He maintains that what the Soviet Union was facing was not a labor shortage, but rather "an overabundance of manpower" resulting from the extremely ineffective utilization of labor power in the economy. The problem originated from a low level of labor productivity. From 1961 to 1970, on an annual average, national income per worker in material production rose by 6.4 percent; from 1981 to 1985 the rate dropped to 4.5 percent. In most organizations, often two or even three people were employed to do a job that could be handled by one worker. According to Mikulsky (quoted in Ellman 1986, 536), superfluous industrial employment in the Soviet Union ranged far above 15 to 20 percent. With an effective economic mechanism, many of those employed might well be redundant.

20. Sophistication in the demands of urban populations is not an unusual phenomenon in the urbanization process. What is peculiar about Soviet urbanization is that, unlike the experience of other urbanized countries, it was achieved fairly rapidly. Moreover, the Soviet Union was already a superpower before urbanization was consummated. See for details, Lewin (1988, 32); Kagarlitsky (1990, 286); Dowlah (1992a, 106-9).

21. Another interesting dimension of Soviet education is that, although women constituted 51 percent of the total population, they constituted 54 percent of the university students and 58 percent of the students in secondary specialized schools.

22. According to Lewin (1988, 48), 60 percent of all specialists with both higher and secondary education, 56 percent of educated specialists, and 40 percent of scientists in the Soviet Union were females.

23. Lewin (1988, 52-56) provides an excellent analysis of the educational, and consequent societal, transformation of the Soviet Union on the basis of Gordon and Komarovsky's "vocational x-ray" of three generations of Soviet society—(1) those (men) born around 1910 who entered the workforce in the 1930s, (2) those (sons) born in the 1930s who joined the labor force in the 1950s, and (3) those (grandsons) born in the 1950s who entered the labor force in the 1970s,—captures the underlying dynamics and mobility of Soviet society during the transition from a predominantly peasant to an industrial, then to a service and information-oriented society. The authors point out that the first generation was predominantly employed in "preindustrial" peasant jobs that required no schooling. The second generation, predominantly employed in industry, required emphasis on skill. A modest portion of this generation also moved to the service and information sectors. The third generation was substantially employed in service and information sectors that required intellectual training. Also see Kagarlitsky (1990, 287-301) and Dowlah (1992a, 106-9).

24. Draper's remarks in this regard are worth quoting:

If any one factor may be said to have shaken the leadership out of its accustomed self-satisfaction and inertia, it is this—the failure to meet the competition of what Gorbachev has referred to as "the capitalism of the 1980's, the capitalism of the age of electronics, and the informatics, computers and robots. It was not simply that the Soviet Union had fallen behind the United States or Western Europe in the new technology, it could not produce what Japan, South Korea and even Taiwan were turning out in mass production and with which they were flooding world markets. (1988, 295-96)

25. Gorbachev puts it succinctly in his book *Perestroika,*

The need for change was brewing not only in the material sphere of life but also in public consciousness. People who had practical experience, a sense of justice and commitment to the ideals of Bolshevism criticized the established practice of doing things and noted with anxiety the symptoms of moral degradation and erosion of revolutionary ideals and socialist values.... There was a growing awareness that things could not go on like this much longer. (1987, 24)

26. Such reforms touched the very nature of the Soviet economic system and also the vested interests of the higher and intermediate-level economic bureaucracy. Therefore, redefining the functions of *Gosplan, Gossnab,* and *Gosbank* became problematic at this stage.

27. Along with the structural and organizational reforms, measures were undertaken to replace, demote, or fire key personnel in various branches of government. For details on personnel matters, see Colton (1987) and Dowlah (1992a, 154-75).

28. By the end of 1988, most ministries and departments, all union republics, and more than 100 associations and intersectoral scientific and technical complexes were granted rights to carry out international trade directly. Such independent international trade constituted 12 percent of imports and 28 percents of exports in 1987, and 32 percent of imports and 22 percent of exports at the beginning of 1988. For details see Shmelev and Popov (1989, 232-33) and Dowlah (1992a, 161-63).

29. In January 1990 the Soviet-led trading bloc Council for Mutual Economic Assistance (COMECON), originally founded in 1949, was dissolved and replaced by the Organization for International Economic Cooperation (OIEC), which aimed at greater integration of the Soviet Union and its former satellite countries into the world economy on the basis of market principles rather than central planning.

30. As Gorbachev (1988a, 420) declared, "perestroika implies not only eliminating the stagnation and conservatism of the preceding period, and correcting the mistakes committed, but also overcoming historically limited, outdated features of social organizations and work needs."

31. This redirection of Soviet foreign relations was accompanied by a substantial modification of Soviet ideology. See Dowlah and Elliott (1991).

Chapter 9

Gorbachev and Democratizing Socialist Economy: Consequences and Contradictions

This chapter continues an examination of the Gorbachev era (1985-1991) in Soviet development as an exemplar of a movement toward a more democratized form of Soviet socialism. The preceding chapter focused on the underlying causes and origins of this democratized version of Soviet socialism and its institutions and policy measures. This chapter extends the analysis of the Gorbachev period to consideration of its economic and political consequences and its tensions and contradictions, which led (as developed in Chapter 10) to the disintegration of the Soviet politico-economic system.

CONSEQUENCES

Economic Reforms

Most of Gorbachev's economic reforms failed to achieve their goals, partly because of obstacles to their implementation. Several top leaders actively supported the expansion of cooperatives (and other forms of private enterprise), including, in addition to Gorbachev, Alexander Yakovlev and Prime Minister Nikolai Ryzhkov. But cooperatives were the most controversial as well as successful component of Gorbachev's economic program and faced serious opposition. Conservative party leaders and members, labor union leaders, and members of some Russian nationalist organizations condemned cooperatives from an ideological perspective, characterizing them as an abandonment of socialism and a move toward capitalism. Economic opposition was stimulated by the significantly higher-than-average incomes of cooperative members (more than twice as high as state factory workers) and the capability of cooperatives, which had the right to set their own prices and did so, to purchase commodities in limited supply at low fixed prices and thereby to divert them from state stores, which sold at lower prices to cooperative markets where they were sold at higher prices. Cooperatives also elicited political opposition from many party and government officials, who perceived them as a potential democratizing threat to their power.

The national government, as a consequence of these divisions over the desirability of cooperatives, alternated between fostering and restricting them. In March 1988, the Ministry of Finance established steeply progressive taxation of cooperative members' salaries, ranging from 50 percent on monthly earnings of 700 rubles, to 70 percent on earnings greater than 1,000 rubles, and 90 percent on salaries above 1,500 rubles. Although the maximum tax rate was later reduced to 35 percent, adverse effects of this tax policy on the progress of the development of cooperatives presumably were significant.[1] In December 1988, the Council of Ministers barred cooperatives from various activities, including several kinds of medical care. State agencies and enterprises often refused to provide raw materials and supplies to cooperatives. Local officials refused to register cooperatives "or dragged out the process, denying them space to operate, harassing them with inspections and petty intrusions" (Smith 1990, 285). Individual and small capitalist private enterprises were often blocked or constrained by similar obstacles, including ideological opposition and ambiguous and undependable ownership rights.

If cooperatives were the most energetic element in the Gorbachev administration's economic reform program, agriculture was the arena of "compromise," described, alternatively, as "weak" (Smith 1990, 232) and "workable" (Desai 1990, 152). After much delay and discussion, a land law was passed by the Supreme Soviet in March 1990. Under this legislation, collective and state farms would continue, but local soviets were authorized to lease land to individuals or groups for life, with the right to bequeath the lease holding to one's inheritors, in exchange for a rental payment set by union or autonomous republics. Alternatively, local soviets could distribute land to such organizations as cooperatives, kholkozy, or sovkhozy under conditions of permanent tenure and payment of taxes. Tenure holders and leases were expected to practice self-financing and cost accounting, without (or with lower) subsidies, and party and state agencies were instructed not to interfere into farm management and marketing decisions. Thus, individuals and groups were expected to exercise the "property right" of control over management and benefits (after payment of taxes or rents). But the Soviet political leadership balked at extending the private property right of alienation; that is, individuals, groups, and organizations could not sell or subdivide the land. Land was to continue to be owned in common by the state as the agency of society as a whole. Also, although the potential for transformation from collective and state farms into individual, family, or cooperative farming under the new land legislation was considerable, the pace of such transformation was expected to be gradual. Gorbachev apparently chose "the less divisive, if slower, Darwinian process of disintegration of the unviable farms" (152) to the more rapid, but politically explosive, strategy of dissolution of collective and state farms and privatization of land itself.

Obstacles to the withdrawal from collective or state farms and the establishment of private farms were substantial. First, the Gorbachev regime gave contradictory signals on private farming, notably by insisting on the retention of public ownership of land. Second, Yegor Ligachev, prominent conservative member of the Politburo and a strong proponent of collective and state farming, was appointed to oversee Soviet agriculture. Third, local party and state administrators and collective farm managers discouraged applications for the establishment of private farms. Fourth, family farming lacked deep cultural roots in the Soviet Union. After the emancipation of the serfs in 1861 and before the Bolshevik Revolution, the village commune was the dominant institution for organizing work and production in the Russian countryside. For a short period before World War I and, of course, during the New Economic Policy (NEP) period, private proprietary framing expanded substantially. This relatively brief experience was shattered by Joseph Stalin's collectivization program. By the 1980s, the dominating influence of the collectivization experience, custom, and the accumulated weight of investment patterns, which favored collective and state farms, reinforced the antiprivate farming policy preferences of local and regional leaderships. By April 1990, "there were only about 20,000 private farms" in the entire Soviet Union. Over 12,000 of these were in Georgia and 5,700 were in Latvia. "Only 240 were registered in the Russian republic and 4 in the Ukraine" (Goldman 1991, 116-17).

Division over the content and rapidity of structural change in agriculture at the center, coupled with bureaucratic opposition to restructuring at regional and local levels, was accompanied by questionable agricultural policies during the Gorbachev era. Four examples will illustrate. First, "subsidies to agriculture and the food industry skyrocketed, ...contributing greatly to the overall state budget deficit." By 1990 "any semblance of balance on Soviet food markets evaporated," with consequent extensions of rationing, longer queues, and ever-higher, exorbitant prices. Net payments from the state budget to the agro-industrial complex rose from 27.6 billion rubles in 1985 (and -3.8 billion rubles in 1982) to a peak of 54.1 billion rubles in 1988. Prices in collective farm markets in 1988 were 2 percent higher than in 1987, 12 percent higher in 1989, and 45 percent higher (and rising) in 1990. Second, subsidies, combined with differential procurement price payments, distorted farm prices and steered production in socially wasteful directions. Subsidies were larger and farm procurement prices were higher to high cost, unprofitable collective and state farms than to low cost, profitable farms. Thus, inefficient farms were both bailed out and encouraged to expand and efficient farms were discouraged. Third, the allocation of investment funds and other resources in agriculture underprovided for "storage, processing and transportation infrastructure." The share of agricultural investment devoted to these neglected areas "fell from 11.5 percent in 1980 to 10.3 percent in 1985, and then recovered to 11.9 percent by 1988," thus registering no real increase for the decade of the 1980s as a whole. Fourth, there was a "surprisingly weak linkage between labor productivity and remuneration." Except for unusually profitable farms, data for the mid-1980s indicate that labor income did not vary significantly with farm profitability. Thus, there was "little incentive from the workers' point of view to improve performance on any farm" (Cook 1992, 203-7).

Perestroika's industrial reforms also created certain dysfunctional managerial consequences. For example, state enterprises were caught in between conflicting demands: the central plan insisted on production of planned gross output, while a reconstituted *Gospriemka* (State Quality Inspectorate) insisted on meeting its quality standards for consumer goods. *Gospriemka* returned goods worth billions of rubles because of inferior quality. This resulted in huge unsold inventories of products, contributing to what came to be called the "paradox of excessive demand and excessive inventories."

Moreover, most industrial reforms proceeded slowly. The "ground-breaking" Law on Socialist Enterprise, in principle, made it possible for any of the nation's 50,000 business enterprises to reorganize themselves outside state control, make a profit, elect their own manager, and be free from detailed direction by higher administrative authorities, as long as they were prepared to pay their own way or go out of business. In practice, the economic ministries, with the support of the party apparatus, "proposed a leisurely, seven-year time-table which would allow them to circumvent the Gorbachev legislation" (Sheehy 1990, 258-59). Gorbachev compromised, accepting the extended timetable, thereby de facto negating by postponement timely and rigorous implementation of his own reform.

Often, actual practices of central planners and state enterprises contradicted stated reform objectives because of bureaucratic and managerial resistance to change. For example, the Enterprise Law of June 1987 envisaged a reduction in state orders to enterprises, at first to 85 percent of enterprise output, then to 70 percent and lower as market processes expanded to fill in the difference between enterprise output and government demand. Enterprise managers were permitted to sell the surplus of output above state orders at prices to be negotiated with whatever customers managers were able to locate. Because negotiated prices were generally higher than state-determined prices, it was expected that this new arrangement would be very profitable and would thereby encourage expanded production and settling of prices at lower, equilibrium, levels.

In practice, however, the new system created significant confusion. First, to reduce transition difficulties, it was decided to shift enterprises producing 50 percent of the nation's output to the new system on January 1, 1988, and the remaining 50 percent one year later. Critics wryly commented that this was akin to shifting half of the nation's cars and trucks to the left side of the road now and shifting the remaining half later. Second, the market infrastructure to implement the new system, notably wholesale suppliers on the one hand and customers on the other, simply did not exist or at least was difficult to locate. Despite the profit incentive associated with obtaining supplies and disposing of a portion of enterprise output outside the planning system, many enterprise managers found it safer and less cumbersome to continue to operate under the old regime. Because a successful shift to the new system would eventually eliminate the need for the economic and ministerial bureaucracy, the ministries had a weak incentive to implement the new system and a strong incentive to acquiesce to managers' requests to continue the old one. Consequently, state orders, instead of dropping to 85 percent (much less 70 percent) of enterprise output, often continued to hover from 90 to 100 percent (Shmelev and Popov 1989, 247-93; Dowlah 1992a, 166-68).

Other major objectives of perestroika, for example, targets of meeting world standards for from 80 to 90 percent of Soviet goods by 1990 remained largely unfulfilled. Conversion of 100 percent of the country's industrial output into the *khozraschet* model by the end of 1989 met the same fate, promised price reforms to reflect scarcity and demand conditions were delayed repeatedly, and broad goals of economic accountability for industrial management remained problematic.[2] Little progress was made in the agrarian sector, the principle of mandatory plan deliveries continued, and RAPO's (Regional Agro-Industrial Associations) sweeping bureaucratic control prevailed in the countryside as almost 90 percent of the rural economy continued to be run by the old administrative methods of command and control.

The limited success in implementing economic restructuring during the Gorbachev years is rooted in several factors. First, perestroika was an evolutionary phenomenon. It proceeded through several stages, and was redefined and reinterpreted in the process. Throughout, Gorbachev steadily intensified his rhetoric and expanded the scope and character of economic restructuring. An initial stage, from roughly early 1985 to early 1987, was characterized essentially by tinkering with the system. Priorities were shifted, from extensive development to intensive development and from the military sector to consumption and investment. Programs were initiated to tighten labor discipline and curb alcoholism. During this first stage, Gorbachev also began a concerted attempt to court elements of the Soviet intelligentsia, notably those active in the media of mass communication, and to stimulate an extension of information, public discussion and debate, and openness to criticism that has been described as historically unprecedented. Evidently, Gorbachev and his associates decided that modernization required initiative and effort from below and thereby accountability, which in turn made provision and dissemination of accurate information essential.

A second stage, from the June 1987 plenum of the CPSU Central Committee to late 1989, was dominated by radical rhetoric but moderate reforms. The party-state monopoly over society and the bureaucratic planning system were essentially retained. But attempts were made to improve that system through somewhat greater delegation of decision-making powers, changing personnel, and expanding the pace of scientific and technological development. Attempts were also made to modify the system by moderate expansion in private and hybrid forms of ownership and adroit management of glasnost and, a bit later, *demokratizatsiya* from above.

A third stage, from late 1989 or early 1990 onward, marked a more radical shift in the direction of perestroika. In 1990 the CPSU relinquished its monopoly power position, thus opening the door for multiparty political pluralism. Also, in 1990, legislation was passed authorizing the abolition of the state's monopoly ownership of the means of production and proposing diversified private and cooperative ownership (Dowlah 1990b, 62). In July 1991, the Soviet government ended centralized resource allocation and administrative direction of the economy. In this stage, Gorbachev came to believe that "instead of being the solution, central planning had become the problem" (Goldman 1991, 26-34). Combined with proposals for market and price reforms, foreign investment, and such institutions as stock exchanges, perestroika had finally become a program for significantly departing from the post-Stalinist consensus on politico-economic institutions and policies.

A second factor explaining why perestroika's rhetoric outpaced its actual implementation was that economic restructuring, even at its best, brought adverse as well as positive consequences for the various classes and groups in Soviet society. The military, for example, generally supported perestroika on the assumption that "a

stronger economy [would] permit qualitative improvements in military capabilities."
But Gorbachev's policy of low growth in military expenditures and maintaining the
status quo in military procurement put the civilian and military sectors on a "colli-
sion course with respect to resource requirements." Managers were attracted by the
"promise of enterprise autonomy" but fearful of heightened uncertainty, including
the "risk of losing an election" by workers, greater insecurity of rewards, and possible disruptions in supplies, losses of subsidies, and plant closures. The intelligentsia were attracted by the opportunities that glasnost gave for "greater criticism and
publication" and for the enhanced rewards which a more market-oriented economy
would bring them, but they had "little institutional power" and were often "mercu-
rial" in their support. Workers would benefit from the "improved productivity, greater
individual rewards, and economic expansion" that perestroika promised. But many
were apprehensive about potential inequality, unemployment, and loss of housing
subsidies. Peasants were attracted by improved incentives and greater reliance on
family farming, but they disliked change, were suspicious of government assurances,
and opposed reductions in agricultural subsidies. Gorbachev's policies, for example,
modernization programs that focused on renovation of existing plants and equipment over new investment projects, favored relatively developed regions, such as
the western parts of the country, over less developed regions, such as Central Asia.
Gorbachev's reforms combined increased centralization of "broad policy powers" at
the upper levels of the party with reduced micromanagement of enterprises by ministries and greater decentralization of day-to-day enterprise management. This pleased
radical reformers within the party but challenged party conservatives, local and regional party authorities, and ministries. In all these instances, perestroika's support
was to a greater or lesser extent offset by popular opposition.

Lacking both unequivocally dictatorial powers over the ruling oligarchy and the
party consensus of the Brezhnev years, Gorbachev relied heavily on "jawboning" or
cajoling in the endeavor to forge a new, reformist, consensus within the party. This
increasingly aggravated party radicals who came to believe that perestroika was more
rhetoric than reality. Boris Yeltsin, who had originally been brought to Moscow by
Gorbachev in 1985, emerged in the late 1980s and early 1990s as a leader of this
group, at first inside, and later outside, the party. Caught between the cautious opposition of the moderates and conservatives and the impatience of the radicals,
Gorbachev's version of perestroika became increasingly mired in apparent indeci-
siveness and ineffectuality. Economically, therefore, perestroika remained largely
unimplemented during most of the latter half of the 1980s.

Measuring Soviet economic performance during the Gorbachev period is somewhat problematic because different sources estimate differently.[3] However, recognizing that Western estimates tend to be somewhat lower and official Soviet estimates
somewhat higher, it is still useful to compare Soviet growth performance in the late
1980s with that of the later years of the Brezhnev era. (The experience of the early
1990s will be discussed in Chapter 10.) In the early 1980s (1980 to 1984), a period
when Gorbachev and his associates believed that stagnation or near stagnation prevailed
in the country, the annual average growth rate of Soviet GNP (see Table 8.2) was 1.9
percent, equal to that of the United Kingdom and less than that of the United States,

Table 9.1
Annual Growth Rates of Soviet GNP, 1985-1989

Years	CIA Estimates	Soviet Estimates	UN Estimates
1985	.08	--	1.6
1986	4.0	4.1	2.3
1987	1.3	3.1	1.6
1988	1.5	5.0	4.4
1989	--	3.5	--

Source: United Nations Economic Outlook (1990).

but still a respectable figure by Western standards.[4] But between 1985 and 1988, according to CIA and DIA (1989) estimates, the average annual growth rate of the economy fell to 1.7 percent. As Table 9.1 shows, the Soviet economy grew at a rate of 0.08 percent in 1985, 4 percent in 1986, 1.3 percent in 1987, and 1.5 percent in 1988. Soviet official sources estimate that the growth of the Soviet economy was 4.1 percent in 1986, 3.1 percent in 1987, and 5 percent in 1988.

A striking feature of the Soviet economy during the late 1980s was an explosion of the government's budget deficit. Gorbachev himself acknowledged on October 19, 1990, "We lost control over the financial situation in the country. This was our most serious mistake in the years of perestroika" (cited in Goldman 1991, 136). As shown in Table 9.2, the budget deficit quadrupled, from 18 billion rubles (2.3 percent of GNP) in 1985 to 91.8 billion rubles (about 10 percent of GNP) in 1989. By 1990 the budget deficit had grown to perhaps 150 billion rubles or more (15+ percent of GNP). In the early years of perestroika, revenues from turnover taxes on alcoholic beverages

Table 9.2
Soviet Fiscal and Monetary Variables, 1985-1990

	1985	1986	1987	1988	1989	1990
M2* (annual % growth rate)	7.5 (1981-85)	8.5	14.7	14.1	14.8	15.3
M2 (% of GDP)	51.2	56.9	61.2	65.5	72.5	--
Monetary Emission (billions of rubles)	--	3.3	5.9	11.7	18.3	26.6
Budget Deficit (billions of rubles)	18.0	47.9	57.1	90.1	91.8	150 +
(% of GNP)	2.3	6.0	6.9	10.3	9.9	15+
State Debt ** (billions of rubles)	142	162	184	312	398	550+
(% of GNP)	18	20	22	36	48	55
Money Income (billions of rubles)	420.1	435.3	452.1	493.5	558.0	652.5

* M2 = Cash + Demand Deposits. ** Internal debt, though probably some is ruble counterpart of Soviet external debt

Source: Compiled from Ellman (1992, 108, 114, 120-22); Cook (1992, 209); Goldman (1991, 135).

fell sharply (by about 200 billion rubles altogether) because of the drop in sales associated with the anti-alcoholism campaign. Revenues also fell because of unanticipated reductions in world energy prices: the value of Soviet petroleum exports dropped substantially (by about 10 billion rubles) between 1984 and 1988. In the late 1980s, the Law on State Enterprises dramatically increased the share of state profits retained by enterprises and correspondingly reduced (by about 8 billion rubles in 1988) enterprise payments to the state budget.

At the same time, government expenditures rose, partly because of unexpected disasters, notably the Chernobyl nuclear power accident and an earthquake in Armenia. Large increases in domestic investment and in machinery imports associated with the endeavor to shift to an intensive growth strategy also swelled government expenditures and thereby the budget deficit. Growing budget deficits may also be attributed in part to substantial and rising subsidies to food and agriculture (amounting to 24 percent of the budget deficit or 12 percent of GNP) and to unprofitable enterprises (about 10 percent of the budget, or 5 percent of GNP) (Nordhaus 1992, 200, 203).[5] Although military spending probably fell somewhat as a result of post-Cold War policies, the Soviet military establishment remained a heavy burden on the Soviet economy and a serious contributor to the budget deficit.[6] Unfinished construction (discussed earlier) was another significant cause of financial disequilibrium in the Gorbachev years, derivative in part from the investment boom instigated by Gorbachev as an element in his program to accelerate a shift from extensive to intensive development. Although the 1986-1990 plan projected a reduction in unfinished construction, in fact it expended significantly, increasing from 79 percent of total investment in 1986 (73 percent in 1973) to more than 100 percent in 1990. The amount of construction that exceeded the planned time limit "exploded in 1988-90, rising from 8.2 billion rubles in 1987 to 13.3 billion in 1988, 39 billion in 1989 and 60 billion in 1990" (Ellman 1992, 119).

As budget deficits expanded, so too did the government's debt which, by the late 1980s, was about 43 percent of the GNP and rising, and by 1990, had tripled relative to 1985. A significant portion of the rising deficits was monetized. As indicated in Table 9.2, the annual rate of growth in M2 (cash + demand deposits) roughly doubled between the first half (7.5%) and the latter half of the 1980s (between 14% and 15% in the years 1987-1990), and the amount of coin and paper currency issued annually beginning in 1986 had grown more than fivefold by 1989 and about eightfold by 1990. By 1989 and 1990, the annual growth rate in the emission of new money had risen to about 50 percent. The result of the accelerating expansion in the money supply was an increasing "ruble overhang," manifested by a growth in M2 as a percent of the GNP (from 51.2 percent in 1985 to 72.5 percent in 1989, as shown in Table 9.2). The ratio of household liquid assets to household income also rose, "from around 0.6 in the 1970s (when there was little ruble overhang) to around 0.95 in 1989" (Nordhaus 1992, 200).

As depicted in the last row of Table 9.2, money income grew vigorously in the Gorbachev years. Between 1985 and 1990, money incomes expanded by 55 percent. Enterprises used their greater autonomy under the law on state enterprises to raise wages. The annual rate of increase in average wages accelerated from 2.6 percent in

1986 to 9.4 percent in 1989 and 12.3 percent in 1990. By 1989 the annual income of collective farmers, both from the collective farms and their private garden plots, rose by double-digit or nearly-double-digit figures. In 1990 the earnings of "the (mainly rural) population from the sale of agricultural products to the state rose by 30 percent mainly as a result of the increase in procurement prices." Incomes earned in cooperatives also rose rapidly, from "2.2 billion roubles in 1988 (the year the law on cooperatives came into force) to 16.8 billion in 1989." In 1990 the increase in earnings by cooperative members was "one-fifth of the total increase in wages" (Ellman 1992, 116). Growth in money income increasingly outstripped increases in production and labor productivity.

As a result of the rapid growth in money incomes, and the unusually expansionary monetary and fiscal policies (relative to slower growth in production and productivity) that underpinned them, excess demands for consumer goods, with their accompanying manifestations of shortages, queues, and higher black market prices, rose substantially. One estimate for the late 1980s is that the prices of consumer goods would have needed to rise by "more than 50 percent to extinguish the [ruble] overhang" (Nordhaus 1992, 200). Chastened by years of economic decline, chronic shortages, and dwindling food supplies at state stores, consumers grew increasingly disappointed with Gorbachev's reforms.

Political Reforms

The pace of the sweeping political changes in Soviet society under the banner of glasnost and *demokratizatsiya* exceeded both common expectation and the pace of economic reform. Gorbachev indeed achieved a Herculean task. Soviet society was changed dramatically. Glasnost made public opinion a serious force for social change and succeeded in sowing the seeds for cultivation of political and civic culture in the Soviet Union. Glasnost effectively repudiated the mythology of Stalin and the command model of socialism, shattered taboos that had dominated the country for generations, and reinstated many prominent dissident activists, such as Andrei Sakharov, radical writers, such as historian Roy Medvedev, and revolutionary Bolshevik thinkers, such as Nikolai Bukharin. The degree of freedom that the media in general enjoyed under Gorbachev's Soviet Union had no parallel in its entire history.[7]

Glasnost opened up the Soviet mind. Besides providing a wide platform for reinterpreting history and facilitating dauntless expression of ecological, societal, humanitarian, and cultural concerns and contributing substantially to thwarting an August 1991 coup perpetrated by Party conservatives, glasnost was responsible for exposing long-suppressed ethnic, nationality-oriented, religious, and social grievances and conflicts that eventually led to Soviet disintegration in late 1991.

Demokratizatsiya was similarly successful. It succeeded in changing Soviet political life for good. Democracy began to take root in Soviet society as ever-greater participation of the masses rejuvenated the processes of governance in the country.[8] In 1989, for the first time in Soviet history, an overwhelming majority—1,500 of the 2,250-member Congress of the People's Deputies—were freely elected through secret ballots.[9] Although the Communist party won the election as a party, many individual party officials were defeated. The Congress of the People's Deputies was thus transformed into the most democratic governmental institution in the entire Soviet history. Discarding its conventional rubber-stamp approach, the new congress played a significant role in national and international policy matters. Heated discussions and fearless opposition on the congress floors became common in Gorbachev's Soviet Union.

In mid-1989 a formal opposition in the nation's parliament, the Inter-regional Deputies Group led by Boris Yeltsin[10] and prominent human rights activist Andrei Sakharov, was allowed to operate. Another revolutionary turning point in Soviet history occurred in February 1990 when Gorbachev formally brought an end to the political monopoly that the Communist party had enjoyed in the Soviet Union since 1917.[11] Thus, a remarkable process began for the transformation of Soviet society from a centralized, authoritarian structure toward a more democratic, pluralistic one. Subsequently, the establishment of a stronger executive presidency in March 1990 accelerated the transfer of power away from the Communist party to the government. The Communist party received a further blow in the March 1990 congressional election, in which non-Communist candidates outnumbered the Communist party candidates in a reconstituted 1,033-member congress.

Like economic reforms, the political reforms of perestroika demonstrated an evolutionary character. The character of glasnost and *demokratizatsiya* began to change especially after the spring of 1988 with the emergence of a myriad of informal and unofficial political, social, and other kinds of groups and associations with diverse political preferences, programs, and constituencies. The elimination of the CPSU's monopoly of political power, thus setting the stage for multiparty political pluralism, marked the next important stage. This stage was also marked by a proliferation of independence movements in the Baltic states, and by Gorbachev's call for "self-determination" of republics, "harmonizing inter-ethnic relations," and efforts to establish "optimal links" between republics and Union governments (1990c, 36-37. During this period, Gorbachev also consolidated his power as president of the Soviet Union. At the Twenty-eighth Congress, Gorbachev called for the complete separation of state and party, asked the CPSU to work within the "bounds of democratic process" as a parliamentary party, and to shun its traditional right to control the management of enterprises, departments, and other government bodies.

Accordingly, the Politburo of the CPSU was reorganized and extended to incorporate leaders from the Soviet Union's fifteen republics and other grassroots organizations; thus, for the first time in Soviet history, representation to the Politburo from all corners of the country was ensured.[12] Second, measures were taken to restrict Politburo activity to party matters and to stop its direct management of the state and economy. State officials, including the head of government and members of the council of ministers, were excluded from the Politburo.

The progress of glasnost resulted in a virtual disappearance of official censorship or control over the media and the freedom of expression of ordinary citizens. Soviet citizens became free to talk to news media, foreign or domestic, and to join virtually any organization, political, economic, or cultural. Newspapers published almost anything, including demands for the disintegration of the country, the overthrow of the CPSU from power, or denouncement of Soviet official ideology—indeed, of socialism itself. And the Soviet state-controlled media, including state-run television, radio, and the news agency TASS, gave coverage to dissident and oppositional activities. In the immediate aftermath of the Twenty-eighth Congress, Gorbachev lifted the party monopoly over the state-run radio and television system, and thus all political movements and organizations had access to the airwaves, including the right to set up their own television and radio stations. A Presidential Council was formed with a position of vice president, and a new union treaty was proposed on the basis of "sovereign republics."

In November 1990, the Supreme Soviet approved a new union based on "optimal links" between the weakened center and the voluntary cooperation of the "sovereign republics." In March 1991, a nationwide referendum gave a mandate to such a union.[13] A Council of Federation, composed of presidents of the constituent republics, was established as the highest collective policy-making body of the country. A Constitutional Court was also created to resolve disputes between the center and the republics.

But these political innovations failed to solve the mounting problems stemming from age-old ethnic and nationality disputes compounded by widespread political turmoil and economic downturn. Indeed, some leading members of the party, representing the military, the KGB, the party, and the government, believed that the new union would so weaken the powers of the central government and strengthen the powers of the several republics as to constitute the demise of the Soviet Union, and evidently they began preparations for a coup to depose Gorbachev. By mid-1991 Soviet society had become so polarized that both conservatives and pro-Western liberals were worried that the country was heading toward anarchy, potential civil war, or even military takeover. Gorbachev, anticipating such dangers and in desperation to keep the Soviet Union together, had sided with the conservatives in the winter of 1990. This not only resulted in a temporary reversal in the reform processes of democratization and liberalization, but also alienated the pro-reform forces. Gorbachev's reversal, although a temporary retreat succeeded by a shift toward the radicals in the spring of 1991, cemented unity among Yeltsin and other pro-reformers, who concluded that the political turmoil and economic downswing that the country faced at that time could not be resolved under a "center" dominated by the Soviet Union or Gorbachev's leadership. The abortive coup of August 1991, which was orchestrated by conservatives as a last ditch attempt to save the country and sustain the Soviet Union as a united geopolitical entity, perilously punctured the legitimacy of both Gorbachev and the Soviet Union that he was trying to save.

Eventually, in December 1991, a weakened Gorbachev was completely bypassed when presidents of the Russian Federation, Ukraine, and Byelorussia declared the cessation of the Soviet Union at the historic Byelorussian city of Minsk.[14] The Minsk declaration, initially signed by these presidents, was responsible for the creation of a new geopolitical entity called the Commonwealth of Independent States (CIS), which replaced the Soviet Union when most of its republics joined this body gradually. The CIS, as an extremely loose confederation of sovereign states, was initially responsible for foreign and defense affairs and other interrepublican governmental affairs. In sharp contrast to the American confederation of the 1770s, the CIS was not aimed at forming a stronger national government. It was, as the signers made clear at the outset, aimed at arresting the momentum toward anarchy and smoothing out the disintegration process of the country.

TENSIONS AND CONTRADICTIONS

Gorbachev's "socialism with a human face" succeeded in resolving several problems stemming from preceding Soviet models of political economy. At the same time, perestroika generated tensions and contradictions of its own. Economically, some of the most serious shortcomings of perestroika were as follows. First, simultaneous emphasis on increasing economic growth and massive economic restructuring was unrealistic. This was especially true in a situation where both acceleration and restructuring of the economy involved radical transformation of the whole economy and society. Economic restructuring causes disruptions of normal patterns of economic relationships. Even if the new institutions and processes are economically progressive in the long run, they may well be dislocative in the short run. For example, if steel mills no longer receive coal and iron by ministerial allotment and have not simultaneously arranged for sales to, say, tractor factories, they will lack both resource inputs to sustain continuity in steel production and the income to purchase those needed inputs. Tractor production, dependent on steel, will then decline, and, with it, depressive repercussions will spread to other sectors. The overall result will be at least reductions in growth rates, possibly absolute contractions in production and employment. Moreover, a pro-growth strategy, even one relying on intensive development, if it entails an expansion in the ratio of investment to national income, will reduce consumption, at least relatively and possibly absolutely. Second, despite the exhortations and rhetoric of Gorbachev and his associates, during at least the initial stages of perestroika, the Soviet Union depended primarily on central planning and state direction for the functioning of the economy. Reform efforts were aimed at achieving higher growth rates without overturning the old economic system or disturbing the internal balance of power. Gorbachev and his advisers mistakenly believed that the main problem of the economy was, in effect, technical, that is, that it lay with the extensive methods of production per se, and concluded that a transition to intensive methods of production, coupled with improvements in the central planning apparatus, would suffice. They failed to realize that the old system was not receptive to scientific and technological progress, indeed to progress at all.[15]

Third, market economy is not automatically self-emergent, nor does it develop rapidly. It requires institutions and social attitudes that, in Western societies, took positive action and emerged over a long period of time. During transition out of the old society, two problematic features of institutional restructuring thus occur at the same time. On the one hand, old institutions tend to be dismantled before new institutions have emerged to supersede them, with growing chaos as a result.[16] For example, the law on state enterprises, which went into effect in the Soviet Union in January 1988, significantly increased the independence of enterprises from central party-state control before the institutions of competition and market economy, which are expected to regulate and constrain enterprise power in Western, industrially advanced capitalist economies, had been created. This led to price increases, assortment changes, output reductions, excessive wage increases, and a worsening of the reliability of the supply system (Ellman and Kontorovich 1992, 23).

Prices rose because increased independence gave enterprises greater opportunity to circumvent state-set prices and the retention of a larger share of profits provided a greater incentive to do so. The same forces encouraged changes in product assortment which, although profitable, were based more on enterprise monopoly power and distorted prices than on greater efficiency and adaptation to buyers' preferences. Outputs were often reduced because state orders dropped below 100 percent, and given the greater resulting flexibility, it was often easier as well as more profitable to reduce output and raise prices. Enterprise directors, especially when elected by workers and armed with new powers to raise prices and to reduce employment, were often quite willing to raise wages. Output reductions and assortment changes, combined with increases in money and credit, retention of larger shares of profits by enterprises, and reductions in centralized allocation of products (according to *Gossnab*, from 13,000 to 618 during 1987-1989), reduced the reliability of the supply system, especially in the construction sector. Moreover, the macroeconomic monetary disequilibrium (described in the preceding section) made enterprises increasingly desirous of exchanging their outputs for scarce goods instead of overabundant rubles. Consequently, the supply system was partially replaced not by wholesale trade but by barter. The resulting disruptions in supplies and "increased inability to obtain the goods necessary for high levels of production and to give reality to money incentives naturally led to declines in production and labor productivity" (24).

On the other hand, the old institutions that do survive in a time of system reform and transition require careful coordination with emerging institutions. For example, what may well be needed in what Gorbachev called a "regulated market economy" is not the abolition of central planning in favor of laissez faire, but reconstruction and redirection of planning, away from party- state control over microeconomic details and toward an overall macroeconomic framework of stability, security, and high-level employment within which the newly emerging decentralized, market-oriented, and private processes can function most efficiently (Dowlah and Elliott 1991). Insofar as the old bureaucratic planning methodologies survive, economic restructuring suffers from the absence of new, needed planning institutions and methodologies at the same time that the simultaneous operation of traditional, centralized planning and management systems and emergent, more decentralized processes conflict and to some extent nullify each other.

Paralleling the economic deficiencies and contradictions of the Gorbachev era were important political tensions. First, vacillation in Gorbachev's economic reforms reflected a fundamenental ambivalence, among both the Party-state elite and the Soviet population at large. Many ordinary Soviet citizens supported perestroika, at least in its early years, insofar as they associated reforms with economic improvement and reduction in abuses by and privileges accorded to members of the party-state apparatus. But, no doubt, most regarded higher prices, lower real wages, unemployment, and cuts in subsidies as an unacceptable trade-off for such reforms. For example, economic advisers told Gorbachev that "he had to end state subsidies to money-losing enterprises as a condition to any real reform, but he understood how the tripling of food prices that would result could tear Soviet society apart" (Parks 1991a, H9). Moreover, Alexander Yakovlev, ideological adviser to Gorbachev, maintained that "a majority

Table 9.3
Distribution of Social Product in the Soviet Union (in percentage)

	A	B	C
Initial situation	55	15	30
Beginning of bureaucratic industrialization	35	30	35
Long-term result	35	20	45

Source: Mandel (1992, 35).

of the popular masses—not everybody, but a majority—want conservative decisions, but made in a democratic way.... They want order, discipline. At that same time, they don't want to return to the totalitarian past" (H9). Similarly, the party in the Gorbachev years, buffeted by the pressures of economic slowdown and the challenges of economic and political reform, including threats to the power and status of the politocracy, lost its Brezhnevian consensus and increasingly divided into factions, with conflicting opinions on perestroika, democratization, and liberalization, and with linkages to and support from different groups and elements in Soviet society.

Caught in these contradictions, Gorbachev walked a tightrope trying, largely unsuccessfully, to forge a new consensus between his more radical advisers and conservative defenders of centralized and authoritarian modes of political and economic decision making in the party and other leading Soviet institutions. He was pressured from the right by his chief rival, Politburo member Ligachev, and other members of the party apparatus, the state bureaucracy, the military, the industrial administration, and finally the aborted August 1991 coup to pursue cautious, managed change. From the left, he was pressed by such associates as Foreign Minister Edward Shevardnadze and Yakovlev to "accelerate the pace of reform, to broaden its scope, and to move boldly toward a free-market economy and full democracy" (Parks 1991a, H9).[17]

Second, after Nikita Khrushchev's critique of Stalinism and the reduction of repressive measures, the Brezhnev regime, confronted with economic slowdown and growing discontent, engaged in a partial "re-Stalinization," characterized by greater constraints on and incarceration of dissidents (often in psychiatric clinics rather than Siberian gulags). The resulting expansion in "surveillance and control" (Goldman 1983, 105) brought with it not only greater human costs, police abuses, and unrest, indicated by demonstrations and strikes, but also a "tremendous increase of non-productive expenditure" and hence a drop in the growth of "productive investment side by side with the relative reduction in consumer outlays" (Mandel 1991, 202).

One, very rough, estimate of "nonproductive" consumption, including arms production, costs of the party and state bureaucracy and the repressive apparatus, and costs of the luxury consumption of the *nomenklatura* based on its special privileges, is provided in Table 9.3. According to this estimate, such consumption (column C), as a percent of Soviet GNP, rose from 30 percent in the 1920s to 35 percent at the outset of Stalinist industrialization. "Productive consumption," that is, consumption necessary for the reproduction of labor power and the physical means of production, fell (from about 55 percent to 35 percent, column A) at the time of initial industrialization, permitting, roughly, a doubling (from 15 to 30 percent) of productive investment (column B) despite some initial expansion in nonproductive consumption. In the post-

Stalinist era, however, nonproductive consumption continued to rise (to 45 percent by the 1980s), notably because of Cold War military expansion and the continued extension of privileges by the party, state, military, and KGB bureaucracies, and productive investment fell (to 20 percent). Thus, over time, the expansion of nonproductive expenditure "reduces or cancels those extra advantages that it was thought possible to achieve by holding down consumption of the producers." Productive consumption was repressed, but productive investment was constrained, indeed ultimately reduced (though maintained at a higher level than prior to industrialization) because of the enlarging tribute distributed unproductively as a result of the "despotism of the bureaucracy" (Mandel 1992, 35).

Gorbachev (correctly) concluded that the abandonment of repression, the freeing of political prisoners, and reliance on persuasion rather than fear were essential to both successful economic performance and political legitimacy. At the same time, from the perspective of continuity of authoritarian rule, pre-Gorbachev Soviet leaders were prudently "reluctant to relax their controls," on the grounds that, judging from historical experience, if "grievances are widespread enough, particularly when there is a shortage of food, large numbers join in [with revolutionary action] spontaneously. There is then a dangerous potential of a chain explosion" (Goldman 1983, 114). Ironically, the easing of repression in the context of economic reform thus constitutes one of the fundamental internal contradictions of the political reform. Popular discontent was rooted in the institutions and policies of the Brezhnev era. But the repression then was so strong that many people hardly dared to voice their discontent. The economic reforms of perestroika solved few of the problems, at least in the short run, but the easing of repression and the more candid, open atmosphere allowed discontent to be expressed. Because the consumption of liberty "whets the appetite for it," the greater the opportunity for open criticism, "the greater the discontent turn[s] angrily on the system," as illustrated pointedly by the revolutions in France (1789), Russia (1917), and Iran (1979) (Kornai 1992, 427). As de Tocqueville (1955, 177) insightfully puts it, "The perilous moment for a bad government is when that government tries to mend its ways."

A third political contradiction pertains to the dynamics of the relationships among economic restructuring, political liberalization, and democratization. In his farewell address made in December 1991, Gorbachev observed that, in 1985, at the outset of his administration,

we were living much worse than people in the [Western] industrialized countries, and we were increasingly falling behind them. The reason was obvious even then. This country was suffocating in the shackles of the bureaucratic-command system. Doomed to cater to ideology and suffer the onerous burden of the arms race, it found itself at the breaking point.... We had to change everything radically. (Cited in Parks 1991a, H9)

For the reasons already indicated, Gorbachev's reform model incorporated significant elements of liberalization and democratization, both in their own right, as a means of creating "more socialism, not less,"[18] and as instruments, to combat bureaucratic inertia and opposition and to generate allies in the campaign to accelerate economic restructuring. But glasnost and *demokratizatsiya* contained dangers as well as opportunities for perestroika. Under glasnost, people were encouraged to ventilate their complaints and voice their demands, thereby exposing corruption and inefficiency and prodding officials to reform. But even if living standards improve, decentralizing and market-oriented economic restructuring tends to cause at least short run dislocations, such as greater inequality, inflation, and unemployment. Once people believe it is safe to complain, they will complain about these dislocative consequences of perestroika, not merely the underlying causes of the need for restructuring. If living standards fail to improve, public complaints are likely to intensify and to be directed against the economic restructuring itself, and against the political leadership propounding that restructuring. "In the end, Gorbachev ran the risk of being mocked for bringing the Soviet people words but no material benefits, glasnost but no perestroika. Moreover, once given glasnost, the public were likely to take that *glasnost* for granted while they focused even more on the failures of perestroika." Thus, the combination of perestroika and glasnost proved to be "combustible." It virtually "predetermined that there would be growing ethnic, political, and social tension clashes, complicating the already difficult process of economic reform" (Goldman 1991, 126).

Democratization, "while necessary, may also have been his [Gorbachev's] undoing." Gorbachev's version of moderate and guided democratization presupposed that the overwhelming majority of the citizenry would share his vision of the future as well as his critique of the past, and that minorities would observe the discipline of a majority rule kept within relatively narrow bounds by the guidance of a successful central leadership supplemented by the persuasive powers of allies among the intelligentsia, the application of whose critical talents would also be kept reasonably narrow in scope. In this way, democratization would constrain the "power abusers and incompetents from the old era" at the same time that it "energized the supporters of perestroika and glasnost." Criticism would occur, but it would be "constructive and disciplined" and would thereby "help, not hurt, the reform process" (105).

In practice, these presuppositions proved to be unduly optimistic. Perestroika did not emerge in response to democratic pressure from below, but as a modernizing reform strategy from above. Political support for perestroika and public confidence in the Gorbachev regime varied with economic performance. As performance deteriorated in the late 1980s and early 1990s, disappointment with the reforms grew. Growing disappointment translated into declining confidence and support, decreased willingness to accept discipline and sacrifice, and increased proclivity to seek alternatives, for example, movements for republic independence.

Thus, democratization, although deemed necessary for economic reform, placed important constraints on its content and pace. The political reforms embodied in democratization strengthened the role and power of the state relative to that of the party and of individuals, non-party associations, regions, localities, and national and ethnic groups relative to the state. These two tendencies weakened the power and position of the center—the Moscow party and its top leadership. Enthusiastic participation in glasnost and the opportunities raised by democratization stimulated the beginnings of a civil society in the Soviet Union, a growing polyarchy of political forums within and outside the Communist party. These emerging alternative platforms and leaderships formed the embryonic foundation of a kind of multiparty pluralism which, especially after the Twenty-eighth Congress of the CPSU held in 1990, began to radicalize. Like the Sorceror's Apprentice, Gorbachev had let loose forces that went beyond his (or the party's) control and eventuated in revolutionary change rather than more reform. Gorbachev's version of democratization thus left unresolved the tension between popular sovereignty and a leading role for the party, of democracy and Leninism. It is perhaps not impossible that a viable blend of these two could occur, for example, through the shared values of leaders and the electorate or through a gradual process of education and "learning democracy" (Kurashvili, cited in White 1992, 72) under auspicious economic circumstances.

At best, however, an attempt to combine the two principles plausibly would contain a powerful element of instability. Party leaders would have to be content with "leading" through persuasion, education, mobilization of public opinion, and compromise and refrain from returning to older patterns of authoritarian rule. The citizenry would need to be satisfied with political participation within the context of a dominant and guiding role by a single party and refrain from pushing forward to a representative system of governance wherein the Communist party had been reduced to a position of one party among several, contributing to democratic debate over public policy, but quite possibly rejected through the ballot box as a party "uniquely qualified to articulate the national interest" (White 1992, 74).

In practice, the emerging political system of the late 1980s combined the worst of both worlds. Voters could reject particular candidates for political office but could not effect a change of regime. Parliamentarians could criticize, articulate grievances, and resist unpopular policies, but they lacked the integration to cohere around an alternative program of government. In Eastern Europe, Communist rule had been externally imposed. When Soviet military support was withdrawn, the Communist regimes lost power in the wake of popular uprisings. The dissolution of the CPSU was much more complicated, but one compelling cause was its failure to articulate "a convincing vision of the Soviet future" that would unite both the leadership and the citizenry, and the accompanying failure, based on the rigidity of party leadership, notably its conservative wing, to "democratize its manner of operation" with sufficient thoroughness and speed. The aborted coup in August 1991, combined with failure by the party leadership to condemn it, sealed the party's fate and thus resolved the tension between party dominance and popular sovereignty, but it did not, by itself (as will be discussed in Chapter 10), provide a basis for stable government in the divided and recessionary society of the later 1990s (74-75).

Because of the relative success of economic rather than political reforms in Hungary, Poland, and Yugoslavia in the 1950s and 1960s, and in China in the late 1970s, it is often held that economic reforms can be easier to accomplish in the context of an authoritarian political environment than political reforms. Economic reforms are more acceptable to oligarchic political leaderships because they are less threatening to existing political power than political reforms. Also, empirically, economic reforms may be politically advantageous to ruling authorities as means of assuaging the demands of the proreform elements in society. Often, socialist governments have orchestrated economic reforms from above but have held back on political reforms. Also, reform experience, notably in China, has shown that privatization and market reforms in agriculture or an "agriculture first" strategy in general may serve to generate momentum for extending reforms to the industrial sector.

By the late 1980s, however, Gorbachev and his associates gave priority to political relative to economic reforms as a key strategy, and they stressed the industrial rather than the rural/agricultural sector as a point of departure. This strategy and sequential arrangement was a tremendous success in the political sphere but yielded relatively less progress in the economic sphere. The Gorbachev leadership argued that one of the crucial reasons for the failure of previous economic reforms in the Soviet Union had been lack of political reforms. They believed that the economic situation they inherited demanded a different strategy and sequential arrangement of reforms than China or Hungary had previously pursued somewhat successfully. The Soviet Union lacked the huge manpower in rural areas that could be transformed into active work forces under a "rural revolution" as had occurred in China. Rather, the Soviet Union had highly educated and skilled urban manpower that was presumably ready for diversified social and political structures. Besides, the Gorbachev leadership concluded that there were many other geographical, historical, political, ideological, social, institutional, and international factors that distinguished the Soviet Union from other socialist countries. Glasnost and *demokratizatsiya* were promoted as a means to foster support for economic reforms as well as to stimulate incentives and greater participation from below.

Gorbachev's unique strategy of simultaneous economic and political reforms, with greater importance given to the political sphere and sequential preference to the industrial sector, resulted in a kind of dialectical relationship. At the earlier stages, glasnost was aimed at eliciting public criticism against the bureaucratic apparatus of the centralized, authoritarian state and mobilizing public support for perestroika. Some latitude was granted to journalists and intellectuals so that the evils of the inherited system could be revealed, and at the same time forces opposed to reforms could be challenged. Liberalization and democratization were expected to be less than the rhetoric implied, but enough to generate support for perestroika.

Glasnost generated unprecedented enthusiasm and rejuvenation in the press and among the masses in Soviet society at large. Millions of people joined public life. The more people became open minded, aware and informed of the actual conditions of the existing society, economy, and polity, the more vocal they became against abuses, corruption, and official privileges, and the more they demanded an extension of glasnost. To accelerate the process of the implementation of economic reforms, Gorbachev found an extended glasnost to be useful as a means of promoting support for perestroika's more radical economic reforms.[19]

Over time, however, the unprecedented democratization, the expanding openness to both domestic and international information and ideas, and the rebirth of civil society contributed to a growing challenge to the monopoly power of the CPSU. The CPSU, on the other hand, remained dominated by conservative forces who believed in orthodox Soviet socialist values and were unwilling to relinquish the party's supreme authority over the state, society, and economy. Facing this situation, Gorbachev was left with options either to transform the party into a more liberal one suited to the needs and challenges of the changed population, or to shift power from the party to the state. Gorbachev apparently tried to do some of both. In the immediate aftermath of the Twenty-eighth Congress, conservative leader Ligachev[20] was retired, a new central committee was formed with a larger number of liberal members, the Politburo was reorganized with circumscribed power, the CPSU was separated from the state, and definitive steps were taken toward multiparty political pluralism. This embryonic stage of political pluralism received special momentum when Yeltsin resigned at the Twenty-eighth Congress.

Gorbachev, who began with rather cautious efforts at easing authoritarianism, rapidly moved toward more radical and widespread democratization. Indeed, democratization went beyond that of many socialist countries that had been experimenting with market-oriented reforms for decades. In the case of China, when economic reforms stimulated demands for political reforms, the authorities crushed those demands. But in the Soviet Union, political reforms stimulated demands for more radical change, and Gorbachev not only approved such demands, he officially encouraged them. After mid-1991, the forces of political change took on a life of their own. Within a few months after the August 1991 coup, the Communist party was outlawed, socialism was abandoned, and, finally, the second-mightiest state on the surface of the earth—the Soviet Union—disappeared from the world map.

NOTES

1 Cooperatives played an important role during the NEP period, as discussed in Chapter 3, during which private enterprises paid only 5.7 percent of their earnings in taxes.

2. Of the four *khozraschet* models described above, the first one appeared to be over-whelmingly popular as about 60 percent of industrial output was produced under this model in 1988; the other models, which emphasized greater accountability, remained less promising.

3. As Bergson (1989, 263-81) points out, neither the CIA estimates nor Soviet official statistics seem to be fully reliable; both enjoy a "relatively privileged status" of reliability in terms of some estimations and lack the same for other spheres. Lack of any simple set of indicators reflecting the overall condition of the Soviet economy, questionable quality of traditional quantitative indicators like national income statistics, and sheer absence of price deflators, make an evaluation of the Soviet economy's performance "notoriously difficult" (Hewett 1989, 55).

4. See for details Cohn (1987, 12) and Dowlah (1992a, 100-101).

5. For details on Soviet budget deficits, see Ofer (1989, 107-61); Gorbachev (1990b, 3-5); Hewett (1989); Nordhaus (1992); Ellman (1992).

6. The late 1980s and early 1990s were characterized by increased accuracy of reporting about the Soviet military. A committee of the Supreme Soviet estimated that military expenditures in 1990 were about 200 billion rubles (about 20 percent of the GNP) (Ellman 1992, 118).

7. Perestroika facilitated, as Falin (1988, 306) writes, the printing of millions of copies of once- disgraced books and the restoration of the stature of scores of cultural figures formerly anathematized for various reasons or for no evident reasons at all.

8. As Brzezinski (1989, 59) remarks, Gorbachev has been "remarkably successful" in creating "a higher degree of individual motivation" and in ensuring greater participation of the masses at all levels of the party and state machineries.

9. The rest were chosen by various public organizations under the Communist party's leadership.

226 The Life and Times of Soviet Socialism

10. Yeltsin was chairman of the Russian republic's parliament at this time. Subsequently, he was elected president of the Russian Federation in a historic election in June 1991. Born on February 1, 1931, in Sverdlovsk in Russia, Yeltsin received his education in industrial engineering. He joined the CPSU in 1961. Gorbachev brought him to Moscow to head the Moscow Communist party in March 1985. A deputy of the Supreme Soviet since 1974, Yeltsin became a candidate member of the Politburo in 1986. A pro-Gorbachev liberal-turned-radical reformer, Yeltsin resigned from the CPSU at the Twenty-eighth Congress in 1990.

11. The repeal of Article 6 of the Soviet constitution, which guarantees a constitutional monopoly of power to the Communist party, was ratified by 1,771 to 264, with 74 abstentions.

12. The old Politburo had thirteen full members, including eleven Russians, one Georgian, and one Ukrainian; eight candidate members including seven Russians and one Byelorussian; and a ten-member Secretariat with one non-Russian. The newly constituted Politburo, in contrast, had twenty four full members drawn from the whole country.

13. Six republics—Armenia, Estonia, Georgia, Latvia, Lithuania and Moldavia—boycotted the referendum.

14. It is, indeed, ironic that the meeting scheduled between Yeltsin and the Ukrainian president at Minsk was originally aimed at stopping the disintegration of the Soviet Union which was sparked by the declaration of independence by Ukraine. Yeltsin was expected to convince Ukraine to stay within the Soviet Union. The meeting, held at a forest dacha by the three presidents of the Russian Federation, Ukraine, and Byelorussia—Yeltsin, Leonid Kravchuck, and Stanislav Shushkevich, respectively—ended with a declaration of the dissolution of the Soviet Union.

15. Gorbachev himself admitted this in his meeting with the leaders of the U. S. Congress. See *New York Times*, June 2, 1990, p.3.

16. "Gorbachev was quite successful in dismantling the old system," notably such elements as "the central bureaucratic apparatus, the official ideology, and the active role of the party in the economy," but he "failed to create a viable new one." The result was "to demolish a system which did function, if far from optimally, and leave in its place a systematic chaos and harmful economic policies" (Ellman and Kontorovich 1992, 31-32).

17. For a discussion of party factions in the late 1980s, see Medvedev (1988, 2).

18. "We are looking within socialism, rather than outside it.... Every part of our program... is fully based on the principle of more socialism and more democracy." "The essence of perestroika is that it unites socialism with democracy" (Gorbachev 1987, 35-36).

19. Gorbachev (1990c, 22) proclaimed, at the Twenty-eighth Congress that without glasnost, Soviet society could "scarcely have reached the new stage in society's revolutionary transformation."

20. Yegor Ligachev was born on November 29, 1920, in Russia. He joined the CPSU in 1944 and became a full member of the party in 1976. A deputy of the Supreme Soviet since 1976, Ligachev was appointed a full member of the Politburo in charge of personnel affairs by Gorbachev in 1985. Ligachev did not serve as a candidate member of Politburo. He represented the conservative wing of the party during Gorbachev's leadership, and he was retired from the party in 1990, following the Twenty-eighth Congress.

Chapter 10

Disintegration of the Soviet Politico-Economic System

Perestroika began as a reform program to achieve modernization through economic restructuring. Under the banners of glasnost and *demokratizatsiya,* brought into being as means to foster perestroika, it escalated into a revolution which, in turn, contributed to disintegration—of the economy and strategic components of its administrative and management structure; of the party/state monopoly of power over information, the communications media, and association; of the Communist party's power monopoly over state and society; and, ultimately, of the multinational state itself as a geopolitical entity. This chapter examines these processes of disintegration.

DISINTEGRATION OF THE SOVIET ECONOMY

Compared to the economic record of Leonid Brezhnev and his immediate successors during the first half of the 1980s, the first three years of the Gorbachev period were neither dismal nor exhilarating. Although the annual growth rate in national income between 1986 and 1988, at 2.8 percent, was a bit lower than that registered for the years from 1981 to 1985 (3.6 percent), both industrial output and agricultural output in the early Gorbachev years grew at annual average rates of 4 and 2.1, respectively, between 1986 and 1988, a bit higher than the growth rates achieved (3.7 and 1) during the period from 1981 to 1985 (compare Tables 10.1 and 8.4). Moreover, growth rates for 1988 rose moderately and were generally higher than those for the early 1980s. Increases in national income in 1988 (4.4 percent) and agricultural output in 1986 (5.3 percent) were especially impressive.

Compared to plan aspirations, however, the economic record of the early Gorbachev years was disappointing. The five year plan adopted in 1986 specified targets of 4.2 percent, 4.6 percent, and 2.7 percent, respectively, for average annual growth rates in national income, industrial output, and agricultural output, which, notably in

Table 10.1
Soviet Economic Growth, 1986-1991 (offical data, percent)

	1989-90	1986	1987	1988	1989	1990	1991
	average (plan)						
National income produced	4.2	2.3	1.6	4.4	2.4	-4.0	-15.0
Industrial output	4.6	4.4	3.8	3.9	1.7	-1.2	-7.8
Agricultural output	2.7	5.3	-0.6	1.7	1.3	-2.3	-7.0

Source: White (1992, 123).

agriculture, were substantially above actual growth rates for the early 1980s. Guide lines for the 1990s specified even higher growth rates, for example 5 percent annually for national income. Actual growth rates for the years from 1986 to 1988 fell below plan targets by more than 30 percent for national income and 14 percent for industrial output. "The failure in Soviet agriculture was particularly striking." Actual growth in that sector was more than 20 percent lower than the (relatively modest) planned growth, and in the first three years of the new administration, "more than 30 billion rubles had to be spent on foreign grain purchases in order to make good domestic shortfalls" (White 1992, 121). Grain production in 1988 alone was 38 million tons below the plan target, and 36 million tons had to be imported to fill the gap.

This less than exuberant economic record undoubtedly contributed to the view among Mikhail Gorbachev and his advisers that making personnel changes, tinkering with the economic administrative structure, and waging a war against alcoholism and absenteeism (highlights of perestroika's early years) were insufficient to make serious inroads on barriers to higher economic performance. It also no doubt reinforced the growing view among perestroika's advocates that political liberalization and democratization were needed to invigorate economic reforms.

The 1989 economic indicators were even more disappointing. The growth rate in gross national product fell from 5 percent to 3 percent and, as indicated in Table 10.1, growth rates in national income, industrial output, and agricultural output also fell significantly. Growth rates in consumer goods were both lower than planned and lower than the rate of growth in investment (the opposite of that projected). Production of some consumer goods, for example, in housing, transportation, and fuels, fell, and shortages of consumer goods became more prevalent.

Other aspects of economic performance reinforced the sense of slowdown, even deterioration. Inflation, which had been gradually increasing between 1986 and 1988, accelerated substantially in 1989. Retail prices rose, according to Central Intelligence Agency estimates, by 6 percent. Including repressed inflation, consumer goods prices, according to official Soviet sources, rose by 7.5 to 10.5 percent (U.S. Congress 1990, 7).

Inflationary pressures, both open and repressed, were fed by rapid increases in money incomes and money wages. Already high in 1988 (9.2 percent), the rate of growth in money incomes rose to 13.1 percent in 1989. Money wages also rose rapidly, indeed more rapidly than labor productivity, in contrast to the experience of the years from 1981 to 1985, when annual average productivity gains (at 3.1 percent) outpaced wage increases (at 2.4 percent). In 1988 average monthly income of workers and office employees rose at 7 percent as compared to annual average productivity increases of 5.1 percent. In 1989 the gap between wage income increases (9.5 percent) and productivity growth (2.3 percent) widened dramatically (*Pravda,* January 28, 1990). As noted earlier, the rapid growth in money wages was based partly on the greater retention of profits by enterprises, which grew by 16 percent in 1989, and the increased allocation of retained profits to enterprise incentive funds, which grew by a remarkable 34 percent (Ellman 1992, 115).

Because of the policy of maintaining stable prices at state stores, real wages and real income officially rose during 1989. Moreover, because of shifts in priorities, the overall rate of growth in consumer goods production in 1989 (4.8 percent) substantially exceeded that in both industrial output (1.7 percent) and heavy industry (0.7 percent) (U.S. Congress 1990, Table C-4) and "thus marked a decisive shift of Soviet industry from its traditional emphasis on heavy industry" (Desai 1990, 147). The actual extent of gains in real income and real wages, however, was moderate. Substantial inflation, both open and repressed, offset much of the income gains. When population growth is incorporated into the calculation, the expansion in per capita real income was actually quite small for 1989—about 1 percent by both official Soviet and CIA estimates. When account is taken of additional costs, real per capita income and real wages probably decreased, particularly for the bottom half of the population. These costs included deteriorating quality and unavailability of goods, proliferation of special distribution channels, longer and more time-consuming lines, extended rationing, higher prices and higher inflation rates in nonstate stores (e.g., collective farm market prices were nearly three times those in state stores in 1989), virtual stagnation in the provisioning of health and education, and the growth of barter, regional autarky, and local protectionism (Schroeder 1992, 98-99).

For the various reasons noted in Chapter 9, the government's budget deficit, which had been rising throughout the late 1980s, both in absolute terms and as a percentage of the GNP, increased sharply yet again in 1989 and reached, by some estimates, more than 13 percent of the GNP. The monetization of the deficit, combined with the rapid growth in money wages and collective farm and cooperative income, caused a rapid growth in the money supply and a larger "ruble overhang," manifested by bank deposits of nearly 340 billion and cash at home estimated at up to 240 billion rubles by 1989 (Desai 1990, 164). The resulting acceleration of inflationary pressures imposed significant hardships on lower income households. Absolute poverty levels increased, especially for such categories as pensioners, the handicapped, large families, and low-paid workers whose money income increases failed to keep pace with higher prices. Poor families (as many as 43 million persons, or about 14 percent of the population) consumed "about a third less meat and milk products in the late 1980s than they had been able to enjoy in the early 1970s" despite the rapid growth in government subsidies, from "about 3.5 billion rubles in the mid 1960s to 84 billion rubles in the late 1980s" (White 1992, 131-32).[1] If the late, no less than the early, 1980s can be characterized in Gorbachev's words as a "pre-crisis," that is, a slowdown in and unacceptably low rates of growth, the early 1990s were years of absolute economic contraction and economic "crisis." In 1990 the GNP dropped by 2 percent, and labor productivity fell by 3 percent. Foreign trade contracted by nearly 7 percent. As shown in Table 10.1, the national income fell by 4 percent. Industrial output and agricultural output also fell, both in the aggregate and for many particular commodities, such as oil (down from 642 million tons in 1988 to 570 million tons in 1990), which caused further reductions in precious hard currencies (White, 1992).

As an examination of the last column of Table 9.2 shows, the various indicators of monetary disequilibrium escalated during 1990. Annual money growth rose to 15.3 percent, and the issuance of cash and currency, although down slightly relative to 1989 (when it rose by 56 percent), still grew by 45 percent. The state debt expanded by nearly 40 percent and became more than half of the GNP. Money incomes rose by 17 percent and money wages grew by 12.3 percent.

Financial disequilibrium created accelerating inflationary pressures. The inflation rate (including both open and repressed inflation), which had reached double-digit levels in 1989, jumped to 19 percent by official Soviet estimates. Thus, real income and real wages fell. Black market prices soared and collective farm prices became "many times higher than those in the state trade" (Ellman 1992, 125). The price index for collective farm markets rose progressively during 1990, from about a 13 percent annual rate in January to a 50 percent rate in December. The index for 1990 as a whole was 145 percent of the 1987 level (as compared to about 113 percent for 1989) (Cook 1992, 211-12). Partly because of escalating inflation, however, farmers were reluctant to part with food in exchange for deteriorating rubles, and the government increasingly purchased food from farms with hard currency or scarce goods. According to Soviet survey studies, shortages of consumer goods became acute. The proportion of a market basket of most important goods more or less freely available in state stores fell from 12 percent in 1988 to 7.5 percent in 1989 and to only 4 percent in 1990. Widespread hoarding and panic buying in response to announcements by the Rhyzkov government in May 1990 of impending large-scale price increases at state stores intensified shortages, disrupted rationing, and mandated both longer queues and greater amounts of time spent in searching for scarce goods.

Thus, by the early 1990s, the retail market for consumer goods, as an orderly process of exchange of money for goods, had collapsed. Monetary disequilibrium thereby was a "major cause" not only of severe economic dislocation, but of the "disintegration of the Soviet economic system." Expanding inflation and recession in the late 1980s and early 1990s and the associated collapse of the retail marketing process, abrogated the tacit social compact between the Soviet leadership and the population. Combined with an apparent inability to devise and implement effective stabilization programs, this contributed significantly to radical changes in social attitudes which "ended the discussion about economic reform and placed the rapid introduction of a western style economic system on the political agenda" (Ellman 1992, 130).

Some stabilization measures were implemented. For example, military spending and state investment were reduced somewhat, and imports of consumer goods expanded, both absolutely and as a share of total imports. Tax revenues rose, both because of new impositions (a sales tax and a tax on wage increases) and because the abandonment of the anti-alcoholism campaign led to a substantial increase in the sales of alcoholic beverages and accompanying revenues from turnover taxes. But other possible programs were effectively blocked or elided. A plan to sell the means of production to "the cooperatives and the population for 1.6 billion roubles was only 2.3 percent achieved." Political opposition effectively blocked reductions in food subsidies and other measures to reduce the government's deficit. A proposal to raise retail prices of consumer goods by about 45 percent was rejected by the Supreme Soviet. The Soviet parliament, against the advice of the Ryzhkov government, also reduced tax rates on enterprise profits. Increased independence and powers of both enterprises and banks stemming from 1987 and 1988 reforms, a failure to develop new institutions to regulate the growth of money and credit, and growing struggles between the center and the republics for control of the banks in the early 1990s left the Soviet Union "with a number of institutions (governments at various levels, enterprises and banks) interested in expanding bank lending and without a suitable institutional framework for controlling the money supply" (127-29).

If in 1990, the Soviet Union, for the first time in the post-World War II period, experienced an economic "recession," 1991 was a year reasonably characterized as a "depression." In the first quarter of the year, the GNP "fell by 8 percent, compared to the same period of 1990, and foreign trade fell by one third" (Morrison 1991, 249). For the year as a whole, as indicated in Table 10.1, national income fell by 15 percent, and industrial and agricultural output fell by 7 percent or more. Consumption dropped by 15 percent and investment by 25 percent. Even more dramatic than the contraction in production and real aggregate demand was the explosive rise in prices associated with runaway increases in money and credit. According to official government figures, the budget deficit grew by 5 times in 1991, credit by 2.1 times, cash by 4.8 times, consumer prices by 1.96 times, and producer prices by 2.4 times (Ericson 1992, 53). The crisis was both deepening and beginning to rival in severity and economic dislocation and pain that found in such capitalist economies as the United States during the 1930s.

The analogy between the depressionary experiences of the Soviet Union and the United States was extended to the domain of institutional and policy reform. As Alexander Yakovlev, a member (together with Gorbachev and Edward Shevardnadze) of the "Perestroika Troika," explained it, "Roosevelt managed to save capitalism by changing it. This is the idea of our *perestroika,* which is aimed at giving our society fundamental equality" (cited in Sheehy 1990, 256). The Roosevelt analogy

> breaks down, however, on one crucial point. Roosevelt acted with the consent of the governed. By the very act of *not* choosing to throw out their leader during the Depression, the American people consented to share the risks and sacrifices their leader asked of them during a period of painful change. (Sheehy 1990, 257)

Gorbachev's economic and political reforms, by contrast, constituted a top-down revolution that was not given legitimacy by a popular mandate. As economic dislocation and disintegration accelerated, popular support, for both Gorbachev and perestroika, also increasingly dissolved.

While the Soviet economy was contracting in the early 1990s, other economic and social indicators also were deteriorating. According to reports in Soviet newspapers, absolute poverty was increasing and by late 1990 afflicted at least 70 million persons or one-fourth of the Soviet population. Unemployment, now officially recognized, was (under) estimated to be 2 million and rising in the 1990 Plan Report. The Ministry of

Internal Affairs reported that 98 percent of 1,100 selected consumers' goods were not regularly available in state retail outlets in the first half of 1990. For example, "medicines became all but unobtainable, and typhoid, cholera, and diphtheria made an unwelcome reappearance. Shortages of foodstuffs and medicines were so bad by the early 1990s that 90 percent of schoolchildren had vitamin deficiencies" (White 1992, 133). Fewer hospitals and schools were built, and the quality of health care and education continued to deteriorate. Pollution and environmental degradation also continued to worsen. For example, in the early 1990s, "almost 130 towns had concentrations of harmful substances in their air that were at least ten times the permitted norm." In some egregious instances, pollution levels were up to 120 times upper legal limits.[2] Partly because of greater liberalization and partly because of deteriorating economic conditions, increasing numbers of Soviet citizens emigrated or wanted to do so. According to official figures, 8,000 persons emigrated in 1986, but "235,000 left in 1989, and more than twice as many left in 1990" (138-39). *Komsomolskaya Pravda*, the party's youth newspaper, reported in 1989 that "before the 1917 Bolshevik Revolution, Russia ranked seventh in the world in per capita consumption, and now it was seventy-seventh," just after South Africa but ahead of Romania (285).

Perhaps the brightest spot in the economic crisis of the early 1990s was the cooperative movement, the legal authorization of which went into effect at the beginning of 1988. In the first two years under the Law on Socialist Enterprise, which launched the cooperatives (and other small proprietary and family enterprises), cooperative output "mushroomed from three hundred million rubles to forty-one billion rubles, accounting for 8 percent of the country's GNP" (264). As noted in the preceding chapter, the number of coops doubled in 1990 (to 245,300), and the number of persons employed in coops grew by the early 1990s to more than 6 million. Moreover, expansion of cooperatives, together with private and hybrid enterprises, helped to offset reductions in output and employment in the state sector and hence served to buffer the overall contraction in the early 1990s. For example, in the Russian republic in 1991, employment fell in state enterprises and organizations (by 4.5 million) and in collective farms (marginally), but rose in leased enterprises (2.3 million), joint stock companies (0.6 million), and private enterprises (0.5 million). Thus, including expansion in employment in cooperatives, overall employment remained fairly stable (IMF 1992, 10). But coops and other small enterprises were not sufficient to completely counter the general trend toward economic collapse. In any event, they were clustered in light consumer goods and services and construction, and had no appreciable effect on industrial output. Moreover, cooperatives and small private businesses, free to determine their own prices, took advantage of conditions of excess demand and consumer goods shortages, and charged what the market would bear.

The result was often unusually high incomes and salaries (and considerable resentment against them). In some instances, coops paid their members "a hundred times as much as an Academician or a minister" or "twice as much in a day as an ordinary worker was able to make in a whole month." As shortages grew, consumers turned increasingly to coops and other small businesses and to black marketeers. In 1990 it was estimated that the Soviet population paid "5 billion rubles above list prices for items other than foodstuffs," nearly three times as much as in 1989. Black markets had created an estimated 100 to 150,000 "underground millionaires," and coops had enabled many other millionaires to flourish by the early 1990s (White 1992, 130, 139). Coops and black markets thus contributed significantly to dramatic increases in income inequality or relative poverty during the late 1980s and early 1990s. Some estimates suggested that income inequalities had actually become greater in the Soviet Union than in the United States.

Worsening economic conditions were attributed, by pro-reform Party factions and economic advisers to too little economic reform. For example, according to Gavriil Popov, a radical economist elected as Moscow's new mayor in March 1990, only thoroughgoing structural change could halt the economic collapse and its attendant anarchy or reemergence of totalitarianism. Such change should incorporate substantial privatization of government enterprises, supplantation of state orders and directives by market exchange processes (including substantial price increases to eliminate most subsidies), and substitution of family-based farming for collective farms. Nikolai Shmelev, another pro-market reformer, has argued, since the late 1980s, that labor productivity is adversely affected by drunkenness, disorderliness, and shoddy work, which he attributes to "excessively full employment." To combat these evils, freely competitive labor markets, with possible unemployment, must be substituted for guaranteed full employment. Specifically, Shmelev proposed "a comparatively small reserve army of labor" above the frictionally unemployed (to be provided the option of a modest, temporary unemployment allowance or "being obliged to work wherever [one] was sent"), that is, "replacing administrative coercion with purely economic coercion" (Shmelev 1987, 9).

Critics from the socialist left, by contrast, generally attributed the Soviet economic deterioration to regressive distributional features of Soviet economy and society. Some of these, for example, the lucrative earnings of "ruble millionaires" and the sharp reductions in real income accompanying price increases by pensioners, the unemployed, and such workers' groups as coal miners, were believed to be a derivative effect of marketization and privatization. Others, for example, the low level of wages and consumption in the Soviet Union as compared to industrialized capitalist countries and the deterioration in collective consumption standards as economic conditions worsened, were attributed in part to continuing conservative party priorities in favor of investment, heavy industry, and the military sector and in part to the siphoning off of "invisible incomes" to some members of the party-state bureaucracy largely in the form of bribes in exchange for the diversion of goods from state enterprises to persons and organizations active in the "underground economy." By 1990, for example, sociologist Tatyana Zaslavskaya (1990) was writing about the "economic exploitation and political oppression of working people by the party-state *nomenklatura*" (43).

Some quantitative indicators of adverse distributional consequences for the Soviet working class of the operation of the Soviet politico-economic system, which apparently worsened during the late 1980s and early 1990s, are as follows (Menshikov 1991, 96-97). First, in the early 1990s, wages were less than 40 percent, and consumption was about 54 percent, of Soviet national income, as compared to from 60 to 70 percent in other industrialized countries. If "invisible incomes" (which rose during the late 1980s and early 1990s as a percentage of wages) are added to official figures for nonwage incomes, the labor share of national income falls to less than 35 percent. Moreover, the ratio of nonwage components of national income (primarily profits and turnover taxes) to wage income rose steadily, from 92 percent in 1980 to 104 percent in 1988, to presumably a still higher percentage by the early 1990s. This ratio of nonwage to wage income was about 75 percent higher than that found in such capitalist countries as the United States. On a per capita basis, the monthly pay of an average Soviet worker was only 40 percent that of an average American worker in 1988, and it undoubtedly fell below that figure in the Soviet recession-depression of 1990-1991.

Second, government spending on health in the Soviet Union had declined to 3 or 4 percent and education to 5 or 6 percent of total government expenditures by the early 1990s, as compared to from 8 to 12 percent and from 10 to 12 percent, respectively, in other developed countries. Housing construction and social welfare spending, in proportion to national income, had also fallen below the levels of the United States and such West European countries as France and the United Kingdom. Third, if the poverty line for the late 1980s in the Soviet Union is set at 75 rubles per month, then about 14 percent of the Soviet population fell below the poverty line, another 16 percent was only slightly above it (75 to 100 rubles per month), and another 33 percent received from 100 to 150 rubles per month. Thus, nearly two-thirds of the Soviet population fell below a modest income of twice that of the poverty level. In short, "most of our [Soviet] workforce was being systematically underpaid" (Menshikov 1991, 96), and perestroika in practice had regressive effects on the division of income both between low-income and high-income recipients and between workers on the one hand and many political leaders, bureaucrats, managers, entrepreneurs, cooperatives, and members of the "underground economy" on the other.

Boris Yeltsin, elected president of Russia in June 1991, worked both sides of these arguments. On the one hand, he increasingly argued that privatization and land reform needed to proceed much more rapidly to stimulate expanded production by small business and farm proprietors. On the other hand, he excoriated inequalities in the power and privileges of Party and bureaucratic leaders, as well as unsatisfactory wages, hours, and working conditions, as major sources of both low productivity and social injustice, and he proposed increased political and economic independence of the republics as the paramount means to remedy both kinds of problems.

Perestroika's radical, conservative, and laborist critics made telling points, each applicable to different aspects of the economic structure, policy, and performance. For example, as noted earlier, Soviet economic growth steadily decreased over time in the post-World War II period, especially in the 1970s and early 1980s. Some part of the growth slowdown can be attributed to exogenous factors, such as bad harvests and lower world oil prices, and to other factors, such as demographic ones, largely beyond the control of the politico-economic system or the policy priorities of its leaders. But some part of the falling growth rates in the late 1970s and early 1980s can be explained by factors integral to the Soviet system, such as overcentralization and lack of indigenous processes for determining rational prices, and by the Soviet leadership's policy priorities, such as reductions in the rate of growth in investment so as to accommodate higher growth rates in consumption. According to Nikolai Ryzhkov, the chairman of the Council of Ministers in 1990, the transition to a market economy could take ten years or more. As he put it in a September 5 interview in *Komsomolskaya Znamya*, "The old cannot be done away with until the new has been created." Insofar as the Soviet economic reform program proceeded cautiously, its institutions and policies would continue to retain vestigial elements of the old regime and thus would continue to exhibit some of its problematic features, such as lower growth rates, low productivity, inefficiency, and imminent stagnation.

On the other hand, insofar as perestroika did succeed in making serious institutional and policy changes, it tended to create economic dislocations, at least in the short run, although in different areas. Freer markets, given considerable pent-up inflationary pressures, were almost bound to generate higher prices. The expansion of cooperatives and the legalization of elements of the underground economy had the plausible consequence of causing greater income inequalities. Attempts to tighten labor and managerial discipline by economic means carried the corollary effects of possible bankruptcy and unemployment. Price increases, as means of reducing subsidies and excess demands for consumer goods, without a significantly expanded "safety net," could not fail to yield sharp cuts in real income and increases in absolute poverty for disadvantaged segments of the population. Budgetary austerity, in the endeavor to lower government deficits, naturally tended to cause deterioration in the provisioning of health, education, and social welfare.

According to the Hungarian economist Janos Kornai (1992), the "classical system" of centralized planning and management, despite its tensions and contradictions, has a certain internal coherence. Given favorable circumstances, it may survive for a more or less extended period. A reform model, by contrast, however well intentioned and theoretically attractive, tries to combine principles—private and public, plan and market, centralization and decentralization, efficiency and security—that are internally incoherent and hence subject to disintegration. Whatever the validity of this proposition as a general, abstract hypothesis, the confluence of institutional forces in the Gorbachev era in several concrete instances combined the worst of both possible worlds and thereby contributed to impasse and economic deterioration.

Two examples will illustrate. First, perestroika did not succeed in establishing a functioning market economy to replace the old system of bureaucratic coordination. But it did succeed in dismantling much of the staff support and authority of the central planning apparatus and in enlarging the decision-making powers of enterprise managers. Managers used their greater autonomy to raise wages and ignore less profitable items and used their monopoly powers and sellers' market conditions to raise prices and lower product quality. This, in turn, increased pressure on local and regional party officials to intervene because they continued to be held accountable by higher party authorities for economic performance of the areas and enterprises under their jurisdiction.

In the absence of genuine market forces and a "reliance on monetary relations as the main medium of economic exchange," it was implausible to suppose that party officials would abandon their roles as economic supervisors and brokers. In any event, local and regional party leaders were disinclined to be supportive of economic reforms. Perestroika was, after all, "foisted on a recalcitrant party apparatus by the Gorbachev leadership." Consequently, in many instances, instructions from the center became stuck in the "sands of bureaucratic inertia." Despite exhortations by the central party leadership to establish family farming, for example, local and regional party authorities simply "ignored farmers wishing to lease land or repeatedly altered the terms of the lease, all the while keeping machinery and fertilizers out of the hands of private farmers." In short, the "impact of perestroika was to disrupt the operation of the central planning system without replacing it with a functioning market mechanism" and without eliciting a "systematic diminution in the party's role in the economy" (Rutland 1993, 207-12).

Second, the Soviet economy, in fact, had a significant market component, beyond that of the coops, small proprietorships, and free markets for agricultural products, namely, the fairly substantial underground economy and its affiliated black markets. As centralized economic authority disintegrated and the underground economy became legalized or partially so, consumers increasingly turned to it to obtain commodities in short supply at state retail outlets. This economy was subject to neither government regulation nor control by textbook competitive market processes that coordinated consumers and producers and elicited adjustments in production in response to changes in market prices, determined by interactions of demand and supply. It went "far beyond raw, unregulated buccaneer capitalism. Power was in the hands of neither those who controlled the means of production nor the proletariat; it had fallen into the hands of those who controlled the means of consumption," that is, what was loosely called the Soviet "mafia" (Sheehy 1990, 311). According to Zaslavskaya (in Sheehy 1990, 315-17), the mafia contained three main elements: (1) corrupt members of the party and state apparatus, who served, on payment of bribes, as patrons to "mafia bosses"; (2) employees in the retail sector, who were "obliged to pay money to the chain that kicks back to the apparat" and who received occasional small payments in exchange for thefts from state stores or for overcharging customers; and (3) corrupt members of the "militia, prosecutors, courts, judges" whose favors were bought by the mafia bosses and the new "coop capitalists" and who, in exchange, provided protection against law enforcement and made it "quite impossible to get social justice" in the courts (1990, 315). In brief, mafia bosses "used their patrons in the ministries to purchase supplies at artificially low state prices," thus reducing supplies at state retail stores and expanding the symptoms of repressed inflation there: queues, searches, and shifts to other sources of supply. They then "used the new laws to sell their products or services at rapacious prices." The result was a "total breakdown in retail trade" (316-17) and circumvention of the use of the price system as a means to stimulate expansions or reallocations in supply by producers in response to consumer preferences. Again, this was not centralized management, textbook market competition, or even a blend of the two, but a deformed fourth alternative emergent from circumstances in which older, centralized institutions had been dismantled (or disintegrated), but new, competitive market institutions under the protection of an established legal and cultural infrastructure had not yet been created.

The data in Tables 10.2 and 10.3, assembled by Russian economist Stanislav Menshikov (1991, 90), give a rough estimate of the "invisible income" significantly attributable to the alliance between members of the party-state bureaucracy and the underground economy. Table 10.2 shows aggregate personal money expenditures in

Table 10.2
Aggregate Personal Money Expenditure in the Soviet Union, 1988
(in billion rubles)

State and cooperative retail trade turnover	366.2
Turnover of extra-rural collective farm market	9.3
Total retail trade turnover	375.5
Paid personal services	62.2
Aggregate visible expenditures on goods and services (figure 3 plus figure 4)	437.7
State taxes and duties	36.2
Personal savings (increments of savings bank holdings)	30.6
Aggregate before-tax and before-savings visible money incomes (5 plus 6 plus 7)	504.5
Personal labour incomes	406.6
Invisible personal incomes (8 minus 9)	97.9

Source: Menshikov (1991, 91).

Table 10.3
Invisible Incomes in the Soviet Economy, 1975-1989
(in billion rubles and in percentage of the wage fund)

	1975	1980	1985	1988	1989 (first half)
Billions of rubles	31.8	52.5	74.3	97.9	55.3
Percent	13.8	17.9	21.1	24.1	25.4

Source: Menshikov (1991, 92).

the Soviet Union for 1988. Expenditures on goods and services include retail trade turnover plus paid personal services. Adding in state taxes and increments to savings accounts, and assuming that expenditures roughly parallel incomes, yields aggregate before tax and before savings "visible" incomes. This figure (504.5 billion rubles in 1988) substantially exceeds personal labor income (406.6 billion rubles). Menshikov designates the difference (nearly 100 billion rubles) as "invisible personal incomes." Invisible incomes, he states,

> can be interpreted as a partial, approximate, but very real reflection of the tribute paid by the population for the existence of a special bureaucratic stratum merged with the shadow economy; it is a part of the social product appropriated with the cash resources illegally taken away from the state and not included in wages or collective farmers' or new cooperators' earnings, let alone pensions, scholarships, or benefits. (1991, 92)

Menshikov's estimates of invisible incomes for 1975 to 1989 (Table 10.3) indicate that they more than tripled in size, from about 32 billion rubles, or less than 14 percent of total wages, to about 100 billion rubles or more, or about 25 percent of total wages. Whatever the precise magnitude of this "tribute," which presumably grew in the early 1990s, its growth gives vivid testimony both to the dilemmas involved in working out a viable blend of central planning and market economy and to the disintegration of the Soviet economic system.

INFORMATION AND COMMUNICATION BREAKDOWN

Gorbachev and his advisers evidently relied on the liberalization of the press, television, and other media of mass communication, greater openness of discussion within the party and economic bureaucracies, enhanced freedom of expression, and expanded communication among members of voluntary associations as integral components of the Soviet socialist reform program. To recapitulate and sharpen earlier discussion, glasnost's advocates expected several major benefits from its establishment and extension. Not the least of these advantages would be improvements in the amount and accuracy of information and thereby the quality of policy discussions and outcomes, the cultivation of allies (notably among the intelligentsia) in the critique and disempowerment of perestroika's opponents among the party/state bureaucracy, the reversal of economic stagnation through heightened workers' energy and labor activism, and an augmented legitimation of the party and popularity of its reformist leadership. As Gorbachev put it to the party's Central Committee in the late 1980s, "The better the people are informed, the more consciously they act, the more actively they support the party, its plans and programmatic objectives" (cited in White 1992, 77).

In addition to these domestic benefits, political liberalization has external advantages. Demonstrating progress in human rights strengthens the likelihood of detente, "facilitates arms control, contributes to a lowering of defense expenditures, and led to renewed inflows of foreign credits, investments, and technology" (Desai 1990, 98). Beyond these advantages, Gorbachev and his leading advisers also expected that, through novels, films, plays, and poetry, as well as the mass media, writers, journalists, and other intellectuals would mold public opinion so as to redefine the "social contract" between the leadership and the population, and thereby radically change social attitudes toward the past, the newly emerging system, and the disciplined and creative work within it.

Judged by more stringent, Western standards, glasnost in the late 1980s and early 1990s was "precarious, ambiguous, and incomplete" (Desai 1990, 97). Freedom of the press and the right to express opinions and to seek and disseminate information was, in practice, qualified by government control over printing presses and paper and by leadership attempts to manipulate or soften public criticism of party-state actions. Imperfect though the extension of political liberties was under the auspices of glasnost, it constituted a powerful element in the transformation and eventual disintegration of the Soviet politico-economic system. Party-state monopoly of control over information and the mass communications media was a strategic component in the Stalinist totalitarian state economy. In shifting to a softer, authoritarian system of rule, Nikita Khrushchev abandoned such instruments of power as dictatorial control by a single, supreme leader and secret police terror, but he retained, among other things, party-state monopoly control over information and communications. Retention of this element of the Stalinist heritage helped the post-totalitarian regimes after Stalin and prior to Gorbachev to survive "by inertia (rather than by direct fear)." The old party and state structures were "still intact, though a little rusty around the edges" (Morrison 1991, 13). By liberalizing public expression and association, the Gorbachev regime obtained several of the benefits summarized above. Glasnost was very popular, especially among intellectuals. But henceforward, another strategic pillar of authoritarian rule was essentially lost. Thereafter, Gorbachev and his associates would not only have to lead by persuasion and cajoling, but having abandoned the party-state monopoly of control over communication, they would have to compete with alternative associations and sources of opinion and information.

By mid-1988, for example, "thirty thousand informal groups involving millions of people" had been established. Maverick publications, such as *Ogonyok*, expanded their subscription lists, from 200,000 in 1987 to "a powerhouse of influence reaching into remote places with a readership of 4.6 million by spring 1990." After Vladislav Starkov refused to obey Gorbachev's directive to resign from the editorship of the Moscow weekly *Argumenty I fakty*, in October 1989, in a flap over an article that had reported that Gorbachev "was no longer the most popular political figure in the Soviet Union," the magazine's circulation soared to 31.5 million (Sheehy 1990, 268-91). Throughout the late 1980s and early 1990s, Soviet newspapers and magazines increasingly conducted public opinion polls in which citizens were queried on all sorts of political and economic issues. This had powerful demonstration effects. Through polls, individuals, anonymously, could discover that public criticism of the regime and its leadership was quite possibly stronger than they had thought and that their own grievances were not unique. Such revelations contributed to additional shifts in attitudes, growth in public opposition, diminution in party-state authority, and thereby to a potentially explosive "revolutionary bandwagon" (Kuran 1991).

This is illustrated by the rapid shift in public attitudes (or evaporation of fear of public expression of one's private views) which appears to have occurred in 1989-1990. Prior to that time, public opinion polls indicated widespread antagonism to such ideological and institutional properties of capitalist market economy as inequality, privatization, and individual initiative. In the fall of 1989, "only 24 percent of the population had positive attitudes toward private property while 36 had negative attitudes. Yet this changed in a matter of months. By the summer of 1990, more than half (55 percent) considered private property admissible" (Levada 1992, 65). In a survey conducted in September 1990, privatization of small businesses, shops, and stores was supported by 73 percent, with only 18 percent opposed. In sharp opposition to Soviet leadership, support for privatization of farm land was 87 percent, with only 7 percent opposed (54 percent, however, opposed privatization of large plants and 61 percent opposed sales of plants to foreigners). Evidently, public attitudes supportive of highly centralized and statist versions of the Soviet politico-economic system were widespread and habituated, but fragile and superficial, "preserved not by conviction, but by political and ideological coercion" (65). In a very short period of time, under glasnost's auspices, and in the context of such events as communism's collapse in Eastern Europe, the disintegration of the party's ideological and communications monopoly; public criticism of the regime, its leaders, and its institutions; and disintegration of the economy, particularly collapse of retail markets, several presumably deeply ingrained attitudes shifted dramatically, and public confidence in the political leadership, now exposed as a kind of "emperor with no clothes," evaporated.

Expansion of public information, communication, and association outside party-state control thus became dynamically unstable in several ways. First, the "taste for political liberty" was not satisfied by "limited tidbits" (Kornai 1992, 575). Liberalization elicited growing demands for fuller informational and associational freedoms, particularly among the intelligentsia, which stimulated greater boldness in actual practice, which in turn caused further adjustments in social attitudes and another racheting upward shift in demands for greater liberties, and so on. Second, public criticism in practice could not be contained within the limits desired by the political leadership. A massive psychological campaign to blame Stalin (and Stalinists) for the failures and deficiencies of Soviet-style socialism created public criticism not only of those aspects of Stalinism (personal tyranny, terror, monopoly of control over the media of mass communication, Stalinist ideology) that Gorbachev and the Soviet reformers were prepared to reject or relinquish, but also other residual elements from the pre-Gorbachev past as well, notably, the party-state monopoly of control over society and economy. The reformers' encouragement of public critique of the "command-administrative" version of Soviet socialism resulted in growing disenchantment (and public expression thereof) with other elements of the "socialist choice," such as state ownership of land and other aspects of reform policy, for example, price increases and reductions of subsidies. Third, glasnost became an integral part of the dilemma between reforms in economic structure and short-run economic performance. As long as economic reform

> scores political and economic successes and satisfaction concurrently increases, the possessors of power can be more lenient on the subject of freedom of speech and association without putting their power in any fundamental danger. But once political and/or economic defeats ensue, the situation becomes strained and the leadership faces a dilemma: either to reimpose (or try to reimpose) the more repressive methods or to face the fact that its indivisible powers may be imperiled. (427-28)

In practice, Soviet economic performance deteriorated significantly in the early 1990s. As it did, the power monopoly of the party and state apparatus in general, not only the party-state monopoly of control over information, communication, and association, began to crumble.

COLLAPSE OF THE PARTY'S MONOPOLY POWER

Political reform, like radical change in economic structure, was not a leading priority of the new administration in its early years. But by the late 1980s Gorbachev increasingly contended that, because of "serious deformations" in Soviet society, especially under Stalin and Brezhnev, "profound democratization" and "radical reform" of the political system had become the party's "most urgent task" and was "at the core" both of economic "restructuring" and the building of a more authentic "socialist democracy" (cited in White 1992, 28-29).

Gorbachev's reform strategy presupposed that it would be possible to democratize the party, state, economy, and society significantly while, at the same time, retain a leading role, if not a literal monopoly of power, for the Communist party. In principle, this perhaps was not impossible, though it presumably would require an unusual set of enabling circumstances, as suggested in the preceding chapter. In practice, the extensions of democratization, both those imposed from above and those that emerged from below and were more or less beyond the leadership's ability to stop, at least short of reimposing severe repression and unleashing a potential civil war, were accompanied by increasing inroads on the party's authority and the dissolution of its monopoly of power.

The mushrooming growth of informal groups and associations, initially approved by the national leadership, constituted, by the late 1980s, a serious grassroots threat to party-state authority. For example, local environmental activists operated throughout the country and a Green Party was established in Ukraine. After the Chernobyl disaster in 1986, antinuclear protesters interrupted nuclear testing and forced the government to abandon or postpone plans to build new nuclear reactors in several instances. Perhaps the most potent of the informal associations was that of the striking coal miners, in Siberia, Ukraine, and elsewhere, in the late 1980s and early 1990s. In July 1989, in the first large-scale strike held since the Bolshevik Revolution, more than 150,000 miners stopped working in Ukraine. The strike spread across Siberia and eventually involved most of the nations's 2.5 million coal miners. The miners protested against egregious working conditions, such as no hot water, virtually no soap, and safety standards that had resulted, among other things, in an average life expectancy of forty-eight years. But their initial demands for improved working conditions escalated into calls for an end to the party's monopoly of power (Sheehy 1990, 281) and, in 1991, for Gorbachev's resignation. The 1989 strikes "brought the government to its knees, forcing promises of higher pay, better working and living conditions, and more rapid economic reform" (Smith 1990, 432). Perhaps more significantly, the strikes vividly challenged the claim by the party-state apparatus that it represented the best interests of the working class and harmoniously balanced workers' needs with those of the rest of society.

The national election of members of the Congress of People's Deputies, in March 1989, as noted in Chapter 8, was a moderate, incremental step in the democratization process rather than an exemplar of robust democracy. Nonetheless, it was a "watershed" in Soviet history because it started the transformation of Soviet politics and the shifting of power away from the Communist party to representative governmental institutions. It was the most democratic election since 1918 and the first post-1918 election in which voters had choices and thereby the opportunity to reject party officials as candidates for public office.[3] Of the 399 candidates, mostly party and government officials, who ran unopposed, 195 were rejected, and a significant plurality (300 to 400) of reform candidates were elected. The 1989 election thus marked the empowerment of tens of millions of voters, the genesis of a political opposition, the beginning of "the real shift of power away from the Communist party and the slow development of a national parliament to challenge the party's monopoly on control," and the "most stunning blow to the Party's prestige since the Bolshevik Revolution." The 1989 election, and the meeting of the congress that followed, "made it all but impossible for party diehards to halt the momentum of reform or to turn back the path of Soviet history" (Smith 1990, 442-47).

The sessions of the Congress of People's Deputies and the all-Union Supreme Soviet which followed continued and solidified the process of differentiation of state institutions from those of the party and thereby the disintegration of the party's power monopoly. The congress clearly established the principle of "parliamentary oversight" of the government and applied that principle, for example, to an investigation and exposure of the role of party and military leaders in using excessive violence in putting down popular demonstrations in Tbilisi, Georgia. The Congress also provided a forum for debate by liberal and radical deputies, thus shifting the arena of debate away from the party's inner sanctums to public view, witnessed by millions on television. The sessions of the Supreme Soviet in 1989 and 1990 established the principle that parliament had the responsibility to confirm the appointment of government ministers, to investigate and oversee such power centers as the military and the KGB, to reject or reshape government proposals (for example, unpopular increases in food prices), and to pass its own, liberalizing legislation, such as a law "banning censorship and permitting any individual or group to operate a newspaper or television station, and a law granting wide powers to local governments, including control of property within their jurisdiction." By 1990 the Supreme Soviet was gradually accumulating power at the expense of the party apparatus and the executive branch. It was "invading the Party's domain [and] usurping its prerogatives"(475). Strictly speaking, the overwhelming majority (85 percent) of the Supreme Soviet were party members and were expected to follow its directives. With the popular mandate from the voters behind them, however, and an accompanying evaporation of party discipline, deputies increasingly acted without guidance from or in defiance of the party.

In July 1989, an organized opposition, known as the Inter-Regional Group, was established, with 316 members from the congress, including 90 from the Supreme Soviet. This group drew support from nationalist deputies from the Baltic republics, Moldavia, Georgia, and Ukraine, and Russian deputies devoted to more rapid economic and political reforms. In September, the group adopted a platform "calling for movement toward a multi-party system, a mixed economy, a free press, a popularly elected head of government, [and] abolition of the Communist Party's monopoly on power" (476-77). In January 1990, the radical reformers in the party established a Democratic Platform. This group adopted a program propounding internal democratization of the party, abandonment of the constitutional guarantee of a dominant position in society for the party, establishment of a multiparty political system, elimination of the *nomenklatura* system for making Party and governmental appointments, and dissolution of party organs in the various economic and security institutions in the Soviet Union. The party was thus polarized into opposing factions. Within six months, the leaders of the Democratic Platform and such radical reformers as Yeltsin resigned from the party and announced their intentions to establish a new "democratic coalition" outside the party. More than 300 Communist deputies to the Russian and Soviet parliaments, as well as some members of the Central Committee, also left the party in the early 1990s. Several republican party organizations seceded from the CPSU, beginning with the Lithuanian party, in December 1989, followed by the Communist parties of Georgia (1990) and Moldavia (1991).

This defection from the party at the top was paralleled by mass desertions at the bottom, especially among working-class members. At a nationwide congress held in mid-1990 to establish an independent labor union outside party control, coal miners resolved, by a 73 percent majority, that "We do not consider the Communist Party our party. We call for a mass exit from the Party" (521). Nearly 260,000 members left the party in 1989. About 4 million more did so in an eighteen-month period from 1990 to 1991. *Komsomol*, the party's youth organization, lost members precipitously (nearly one-quarter of its membership in 1990) and was dissolved in 1991, after the aborted August coup (White 1992, 253). By the early 1990s, only 55 percent of Party members polled supported the "socialist choice." Eighty percent surveyed in summer 1990 did not believe the party "was capable of restructuring itself and leading the country out of its crisis." The party's standing among the Soviet public also dropped sharply. Public trust in the CPSU, as recorded in public opinion polls, fell from 37 percent to 27 percent during 1989. By July 1990, only 14 percent "completely trusted" the party and 38 percent had "absolutely no confidence" in it (White 1992, 256).

Gorbachev's interrelationships with the party evolved over time. Initially, he clearly hoped to reform the party from within. By 1987 he permitted the formation of rival groups and informal associations. By 1989 a national parliament had been established, with Gorbachev as its Chairman, which served as a serious rival to the party and thereby challenged its power monopoly. By 1990 rapidly changing circumstances propelled Gorbachev on to yet another stage in party-state relations. Early in the year, he proposed, and obtained approval from both the party's Central Committee and the Supreme Soviet, for a dual innovation combining (1) abandonment of constitutional guarantees of a "leading and guiding" role for the party in Soviet society and (2) establishment of a strong, executive presidency, with Gorbachev as the first occupant of that office.

Several factors evidently led to this decision: frustration over the intransigence of conservatives, both at top levels and throughout the party bureaucracy; the object lesson given by the overturning of Communist regimes in Eastern Europe, which had rigidly refused to reform; the vulnerability of Gorbachev's power base within the party; and the growing breakdown of central decision-making authority. The party's surrender of legally guaranteed dominion over state and society did not destroy its power base, for it retained vast properties, control over patronage through the *nomenklatura* system, significant control over the media of mass communication, and a dominant position in the armed forces, the economic bureaucracy, the KGB, and the police. But it accepted the principle of political competition. Henceforward, the party would exist and function as a "vanguard" "only as a democratically recognized force." Its status would not be "imposed through constitutional endorsement" (Gorbachev, cited in Smith 1990, 512). A Law on Public Associations, approved by the Supreme Soviet in October 1990, subsequently provided the legal framework for multiparty political competition. By late 1991, over 300 parties, representing a wide range of opinion, had been established, although most of them were not officially registered.

The institution of an executive presidency strengthened the power of the state relative to the party. "The Politburo and the Central Committee were being superseded by the new mechanisms of elected government, a presidency, and the Supreme Soviet." Two additional political changes completed the process. First, at the Twenty-eighth Party Congress, held in July 1990, with the departure of five members of the government from the Politburo, all remaining overlap between party and state appointments at the top of the power pyramid (except for Gorbachev's) was severed. Hence, all policy-making power at the top level was now completely shifted from the party to government institutions. There was no longer any reason "to consult the Politburo beforehand on government policy; it was left to deal with Party affairs." Because of the traditionally strategic role of the Party in policy discussions and decisions, this constituted "an irreparable and potentially fatal loss of power" (Smith 1990, 486, 528). Second, in December 1990, the Congress of People's Deputies voted to replace the Council of Ministers by a cabinet, whose members were nominated by the president, and accountable to him, subject to approval by the Supreme Soviet.

In principle, the executive presidency strengthened the power of the chief executive officer relative to parliament as well as to the party, especially when emergency powers to stabilize Soviet sociopolitical life were extended to Gorbachev in September 1990 for eighteen months. Executive power was limited, however, in two ways. First, the president served for a fixed term, with a two-term limit. He was subject to impeachment (by two-thirds vote of the congress), his ministerial appointments were subject to approval by the Supreme Soviet, it could instigate the resignation of the entire cabinet by a vote of no-confidence, and provision was made for overriding the president's veto of parliament's legislation. Second, in practice, Gorbachev's powers were severely constrained. Indeed, by the early 1990s, he was "the least powerful leader the Soviet Union had yet experienced." His presidential decrees were often "ignored or even rejected by the [republic and local] bodies that were responsible for implementing them." Moreover, "the authority of the central government, for so long unchallengeable, was undermined by the decision (during 1990) of all fifteen union republics to declare their laws sovereign over those of the Soviet Union as a whole" (White 1992, 68). Thus, though the power of the party diminished relative to that of the state, the authority of the central government over its constituent political entities, no less than that of the party, fell precipitously in the early 1990s.

The relationships between party and state at the republic and local levels were more complex. On the one hand, party conservatives were typically stronger at the republic and local levels than in the country as a whole. In mid-1990, for example, a Russian Communist party was established, and Ivan Polozkov, a prominent conservative, was elected as its leader. On the other hand, the 1990 republic and local elections provided for greater choice than in the previous year, and radicals were swept into office in large numbers, especially in major cities. Their "stunning" victories "changed the political map of the country." In Moscow, for example, a coalition dubbed the Bloc of Democratic Russia won 64 percent of the seats in the city council to the party's 20 percent, and elected economist Gavriil Popov and political scientist Sergei Stankevich as mayor and deputy mayor, respectively. In Leningrad, Democratic Election 90 won 68 percent of the city council seats and elected law professor Anatoly Sobchak as mayor. Elsewhere, democratic activists typically either controlled city councils in urban areas or constituted aggressive minorities. Because a significant number also served on the Supreme Soviet, they were often in a position both to draft legislation that delegated power to local governments and to "carry out the laws that they themselves had written" (Smith 1990, 530, 533).

These new city councils served to countervail the local party apparatuses and, indeed, to challenge the central state power structure, by promoting market economy and usurping party and central state functions. In April 1990, in an attempt to thwart

Lithuania's bid for independence, Gorbachev imposed a trade embargo. The Lithuanians responded by proposing barter exchanges to city governments: Lithuanian "textiles, clothing, fabrics, bricks, and a variety of services" for "oil, gas, and raw materials, as well as for spare parts and industrial goods." The value of goods exchanged in each direction, which totaled nearly 1 billion rubles, "signified a staggering breakdown of centralized economic control and defiance" of the central governmental authority (Smith 1990, 535, 538).

In Moscow, the city council established a new independent newspaper to break party control of the mass media and negotiated agreements with Western publishing interests to establish two new printing plants. The Moscow city council also used the powers of local government to foster market economy. It shifted priorities by cutting back on industrial construction and expanding housing, schools, and clinics; transferred ownership of state-owned housing to the renter-occupants; issued contracts to private (both cooperative and capitalist) enterprises to repair streets and construct highways; established new avenues of trade outside centralized control by negotiating swaps with rural provinces to exchange manufactured goods for agricultural products and secured from Prime Minister Ryzhkov control over 12.5 percent of the output of Moscow-based enterprises for that purpose; and reduced constraints on cooperatives and stimulated new businesses by serving as coowner with private domestic or foreign enterprises in joint ventures. In these ways, democratic insurgents adapted V. I. Lenin's revolutionary slogan of "All Power to the Soviets," and both expanded the powers of local governments relative to the party and the central government and used those powers to implement a version of perestroika that went beyond Gorbachev's vision of "socialist democracy" to a kind of social democratic and municipally based mixed economy.

Thus, by mid-1991, substantial inroads had been made into party authority by new governmental institutions, and centralized party and state power structures had been seriously undermined by both public and private agencies at republic and local levels. In this context, the halfhearted and unsuccessful August 1991 coup undertaken by prominent party and state leaders provided the immediate impetus for President Boris Yeltsin's suspension and the subsequent ban of the party in Russia, thereby bringing the vanguard role of the party to a formal and official close.

DISINTEGRATION OF THE SOVIET MULTINATIONAL STATE

The Soviet Union, according to its 1977 constitution, was an "integral, federal, multinational state." In principle, the Soviet Union was a voluntary association with the right to secede by each of its members; a separation of powers provided for substantial republic and local self-government; and each republic (and autonomous republics, regions, and units therein) was so constituted that a particular nationality predominated and exercised significant cultural autonomy. In practice, the whole country functioned upon the basis of a unitary and centrally determined plan and budget; central decisions could be imposed on lower units; the party exercised unifying oversight throughout; the overwhelming majority of industrial output in 1989 was produced under the auspices of all-union ministries (57 percent) or joint union-republic ministries (37 percent); and "cultural autonomy" was more or less restricted to artistic events, dancing groups, and language (White 1992, 145-46).

Russia, the largest republic, accounted for about 51 percent of the total Soviet population in 1989, shared a common linguistic and religious heritage (Russian Orthodoxy) with two other Slavic republics (Ukraine and Byelorussia, together accounting for an additional 19 percent of the population), and constituted from 13 to 40 percent of the population of such other republics as Byelorussia, Kazakhstan, Kirzigia, and Ukraine. The Central Asian republics, primarily Turkic and Muslim, accounted for about another 15 percent. The remainder of the Soviet population was located in the Baltics (acquired by a Soviet-Nazi pact in 1939), Transcaucasia, and Moldavia.

At the outset of the Gorbachev era, in 1985, "nationalities policy" was "at the bottom" of the leadership's priorities. It was not identified as a major problem until 1988 and was not even discussed by the party's Central Committee until 1989. Thereafter, it "came to dominate everything, posing a threat to the very existence of the Soviet Union as a state" (Morrison 1991, 136). This neglect of inter-republic and nationalities issues may be attributed in part to Gorbachev's lack of experience and interest and in part to official Soviet doctrine, which held that international and interrepublic relations were essentially unified and harmonious on the grounds that working class solidarity outweighed any residual differences based on language, religion, and ethnicity.[4]

In fact, Gorbachev inherited a country that was "fragmented" and "secretly seething with national tensions" (Smith 1990, 295). These included, among others, territorial disputes degenerating into civil war (between Armenians and Azerbaijanis), demands for secession and political independence (the Baltics and, later, Moldavia, Georgia, and Ukraine), interethnic violence (Central Asia), and rising nationalism and demands for greater politico-economic autonomy and reduction of control by the Center (Russia) (Lapidus 1989). Several grievances were shared widely by the republics. Deteriorating economic performance stimulated feelings in many republics that they were sacrificing too much for the common good. Relatively affluent or "surplus" republics, notably Russia and those on the western tier of the Soviet Union (Moldavia, Byelorussia, Georgia, the Baltics, Ukraine), complained that they were being made to subsidize excessively the "deficit" republics (for example, those in Central Asia). "According to Russian calculations," for example, "the republic paid in more than 100 billion rubles to the Soviet budget each year, but got only just over 30 billion back" (Morrison 1991, 161). Republics exporting large amounts of raw materials, such as petroleum, pressed multiple grievances. They claimed they were functioning as natural resource cows for other republics; the interrepublic terms of trade were set inequitably against their interests; and the prices of such commodities as oil, electricity, and natural gas were being set by central authorities at levels below world market prices, to their disadvantage. The Russian republic, for example, produced more than half of the coal, nearly two-thirds of the natural gas, and more than 90 percent of the petroleum in the Soviet Union. Its leaders and representatives to the Soviet Congress of Deputies from 1989 to 1991 frequently remonstrated with their parliamentary colleagues about what they perceived as excessive burdens on Russia in the name of the common Soviet good.

Another set of formidable regional and local grievances pertained to pollution and environmental destruction. It has often been observed that capitalist market economies are especially susceptible to the degradation of the environment because environmental costs are largely "external" to the profit-making calculi of individual business firms. Economic systems characterized by centralized planning and management, in principle, should be in a superior position to calculate and act on "social" costs and benefits beyond the confines of individual firms. In practice, because of the high priority given to heavy industry and the geographic distance between central planners and the effects on the local environment, including nuclear accidents and waste disposal, centralized decision- making bodies tended to neglect environmental issues, notably in areas of raw material extraction, such as Siberia, Ukraine, and the Baltics. Central planners and ministries "simply [did] not care about the environmental impact of their economic decisions." And because central planners and administrators exercised the primary authority to decide the location of industrial plants and natural resource development, republics quite naturally "blame[d] Moscow for their pollution problems" (Desai 1990, 135).

In the totalitarian and post-totalitarian political contexts of Stalin and his successors down to the mid 1980s, these kinds of grievances were more or less successfully repressed. At the same time, national minorities were granted extensive linguistic autonomy, and the national-territorial principle was placed at the base of the state's political administration. Although the powers thus granted to nationalities and republics were limited, the multinational structure of the Soviet Union was thereby given constitutional recognition .This established a mode of representation in which, instead of the harmonious resolution of the nationalities issues originally envisioned, "sectional interests, denied any other means of expression, could in practice take only the form of nationalism" (White 1992, 157). Thus, the Soviet Union was like a system under pressure, ready to burst "at its weakest points when that pressure is abruptly released" (Smith 1990, 295), as it was released under the impetus of glasnost and democratization. Once Gorbachev

> enshrined the principle that power should flow from below, through democratic elections, local politicians were responsible not to Moscow, but to their voters.... To avoid being displaced by more radical popular forces, they would have to give at least the appearance of fighting for sovereignty and power in reality, not just in words. It was this dynamic which explained why orthodox Communists, who had previously followed Moscow obediently, suddenly began championing republican rights in 1991. (Morrison 1991, 188)

The Baltic republics, notably Lithuania, provide an early, and classic, illustration of tensions which, in the politico-economic context of the late 1980s and early 1990s, were virtually bound to take a vividly nationalist and separatist form. Nationalist popular front movements (Sajudis in Lithuania) emerged in the three Baltic republics in the summer of 1988. The level of economic development in the Baltics was higher and their experience with both capitalism and representative government (during the period between the two world wars) was greater than that of the other republics. Consequently, Baltic support for perestroika and for Gorbachev and the radical wing of the Communist party against the conservatives was both plausible and welcomed. At each step in the process of political and economic change in the late 1980s to early 1990s, however, the policy positions of these nationalist movements were out in front of both Gorbachev and his more radical advisers. The founding congress of Sajudis, for example, in October 1988, propounded Lithuanian "sovereignty" (that is, autonomy, though within the Soviet Union).

In a stunning upset and complete rejection of the Communist party in the May 1989 elections for the new Soviet Congress of People's Deputies, Sajudis candidates were elected to thirty nine out of forty two seats. (Lithuanians constituted 80 percent of the total population of Lithuania.) "Without actually controlling the Lithuanian government, Sajudis could now drive the political agenda as the recognized voice of the people in Lithuania." Within a few months, Lithuanian was declared the official language of the republic; the national flag and anthem were resurrected; the Lithuanian parliament "passed a sovereignty law giving it veto power over Soviet laws [and] proclaimed that all property in its territory should be Lithuanian, not Soviet" (Smith 1990, 355-62); and the Catholic Church substantially expanded its religious services and public profile. Several political parties were established in Lithuania, well in advance of the revision of Article 6 of the Soviet constitution (which abandoned the officially privileged position of the Communist party of the Soviet Union). A Sajudis newspaper was established, which proceeded to expound Lithuanian grievances, such as the privileged employment and salaries of Russian immigrants, environmental and nuclear concerns, and excessive control by central authorities over the republic's economy. On August 23, 1989, on the fiftieth anniversary of the Nazi-Soviet pact (published by the Gorbachev government as a part of glasnost), somewhere between 1 and 2 million people formed a "human chain" linking the capitals of the three Baltic republics in a massive protest demonstration. Under the leadership of Algirdas Brazauskas, a supporter of Gorbachev and perestroika, the Lithuanian Communist party aligned itself more closely with the nationalist popular front on various issues, such as economic autonomy and republic control over property, investment, and industry within its borders. In December, the Lithuanian Communist party declared its separation from the Communist party of the Soviet Union. (The Lithuanian Komsomol had declared its independence from its parent Soviet organization in June).

In 1990 and 1991, the challenge posed to the unity and integrity of the Soviet Union by Baltic nationalism escalated under the impetus of democratization. In the elections to the Lithuanian parliament in February-March 1990, Sajudis candidates won more than two-thirds of the seats (97 out of 141), the Brazauskas wing of the Lithuanian Communist party (which was also committed by this time to full "independence"), won an additional 25, and Vytautas Landsbergis, the leader of Sajudis, was elected chairman. In March, the parliament formally declared Lithuania's independence on the basis of its 1938 constitution, followed by similar, though somewhat milder, declarations of independence by Estonia and Latvia. Under Soviet pressure, Lithuania's declaration of independence was suspended in June 1990, and, in January 1991, Soviet troops were called upon to restore central authority. But by this time, the tide had turned. As mentioned earlier, all fifteen republics during 1990 asserted the "sovereignty" of their laws over those of the Soviet Union, and Lithuania received strong moral support from Yeltsin, as chairman of the parliament of the Russian republic. In the spring of 1991, in a voter turnout of 84 percent, over 90 percent of the voters supported full independence for Lithuania. During 1990 and 1991, all three Baltic republics "steadily withdrew from the work of all-union bodies,... suspended contributions to the Soviet Union budget,... and began to adopt their own budgets and to make preparations for the issuing of their own currencies." Shortly after the attempted August 1991 coup, the Soviet Union Council of State "formally approved their independent status and they were admitted into the United Nations and other international organizations" (White 1992, 164).

The assertion of nationalism, to take a second example, was more divisive in Russia than in the Baltics. Right-wing nationalists, like nationalists in other republics, supported greater republic-level cultural and economic autonomy and a "Russia-first" policy. This "fundamentalist" wing of Russian nationalism excoriated Communist rule for plundering Russia's natural resources, desecrating its churches, depleting its treasury, and engaging in a mindless industrialization and urbanization. On the other hand, often in alliance with the conservative wing of the Communist party, right-wing nationalists criticized market economy and democratization; yearned for order and authoritarian rule imposed by the army and police as an antidote to moral, economic, and political disintegration; and distrusted what they viewed as the excessive influence of both the West and Jews on Soviet society.

For Russian politicians such as Yeltsin, Russian national concerns merged with the desire for decentralization of power. First, Yeltsin contended, Russia lacked the "state institutions through which it could manifest its power and authority," such as its own internal security system, scientific associations, party organizations, even its own television station. Second, Russia in effect was absorbed into the Soviet Union and lacked the status and autonomy accorded other republics. For example, in contrast to Ukraine and Byelorussia, Russia was not represented in the United Nations. The proportion of enterprises within its territory under all-union jurisdiction (72 percent) was higher than the average. Third, the impetus for economic and political reform at the center was constrained by the greater role there of conservatives and Gorbachev's proclivity to placate them, the tendency for reforms to be held down to a pace permitted by the lowest common denominator, the inclination of the center to place excessive priority on heavy industry and the military, the desire to hold on to centralized power, and the fear that devolution of power could cause Soviet disintegration. Consequently, Yeltsin concluded, the role of the center had to be "sharply reduced" because "radical changes would not come from there." The "vertical bureaucratic pivot" on which the country rested "had to be destroyed, and we had to begin a transition to horizontal ties with greater independence of the republic states" (Yeltsin cited in Morrison 1991, 143).

Once elected as chairman of the Russian Supreme Soviet, in May 1990, and with the firm support of about one-third of its membership, Yeltsin endeavored to implement a program based on this perspective. In June the Russian Congress of People's Deputies declared Russian state sovereignty, including control over Russian natural resources and the right to secede. Republic-level state institutions began to be established: among others, a Russian Communist party, a labor union organization, a Komsomol, and an Academy of Sciences, in 1990, and a republican KGB and radio and television station, in 1991. The republic's constitution was revised to abolish the Communist party's leading role in society. Yeltsin's position (and that of Russian independence) was enhanced by the establishment of a presidential system in Russia and by his election to that post, in June 1991, by nearly three-fifths of those voting.

Responding to these developments, Gorbachev, in 1990, proposed a "new union treaty" which would constitute a voluntary association of republics, a "real union of sovereign states," and would supplant the 1922 treaty which founded the Soviet Union. A year later, in March 1991, after much discussion, both within the party and among the various republics, a revised draft of the treaty was published. It was, in effect, Gorbachev's last chance to salvage the Soviet Union as a multinational state, albeit in extremely weakened form. In an all-union referendum held in March, with an 80 percent voter turnout, 76.4 percent voted in favor of a question that asked whether or not they approved the preservation of the Soviet Union as a "renewed federation of equal sovereign republics in which the human rights and freedoms of any nationality will be fully guaranteed." Gorbachev's victory was somewhat hollow in view of the fact that voters in the Baltic republics had already expressed their desire for full independence, and three other republics (Moldavia, Georgia, and Armenia) declined to participate in the referendum. In April 1991, however, in the 9 + 1 Agreement, the remaining nine republics plus Gorbachev as Soviet president agreed to conclude a new union treaty within three months, to be followed within six months by a new constitution and then by elections to all "union organs of power."

Yeltsin had now stood for popular election on three occasions, whereas Gorbachev had never done so. As a corollary, Russians, for the first time in their history, had become citizens, not subjects, "able to exercise popular sovereignty in choosing their own leader." By solidifying the process of democratization, the election also "weakened the legitimacy of the Soviet Union as a state and strengthened that of Russia" at the same time as it weakened the "socialist choice" exemplified by the Soviet state and enhanced the legitimacy of more radical perspectives on politico-economic change associated with Yeltsin and his allies (Morrison 1991, 267-68).

Political liberalization and democratization, in Russia as in the Baltics, contributed significantly to the disintegration of the Soviet multinational state. Liberalization extended the range of political discourse and made it increasingly difficult to constrain criticism of the center. Democratization, given the "national-territorial principle" of political organization, led to increasing pressures for devolution of political authority, that is, to strengthening of the power of the republics at the expense of the federal state. Through the elections of 1989, "popular sovereignty through the ballot" replaced the party's "democratic centralism" as the "legitimizing factor" in Soviet politics. "For the republics, this meant, in effect, there was the possibility of self-determination. In 1990, elections for republican parliaments made the process irreversible" (Morrison 1991, 137).

The federal party's response to growing national tensions and demands for greater autonomy or independence was too little and too late, lagging behind the rapidly changing pace of events and offering partial solutions that had little practical effect. In early 1989, a set of directives on Soviet-republic level economic relations were published in which "up to 36 percent of industrial production" would be transferred to local control "(the existing figure was only 5 percent), with much higher levels—up to 72 percent—in Georgia and the Baltic republics." By the time a platform embodying the principle implied by this directive ("strong center and strong republics") was approved by the party's Central Committee, in September, several republics, notably Russia and those on the western tier of the Soviet Union, had arrived at the view that "only a reconsideration of the very bases of Soviet statehood" would satisfy their aspirations (White 1992, 178).

The Treaty on the Union of Sovereign States, which emerged from ensuing negotiations and was scheduled for prospective adoption on August 20, 1991, defined the proposed new Soviet Union, in effect, as something in between a federal state and a confederation. On the one hand, the new Soviet Union, as described by the first clause of the treaty, was to be a "sovereign federal, democratic state" under international law, with specified powers, namely, those of defense, foreign policy, energy, transportation, and communications. On the other hand, (1) this new "state" was to be established by a "merger of equal republics," all of which were also to be "sovereign states" and "full-fledged members of the international community"; (2) the federal state was to exercise its authority "within the limits of powers voluntarily delegated to it" by its constituent republics and, for the most part, jointly with them; and (3) the republics would have final authority over taxation and the budget, and in all other matters, republican laws would take precedence over those of the Soviet Union.

Clearly, this new treaty "spelled doom for the old centralized Soviet Union and its structures"—the central planners, the central government and the Soviet parliament, the KGB, and the military and defense industries. As such, "it was a transitional arrangement on the road to the disintegration of a great empire." Its devolution of political authority to the republics threatened to make any notion of a single military command and control system untenable. Its decentralization of budgetary control to the republics, particularly given Yeltsin's stated platform which incorporated proposals for significant expansions in working-class living standards and substantial reductions in Russian contributions to the central budget, threatened major cuts in military spending and de facto surrender of the Soviet position as a world superpower. Its delegation of control over property and natural resources to the republics and its abandonment of commitment to the "socialist choice," especially given Gorbachev's shift toward the radicals after the spring of 1991 and Yeltsin's curb of the party's influence in Russia and his proposals concerning land reform and privatization, indicated that the "real struggle" was between the "empire savers" and the leading conservative figures embedded in the "old structures of the unitary state" and the "emerging forces of private businessmen, the criminal bourgeoisie and intellectuals who were hoping to replace them" (Morrison 1991, 258-75).

It was these threats that evidently led to the attempted coup, one day before the signing of the new union treaty. One may reasonably debate whether the coup could have worked had the plotters been more proficient and ruthless or had Yeltsin been less courageous during the coup or less successful in cultivating key figures in the army and the KBG before it happened. In any event, the coup discredited the draft treaty and accelerated the process of the disintegration of the Soviet multinational state. All the trends of the years from 1989 to 1991 continued, but at an escalating pace, after August. By the end of the year, all of the republics except Russia had issued declarations of independence. It became clear that "only a much looser confederation would satisfy the aspirations of the republics that still wished to establish some kind of association" (White 1992, 182). Even after the coup, Yeltsin was apparently willing to negotiate some new form of union. But a declaration of independence by Ukraine (on August 24), followed by a referendum, on December 1, in which 90 percent of those voting supported a fully independent Ukraine, appears to have persuaded Yeltsin to join Ukraine and Byelorussia, on December 8, in establishing a Confederation of Independent States to supplant the old Soviet Union and renounce its 1922 founding treaty. By additional agreement, on December 21, eight other republics (that is, all of the original fifteen except the new Baltic states and Georgia) joined the confederation, and the Soviet Union was declared to have "ended its existence." Thus, liberalization and democratization led ultimately "not just to the end of the Communist system but to self-determination and the break-up of the imperial state" (Morrison 1991, 289).

NOTES

1 Subsidies on food items in 1989 reached nearly 20 percent of the government's budget (Desai 1990, 172).

2. Feshbach and Friendly (1992) describe health and nature in the Soviet Union during the Gorbachev era as "under siege," and characterize the severe deterioration of public health and the environment there as de facto "ecocide." They observe that ecological and environmental activists were at the forefront of anti-Communist political movements in the Baltics in the late 1980s and that similar movements throughout the Soviet Union in the early 1990s played a significant role in the Soviet collapse.

3. The law governing the 1989 elections required the winner to receive 50 percent or more of the vote. It allowed voters to vote against, as well as for, a candidate, by crossing out his name. If enough voters did so, he could thus lose, even though he ran for office unopposed.

4. "As a matter of self-criticism," Gorbachev stated in a speech before the June 1990 party congress (cited in Smith 1990, 296), "one has to admit that we underestimated the force of nationalism and separatism that were hidden deep within our system... creating a socially explosive mixture."

References

Adams, Arthur E. 1972. *Stalin and His Times*. New York: Holt, Rinehart and Winston.

Adoratsky, V., ed. 1935. *Karl Marx: Selected Works in Two Volumes*. Moscow: Cooperative Publishing Society.

Aganbegyan, Abel. 1988a. *The Economic Challenge of Perestroika*. Bloomington: Indiana University Press.

———, ed. 1988b. *Perestroika 1989*. New York: Charles Scribners Sons.

Arendt, Hannah. 1966. *The Origins of Totalitarianism*. New York: Harcourt, Brace.

Aslund, Anders. 1989a. Soviet and Chinese Reforms—Why They Must Be Different. *The World Today,* November; 190-91.

———. 1989b. *Gorbachev's Struggle for Economic Reform*. Ithaca, N.Y.: Cornell University Press.

Asselain, Jean-Charles. 1984. *Planning and Profits in Socialist Economies*. London: Routledge and Kegan Paul.

Bailes, Kendall E. 1978. *Technology and Society Under Lenin and Stalin*. Princeton, N.J.: Princeton University Press.

Balinky, Alexander. 1970. *Marx's Economics*. Lexington, Mass: Heath Lexington Books.

Ball, Alan. 1991. "Private Trade and Traders during NEP." In *Russia in the Era of NEP*, edited by Sheila Fitzpatrick. 105-20. Bloomington: Indiana University Press.

Baran, Paul A. 1952. "National Economic Planning." In *A Survey of Contemporary Economics*, Vol. 2, edited by Bernard F. Haley. Homewood, Ill.: Richard D. Irwin.

———. 1957. *The Political Economy of Growth*. New York: Monthly Review Press.

Bergson, Abram. 1961. *The Real National Income of Soviet Russia Since 1928*. Cambridge, Mass.: Harvard University Press.

———. 1964. *The Economics of Soviet Planning*. New Haven: Yale University Press.

———. 1987. "Comparative Productivity: The USSR, Eastern Europe, and the West." *American Economic Review* 77:342-57.

———. 1989. *Productivity and the Social System: The USSR and the West*. Cambridge, Mass: Harvard University Press.

Bergson, Abram, and Simon Kuznets. 1963. *Economic Trends in the Soviet Union*. Cambridge, Mass.: Harvard University Press.

Bergson, Abram, and Herbert Levine, eds. 1983. *The Soviet Economy: Toward the Year 2000*. London: Allen and Unwin.

Berliner, Joseph S. 1952. "The Informal Organization of the Soviet Firm." *Quarterly Journal of Economics*. August.

———. 1976. *The Innovation Decision in Soviet Industry*. Cambridge, Mass.: MIT Press.

———. 1981. "The Prospects for Technological Progress." In *The Soviet Economy: Continuity and Change*, edited by Morris Bornstein, 293-312. Homewood, Ill.: Richard D. Irwin.

Bettleheim, Charles. 1975. *The Transition to Socialist Economy*. Atlantic Highlands, N.J.: Humanities Press.

———. 1976. *Class Struggles in the USSR*. New York: Monthly Review Press.

Bettleheim, Charles and Bernard Chavance. 1981. "Stalinism as the Ideology of State Capitalism." *The Review of Radical Political Economics* 13:40-54.

Bialer, Seweryn. 1980. *Stalin's Successors: Leadership, Stability, and Change in the Soviet Union*. Cambridge, England: Cambridge University Press.

———. 1983. "The Political System." In *After Brezhnev: Sources of Soviet Conduct in the 1980s*, edited by Robert Byrnes, 1-67. Bloomington: Indiana University Press.

———. 1987. "The Soviet Union in a Changing World." In *The Soviet Union in Transition*, edited by Kinya Niiseki, 4-17. Boulder, Colo.: Westview.

———, ed. 1989. *Politics, Society, and Nationality Inside Gorbachev's Russia*. Boulder, Colo.: Westview.

Bideleux, Robert. 1985. *Communism and Development*. New York: Methuen.

Bim, Alexander S., Derek C. Jones, and Thomas E. Weisskopf. 1993. "Hybrid Forms of Enterprise Organization in the Former USSR and the Russian Federation." *Comparative Economic Studies* 35:1-38.

Blackburn, Robin. 1991. *After the Fall: The Failure of Communism and the Future of Socialism*. New York: Verso.

Blackwell, William L. 1970. *The Industrialization of Russia*. Arlington Heights, Illinois. Richard D. Irwin.

Boffa, Giuseppe. 1961. *Inside the Khrushchev Era*. Translated by Carl Marzani. New York: Marzani & Munsell.

Bornstein, Morris, ed. 1969 and 1979 editions. *Comparative Economic Systems: Models and Cases*. Homewood, Ill.: Richard D. Irwin.

———. 1981. *The Soviet Economy: Continuity and Change*. Homewood, Ill.: Richard D. Irwin.

———. 1985. "Improving the Soviet Economic Mechanism." *Soviet Studies* 37:1-30.

———. 1987. "Soviet Price Policies." *Soviet Economy* 3:96-134.

Bova, Russell. 1992. "The Soviet Economy and International Politics." In *The Disintegration of the Soviet Economic System*, edited by Michael Ellman and Vladimir Kantorovich. New York: Routledge.

Bregante, Nieves. 1989. "Nationalist Unrest in the USSR and the Challenge to the Gorbachev Leadership." In *Gorbachev's Agenda*, edited by Susan Clark, 85-108. Boulder, Colo.: Westview.

Breslauer, George W. 1980. "Khrushchev Reconsidered." In *The Soviet Union Since Stalin*, edited by Stephen Cohen et al., 50-70. Bloomington: Indiana University Press.

———. 1982. *Khrushchev and Brezhnev as Leaders: Building Authority in Soviet Politics*. London: Geroge Allen and Unwin.

Brezezinski, Zbigniew. 1989. "An Increasingly Sterile System." In *Perestroika: How New is Gorbachev's New Thinking?*, edited by Ernest W. Lefever and Robert D. Vander Lugt, 55-62. Washington D.C.: Ethics and Public Policy Center.

Brovkin, Vladimir. 1990. "Revolution From Below: Informal Associations in Russia 1988-1989." *Soviet Economy* 2:233-57.

Brower, Daniel R. 1989. "The City in Danger: The Civil War and the Russian Urban Population." In *Party, State, and Society in the Russian Civil War*, edited by Diane P. Koerner, William G. Rosenberg, and Ronald G. Suny, 58-80. Bloomington: Indiana University Press.

Brown, Archie. 1980. "The Power of the General Secretary of the CPSU." In *Authority, Power and Policy in the USSR*, edited by T. H. Rigby, Archie Brown and Peter Reddaway, 135-57. New York: St. Martin's Press.

————.1989. "Ideology and Political Culture." In *Politics, Society, and Nationality inside Gorbachev's Russia*, edited by Seweryn Bialer, 1-40. Boulder, Colo.: Westview Press.

————. 1990. "Gorbachev's Leadership: Another View." *Soviet Economy* 6:141-54.

Brus, Wlodzimierz. 1972. *The Market in a Socialist Economy*. London: Routledge and Kegan Paul.

————. 1973. *The Economics and Politics of Socialism*. London: Routledge and Kegan Paul.

————. 1975. *Public Ownership under Socialism*. London: Routledge and Kegan Paul.

Brus, Wlodzimierz, and Tadeusz Kowalik. 1983. "Socialism and Development." *Cambridge Journal of Economics* 7:243-255.

Bukharin, N. I. 1964. *The Politics and Economics of the Transition Period*. Translated by K. J. Tarbuck. London: Routledge and Kegan Paul.

————. 1967. *The Path to Socialism in Russia: Selected Works*. Edited by S. Heitman. New York: Omicron.

————. 1966. *Imperialism and World Economy*. New York: Howard Fertig.

————. (1982). *Selected Writings on the State and the Transition to Socialism*. Edited by Richard B. Day. Armonk, New York: M.E. Sharpe.

Bukharin, Nikolai, and E. A. Preobrazhensky. 1969. *The ABCs of Communism*. Baltimore, Md: Penguin Books.

Burganov, Agdas. 1990. *Perestroika and the Concept of Socialism*. Moscow: Novosti Press.

Campbell, Robert W. 1960, 1966. *Soviet Economic Power*. Boston: Houghton Mifflin.

————. 1983. "The Economy." In *After Brezhnev: Sources of Soviet Conduct in the 1980s*, edited by Robert Byrnes, 68-124. Bloomington: Indiana University Press.

————. 1989. "The Soviet Future: Gorbachev and the Economy." In *Gorbachev and the Soviet Future*, edited by Lawrence Lerner and Donald Treadgold, 44-64. Boulder, Colo.: Westview.

————. 1992. *The Failure of Soviet Economic Planning*. Bloomington: Indiana University Press.

Carr, E. H. 1952, 1953, 1966 editions. *The Bolshevik Revolution, 1917-1923*. Vol. 2. New York: Macmillan, and Baltimore, Md: Penguin.

————. 1958. *Socialism in one Country*. Vol.1. London: Macmillan.

————. 1972. *Socialism in one Country: 1924-1926*. London: Penguin Books.

Carr, E. H. and R. W. Davies. 1969 and 1974 editions. *Foundation of a Planned Economy, 1926-1929*. New York: Macmillan, and London: Penguin Books.

CIA (Central Intelligence Agency). 1985. *Handbook of Economic Statistics*. Washington D.C.: Directorate of Intelligence.

CIA and DIA (Central Intelligence Agency and the Defense Intelligence Agency). 1989. *The Soviet Economy in 1988: Gorbachev Changes Course*. Washington D.C.: Directorate of Intelligence.

Clark, Susan L., ed. 1989. *Gorbachev's Agenda*. Boulder, Colo.: Westview Press.

Cliff, Tony. 1974. *State Capitalism in Russia*. London: Pluto Press.

————. 1978. *Lenin, Vol. 3, Revolution Besieged*. London: Pluto Press.

———. 1979. *Lenin,* Vol. 4, *The Bolsheviks and World Communism.* London: Pluto Press.

Cohen, Stephen F. 1974. *Bukharin and the Bolshevik Revolution: A Political Biography 1888-1938.* New York: Alfred A. Knopf.

———. 1977. Bolshevism and Stalinism. In *Stalinism: Essays in Historical Perspective,* edited by Robert Tucker, 3-29. New York: Norton and Company.

———. 1980. "The Friends and Foes of Change: Reformism and Conservatism in the Soviet Union." In *The Soviet Union Since Stalin,* edited by Stephen Cohen, Alexander Rabinowitch, and Robert Sharlet, 11-31. Bloomington: Indiana University Press.

———. 1985. *Rethinking the Soviet Experience. Politics and History since 1917.* Oxford: Oxford University Press.

Cohn, Stanley H. 1969. *Economic Development in the Soviet Union.* Lexington, Mass.: Heath.

———. 1970. "General Growth Performance of the Soviet Economy." In *Economic Performance and Military Burden in the Soviet Union,* U.S. Congress, Joint Economic Commit tee. Washington D.C.: U.S. Government Printing Press.

———. 1987. "Soviet Intensive Economic Development in Perspective." In *Gorbachev's Economic Plans,* U. S. Congress, Joint Economic Committee.1:10-26. Washington D.C.: U.S. Government Printing Press.

Colton, Timothy J. 1987. "Approaches to the Politics of Systemic Economic Reform in the Soviet Union." *Soviet Economy* 3:145-70.

Conquest, Robert. 1967. *Power and Policy in the USSR: The Struggle for Stalin's Succession.* New York: Harper and Row.

———. 1968. *The Soviet Police System.* New York: Praeger.

Cook, Edward C. 1992. "Agriculture's Role in the Soviet Economic Crisis." In *The Disintegration of the Soviet Economic System,* edited by Michael Ellman and Vladimir Kantorovich. New York: Routledge.

Corrigan, Philip, Harvie Ramsay, and Derek Sayer. 1978. *Socialist Construction and Marxist Theory.* New York: Monthly Review Press.

Cox, Robert. 1991. "'Real Socialism' in Historical Perspective." In *Communist Regimes, the Aftermath: Socialist Register 1991,* edited by Ralph Miliband and Leo Panitch, 169-93. London: Merlin Press.

D'agostino, Anthony. 1988. *Soviet Succession Struggles.* Boston: Unwin Hyman.

Dahl, Robert A., and Charles E. Lindblom. 1953. *Politics, Economics and Welfare.* New York: Harper Torchbooks.

Dallin, Alexander and Boris Nicolevsky. 1947. *Forced Labor in Soviet Russia.* New Haven, Conn.: Yale University Press.

Dallin, Alexander, and Condoleeza Rice. eds. 1986. *The Gorbachev Era.* Stanford, Calif.: Stanford Alumni Association.

Daniels, Robert. 1965. *The Stalin Revolution.* Boston: D. C. Heath.

———. 1988. *Is Russia Reformable?* Boulder Colo.: Westview Press.

Davis, R. W. 1990. "Gorbachev's Socialism in Historical Perspective." *New Left Review.* January/February 5-27.

Day, Richard B. 1973. *Leon Trotsky and the Politics of Economic Isolation.* Cambridge, England: Cambridge University Press.

Degras, Jane. 1962. "Anatomy of Tyranny: Khrushchev's Attack on Stalin." In *Russia Under Khrushchev,* edited by Abraham Brumberg, 77-84. New York: Frederick A. Praeger.

Desai, Padma. 1989, 1990. *Perestroika in Perspective: The Design and Dilemmas of Soviet Reform.* Princeton, N.J.: Princeton University Press.

De Tocqueville, Alexis. 1955. *Democracy in America.* New York: Oxford University Press.

Deutscher, Issac. 1960. *Russia in Transition.* New York: Grove Press.

————. 1966. *Ironies of History: Essays on Contemporary Communism.* London: Oxford University Press.

————. 1967. *The Unfinished Revolution: Russia 1917-1967.* New York: Oxford University Press.

Dobb, Maurice. 1928. *Russian Economic Development Since the Revolution.* New York: E. P. Dutton.

————. 1948 and 1966 . *Soviet Economic Development Since 1917.* London: Routledge and Kegan Paul.

————. 1955. *On Economic Theory and Socialism.* London: Routledge and Kegan Paul.

Dohan, Michael, and Edward Hewett. 1973. *Two Studies in Soviet Terms of Trade, 1918-1970.* Bloomington: International Development and Research Center, Indiana University.

Dornberg, John. 1974. *Brezhnev: The Masks of Power.* New York: Basic Books.

Dowlah, A. F. 1990a. "Perestroika: Soviet Political Economy in Transition." Ph.D. Diss. University of Southern California.

————. 1990b. *Perestroika: An Inquiry Into Its Historical, Ideological and Intellectual Roots.* Stockholm, Sweden: Bethany Books.

————. 1992a. *Soviet Political Economy in Transition.* Westport, Conn.: Greenwood Press.

————. 1992b. "Theoretical Expositions of the Centralized and Decentralized Strands of Socialist Economic Thoughts." *International Journal of Social Economics* 19:210-58.

————. 1993. "Soviet Socialism: The Era of War Communism." *International Journal of Social Economics* 20:57-83.

Dowlah, A. F., and John E. Elliott. 1991. "Gorbachev's Critique and Vision of Soviet Socialism." *International Journal of Social Economic.* 18:139-74.

Draper, Hal. 1977. *Karl Marx's Theory of Revolution,* Vol. 1, *State and Bureaucracy.* New York: Monthly Review Press.

Draper, Theodore. 1988. "Soviet Reformers: From Lenin to Gorbachev." *Dissent* 287-301.

Drewnowski, Jan. 1969. "The Economic Theory of Socialism: A Suggestion for Reconsideration." In *Comparative Economic Systems,* edited by Morris Bornstein, 110-127. Homewood, Ill.: Richard D. Irwin.

————, ed.. 1982. *Crisis in the East European Economy.* London: Croom Helm.

Edeen, Alfred. 1958. *Russia's New Middle Class.* Santa Monica, Calif.: Rand Corporation.

Elliott, John E. 1976. "Marx and Contemporary Models of Socialist Economy." *History of Political Economy* 151-84.

————.1980. "Marx and Engels on Communism, Scarcity, and Division of Labor." *Economic Enquiry* 275-92.

————, ed. 1981. *Marx and Engels on Economics, Politics and Society.* Santa Monica, Calif: Goodyear.

————. 1984. Contending Perspectives on the Nature of Soviet Economic Society. *International Journal of Social Economics* 11:40-61.

————. 1985. *Comparative Economic Systems.* Belmont, Calif.: Wadsworth.

————. 1989. "Gorbachev's Perestroika." *Contemporary Policy Issues* 35-52.

Ellman, Michael. 1979. *Socialist Planning.* New York: Cambridge University Press.

————. 1986. "The Macroeconomic Situation in the USSR—Retrospect and Prospect." *Soviet Studies* 38:530-42.

————. 1992. "Money in the 1980s: From Disequilibrium to Collapse." In *Disintegration of the Soviet Economic System,* edited by Michael Ellman and Vladimir Kantorovich. New York: Routledge.

Ellman, Michael, and Vladimir Kantorovich. 1992. *The Disintegration of the Soviet Economic System.* New York: Routledge.

Engels, Frederick. 1935. "Socialism: Utopian and Scientific." In *Karl Marx: Selected Works in Two Volumes*, edited by V. Adoratsky. Moscow: Cooperative Publishing Society.

————. 1939. *Anti-Duhring*. New York: International Publishers.

Ericson, Richard E. 1988. "The New Enterprise Law." *Hariman Institute Forum*, February, 1-8.

Erlich Alexander. 1960. *The Soviet Industrialization Debate*. Cambridge, Mass.: Harvard University Press.

Falin, Valentin M. 1988. "Glasnost: Getting at the Roots." In *Perestroika 1989*, edited by Abel Aganbegyan, 281-308. New York: Charles Scribners Sons.

Farber, Samuel. 1990. *Before Stalinism: The Rise and Fall of Soviet Democracy*. Cambridge, England: Polity Press.

Feshbach, Murray and Alfred Friendly, Jr. 1992. *Ecocide in the USSR: Health and Nature under Siege*. New York: Basic Books.

Filtzer, D. 1987. "Labor." In *Khrushchev and Khrushchevism,* edited by Martin McCauley, 118-35. Bloomington: Indiana University Press.

Fitzpatrick, Sheila. 1978, 1984. *Cultural Revolution in Russia, 1928-1931*. Bloomington: Indiana University Press.

————. 1989. "New Perspectives on the Civil War." In *Party, State, and Society in the Russian Civil War,* Edited by Diane P. Koerner, William G. Rosenberg, and Ronald G. Suny, 3-23. Bloomington: Indiana University Press.

————. 1991. *Russia in the Era of NEP.* Bloomington: Indiana University Press.

Franklin, Bruce, ed. 1972. *The Essential Stalin: Major Theoretical Writings, 1905-52.* New York: Doubleday.

Freidberg, Maurice, and Heyward Isham, eds. 1987. *Soviet Society under Gorbachev: Current Trends and the Prospects for Reform*. New York: Sharpe.

Friedrich, Carl J., and Zbigniew Brezezinski. 1956. *Totalitarian Dictatorship and Autocracy*. Cambridge, Mass.: Harvard University Press.

Gabrisch, Hubert ed. 1989. *Economic Reforms in Eastern Europe and the Soviet Union*. Boulder, Colo.: Westview Press.

Galbraith, John Kenneth and Stanislav Menshikov. 1988. *Capitalism, Communism, and Coexistence*. Boston: Houghton Mifflin.

Gelb, Michael. 1981. "Roots of Soviet Industrial Management." *Review of Radical Political Economics* (Spring): 15-57.

Getzler, Israel. 1983. *Kronstadt 1917-1921: The Fate of Soviet Democracy*. Cambridge, England: Cambridge University Press.

Gey, Peter. 1952. *The Dilemma of Democratic Socialism*. New York: Columbia University Press.

Gey, Peter, Jiri Kosta, and Wolfgang Quaisser, eds. 1987. *Crisis and Reform in Socialist Economies*. Boulder, Colo.: Westview Press.

Gill, Graeme. 1987. "Khrushchev and Systemic Development." In *Khrushchev and Khrushchevism,* edited by Martin McAuley. Bloomington: Indiana University Press.

Glazov, Yuri. 1985. *The Russian Mind Since Stalin's Death*. Dordrecht, Netherlands: D. Reidel Publishing Company.

Goldman, Marshall I. 1983. *U.S.S.R. In Crisis: The Failure of an Economic System*. New York: Norton and Company.

————. 1987. *Gorbachev's Challenge: Economic Reform in the Age of High Technology*. New York: Norton and Company.

————. 1991. *What Went Wrong with Perestroika*. New York: Norton and Company.

Gooding, John. 1990. "Gorbachev and Democracy." *Soviet Studies* 42:195-231.

Gorbachev, Mikhail S. 1987. *Perestroika: New Thinking For Our Country and the World*. New York: Harper and Row.

————. 1988a. "Document: The Revolution and Perestroika." *Foreign Affairs* 410-25.

————. 1988b. *Gorbachev at the Summit: Speeches and Interviews, February 1987-July 1988*. New York: Richardson, Steirman and Black.

————. 1990a. *Towards a Humane and Democratic Socialist Society*. Moscow: Novosty Press.

————. 1990b. "Gorbachev Addresses Party Conference." *News and Views from the USSR*, June 21, 1-24.

————. 1990c. "The Full Report Given By Mikhail Gorbachev at the Twenty-eighth Congress of the Communist Party of the Soviet Union." *News and Views from the USSR*, July 5, 1-46.

————. 1990d. "Gorbachev's Concluding Remarks at the Twenty-eighth Communist Party Congress." *News and Views from the USSR*, July 12, 1-17.

Gregory, Paul R. 1989. "Soviet Bureaucratic Behavior: Kohzyaistvenniki and Apparatchiki." *Soviet Studies* 511-25.

————. 1990. *Restructuring the Soviet Economic Bureaucracy*. New York: Cambridge University Press.

Gregory, Paul R., and Robert C. Stuart. 1981, 1986, 1990. *Soviet Economic Structure and Performance*. New York: Harper and Row.

Greshchenkron, Alexander. 1965. *Economic Backwardness in Historical Perspective*. New York: Praeger.

Grossman, Gregory. 1965. "Notes for a Theory of the Common economy." In *Soviet Studies*. October. Reprinted in *Comparative Economic Systems*, edited by Morris Bornstein. Homewood, Ill: Richard D. Irwin.

Grossman, Gregory. 1976. "Notes on the Illegal Private Economy and Corruption." In *Soviet Economy in a Time of Change*, Joint Economic Committee, 834-55. Washington D.C.:U.S. Government Printing Press.

————. 1977. "The Second Economy in the USSR." *Problems of Communism* 26:25-40.

————. 1985. *A Transitional View of the Soviet Second Economy*. Durham, N.C.: Berkeley-Duke Occasional Papers on the Second Economy in the USSR.

Gruchy, Allen Gerfield. 1977. *Comparative Economic Systems: Competing Ways to Stability, Growth and Welfare*. Boston: Houghton Mifflin.

Halliday, Fred. 1991. "The Ends of Cold War." In *After the Fall: The Failure of Communism and the Future of Socialism*, edited by Robin Blackburn, 78-99. New York: Verso.

Hanson, Philip. 1987. "The Soviet Twelfth Five Year Plan." In *The Soviet Economy: New Course?*, edited by Reiner Weichhardt, 10-28. Brussels: NATO Economics Directorate.

Hardt, John P. and Richard F. Kaufman. 1987. "Gorbachev's Economic Plans: Prospects and Risks." In *Gorbachev's Economic Plans*, U.S. Congress, Joint Economic Committee, vii-xix. Washington, D.C.: U.S. Government Printing Press.

Hatch, John B. 1991. "Labor Conflict in Moscow, 1921-1925." In *Russia in the Era of NEP*, edited by Sheila Fitzpatrick, 58-71. Bloomington: Indiana University Press.

Hauslohner, Peter. 1987. "Gorbachev's Social Contract." *Soviet Economy* 1:54-89.

————. 1989. "Politics Before Gorbachev: De-Stalinization and the Roots of Reform." In *Politics, Society, and Nationality Inside Gorbachev's Russia*, edited by Seweryn Bialer, 41- 90. Boulder, Colo.: Westview Press.

Hayek, Friedrich von ed. 1935. *Collectivist Economic Planning*. New York: Augustus M. Kelley.

Heller, Mikhail and Aleksander Nekrich. 1986. *Utopia in Power*. New York: Summit Books.

Hewett, Ed A. 1988. *Reforming the Soviet Economy: Equality versus Efficiency*. Washington D.C.: Brooking Institution.

————. 1989. *"Perestroyka* and the Congress of Peoples Deputies." *Soviet Economy* 1:47-69.

Hilferding, Rudolf. 1971. "State Capitalism or Totalitarian State Economy?" In *Essential Works of Marxism*, edited by Irving Howe. New York: Bantam Books.

Hohmann, Hans-Hermann. 1987. "Gorbachev's Approach to Economic Reforms." In *The Soviet Economy: A New Course,* 29-46. Brussels: NATO Colloquium.

Holzman, Franklyn D. 1955. *The Fiscal and Monetary Problems of a Planned Economy.* Cambridge, Mass.: Harvard University Press.

Hook, Sidney. 1955. *Marx and the Marxists: The Ambiguous Legacy.* Princeton, N.J.: D. Van Nostrand Company.

Horvat, Branko. 1964. *Towards a Theory of Planned Economy.* Belgrade: Yugoslav Institute of Economic Research.

———. 1982. *The Political Economy of Socialism.* Armonk, N. Y: Sharpe

Hough, Jerry F. , and Merle Fainsod. 1979. *How the Soviet Union is Governed.* Cambridge, Mass.: Harvard University Press.

Howard, Michael C., and John E. King. 1989. *A History of Marxian Economics.* Princeton, N. J.: Princeton University Press.

Howe, Irving, ed. 1986. *Essential Works of Socialism.* New Haven, Conn.: Yale University Press.

———. 1988. "Thinking About Socialism: Achievements, Failures and Possibilities." *Dissent* 509-25.

Hunter, Holland and Janusz M. Szyrmer. 1992. *Faulty Foundations: Soviet Economic Policies, 1928-1940.* Princeton, N.J.: Princeton University Press.

Hutchings, Raymond. 1969. "Periodic Fluctuations in Soviet Industrial Growth Rates." *Soviet Studies* 20:331-52.

———. 1971. *Seasonal Influences in Soviet Industry.* London: Oxford University Press.

———. 1982. *Soviet Economic Development.* Oxford: B. Blackwell.

IMF (International Monetary Fund). 1992. "Russian Federation." In *Economic Review.*

Jasny, Naum. 1951. *The Soviet Economy during the Planning Era.* Stanford, Calif.: Stanford University Press.

———. 1961. *Soviet Industrialization, 1928-1952.* Chicago: University of Chicago Press.

———. 1972. *Soviet Economists of the Twenties.* Cambridge, England: Cambridge University Press.

Johnson, Chalmers, ed. 1970. *Change in Communist Systems.* Stanford, Calif.: Stanford University Press.

Johnson, D. G. and K. McC. Brooks. 1983. *Prospects for Soviet Agriculture in the 1980s.* Bloomington: Indiana University Press.

Kagarlitsky, Boris. 1990. *The Dialectic of Change.* London: Verso.

———. 1992. *Disintegration of the Soviet Monolith.* Translated by Renfrey Clark. New York: Verso.

Karol, K. S. 1988. "Gorbachev and the Dynamics of Change." In *Socialist Register,* edited by Ralph Miliband, Leo Panitch, and John Saville, 12-36. London: Merlin Press.

Katz, Abraham. 1972. *The Politics of Economic Reform in the Soviet Union.* New York: Praeger.

Kaufman, Richard F. 1987. "Industrial Modernization and Defense in the Soviet Union." In *The Soviet Economy: A New Course?,* edited by Reiner Weichhardt, 247-62. Brussels: NATO Colloquium.

Kellen, Konrad. 1961. *Khrushchev: A Political Portrait.* New York: Praeger.

Kelley, Donald R. 1987. *Soviet Politics from Brezhnev to Gorbachev.* New York: Praeger.

———, ed. 1980. *Soviet Politics in the Brezhnev Era.* New York: Praeger.

Kemme, David M. 1989. "The Chronic Shortage Model of Centrally Planned Economies." *Soviet Studies* (July): 345-64.

Koerner, Diane P. 1989. "Urbanization and De-urbanization in the Russian Revolution and Civil War." In *Party, State, and Society in the Russian Civil War,* edited by Diane P. Koerner, William G. Rosenberg, and Ronald G. Suny, 81-104. Bloomington: Indiana University Press.

Koerner, Diane P., William G. Rosenberg and Ronald G. Suny, eds. 1989. *Party, State, and Society in the Russian Civil War.* Bloomington: Indiana University Press.

Kolakowski, Leszek. 1977. "Marxist Roots of Stalinism." In *Stalinism: Essays in Historical Interpretation,* edited by Robert Tucker, 283-98. New York: Norton and Company.

———. 1978. *Main Currents of Marxism,* Vol. 2. Oxford: Clarendon Press.

Kornai, Janos. 1957. *Overcentralization in Economic Administration.* London: Oxford University Press.

———. 1980. *Economics of Shortage.* Amsterdam: North-Holland.

———. 1984. "Adjustment to Price and Quantity Signals in a Socialist Economy." In *The Economics of Relative Prices,* edited by Bela Csikos-Nagy, Douglas C. Hauge, and Graham Hall, 60-77. London: Macmillan.

———. 1989. "The Hungarian Reform Process: Visions, Hopes, and Reality." In *Remaking the Economic Institutions of Socialism,* edited by Victor Nee and David Stark, 32-94. Stanford, Calif.: Stanford University Press.

———. 1990. *Vision and Reality, Market and State.* New York: Routledge.

———. 1992. *The Socialist System: The Political Economy of Communism.* Princeton, N.J.: Princeton University Press.

Koslov, G. A. 1977. *Political Economy: Socialism.* Moscow: Progress Publishers.

Kostakov, Vladimir G. 1987. "Employment: Scarcity or Surplus?" *Soviet Review* 20-36.

Kowalik, Tadeusz. 1989. "On Crucial Reform of Real Socialism." In *Economic Reforms in Eastern Europe and The Soviet Union,* edited by Hubert Gabrisch, 23-59. Boulder, Colo.: Westview Press.

Kuran, Timur. 1991. "The East European Revolution of 1989: Is it Surprising That We Were Surprised?" *American Economic Review* (May) 81:2-5.

Kurtzweg, Laurie. 1987. "Trends in Soviet Gross National Product." In *Gorbachev's Economic Plans.* U.S. Congress, Joint Economic Committee, 1:126-65. Washington D.C.: U.S. Government Printing Office.

Kushnirsky, Fyodor I. 1988. "Soviet Economic Reforms: An Analysis and a Model." In *Reorganization and Reform in the Soviet Economy,* edited by Susan Linz and William Moskoff, 44-72. Armonk, N.Y.: Sharpe.

———. 1989. "The New Role of Normatives in Soviet Economic Planning." *Soviet Studies* 526-42.

Kuusinen, O., ed. 1961. *Fundamentals of Marxism-Leninism.* Moscow: Foreign Language Publishing House.

Lane, David . 1985. *Soviet Economy and Society.* Oxford: Basil Black.

———. 1986. *Labor and Employment in the USSR.* Brighton, England: Wheatsheaf Books.

———. 1992. *Soviet Society Under Perestroika.* New York: Verso.

Lange, Oscar. 1943. *The Working Principles of the Soviet Economy.* New York.

Lapidus, Gail W. 1989. "State and Society: Toward the Emergence of Civil Society in the Soviet Union." In *Politics, Society, and Nationality Inside Gorbachev's Russia,* edited by Seweryn Bialer, 121-148. Boulder, Colo.: Westview Press.

———. 1990. "Gorbachev and the National Question: Restructuring the Soviet Federation." *Soviet Economy* 3:201-50.

Laqueur, Walter. 1990. *Stalin: The Glasnost Revelations.* London: Unwin Hyman.

Lavigne, Marie. 1974. *The Socialist Economies of the Soviet Union and Europe.* White Plains, N.Y.: International Arts and Sciences Press.

Lenin, Vladimir I. 1922. *Will the Bolsheviks Maintain Power?* London: The Labor Publication Company Limited.

———. 1967. "What is to be Done." In *Selected Works in Three Volumes,* 91-256. New York: International Publishers.

————. 1974. "The State and Revolution." In *Selected Works, One Volume Edition*, 264-352. New York: International Publishers.

Lerner, Abba P. 1934. "Economic Theory and Socialist Economy." *Review of Economic Studies* 2:51-61.

Levada, Iurii. 1992. "Social and Moral Aspects of the Crisis: Their Sources and Consequences." In *Disintegration of the Soviet Economic System*, edited by Michael Ellman and Vladimir Kantorovich. New York: Routledge.

Lewin, Moshe. 1974. *Political Undercurrents in Soviet Economic Debates: From Bukharin to the Modern Reformers*. Princeton, N.J.: Princeton University Press.

————. 1975. *Lenin's Last Struggle*. London: Pluto Press.

————. 1977. "The Social Background of Stalinism." In *Stalinism*, edited by Robert Tucker, 111-36. New York: Norton and Company.

————. 1988. *The Gorbachev Phenomenon: A Historical Interpretation*. Berkeley: University of California Press.

————. 1989. "The Civil War: Dynamics and Legacy." In *Party, State, and Society in the Russian Civil War*, edited by Diane P. Koerner, William G. Rosenberg, and Ronald G. Suny, 399-422. Bloomington: Indiana University Press.

Liberman, E. G. 1971. *Economic Methods and the Effectiveness of Production*. White Plains, N.Y.: International Arts and Sciences Press.

Linden, Carl A. 1966. *Khrushchev and the Soviet Leadership*. Baltimore, Md.: The John Hopkins University Press.

Lovell, David W. 1984. *From Marx to Lenin: An Evaluation of Marx's Responsibility for Soviet Authoritarianism*. New York: Cambridge University Press.

MacKenzie, David and Michael W. Curran. 1991. *A History of the Soviet Union*. Belmont, CA: Wadsworth Publishing Company.

McPherson, C. B. 1977. *The Life and Times of Liberal Democracy*. New York: Oxford University Press.

Malle, Silvana. 1985. *The Economic Organization of War Communism, 1918-1921*. Cambridge, England: Cambridge University Press.

Mandel, Ernest. 1979. *Trotsky: A Study in the Dynamic of his Thought*. London: NLB

————. 1991. "The Roots of the Present Crisis in the Soviet Economy." In *Socialist Register 1991: Communist Regimes, the Aftermath*, edited by Ralph Miliband and Leo Panitch. New York: Monthly Review.

————. 1992. *Power and Money*. New York: Verso.

Marx, Karl. 1935. *Karl Marx: Selected Works in Two Volumes*. Edited by V. Adoratsky. Moscow: Cooperative Publishing Society.

————. 1973. *Critique of the Gotha Program*. In *Selected Works in Three Volumes*, Vol.1, *Karl Marx and Frederick Engel*, 1:9-25. Moscow: Progress Publishers.

————. 1977. *Capital: A Critique of Political Economy*, Vol 1. Introduced by Ernest Mandel. New York: Vintage Books.

Marx, Karl and Frederick Engels. 1936. *Karl Marx-Frederick Engels: Correspondence 1848-1895*. New York: International Publishers.

————. 1948. *Communist Manifesto*. New York: International Publishers.

McAuley, Alastair. 1979. *Economic Welfare in the Soviet Union*. Madison: University of Wisconsin Press.

————, ed. 1987. *Khrushchev and Khrushchevism*. Bloomington: Indiana University Press. 138-55.

McAuley, Mary. 1966. *Labor Disputes in Soviet Russia, 1957-1965*. Oxford: Clarendon Press.

————. 1989. Bread without the Bourgeoisie. In *Party, State, and Society in the Russian Civil War,* edited by Diane P. Koerner, William G. Rosenberg and Ronald G. Suny. 158-179. Bloomington: Indiana University Press.

McCauley, Martin. Ed. 1987. *Khrushchev and Khrushchevism.* Bloomington: Indiana University Press.

Medvedev, Roy. 1971, 1976. *Let History Judge: The Origins and Consequences of Stalinism.* Nottingham, England: Spokesman Books.

————. 1979. *On Stalin and Stalinism.* Oxford: Oxford University Press.

————. 1988. "Soviets Restore Stalin's Victims." *Los Angeles Times,* February 21, vol. 2.

Medvedev, Roy, and Zhores A. Medvedev. 1976. *Khrushchev: The Years in Power.* New York: Columbia University Press.

Menshikov, Stanislav. 1991. *Catastrophe or Catharsis? The Soviet Economy Today.* London: Verso.

Mesa-Lago, Carmelo, and Carl Beck, eds. 1975. *Comparative Socialist Systems: Essays on Politics and Economics.* Pittsburgh: University of Pittsburgh Center for International Studies.

Milanovic, Branko. 1989. *Liberalization and Entrepreneurship: Dynamics of Reform in Socialism and Capitalism.* Armonk, N.Y.: Sharpe.

Miliband, Ralph. 1983. *Class Power and State Power.* London: Verso.

Miliband, Ralph, and Leo Panitch, eds. 1991. *Socialist Register 1991: Communist Regimes, the Aftermath.* New York: Monthly Review.

Miliband, Ralph, Leo Panitch, and John Saville, eds. 1988. *Socialist Register 1988.* London: Merlin Press.

Millar, James R., ed. 1971. *The Soviet Rural Community.* Urbana: University of Illinois Press.

————. 1981. "The Prospects for Soviet Agriculture." In *The Soviet Economy: Continuity and Change,* edited by Morris Bornstein, 273-292. Homewood, Ill.: Richard D. Irwin.

————, ed. 1987. *Politics, Work, and Daily Life in the USSR.* New York: Cambridge University Press.

Miller, David. 1989. *Market, State, and Community: Theoretical Foundations of Market Socialism.* Oxford: Clarendon Press.

Miller, David, and Saul Estrin. 1989. "A Case for Market Socialism: What does it mean? Why should we favor it?" *Dissent* 359- 67.

Miller, Robert F. 1987. "The Soviet Economy: Problems and Solutions in the Gorbachev View." In *Gorbachev At The Helm: A New Era in Soviet Politics,* edited by Robert Miller et al., 108-35. London: Croom Helm.

————. 1989. "Theoretical and Ideological Issues of Reform in Socialist Systems: Some Yugoslav and Soviet Examples." *Soviet Studies* 430-48.

Mishan, Edward J. 1969. *Welfare Economics.* London: North-Holland Publishing Company.

Morrison, John. 1991. *Boris Yeltsin: From Bolshevik to Democrat.* New York: Penguin.

Moore, Barrington, Jr. 1967. *Social Origins of Dictatorship and Democracy.* Boston: Beacon Press.

————. 1951. *Soviet Politics—The Dilemma of Power.* Cambridge, Mass.: Harvard University Press.

Moorsteen, Richard, and Raymond Powell. 1966. *The Soviet Capital Stock.* Homewood, Ill.: Richard D. Irwin.

Nee, Victor, and David Stark, eds. 1989. *Remaking the Economic Institutions of Socialism.* Stanford, Calif.: Stanford University Press.

Nordhaus, William D. 1992. "Macroeconomic Stabilization in the USSR." In *The Road to Capitalism,* edited by David Kennet and Marc Liberman. New York: Dryden.

Nove, Alec. 1964. *Economic Rationality and Soviet Politics or Was Stalin Really Necessary?* New York: Praeger

————. 1969. *An Economic History of the USSR*. London: Penguin Press.

————. 1977 & 1980. *The Soviet Economic System*. London: George Allen and Unwin.

————. 1987. Radical Reform: Problems and Prospects. *Soviet Studies* 39:452-67.

————. 1990. *Studies in Economics and Russia*. London: Macmillan.

————. 1991. *The Economics of Feasible Socialism Revisited*. London: Harper.

————. 1992. "The End of Sovietology: Rejoinder to Roberts." *Critical Review* 6:451-55.

Nuti, D. M. 1986. "Michael Kalecki's Contribution to the Theory and Practice of Socialist Planning." *Cambridge Journal of Economics* 10:333-53.

Ofer, Gur. 1989. "Budget Deficit, Market Disequilibrium and Soviet Economic Reforms." *Soviet Economy.* 2:107-61.

Orlovsky, Daniel T. 1989. "State Building in the Civil War Era: The Role of Lower-Middle Strata." In *Party, State, and Society in the Russian Civil War,* edited by Diane P. Koerner, William G. Rosenberg, and Ronald G. Suny, 180-209. Bloomington: Indiana University Press.

Ossowski, Stanislaw. 1963. *Class Structures in the Social Consciousness*. New York: Free Press.

Oxenfeldt, A. R. 1965. *Economic Systems in Action: The United States, the Soviet Union and France.* New York: Holt, Rinehart and Winston.

Parks, Michael. 1991a. "Shifting the Ashes of an Epoch." *Los Angeles Times,* December 31, H1, H8-H9.

————. 1991b. "Epilogue: Finding Meaning in the Chaos." *Los Angeles Times,* December 31, H10.

Preobrazhensky, E. A. . 1965. *The New Economics*. Oxford: Oxford University Press.

Remington, Thomas F. 1984. *Building Socialism in Bolshevik Russia*. Pittsburgh: University of Pittsburgh Press.

Remington, Thomas F., ed. 1989. *Politics and the Soviet System*. New York: St. Martin's Press.

Rigby, T. H. 1968. *The Stalin Dictatorship*. Sydney: Sydney University Press.

————. 1968. *Communist Party Membership in the USSR: 1917-1967.* Princeton, N.J.: Princeton University Press.

————. 1977. "Stalinism and the Mono-Organizational Society." In *Stalinism: Essays in Historical Transformation,* edited by Robert Tucker, 53-76. New York: W. W. Norton.

————. 1979. *Lenin's Government: Sovnarkom, 1917-1923*. Cambridge, England: Cambridge University Press.

Rigby, T. H. and Ferenc Feher, eds. 1982. *Political Legitimation in Communist States*. New York: St. Martin's Press.

Rigby, T. H., Archie Brown, and Peter Reddaway, eds. 1980. *Authority, Power and Policy in the USSR*. New York: St. Martin's Press.

Roberts, Paul Craig. 1971. *Alienation and the Soviet Economy*. Albuquerque: University of New Mexico Press.

Robinson, Joan. 1960. *An Essay on Marxian Economics*. London: Macmillan

Roeder, Philip G. 1988. *Soviet Political Dynamics*. New York: Harper and Row.

Rosefielde, Stephen. 1981. "How Reliable are Available Estimates of Forced Concentration Camp Labor in the Soviet Union." *Soviet Studies* (October) 32:4.

Rosenberg, Arthur. 1967. *A History of Bolshevism*. Garden City, N.Y.: Anchor Books.

Rosenberg, William G. 1991. "NEP Russia as a Transitional Society." In *Russia in the Era of NEP,* edited by Sheila Fitzpatrick. Bloomington: Indiana University Press.

Rostow, W. W. 1990. *The Stages of Economic Growth,* 3rd ed. Cambridge, England: Cambridge University Press.

Rutland, Peter. 1992. "The End of the Soviet Union: Did it Fall, or Was it Pushed?" *Critical Review* 8:565-78.

————. 1993. *The Politics of Economic Stagnation in the Soviet Union*. New York: Cambridge University Press.

Schapiro, Leonard. 1960. *The Communist Party of the Soviet Union*. New York: Random House.

————. 1966. *The Origins of the Communist Autocracy*. Cambridge, Mass.: Harvard University Press.

————. 1971. *The Communist Party of the Soviet Union*. 2nd ed. New York: Vintage Books.

————. 1984. *The Russian Revolutions of 1917*. New York: Basic Books.

————. 1985. *1917: The Russian Revolutions and the Origins of Present Day Communism*. Harmondsworth, England: Penguin.

Schroeder, Getrude E. 1987. "Anatomy of Gorbachev's Economic Reform." *Soviet Economy* 3:219-41.

————. 1988. "Organizations and Hierarchies: The Perennial Search for Solutions." In *Reorganization and Reform in the Soviet Economy*, edited by Susan Linz and William Moskoff, 3-22. Armonk, N.Y.: Sharpe.

————. 1989. "Perestroika of Ideology." In *Western Perceptions of Soviet Goals: Is Trust Possible?*, edited by Klaus Gottstein, 24-39. Boulder, Colo.: Westview Press.

————. 1990. "Economic Reform of Socialism: The Soviet Record." In *Annals of the American Academy of Political and Social Sciences* (January): 35-43.

————. 1992. "Soviet Consumption in the 1980s: A Tale of Woe." In *The Disintegration of the Soviet Economic System*, edited by Michael Ellman and Vladimir Kantorovich. New York: Routledge.

Schroeder, G. E., and B. S. Severin. 1976. "Soviet Consumption and Income Policies in Perspective." In *Soviet Economy in a new Perspective*, U. S. Congress, Joint Economic Committee. Washington D.C.: U.S. Government Printing Press.

Schwartz, Harry. 1965. *The Soviet Economy Since Stalin*. Philadelphia: J. B. Lippincott.

Selucky, Radoslav. 1972. *Economic Reforms in Eastern Europe*. New York: Praeger.

————. 1979. *Marxism, Socialism, Freedom: Towards a General Democratic Theory of Labor-Managed Systems*. New York: St. Martin's Press.

Service, Robert. 1979. *The Bolshevik Party in Revolution*. London: Macmillan Press.

Shahnazarov, G. 1974. *Socialist Democracy*. Moscow: Progress Publishers.

Sheehy, Gail. 1990. *The Man Who Changed the World: The Lives of Mikhail S. Gorbachev*. New York: Harper Collins.

Shlapentokh, Vladimir. 1988. *Soviet Ideologies in the Period of Glasnost*. New York: Praeger.

Shmelev, Nikolai. 1987. "Advances and Legacies." *Daily Report: Soviet Union*. June 18, 1-20.

Shmelev, Nikolai, and Vladimir Popov. 1989. *The Turning Point: Revitalizing the Soviet Economy*. New York: Doubleday.

Skocpol, Theda. 1979. *State and Social Revolutions*. Cambridge, England: Cambridge University Press.

Smith, Gordon. 1988. *Soviet Politics: Continuity and Contradictions*. London: Macmillan.

Smith, G. A. E. 1987. "Agriculture." In *Khrushchev and Khrushchevism*, edited by Martin McCauley, 95-117. Bloomington: Indiana University Press.

Smith, Hedrick. 1990. *The New Russians*. New York: Random House.

Solo, Robert A. 1967. *Economic Organizations and Social Systems*. New York: Bobbs-Merill.

Stalin, Joseph. 1939. *From Socialism to Communism in the Soviet Union*. Toronto: New Era Publishers.

————. 1939. *Foundations of Leninism*. New York: International Publishers.

————. 1945. *Joseph Stalin: Selected Writings*. New York: International Publishers.

————. 1952. *Economic Problems of Socialism in the U.S.S.R.* New York: International Publishers.

————. 1973. *The Essential Stalin*. London: Croom Helm.

Stark, David. 1989. "Coexisting Organizational Forms in Hungary's Emerging Mixed Economy." In *Remaking the Economic Institutions of Socialism*, edited by Victor Nee and David Stark, 137-168. Stanford, Calif.: Stanford University Press.

Stone, Lawrence. 1971. "Theories of Revolution." In *Revolution: A Reader*, edited by Bruce Mazlish et al., 44-56. New York: Oxford University Press.

Swianiewicz, Stanislaw. 1965. *Forced Labor and Economic Development*. New York: Oxford University Press.

Szeleneyi, Ivan. 1989. "Eastern Europe in an Epoch of Transition: Toward a Socialist Mixed Economy." In *Remaking the Economic Institutions of Socialism*, edited by Victor Nee and David Stark, 208-32. Stanford, Calif.: Stanford University Press.

Szymanski, Albert. 1979. *Is the Red Flag Flying?* London: Zed Press.

Talmon, Jacob L. 1952. *The Origins of Totalitarian Democracy*. London: Secker and Warburg.

———. 1981, 1991. *Myth of the Nation and Vision of Revolution: Ideological Polarization in the Twentieth Century*. New Brunswick, N.J.: Transaction Publishers.

Tarasulo, Issac J., ed. 1989. *Gorbachev and Glasnost: Viewpoints from the Soviet Press*. Wilmington, Del.: SR Books.

Teague, Elizabeth. 1987. "Gorbachev's Human Factor Policies." In *Gorbachev's Economic Plans,* U. S. Congress, Joint Economic Committee, 2:224-39. Washington, D.C.: U.S. Government Printing Press.

———. 1989. "Perestroika: Who Stands to Gain, Who Stands to Lose?" In *Gorbachev's Agenda*, edited by Susan Clark, 57-84. Boulder, Colo.: Westview Press.

Treadgold, Donald W. 1972. *Twentieth Century Russia*. Chicago: Rand Mcnally.

———. 1976. *Lenin and his Rivals*. Westport, Conn.: Greenwood Press.

Tucker, Robert C. 1971. *The Soviet Political Mind: Stalinism and Post-Stalin Change*. New York: W. W. Norton.

———. 1973. *Stalin as Revolutionary, 1879-1929: A Study in History and Personality*. New York: W. W. Norton.

———, ed. 1975. *The Lenin Anthology*. New York: W. W. Norton.

———, ed. 1977. *Stalinism: Essays in Historical Interpretation*. New York: W. W. Norton.

———. 1990. *Stalin in Power: The Revolution from Above*. New York: W. W. Norton.

Ulam, A. B. 1973. *Lenin and Bolsheviks: The Intellectual and Political History of the Triumph of Communism in Russia*. London: Fontana.

———. 1976. *A History of Soviet Russia*. New York: Praeger.

U.S. Congress. 1982. *USSR: Measures of Economic Growth and Development, 1950-80*. Washington D.C.: U.S. Government Printing Office.

———. 1990. *The Soviet Economy Stumbles Badly in 1989*. A Report presented by the Central Intelligence Agency to the Technology and National Security Subcommittee of the Joint Economic Committee. Washington, D.C.: U.S. Government Printing Office.

Volten, Peter M. E. 1982. *Brezhnev's Peace Program*. Boulder, Colo.: Westview Press.

Wadekin, Karl-Eugene. 1973. *The Private Sector in Soviet Agriculture*. Barkeley Calif.: University of California Press.

———. 1982. *Agrarian Policies in Communist Europe: A Critical Introduction*. Totowa, N.J.: Rowman and Allanheld.

Werth, Alexander 1961. *Russia under Khrushchev*. New York: Hill and Wang.

White, Stephen. 1990. "Democratization in the USSR." *Soviet Studies* 42:3-25.

———. 1992. *Gorbachev and After*. New York: Cambridge University Press.

Wiles, Peter J. D. 1962. *The Political Economy of Communism*. Cambridge, Mass.: Harvard University Press.

———. 1977. *Economic Institutions Compared*. Oxford: Blackwell.

————. 1982. "The Worsening of Soviet Economic Performance." In *Crisis in the East European Economy,* edited by Jan Drewnowski, 143-63. London: Croom Helm.

Winiecki, Jan. 1986a. "Are Soviet-type Economies Entering an era of long-term Decline?" *Soviet Studies* 38:325-48.

————. 1986b. "Soviet-Type Economies: Considerations For the Future." *Soviet Studies* 38:543-61.

————. 1989a. *The Distorted World of Soviet-type Economies.* London: Routledge.

————. 1989b. "CPEs Structural Change and World Market Performance: A Permanently Developing Country Status?" *Soviet Studies* (July): 365-81.

————. 1990. "Obstacles to Economic Reform of Socialism: A Property Rights Approach." *Annals of the American Academy of Political and Social Science* (January): 65-71.

Woody, Sylvia. 1989. *Gorbachev and the Decline of Ideology in Soviet Foreign Policy.* Boulder, Colo.: Westview Press.

Yanowitch, Murray. 1963. "The Soviet Income Revolution." *Slavic Review* (December).

————. 1977. *Social and Economic Inequality in the USSR.* White Plains, N.Y.: Sharpe.

Yeltsin, Boris. 1990. *Against the Grain.* New York: Summit Books.

Zaslavskaya, Tatyana. 1988. "Friends or Foes? Social Forces Working for and against Perestroika." In *Perestroika,* edited by Abel Aganbegyan (1988b), 255-80. New York: Charles Scribners Sons.

————. 1990. *The Second Socialist Revolution.* Bloomington: Indiana University Press.

Zemtsov, Ilya, and John Farrar 1989. *Gorbachev: The Man and the System.* New Brunswick, N.J.: Transaction Publishers.

Zysman, John. 1983. *Governments, Markets and Growth: Financial Systems and the Politics of Change.* Ithaca, N.Y.: Cornell University Press.

Index

About the Authors

ALEX F. DOWLAH is Assistant Professor of Economics at SUNY-Canton. Dr. Dowlah has published a previous book called *Soviet Political Economy in Transition: From Lenin to Gorbachev* (Greenwood, 1992).

JOHN E. ELLIOTT is Professor of Economics at the University of Southern California. Dr. Elliott is the author of many books and journal articles published in *Quarterly Journal of Economics, Economic Inquiry, History of Political Economy, Review of Social Economy, Journal of Economic Issues, Journal of Post Keynesian Economics* and others.

ISBN 0-275-95629-6

HARDCOVER BAR CODE